DATE DUE

MAR 2 8 1998		
AUG 1 7 1998		
GAYLORD		PRINTED IN U.S.A.

To Renew Books
PHONE (510) 258-2233

Contemporary Parenting

Understanding Families

Series Editors: *Bert N. Adams, University of Wisconsin*
David M. Klein, University of Notre Dame

This book series examines a wide range of subjects relevant to studying families. Topics include parenthood, mate selection, marriage, divorce and remarriage, custody issues, culturally and ethnically based family norms, theory and conceptual design, family power dynamics, families and the law, research methods on the family, and family violence.

The series is aimed primarily at scholars working in family studies, sociology, psychology, social work, ethnic studies, gender studies, cultural studies, and related fields as they focus on the family. Volumes will also be useful for graduate and undergraduate courses in sociology of the family, family relations, family and consumer sciences, social work and the family, family psychology, family history, cultural perspectives on the family, and others.

Books appearing in **Understanding Families** are either single- or multiple- authored volumes or concisely edited books of original chapters on focused topics within the broad interdisciplinary field of marriage and family.

The books are reports of significant research, innovations in methodology, treatises on family theory, syntheses of current knowledge in a family subfield, or advanced textbooks. Each volume meets the highest academic standards and makes a substantial contribution to our understanding of marriages and families.

The National Council on Family Relations cosponsors with Sage a book award for students and new professionals. Award-winning manuscripts are published as part of the **Understanding Families** series.

Multiracial Couples: Black and White Voices
Paul C. Rosenblatt, Terri A. Karis, and Richard D. Powell

Understanding Latino Families: Scholarship, Policy, and Practice
Edited by Ruth E. Zambrana

Current Widowhood: Myths & Realities
Helena Znaniecka Lopata

Family Theories: An Introduction
David M. Klein and James M. White

Understanding Differences Between Divorced and Intact Families
Ronald L. Simons and Associates

Adolescents, Work, and Family: An Intergenerational Developmental Analysis
Jeylan T. Mortimer and Michael D. Finch

Families and Time: Keeping Pace in a Hurried Culture
Kerry J. Daly

No More Kin: Exploring Race, Class, and Gender in Family Networks
Anne R. Roschelle

Contemporary Parenting: Challenges and Issues
Edited by Terry Arendell

Terry Arendell
EDITOR

Contemporary Parenting
Challenges and Issues

UNDERSTANDING
FAMILIES

SAGE Publications
International Educational and Professional Publisher
Thousand Oaks   London   New Delhi

For information:

SAGE Publications, Inc.
2455 Teller Road
Thousand Oaks, California 91320
E-mail: order@sagepub.com

SAGE Publications Ltd.
6 Bonhill Street
London EC2A 4PU
United Kingdom

SAGE Publications India Pvt. Ltd.
M-32 Market
Greater Kailash I
New Delhi 110 048 India

Printed in the United States of America

Library of Congress Cataloging-in-Publication Data

Main entry under title:

Contemporary parenting: Challenges and issues/editor, Terry Arendell.
    p.   cm. — (Understanding families; v. 9)
    Includes bibliographical references (p.   ) and index.
    ISBN 0-8039-7268-7 (cloth).—ISBN 0-8039-7269-5 (pbk.)
    1. Parenting—United States. 2. Family—United States.
I. Arendell, Terry. II. Series
HQ755.8.P3793   1997   97-4678
649'.1—dc21

97 98 99 00 01 02 03 10 9 8 7 6 5 4 3 2 1

Acquiring Editor:	Margaret Zusky
Editorial Assistant:	Renée Piernot
Production Editor:	Sanford Robinson
Production Assistant:	Denise Santoyo
Typesetter/Designer:	Marion Warren
Indexer:	Cristina Haley
Cover Designer:	Ravi Balasuriya
Print Buyer:	Anna Chin

Contents

Acknowledgments   vii

1. A Social Constructionist Approach to Parenting   1
   Terry Arendell

2. Parenting in American Society: A Historical Overview
   of the Colonial Period Through the 19th Century   45
   Maris A. Vinovskis and Stephen M. Frank

3. Who's Parenting? Trends and Patterns   68
   Ronald L. Taylor

4. Doing Parenting: Mothers, Care Work, and Policy   92
   Demie Kurz

5. The Social Construction of Fatherhood   119
   Kathleen Gerson

6. Divorce and Remarriage   154
   Terry Arendell

7. Lesbian and Gay Families   196
   Katherine R. Allen

8. Children and Gender   219
      Scott Coltrane and Michele Adams

9. Employment and Child Care   254
      Jennifer Glass and Sarah Beth Estes

10. An Agenda for Family Policy in the United States   289
      George T. Martin, Jr.

Name Index   325

Subject Index   335

About the Editor   349

About the Contributors   350

Acknowledgments

Putting an anthology together, I have discovered, is not unlike parenting: frustrating at times, but rewarding and growth enhancing overall. In this regard especially, I acknowledge my son, Rob, who offered me direct experience with and taught me so much about parenting and the value of humor; my daughter-in-law, Stephanie, who is enhancing my understanding about the joys of extended family; and my brother, Randy, whose support remains invaluable. Friendships were enhanced and new ones formed, including with the contributors to this volume, during the book's development. To friends too numerous to mention specifically, I extend my gratitude. For their invaluable contributions to the nitty-gritty, necessary work of everyday activities including, among other things, library research, proofreading, and referencing, and for their good cheer, I especially thank Margaret Harris, Pam Herd, and Suzanne Jones.

This volume evolved under the sponsorship of several editors, and I extend my sincerest appreciation to each of them. The proposal was conceived initially under the oversight and with the support of Sage Publications editor Mitch Allen. Linda Thompson of the University of Wisconsin–Madison shepherded the proposal through anonymous reviewers and several revisions, and the volume was accepted for joint publication by Sage and the National Council on Family Relations book series. Subsequently, the work came to be included in the Understanding Families series, skillfully edited by Bert N. Adams and

David M. Klein and guided further by Margaret Zusky, acquisitions editor at Sage. I am delighted to have the book be a part of this rich, diverse, and important series. Working with David, Bert, and Margaret has been a pleasure, and the book is possible only because of their support, involvement, and commitment, to say nothing of their good humor and patience.

1

A Social Constructionist
Approach to Parenting

TERRY ARENDELL

Parenting is an umbrella term that encompasses the array of activities and skills performed by adults who provide child rearing and child caregiving. Parenting entails a series of actions on the part of parents to promote the development of their children (Brooks, 1996). More specifically, it is

> a process composed of tasks, roles, rules, communication, resources and relationships . . . . Parenting "involves the skillful and creative use of knowledge, experience, and technique [Horowitz, Hughes, & Pardue, 1982, p. 2]." (Horowitz, 1993, p. 45)

Children require physical care, nurturance, material provision, protection and supervision, and logistical support for handling both the routine and the unfamiliar. They need guidance and encouragement in their development—cognitive, physical, social, emotional, moral, sexual, spiritual, cultural, and educational, more generally. The young need direction in skill development that facilitates or provides warmth, demandingness, balance of power, communication, positive role modeling, and conflict resolution (Small & Eastman, 1991, p. 457). The bulk of these needs is met by parents.

1

This book examines central issues related to and affecting parenting in the contemporary United States. These selected topics include (in chapter order) historical developments in parenting; demographic trends; mothering and motherhood; changes in fathering; divorce, remarriage, and stepparenting; gay and lesbian parenting; the engenderment of children; employment and child care; and family policies and policy needs. Our contributions provide both descriptive overviews and explanatory arguments. These draw from a wide array of materials and empirical studies including, in varying ways, our own research and conceptualizations. Our intention is that this book provide a much needed collection of original writings on major issues pertaining to parenting in today's society.

We make no claims that this is a fully comprehensive volume on contemporary parenting. Such an endeavor would require multiple editions, and even then there would likely be gaps in the coverage, given the complexity and heterogeneity of contemporary American society, the fast pace of social change, the contested character of many issues pertaining to the family, and scholars' limited access to the interiors of families. We hope that this book finds a wide audience, student and nonstudent as well as parent and nonparent. We will be delighted if it contributes to a fuller discussion of contemporary parenting and its social dimensions, locations, and significance.

The contributors to this volume are trained in various perspectives and represent different academic disciplines including sociology, history, family studies, and African American studies. Even with these disciplinary variations, however, we all subscribe generally to a sociological perspective in this work. Paraphrasing Mills's (1959) characterization, the sociological perspective asserts that to understand any social phenomenon requires the linking of the personal or biographical to the societal or historical. A consideration of parenting, then, necessitates recognition of the complex interrelatedness of history, institutions, ideologies, interaction, and experience. Such an approach moves us beyond thinking of parenting only as an individual activity shaped by personal characteristics, psychological dynamics, experiences, and values.

What follows in this introductory chapter is an explication of our shared conceptual framework: a sociological perspective and, more specifically, the social constructionist approach. From there, I move into an overview of some of the central challenges and tasks facing contemporary parents and parenting as an activity and to a discussion of the family as an institution. Demographic trends and immigration patterns are summarized. Then I briefly discuss the primary systems of stratification—race and ethnicity, economic, and gender—and their influences on and challenges to child rearing. Concluding the chapter is a brief consideration of the personal costs and rewards in parenting and the predominant kinds of parenting styles in the United States. In this final section, I summarize the findings on parenting variations and priorities by socioeconomic status, race, and ethnic status. The meanings and consequences of these are themselves socially constructed, varying historically and regionally and revealing social, economic, and political inequalities (Collins, 1989; Zinn, 1989). Although these latter topics are not fully addressed in the volume, I stress their significance here.[1]

The Social Constructionist Perspective

Throughout the volume, we use a social constructionist perspective (e.g., see Atwood & Ruiz, 1993; Gergen & Gergen, 1984; Schwandt, 1994), one of several predominant conceptual frameworks within sociology (and other social sciences).[2] This conceptual framework, as applied to parenting, holds the following presuppositions: Children's care and needs must be made sense of; they are not responded to simply out of biological instinct on the part of those who conceive or give birth to them or who assume their care. That is, human parenting is not only or even predominantly the outcome of biological imperatives or genetic imprinting. Parenting activities are not "natural" behaviors derived from the capacity to reproduce.[3] How children are cared for, reared, and socialized into group life are social processes—dynamic, open-ended, and mutable. Multidimensional and complex, parenting entails various behaviors, skills, and objectives learned through participation in the social community. Even the capacities to nurture and empathize with others, although intrinsic to being human, are developed through learning. Parent-child relationships are formed and sustained through social interaction, and relationships and experiences are interpreted and assigned meaning (e.g., Atwood & Ruiz, 1993; Gubrium & Holstein, 1990).

Parenting is *situated* in place and time; it does not occur in a social vacuum but rather is integrally interlinked with and shaped by demographic changes, historical events and patterns, cultural norms and values, systems of stratification, family developments and arrangements, and shifts in societal organization and structure. Each of these is an outcome of social interaction and is maintained or transformed through collective action.

The activities and objectives of parenting, beyond those of basic survival, can vary in relation to the respective social context and historical moment. How parental care and guidance are provided, their logistics, by whom, and how they are valued by the larger group all are subject to collective definition. Cultural meanings about parenting and parenthood are based on tradition, practice, and ideology. Although the broad objectives of child rearing may be similar and even relatively stable—such as achieving positive outcomes in children's growth, development, intellectual functioning, emotional well-being, and social and moral character—how these are defined and understood to be achieved are subject to reinterpretation and reconstruction. The products of interaction and the goals of parenting change as circumstances and understandings shift. As social change occurs, expectations of parents change. So, too, do individual parents' expectations change as their perceptions, skills, concerns, objectives, and circumstances evolve and as children grow and develop, presenting different needs, demands, and interests.

Meanings, according to the constructionist perspective, are continuously reshaped and redefined. The dynamic and contested character of meanings applies to the family (and, by logical extension, to parenting), as Stacey (1993), for instance, asserted, noting that anthropological and historical studies illustrate that the family is "an ideological, symbolic construct that has a history and a politics" (p. 545). Individuals' definitions of parenting are shaped by multiple influences. These include, among others, experiences in the family of origin; the character of interpersonal relationships; socioeconomic class status and ethnic or minority group membership; beliefs about the contemporary family and modern society more generally; notions about the probable future; evaluations of personal well-being;

economic realities, possibilities, and priorities; psychological well-being; and assessments of rewards and costs to be gained from parenting.

Parenting priorities, actions, and choices are constrained in differing ways and to varying degrees by the social positions families occupy (Belsky, 1984; LeVine, 1988; Small & Eastman, 1991). That is, parents' range of options and the opportunities perceived are framed by structural and historical realities. Differences in values, knowledge and educational levels, and access to resources contribute to variations. More specifically, religious teachings, ethnic and community identities and backgrounds, immigrant status, and economic circumstances and experiences are important contributors to family realities and parenting differences (Crockenberg, 1987; Ogbu, 1981, 1987).

Tensions, contradictions, and conflicts are recognized within this conceptual approach, not glossed over or ignored. They are seen to exist, or potentially exist, not only between family members—in their relationships and interactions—but also between the practices and ideologies of parenting and other social institutions, especially the economy and workplace. Beliefs held and societal location are central to perceived interests and conflicts of interest.

Finally, for purposes of this volume, the social constructionist perspective sees assessments of and judgments about parenting behaviors and styles as being entwined with the theories dominant at the time that are also cultural products—contextual and emergent. Knowledge, such as about child development and parenting strategies, both reflects and reinforces ideologies. These, too, always are in flux. In brief, parenting and parenthood are inseparable from the cultural understandings of and beliefs about childhood as well as the structural realities within which they are situated. Parenting, then, is constantly changing and being reformed and reformulated. All social phenomena, in sum, are dynamic, mutable, and emergent.

Parenting in Contemporary Society

The challenges confronting child-rearing parents are vast. Some are economic stress and poverty; the isolation of individual family units; demands of the workplace, which can conflict with family needs;

inadequate, inferior, and/or unaffordable child care; and an array of individual needs, both children's and parents'. The prolonged period of children's economic dependency and education together with the expansion of a consumer orientation and mass marketing aimed at them, the power of peer groups, and uncertainty about youths' future employment prospects are problems especially facing parents of older children.

Positioned in custom and continuously influenced by scholarly, religious, economic, and political developments, to name some of the predominant forces, the activities constituting parenting and its objectives are not necessarily congruent. For instance, parents need to retain authority and control over their children even as they promote their independence and autonomy. American parents, rather than encouraging *familism*—"deference and allegiance to senior family members and collective support of siblings throughout life (Triandis et al., 1982)—as do many cultures, stress independence and self-reliance" (Baumrind, 1993, p. 1301). The focus on autonomy in contrast to family allegiance, however, varies by racial ethnic groups with Latinos, Asian Americans, and Native Americans continuing to stress familism or its cultural equivalent more so than other groups (e.g., Shon & Ja, 1992; Vega, 1992; Yellowbird & Snipp, 1994). Especially recent immigrants stress kinship obligations and loyalty, more in keeping with their home cultures. Families trying to resist the cultural press toward the fostering of autonomy and self-direction within children contend with conflicts of values and the need to acculturate. The emphasis on autonomy is advantageous, arguably, to life in American society with its competitive capitalist economy and individualist ethic, especially in the middle and upper income classes. But, at the same time, this focus diminishes parental and familial authority, particularly among older children. Also, children are not merely passive recipients of parental actions and decisions but are themselves active agents in the family, although typically less powerful than adults.

PARENTING AND THE FAMILY

Parenting remains lodged in the family, even as the family as an institution undergoes and adjusts to numerous significant changes.

Indeed, as many of the traditional functions performed by the family have been moved out of the household and more squarely into the economy, often now available as services for a fee, child rearing has become a more specialized family activity (e.g., Hareven, 1994; Zaretsky, 1976). Nearly all children are raised by the mothers who give birth to them, and a majority of children—even in this era of divorce, maternal custody, and out-of-wedlock births—also live, during at least part of their early childhoods, with their fathers. Although increasing numbers of children spend large amounts of time outside of the family in paid care and school, most child rearing and caretaking occurs within family units. And parents oversee, at least to some extent, children's day care and education, which takes place outside the family. The family is where children form primary attachments (e.g., Bowlby, 1969; Bretherton, 1993) and develop their identities and social selves (e.g., Epstein, 1991).

The American social context in which adults form families and parent children is radically different from that of a century ago. So, too, are children's and most adults' activities. Although the family has never been static (e.g., Hareven, 1994), the pace and array of changes experienced in this century are staggering. About 100 years ago, most American families were living on farms or in small communities and children were engaged both in economically productive and educational activities, although typically less of the latter. Steadily, children were moved out of their roles as productive contributors to the family and into longer periods of dependency and formal education. Today's youths experience many more years of schooling, have little (if any) contact with agricultural life or basic subsistence, and do not contribute to a family's economic resources but rather depend on and deplete them (see, e.g., Demos, 1986; LeVine & White, 1992). As the conditions, definitions, and activities of childhood shifted over the decades, the meaning of parenting and, to varying degrees, the activities of child rearing evolved (LeVine & White, 1992; Zelizer 1985). Additionally, the historical tradition of reciprocity in which adult children, in turn, provided care for their aging parents is mostly ended, especially in the white middle class but increasingly among other groups and socioeconomic classes as well.

The meaning of childhood has evolved in conjunction with social changes, as Vinovskis and Frank detail in this volume (Chapter 2).

More specifically, over the past century, North American children acquired far greater emotional value even as their economic value disappeared (Engstler & Luscher, 1991; Gordon, 1983). Describing this transformation, the sociologist Zelizer (1985) noted that

> the expulsion of children from the "cash nexus" at the turn of the past century, although clearly shaped by profound changes in the economic, occupational, and family structures, was also part of a cultural process of "sacralization" of children's lives. The term sacralization is used in the sense of objects being invested with sentimental or religious value. (p. 11)

This major alteration may now itself be undergoing change; the heavy emphasis on and intense investment in affective value assigned to children since the latter part of the 19th century "may well have reached a plateau as a result of new pressures placed on the family" (Ambert, 1994, p. 532). Furthermore, parents and children spend less direct time with each other than they did in the past, especially as mothers are employed and fathers often are disengaged from child rearing and care, whether or not they are actually present in the home. Parents contribute to this relative disengagement directly by emphasizing steadily increasing levels of autonomy and independence (Presser, 1989). The emerging form of parenting is one of *supportive detachment,* suggested Demo (1992), who concluded that this is an adaptive and functional strategy. Some, however, lament this trend, arguing that it is harmful to children. For example,

> As men and women increase their commitment to their own self-fulfillment, they necessarily reduce their commitment to sacrificing personal pursuits for their children's welfare. . . . It is clear that parents have become more aware of the costs of raising children and are less willing to make unconditional commitments to their children. (Uhlenberg & Eggebeen, 1986, pp. 36-37)

Child care and development are increasingly the purview not only of parents or the dictates of religious institutions but also of professionals. More is known about the nuances and course of child development—physical, social, psychological, and cognitive. Parenting also is an arena for professional intervention and direction. Ambert (1994) summarized the evolution of influences on child rearing in recent decades:

> In the past century, under Western masculine hegemony, parenting has been successfully encoded in religious strictures, then moralized, medicalized, psychologized, psychiatrized, and more recently legalized (Hendrick, 1990; see also Morgan, 1985; Schutze, 1987)—frequently all of these together in the past decade. . . . Parenting is constantly being constructed according to the ideologies and paradigms of those sciences and professions that happen to dominate at any point in time in terms of dictating what is good for children. Once what is "in the best interest of the child" has been defined, what parents should be and should do is implicitly and explicitly constructed. Whatever notions of childhood predominate will thus shape the form that parenting should take. (p. 530)

The body of basic civic and protective rights accorded to children is steadily, if slowly, expanding. The growth of state intervention into the family is attributed to the interrelated crises in Western capitalism and the social welfare state by the social theorist Morgan (1985, p. 5; see also Abramovitz, 1988; Fraser, 1989; Gordon, 1990). The state, especially through its social welfare policies, attempts to minimize the adverse effects of the breakdown of traditional institutions and community and economic cycles (Martin, 1990). With this expansion of state authority, parents both acquire new and lengthened obligations and lose authority with respect to their offspring. Parents are curtailed in decision making in arenas such as health care, education, child employment, and discipline and punishment, areas that traditionally were defined as the purview of individual families. American children will gain more basic rights, according to the European theorist Therborn (1993), drawing from his comparative research, whereas parents will witness a further reduction in their discretionary authority, including with respect to discipline. Therborn argued that private patriarchal authority, in general, will continue to decline (see also Morgan, 1985), more in keeping with the trends in the Scandinavian countries and opening the way for more alterations in parenting and parent-child relationships.

A significant player in nearly all contemporary families, unlike in the first five or so decades of this century, is television (e.g., Berry & Asamen, 1993). Specifically,

About 98 percent of U.S. homes have television sets, more than have indoor toilets or telephones. Children begin watching television before their first birthday and have favorite programs by their second or third birthday. Children watch television 2-4 hours a day, spending more time viewing than doing any one other thing except sleeping. (Dorr & Rabin, 1995, p. 323)

Furthermore, more than half of American households have videocassette recorders and cable television, vastly increasing the available viewing options (Dorr & Kunkel, 1990).

Television, on about 7 hours a day in the average American home (Dorr & Rabin, 1995), diverts family members' attention away from each other and competes with other possible family activities (Condry, 1993). Although the extent of the influence of television programs and advertising on children is controversial, "The more hours of 'regular television' children watch, the more they hold traditional sex-role attitudes, behave aggressively, and want advertised products" (Dorr & Rabin, 1995, p. 333). Children who watch greater amounts of television have poorer quality social relationships, have fewer interpersonal interactions, and perform less well in school. Such children also are less healthy, eat more snack foods, and are overweight (e.g., Graves, 1993). On the positive side, children learn facts, become less prejudiced, and increase their interpersonal skills by viewing particular television programs (Dorr & Rabin, 1995, p. 323; Graves, 1993).

Both television programming and advertising often present stereotypical images, especially of minorities, women, and the aged. Aggression and violence, material consumption, sexual activity, and quick gratification are disproportionately portrayed. Young children, who are less experienced in discriminating among messages and images, are most vulnerable to these effects (e.g., Berry & Asamen, 1993). Thus, in households where television viewing is commonplace and relatively unmonitored, parents may well be competing with television and its offerings in their efforts to teach their offspring particular values. Parents must make decisions about the role of television and videos in their family lives. In general, parents do far less monitoring of their children's television viewing than they might, and their viewing habits are mirrored by their children (e.g., Palermo, 1995).

PRIMARY CULTURAL IDEOLOGIES

The family was seen and conceptualized over the past century and a half as a *private* sphere with objectives, values, and norms distinct from the *public* sphere (e.g., Parsons, 1955, 1964). This ideology—the "separate spheres doctrine"—which posits that the family is a private, autonomous, and self-sufficient unit, has been soundly critiqued, particularly by feminist and critical theorist scholars who highlight the irrevocable interrelationships between family and other social institutions (Keniston & Carnegie Council on Children, 1977; Thorne, 1982; Zaretsky, 1976). Despite such critiques, this view of the family persists, held by the public at large and by some scholars who build it into or accept it as an underlying premise of their conceptual models (for critiques, see Cheal, 1991; Morgan, 1985).

Other enduring cultural beliefs include the assumptions of a universal nuclear family, the consequence of the biological imperative; family harmony; parental determinism with socialization being one-way, parent to child; and the view that the family of the past was stable and harmonious (Skolnick & Skolnick, 1994). These typically are interlinked with the separate spheres doctrine. In their critiques, feminist and critical theorist scholars examine and illustrate how these beliefs obscure the dynamics of family life (e.g., Morgan, 1985; Osmond & Thorne, 1993; Rapp, 1982; Thorne, 1982). Hochschild's (1997) recent work further deconstructs conventional assumptions, especially those of the alleged dualism between family and market and nurturance and individualism.

The tenacity of traditional ideologies contributes to the national debates about the state of the family and to the numerous cultural contradictions that surround and shape families (e.g., Dizard & Gadlin, 1990; Wolfe, 1989). Tensions persist between the values of separation and commitment, competition and cooperation, autonomy and intimacy, utilitarian individualism and love, and obligation and freedom (Berger & Berger, 1983; Swidler, 1980). "Most Americans are, in fact, caught between ideals of obligation and freedom" (Bellah, Madsen, Sullivan, Swidler, & Tipton, 1985, p. 102; see also Dahlstrom, 1989). The theorist Flax (1987, p. 51), for example, observed that Western culture appears to be in the middle of a fundamental transformation: "A 'shape of life' is growing old," involving a shift that "may be as radical as the shift from medieval to a modern society," and yet is little understood (see also Cheal, 1991; Morgan, 1985). Parenting is not immune from the tensions and contradictions within a culture. A critic of these developments, Popenoe (1988), for example, argued,

> With the rise of what is sometimes called "late modernization," self-fulfillment has become one of the paramount cultural values. This means that familism and the family today face what can reasonably be described as an unprecedented, adverse cultural climate. (p. 329)

DEMOGRAPHIC TRENDS

Demographic trends are major factors in parenting and the diversity of American family life. Significant racial ethnic variations prevail in demographic trends and family arrangements (see Chapter 3). Family arrangements in which children are reared are so varied that the definition of family itself has become subject to debate. Seeking to avoid the conventional restrictive definition as well as ones so broad as to become meaningless, Bould (1993) proposed a middle-range definition that has particular salience for families engaged in parenting: "The family can be defined as the informal unit where those who cannot take care of themselves can find care in time of need" (p. 138).

A primary demographic trend of recent decades is the shift to smaller families. This pattern is a result of steady declines in both the fertility rates and birthrates, a rising number and proportion of families headed by unmarried women, high marital separation and divorce rates, and the closer spacing of births so that parents spend fewer years engaged in child rearing. Other significant trends include the high rates of remarriage and stepparent family formation, the return of young adult children to live at home, and, for those who remain married, increasing numbers of years spent together as couples. With the dramatic decline in childbirth mortality and the overall increases in longevity, most parents now live to see their youngest children move into adulthood. More and more children have grandparents and even great-grandparents living.

Parenting occurs in various family arrangements. Nuclear families, defined as those having both biological parents and full brothers and sisters present, account for the living arrangements of one out of two children, according to 1991 census data (the latest year for these specific assessments). The remaining children live in homes that include, for example, a single parent, stepparent, grandparent, or another relative or nonrelative (Furukawa, 1994). Child rearing occurs in single-parent families formed by parents' divorces, births to parents not married or living together, or adoption. The majority of single-parent families are mother headed, and nonresidential fathers, for the most part, provide little in the way of parenting (e.g., Arendell, 1996). Parenting takes place in stepparent households in which a biological parent, usually the mother, is married to or living in a marital-like relationship with a person who is not the biological father of her children. Gay and lesbian couples or individuals parent. So, too, do grandparents rear grandchildren. Adoptive and foster parents care for and raise children. Parenting experiences and challenges vary, in differing ways and to different extents, by parenting arrangement (Schwartz, 1994; see also Allen & Baber, 1992), as various contributors to this volume show and discuss.

IMMIGRATION

Since the mid-1960s, a surge of immigration into the United States has occurred, largely an outcome of the 1965 Immigration Act that abolished the discriminatory national-origin quotas. The proportion of immigrants who are Asian or Latino increased dramatically. Whereas European immigrants still made up more than half of those coming into the United States in the 1950s, they constituted only 10% by the 1980s. This trend has reversed somewhat; of all immigrants who entered the United States in the first part of the 1990s, a result of the 1986 Immigration Reform and Control Act, Europeans comprised 17%. Asian immigrants, a small but rapidly growing group, include especially Filipinos, Chinese, Vietnamese, Koreans, and Asian Indians. Latinos, the fastest growing segment of the U.S. population overall, include Mexicans, Puerto Ricans (who are U.S. citizens but who often are treated in analyses as if they are immigrants), Cubans, Salvadorans, Dominican Republicans, Colombians, Venezualans, and persons from other Central and South American nations. Seeking economic opportunity and escaping political oppression are two primary motivations for this migration (Feagin & Booher Feagin, 1996; Zinn, 1994; see also Taylor, 1994, more generally).

As has been the case throughout American history, immigrant parents face some unique challenges in the rearing of their children. Coming from an array of cultures, immigrants bring with them varied ideals about family life and different fertility rates and birthrates. Discrimination in the United States—based on race, ethnicity, and religion—has not disappeared and is a factor in immigrant child rearing. Holding the cultural values and norms of their native society, immigrant parents try to bring up their children in ways that are important and familiar to them even as they try to help them adjust and succeed in the new society. Their children become *bicultural,* appropriating norms and values of the two cultures, although many of the parents do not or do so to a lesser degree. Children's, particularly younger ones', expectations and opportunities for acculturation are mediated both by parents and by the extended family network (Garcia Coll & Meyer, 1993; Garcia Coll, Meyer, & Brillon, 1995, p. 200). Different expectations and desires for acculturation can be a major area of intrafamilial tension and conflict (Shon & Ja, 1992). Immigrants vary dramatically in their socioeconomic situations, levels of literacy, and professional or occupational training or readiness; each specific immigrant group confronts somewhat unique issues.

All parents, irrespective of family composition or group membership, face innumerable challenges in rearing children in contemporary society. Yet, and more specifically, the intertwined systems of economic, race and ethnic, and gender stratification endemic to American society influence parenting as a process, parenthood as a status, and the character and quality of the experiences of both parenthood and childhood.

Systems of Stratification

RACE AND ETHNICITY

Race and ethnicity, together with class and gender, constitute interacting hierarchies of resources and rewards that condition the material realities, parenting activities, and subjective experiences of family life. "Marriage patterns, gender relations, kinship networks, and other family characteristics result from the social location of families, that is, where they are situated in relation to societal institutions allocating resources" (Zinn, 1989, pp. 73-74).

Members of groups holding minority status in the United States on the basis of racial and ethnic identity must ready their children for participation and survival in a society still stratified by race and ethnicity. They must cope with and prepare their offspring for the economic consequences of racism, discrimination, and prejudice while at the same time trying to foster positive self-esteem and a sense of belongingness. How these objectives are explicitly defined and met (or are attempted to be met) vary according to circumstance. For example, African American parents who live in predominantly black communities show less concern about discrimination in their parenting and are less psychologically stressed than their counterparts who live in predominantly white communities (McAdoo, 1985; Taylor, Chatters, Tucker, & Lewis, 1990).

Given that racial and ethnic minorities are positioned disproportionately in the lower socioeconomic strata, the intersections of class and race or ethnicity are complex, and their influences on parenting are multifaceted. In addition to poverty, more prevalent among minority populations are unemployment, underemployment, and downward mobility following job loss (Garcia Coll et al., 1995; Wilson, 1996). These groups' parenting practices are entwined with strategies for coping with economic hardships and uncertainty. Many studies of racial ethnic families confound the effects of poverty and employment insecurity with minority status.

ECONOMIC STRATIFICATION

The American family has been impacted directly in recent decades by enormous changes in the nature of work and the workplace. "Today's parents face what may be unprecedented levels of social and economic stress" (Zigler, 1995, p. xi). These developments include, for example, deindustrialization and the transferring of manufacturing abroad, corporate downsizing and restructuring, and the steady expansion of the service sector that typically affords workers lower wages, less job security, and fewer benefits. The consequences of these developments on families vary and are tied to social position, especially racial patterning (Wilson, 1987, 1996; Zinn, 1989).

Particularly those engaged in working-class occupations have experienced job uncertainties and layoffs. Workers without college educations have encountered the largest decline in real wages, and the gap between the professional middle class and the working class has widened in the past 20 years (Rubin, 1976/1992). But the middle class is not immune from the effects of a changing economy and the globalization of production as witnessed, for example, by downsizing and the elimination of formerly secure middle-management positions (Newman, 1988).

Family income disparities are great and increasing, with the highest fifth of earners in 1993 obtaining 46.2% of all household income while the bottom fifth received only 4.2%. Moreover, between 1977 and 1993, the income of the top 5% went from 16.8% to nearly 20%. Inequality of wealth, as well as of incomes, has risen and is greater than it has been at any time since the 1920s (U.S. Bureau of the Census, 1995).

Median weekly earnings are lower now in terms of real purchasing power than they were in the 1970s (Folbre & Center for Popular Economics [CPE], 1995; Rubin, 1992). With the demise of the "family wage," families require two earners to maintain a moderate standard of living. Over the past two decades,

> only those families who were able to send another person, usually a wife and mother, into paid employment have been able to increase their total income. They did so at the expense of time previously devoted to family labor, including child care. (Albelda, Folbre, & CPE, 1996, p. 72; see also Presser, 1989; Sidel, 1996)

More specifically, in 1994, the median family income of families with two earners was $48,970, whereas that of families with one earner was $27,145. The gap between income earners with dependent children and those without them also has increased so that the per capita income for individuals with minor dependents is significantly less than it is for those without them (U.S. Bureau of the Census, 1995; U.S. Department of Labor, 1995).

Growing numbers of workers earn only the minimum wage, insufficient to bring a family out of poverty. A third of all poor families have at least one family member who works a minimum of 30 weeks during the year (Albelda et al., 1996). The recent increase in the minimum wage, raising the hourly pay from $4.25 to $4.75 in 1996 and to $5.15 by September 1997, is too low to eradicate family poverty. Additionally, unemployment rates have drifted upward. They averaged about 4.4% in the 1950s, 6.2% in the 1970s, and 6.5% in the years 1990 through 1994. African Americans and Latinos have significantly higher rates of unemployment than do whites and Asian Americans (U.S. Bureau of the Census, 1995).

The rate of child poverty has increased almost steadily since the mid-1960s. Several factors are involved: the increase in mother-only families; the persistence of gender stratification, occupational segregation in the workplace, and inadequate wages to women; the underpayment of child support; the inadequacy of the minimum wage; and the declining value of public assistance (e.g., Hoff-Ginsberg & Tardiff, 1995; Sidel, 1996). Constituting just over one quarter of the nation's population, children make up two fifths of the poor. Fully 23% of children under 18 years of age are poor, and the very young have even higher rates of poverty, approximating 30%. Moreover, racial and ethnic minority children are at particular risk of impoverishment. African American and Latino children are especially likely to be poor—46% and 41%, respectively, compared to 14% of all non-Hispanic white children (U.S. Bureau of the Census, 1995; see also Lerner, Castellino, Terry, Villarruel, & McKinney, 1995). Family composition is a central factor in child poverty; whereas more than half (54%) of children living with single mothers are poor, only one of every six (12%) children living in married, two-parent families is poor. Female-headed households are more than five times as likely to be poor as are married-couple families (35.6% vs. 6.5%). These trends constitute the racialization and feminization of poverty (Dickerson, 1995).

Social benefits do not meet the needs of poor families (e.g., Brooks-Gunn, 1995; Martin, 1990). For example, in 1993, the families of 40% of poor children received no Aid to Families with Dependent Children (AFDC), and only 44% of poor families received food stamps. About half of all food stamp recipients are children, yet about

4 million children under age 12 live in households with insufficient food, and one third to one half of impoverished children receive fewer calories and less nutrition than the federally recommended levels for normal learning and thinking (Albelda et al., 1996, p. 35; Vobejda, 1995). Poor children are more than twice as likely as others not to finish high school, to have much lower achievement test scores than children from high-income families, to suffer from various serious physical and mental ailments, and to experience fatal accidental injuries (Albelda et al., 1996, p. 27; Finlay, 1995; Lerner et al., 1995). The fastest growing group of homeless is families with children (Lee et al., 1990); the 1994 U.S. Conference of Mayors' report indicated that children make up approximately 40% of the homeless population (Sidel, 1996, p. 149; see also Lee et al., 1990).

The welfare reform bill, the Personal Responsibility and Work Opportunity Reconciliation Act of 1996, was passed by Congress and signed by President Clinton in the summer of 1996. According to Children's Defense Fund analyses, the bill will significantly worsen the situation for low-income and poor families. The new legislation terminates the AFDC program, the primary cash aid program for families, and also ends or dramatically alters numerous other programs aimed at assisting the poor, returning monies to the states in the form of block grants. The Children's Defense Fund predicts that child poverty will increase by 12%—another 1.1 million children—and that 12 million poor families will lose or have major reductions in food stamp assistance. Families with children will bear some 70% of the cuts in the food stamp program; hardest hit will be those families whose total incomes fall below half of the poverty line (Aravosis, 1996).

It is poverty, not public assistance per se, that is linked to poor child outcomes. "The findings may also mean that if families move from being 'welfare poor' to 'working poor,' the overall life chances of the children in these families will not be enhanced" (Zill, Moore, Smith, Steif, & Coiro, 1995, p. 55). In brief, the stresses and uncertainties of daily life are greater for those without adequate economic means. Poverty both adds obstacles to parenting and curtails access to necessary resources. The high rate of child poverty—nearly one in four children—precludes, except rhetorically, holding on to any romantic views that Americans "love" children, value them as the future, or appreciate the work of parenting.

> If sentiments are to be taken as evidence, Americans are indeed a nation in love with children. However, sentiments do not tell the whole story. I am prepared to assert that in spite of popular rhetoric, we do *not* really like children—not as a nation. . . . While it is true that many children turn out well, it is also true that substantial numbers are experiencing a formidable array of preventable burdens of ignorance, illness, suffering, failure, humiliation and lost opportunities. Every relevant national indicator suggests that our children are in a state of what David Hamburg, president of Carnegie Corporation of New York, refers to as "inadvertent neglect" [Hamburg, 1990, p. 5]. They are victims of institutional-level neglect. (Goetting, 1994, pp. 81-82)

GENDER STRATIFICATION

Parenting, as has long been the situation, is done disproportionately by mothers in American society, and both—parenting and mothers— are devalued, a reality Kurz explores in this collection (Chapter 4). Research evidence is consistent in the finding that fathers, in general, do far less parenting work than mothers and that most men view their parenting involvement as discretionary (e.g., Blair & Johnson, 1992; Tiedje & Darling-Fisher, 1993; for reviews, see Arendell, 1996; Pleck, 1996). Maternal child rearing is evidence of the persistence of gender hierarchy. Other phenomena that attest to gender stratification are occupational segregation, wage differentials, women's political under-representation, and mothers' "double days."

Mothers now couple their traditional domestic and parenting roles with those of income earning. Their employment has tripled over the past 30 years (U.S. Bureau of the Census, 1995). Specifically, 75% of all mothers of dependent children and more than half of mothers of infants are working for pay (U.S. Department of Labor, 1995). Much on the home front, however, remains unchanged.

The "second shift," in which women continue to handle the bulk of domestic and parenting work even as they carry employment, persists (Hochschild with Machung, 1989). Although some changes are occurring (Pleck, 1996), relatively few men have significantly increased their contributions to household and child-rearing work. A

1992 survey found that employed mothers of minor children invest about 61 hours per week in both paid and unpaid work, whereas their male counterparts put in about 46 hours (Galinsky, Bond, & Friedman, 1993; see also Douthitt, 1988; Seidler, 1992).

> The fact that women continue to do two or three times as much nonwage family labor as their husbands or partners is compelling evidence that family labor remains gendered and that popular descriptions of changes in marital, family, and gender roles are overstated. (Demo & Acock, 1993, p. 330; for review, see Thompson & Walker, 1995)

Additionally, a gender gap in perception exists, with men overestimating the number of hours they contribute to domestic and parenting work (Backett, 1982, 1987; McBride & Mills, 1993). In general, women are dissatisfied with men's limited parenting and domestic involvement, whereas men either are not or are much less so (e.g., Cowan & Cowan, 1987, 1988; Cox, Owen, Lewis, & Henderson, 1989). More specifically, "While both mothers and fathers indicate that they want more father participation in child care, mothers seem to want even more father participation than do their husbands" (Dickie, 1987, p. 138). Showing the complexity of father involvement, Gerson teases out three dominant patterns of men's parental participation and attitudes in her contribution to this book (Chapter 5).

Gender inequity has consequences beyond workloads. For instance, many married women, especially employed mothers, resent men's lack of full participation in the home and resistance to change. This is a contributing factor to women's disenchantment with marriage (e.g., Arendell, 1995; Finlay, Starnes, & Alvarez, 1985; Riessman, 1990). Stacey (1993) put it this way:

> It strikes me as a sad, revealing commentary on the benefits to women of the traditional nuclear family that, even in a period when women retain primary responsibility for maintaining children and other kin, when most women continue to earn substantially less than do men with equivalent cultural capital, and when women and their children suffer substantial economic decline after divorce, so many regard divorce as the lesser of two evils. (p. 546)

In turn, many men resent women's demands for change, feeling unfairly pressured and unappreciated (e.g., Hochschild with Machung, 1989; Weiss, 1990). Another outcome of gender inequity in family life and, more specifically, of women's role as primary parent is maternal custody in divorce. I provide a fuller discussion of divorce, remarriage, and stepparenting later in this volume (Chapter 6).

Gender inequity perpetuates the traditions of patriarchy and models inequality to children rather than showing and preparing them for equitable relationships (e.g., Okin Moller, 1989; Thorne, 1993). Gender is about power:

> The imposition of an ideology of two genders and the differential evaluation of these differences have one universal outcome: systems of gender stratification in which males have greater claims on and access to the scarce resources—power, prestige, and property—of a society than do females. (Ferree & Hess, 1987, p. 22)

Still, despite the uneven rates of change and although the majority of women earn less than do men, women's employment is altering marital dynamics and the balance of power between the genders. This is occurring in racial ethnic families as well as in Anglo ones (e.g., Zinn, 1989).

The gender socialization of children is one of the challenges facing contemporary parents. The family is the nursery and workshop of gender identity and, as Epstein (1991) noted, "The literature now documents the unfolding of 'core gender identity' in boys and girls within the first two years of life" (p. 848; see also Cahill, 1986, 1994; West & Zimmerman, 1987). Given the structural arrangements of early child care and rearing, in which women do the overwhelming bulk of parenting and caregiving, children are socialized into gendered identities (e.g., Chodorow, 1978, 1989; Epstein, 1991). That is, they are being prepared to assume more or less conventional gender roles, including future parental ones. In addition to having gender differences modeled by their parents and acquiring gendered identities through interaction and family socialization, children participate in a culture organized along gender lines. This environment perpetuates an ideology that espouses gender differences, including women's "innate" capacity for nurturing and caregiving. Even children reared by those lesbian and gay parents who are committed to greater openness about gender and sexuality are influenced by the gender-stratified and heterosexist (a related phenomenon) society, as Allen shows in her much broader discussion in this collection (Chapter 7). Parents attempting to rear less gender-differentiated children must contend with these cultural pressures. Coltrane and Adams explore more fully the gender socialization of children and related issues in this volume (Chapter 8).

Within this context—historical, social, economic, and cultural—individuals raise their children. What follows is an overview of the satisfactions and costs in parenting. Also summarized are the predominant styles of parenting and variations by socioeconomic status and minority group membership.

Personal Costs and Rewards in Parenting

Parenting can be an enormously satisfying, rewarding, enriching, and growth-promoting activity. It also can be frustrating, stress producing, isolating, and lonely. For many (and perhaps most) parents, parenting varies, being enormously satisfying and seemingly easy at times as well as confounding, difficult, and burdensome at other times. This is not unique to these times. "The sheer magnitude, diversity, and unending nature of parenting tasks can strain the most devoted parent. 'Parenting, with all its joys and pains, has always been hard' [Horowitz et al., 1982, p. 9]" (Horowitz, 1993, p. 48). Some predict that parenting, given various social trends, will become even more challenging. Ambert (1994), for example, asserted that "as children's environments have become more complex, more dangerous, and less supportive, we can expect parenting to become more difficult" (p. 535). Given women's primary roles in parenting and the slow pace of gender role change, the future increase in parenting burdens will fall disproportionately on mothers.

Individuals' transitions to parenthood can be complicated and difficult, often in unanticipated ways (e.g., Cowan & Cowan, 1988; LaRossa & LaRossa, 1981, 1989). Persons becoming parents bring a complex and unique history to their entry into and engagement in parenting. Additionally, women and men seem to experience the transition differently, with men finding it a more difficult process (Cowan & Cowan, 1987, 1988; Crnic & Booth, 1991). The move into parenthood is affected by various phenomena: the social context generally; personal, spousal, and familial expectations and experiences; family-of-origin experiences; age; level of education; occupational status and security; and psychological, social, and economic resources.

Certainly the economic cost of rearing children is escalating and is a factor in the growing gap between those who remain childless and those who parent. The actual estimates are daunting. According to government calculations, the probable cost for raising a child to age 18, not including the cost of college or inflation, is $106,890 for a two-parent family making less than $33,700 a year, $145,320 for a two-parent family making between $33,700 and $56,700 a year, and $211,830 for a two-parent family making more than $56,700 a year. A one-parent family making less than $33,700 annually will spend $101,580, whereas one making more than $33,700 will spend $213,240 (U.S. Department of Agriculture, 1995).

A leisure gap exists between those adults engaged in child rearing and those not. Parents, particularly employed mothers of young children, experience both a time and a sleep deficit (Hochschild with Machung, 1989; Presser, 1989; Schor, 1992). Child care is becoming a major family and social issue (e.g., Cherlin, 1995), a discussion Glass and Estes provide in this book (Chapter 9). The work of arranging and monitoring child care typically is done by mothers.

Parents must contend with the reality that their children face a future likely to witness as yet unrecognized or unknown technological and other social changes that will further alter, possibly dramatically, American life. Just in the past several decades, for example, the changes wrought in children's education and their future employment prospects by the development and widespread availability of personal computers and advances in the telecommunications network are vast. One immediate impact of these developments has been a reduction in the amount of time parents and children spend in interaction with each other. The longer term effects of these changes on family life and parents' effectiveness in preparing their offspring for uncertain futures remain to be seen.

Relatively little is known about parental satisfaction and dissatisfaction, which "is surprising because the issue of parental satisfaction is one of central importance to American society, as well as to the many individuals who invest a lifetime to parenting" (Hamner & Turner, 1996, p. 5). What findings do exist offer a paradoxical evaluation. That is, on the one hand, parents report high levels of personal satisfaction with parenting. On the other hand, parenting has negative consequences for parents' psychological well-being and general life satisfaction (Goetting, 1986; McLanahan & Adams, 1987). Mothers are more satisfied overall with parenting than are fathers. Parental satisfaction is entwined with perceived marital quality, more so for men than for women (e.g., Cowan & Cowan, 1985, 1987; Cox et al., 1989; Volling & Belsky, 1991). In general, and not surprisingly given their much greater involvement in parenting work, women show greater parental strain over the course of child rearing than do men. Strain is not necessarily a negative phenomenon; it "may indicate greater emotional intimacy and, as such, is a positive sign of a close relationship" (Scott & Alwain, 1989, p. 500). Indeed, both mothers and children, in general, report that children feel more closely attached to their mothers than to their fathers (Lamb & Oppenheim, 1989; see also Basow, 1992).

Parental Characteristics and Parenting Styles

More than a decade ago, Belsky (1984) and Belsky, Robins, and Gamble (1984) conceptualized parenting and child outcomes and specified the factors influencing them. The model retains a position of prominence in the literature on parenting competency (e.g., Brooks, 1996; Hamner & Turner, 1996; Small & Eastman, 1991). Parental characteristics, child characteristics, and social context are the three major influences. Parental characteristics include developmental history and personality. High levels of psychological health and well-being and overall maturity contribute to high parental functioning. Child characteristics entail temperament, personality, mood, and activity level. "Children come with their own temperaments, patterns of

growth, sexual gender, birth position, and a particular social, historical time in which they live. All these factors affect the process of
parenting" (Brooks, 1996, p. 4). Lowered parental functioning is more
likely with children who are temperamentally more difficult. Three
distinct sources of social stress and support promote or undermine
parental competence: the marital relationship, networks, and employment. By providing emotional support, instrumental assistance, and
social expectations, social support influences parenting positively
(Belsky, 1984, p. 87). Facets of the marital relationship, more specifically, that affect parenting are emotional support, cognitive support
or agreement in child care, and physical support or sharing child care
(Dickie, 1987, p. 121). Parents influence children's development—
cognitive, social, and personality—as well as behavior by the style of
their interactions (e.g., Baumrind, 1978, 1993; Webster-Stratton,
1990). Belsky (1984), in a widely cited article, concluded,

> Across childhood, parenting that is *sensitively* attuned to children's
> capabilities and to the developmental tasks they face promotes a variety
> of highly valued developmental outcomes, including emotional security,
> behavioral independence, social competence and intellectual achieve-
> ment. (p. 85; emphasis in original)

"Parenting has been described as the most challenging and complex
of all the tasks of adulthood," and yet little is offered in the way of
guidance, support, or preparation for parenthood (Zigler, 1995,
p. xi). Few people receive much preparation for parenting (e.g.,
LeMasters & DeFrain, 1989). Nor do many parents have much, if any,
education in child development. Parent education programs are now
widespread, and studies of their overall effectiveness demonstrate
their utility. More effective child-rearing methods and approaches can
be acquired (e.g., Baumrind, 1993; Patterson, 1978; Zill et al., 1995).
Parents who are knowledgeable about child developmental stages and
processes are better equipped to relate appropriately to their children
and to have realistic expectations of them.

   Three parenting approaches predominate in the United States:
authoritative, authoritarian, and permissive. Embedded in parenting
styles are the dimensions of warm-hostile and autonomy-control.
Authoritarian parents typically are highly controlling and lacking in

warmth in their interactions, whereas permissive parents are noncontrolling, nondemanding, and warm in their interactions. Authoritative, or democratic, parents are controlling and demanding *but also* are warm, receptive, and rational in their relations with children (Horowitz, 1993, pp. 53-54). Multifaceted, authoritative parenting encompasses "a high degree of warmth or acceptance, a high degree of psychological autonomy or democracy, and a high degree of behavioral control" (Steinberg, Elmen, & Mounts, 1989, p. 1425). Authoritative parents are highly invested in rearing their children and committed to them. They sacrifice personal pleasures to be with them, believing they are the most competent caregivers, and view their children more positively (Baumrind, 1993, p. 1308; Greenberger, Goldberg, Hamill, O'Neil, & Payne, 1989; Greenberger & O'Neill, 1990).

Some cultural and racial group variability exists with respect to the use and effectiveness of parenting approaches and the ways in which the approaches are combined (e.g., Baumrind, 1971, 1972, 1978; Chao, 1994). Yet a growing body of work suggests that, in general, authoritative parenting is the most conducive for fostering positive child outcomes and promotes instrumental social competence consistent with the ideologies dominant in U.S. society (Baumrind, 1978). Baumrind (1993) concluded,

> Children from different sociocultural niches whose parents are authoritative—that is, both firm disciplinarians (demanding) and warm, receptive caregivers (responsive)—tend to be well adjusted and competent [Dornbusch, Ritter, Lederman, Roberts, & Fraleigh, 1987; Maccoby & Martin, 1983; Steinberg et al., 1989]. (p. 1308)

For instance, school performance, a common measure of child development, is positively correlated with authoritative parenting, although these findings are, to date, most evident for white youths (Chao, 1994; Dornbusch et al., 1987; Steinberg et al., 1989). Other researchers have found authoritative parenting to be closely linked to children's successful adjustment to their parents' marital transitions (Hetherington, 1987, 1993; Maccoby & Mnookin, 1992). Furthermore, authoritative parents both monitor their children's television viewing more and are more concerned about the effects of advertising than are parents who use other types of parenting approaches (Carlson & Grossbart, 1988).

Variations by Class and Race and Ethnicity

SOCIOECONOMIC STATUS

Socioeconomic class status accounts for a large measure of parenting differences in parenting styles (Staples, 1988). Both external factors related to class membership (such as access to resources) and internal characteristics (such as personality) influence parenting (Crouter & McHale, 1993). Parents' socioeconomic status, values, child-rearing beliefs, and actual behaviors are interrelated. More specifically, values and child-rearing beliefs mediate between class status and child-rearing behaviors. At the same time, parenting practices are more varied than the values and beliefs held about parenting alone would suggest (Kohn, 1979; Luster, Rhoades, & Haas, 1989). Furthermore, because diversity exists both within and across socioeconomic class strata and within racial ethnic groups, general characterizations of distinctive parenting approaches and priorities by group must be qualified. A racial ethnic group's parenting practices and beliefs must be viewed in the context of its history and social situation.

One of the major difficulties in assessing parenting variations by socioeconomic class status is the middle-class bias typically inherent in both research and comparative assessments of parenting; Ogbu (1988) termed this bias "middle-class centric." That is, middle class practices and values are used as normative (Garcia Coll & Meyer, 1993; Ogbu, 1981, 1985), drawn on as the standard by which to evaluate variations. "Seeing differences as deficits basically presumes that these families are impaired by their social, cultural, racial, and economic status, and, therefore, that there is a need to resocialize them to White, Anglo-Saxon middle-class norms [Bronfenbrenner, 1985]" (Garcia Coll et al., 1995, p. 191).

Parenting is more difficult when economic uncertainty and hardship prevail; poor parents' children are "the walking wounded" (Sidel, 1996, p. 141). Poverty affects the quality of life and, thus, family dynamics and parenting in innumerable ways (e.g., Lerner et al., 1995). Psychological stress related to low income status and economic hardships is a major one (Dodge, Pettit, & Bates, 1994; McLoyd, 1990; Ogbu, 1981, 1987). When under great economic pressure, parents overemphasize obedience, withhold affection, rely on corporal punishment as a means of control, are inconsistent in their disciplining, and are inadequately responsive to their children's socioemotional needs (Garrett, Ng'Andu, & Ferron, 1994; Hashima & Amato, 1994).

But variations exist beyond those characterizing the poor relative to the nonpoor. For instance, parents of higher socioeconomic status generally seek to promote initiative and independent thought in their children. They see their parental role as being one that fosters development, and they use more diverse and interactive verbal skills. By contrast, parents of lower socioeconomic status stress children's conformity to societal expectations and exert their authority to achieve that conformity. They are more directive of their children in everyday interactions. Parents of lower income groups are more likely to resort to physical punishment, whereas higher income parents rely more on verbal interactions and reasoning as well as "psychological" techniques of discipline such as appeals to guilt. Parents of higher educational and income status are more confident and certain about the efficacy of their parenting with respect to their abilities to enhance their children's development (Luster & Kain, 1987). Middle and upper income parents are more likely to promote egalitarian relationships within their families (Hoff-Ginsberg & Tardiff, 1995, p. 165) and to offer greater and more consistent amounts of cognitive stimulation (Hoff-Ginsberg & Tardiff, 1995, p. 182; Kohn, 1979; Luster et al., 1989). Furthermore, higher income parents are more likely to adhere to and practice parenting approaches consistent with the current child developmental literature and so are more likely to alter their parenting styles in response to advances in the child development and parenting literature than are lower income parents (Garcia Coll et al., 1995; Hamner & Turner, 1996).

Intersecting with socioeconomic variations in parenting are ones related to race and ethnicity (Ogbu, 1987), even though most minority group members share many of the dominant culture's parenting values, practices, and objectives. For instance,

These parents [ethnic and minority] . . . have distinct beliefs, attitudes, values, and parenting behaviors that overlap with, but are also unique from, the dominant culture in the United States. These unique features refer to basic conceptualizations such as the definition and roles of the family; parental beliefs about the determinants of development, including what, how and who may foster or hinder a child's development; as well as what aspects of a child's development are most important (i.e., discipline vs. intelligence) and what the definition of competence is in each of these areas. It is also our contention that most ethnic and minority parents consider what they believe and do (as divergent as it may be from dominant culture parenting norms) to be in the best interest of their children and/or their family system. (Garcia Coll et al., 1995, p. 190)

Briefly considered now, in the order of their relative proportions of the current American population (see Chapter 3 of this volume), are the racial/ethnic parenting practices of African Americans, Hispanics, Asian Americans, and Native Americans.

AFRICAN AMERICANS

African Americans comprise the largest minority group in the United States, making up approximately 13% of the population. Diversity in values and regional differences characterize African American families nationally (Staples, 1988). The vast majority of blacks, however, live in urban areas, often in concentrated inner-city sections. Thus offering children protection and safety are typical parental objectives, and coping with economic uncertainty and hardship are common necessities. Historically, more attention has been directed at low-income and poverty-stricken black families; this has begun to change, however, particularly with analyses of data collected in the National Survey on Families and Households. Nonetheless, relatively little is yet known about the diversity of the development and socialization of African American children (Taylor et al., 1990).

Extended kin networks are a significant facet of black family life. In general, blacks emphasize children's compliance to and respect for adult authority and attempt to foster pride in racial identity even as adaptive skills for coping in a racially and economically stratified society are taught. Racial socialization is a central facet of parenting for those living in relatively more integrated communities and by more highly educated parents (McAdoo, 1991; Taylor et al., 1990). Positive self-identity and perseverance are emphasized (Willis, 1992). Stressed by many families is the significance of religion and the church, education, the importance of the oral tradition, and flexibility and interchangeability of family roles (e.g., Collins, 1989; Gibbs, 1989). Interpersonal skills and recognition of one's own and others' feelings are promoted. Confrontation for perceived wrongs is encouraged. Nonverbal communication skills are taught and expected to be refined (Rashid, 1985). Community and family members are expected to balance individual needs and rights with those of the larger group. Additionally, reciprocity is stressed (Rashid, 1985).

Historically, blacks have used harsher disciplinary measures, including corporal punishment. In general, this remains the pattern (Hale-Benson, 1986), as does a parent centeredness rather than a child centeredness. Yet considerable variation in disciplining prevails, related especially to class status, neighborhood dynamics and safety, and church affiliation and participation (Kelley, Power, & Wimbush, 1992). In addition to biological mothers, grandmothers and aunts play particularly strong roles in the parenting of black children (Crawley, 1988; McAdoo, 1993).

HISPANICS

Hispanics, the category of people identified primarily by their Spanish origin and use of the Spanish language, are the second largest minority group in the United States. As a consequence of high fertility rates and immigration, Hispanics are expected to become the largest ethnic group within the next decade. This is a particularly heterogeneous population, representing numerous cultures and cultural backgrounds. Migration and stage of acculturation, variations in political and economic backgrounds, regional differences, class status and mobility rates, and outmarriage all contribute to the pluralistic character of the Hispanic population (Vega, 1992; Zuniga, 1992). Offsetting the heterogeneity, in addition to the common language, is the heritage and practice of Catholicism.

Most Hispanics live near to and have frequent interactions with family members; extended families are normative. With the exception of Puerto Ricans, who have a high rate of marital dissolution and out-of-wedlock births, there is a high level of family stability. In comparison to other groups, Hispanics are generally more family oriented, continuing to stress the ideology and practices of *familism* (Vega, 1992). Thus family loyalty is paramount, as is interdependence rather than autonomy and individualism. "Personalism is another enduring Hispanic cultural value that emphasizes the inner importance, dignity, and respect of an individual, in contrast to the individual's relative social and economic status which is commonly emphasized in the Anglo culture" (Garcia Coll et al., 1995, p. 197).

Children are valued highly, and there is a strong focus on child rearing. Older siblings, extended kin, and *compadres* all participate in the caregiving and rearing of children. Parenting of the very young tends to be indulgent; young children are to be placated rather than controlled (Vega, 1990). Providing nurturance and protection are areas of emphasis, whereas achievement and the reaching of developmental points in accordance with a timeline hold a relaxed approach (Martinez, 1988, 1993).

Good behavior is expected from children. Interpersonal attentiveness and responsiveness are valued and promoted; so, too, is a sense of belongingness (Harwood, 1992; Martinez, 1988, 1993; Roland, 1988). Disciplinary strategies are similar to mainstream culture. Even among low-income mothers, authoritarian parenting no longer prevails. Martinez (1988, 1993), for example, found comparable proportions of authoritative and authoritarian parenting among parents who had limited amounts of education.

Paternal authority continues to be valued highly. Mother-child relationships are expected to be strong and lasting and are emphasized as the core of family life throughout the various subcultural groups. Sons are given more freedom than are daughters.

ASIAN AMERICANS

As is the case with African Americans and Hispanics, the category of Asian Americans encompasses a wide array of cultural traditions and nationalities, and so generalizing about parenting practices, beliefs, and objectives must be done with caution. Also, similarly, variations in Asian American parenting have received relatively little systematic attention.

The philosophies of Confucianism and Buddhism, along with influences from other Eastern philosophical systems, play particular roles in Asian American family life (Kelley & Tseng, 1992; Vega, 1990) and are the primary source of variation in comparison to Anglo and other family practices when socioeconomic status is held constant. The family as a collective is emphasized, whereas individualism and autonomy are downplayed and even discouraged. Hierarchical roles, as established within Confucianism, are followed; thus relationships, including parent-child ones, are strictly prescribed. Adherence to these rules and roles carries significance and reflects on the family and extended kinship or clan network, not merely the individual. Thus conformity is highly valued and expected (Chao, 1994; Shon & Ja, 1992).

Children are taught obedience, self-discipline, moderation, appreciation for order and hierarchy, minimization of conflict and tension, respect for the elderly, and "proper development." Babies and toddlers are nurtured and treated leniently, even permissively, because they are believed to be incapable of understanding. However, by the "age of understanding," acquired during the period between 3 and 6 years of age, parents become stricter and more demanding (Garcia Coll et al., 1995; Kelley & Tseng, 1992; Lin & Fu, 1990; Shon & Ja, 1992).

The rearing and nurturance of children is highly valued. Formal education and academic success are stressed, an important element in Confucianism, as a means for honoring the family and a strategy for upward mobility. Much parenting effort goes into children's schooling (Chao, 1994; Shon & Ja, 1992). Parental sacrifices are to be understood and acknowledged and then later rewarded by adult children who provide care and support to their parents. Because of the emphasis on conformity, success, and hard work, Asian Americans sometimes are characterized as the "model minority."

Patriarchal authority persists, and mothers are the emotional caretakers of both husbands and children. Mothers, particularly, are integrally involved in children's development, decorum, and activities. Parenting or child rearing is seen as "child training" or teaching. Parental care, involvement, and concern are synonymous with firm control and guidance of children (Chao, 1994; Kelley & Tseng, 1992). Interpersonal and social relationships are emphasized, as is harmony that is attained through proper conduct and attitudes. Confrontation is avoided. Conformity is promoted through shaming; withdrawal of family affection and support and community disapproval are key child-rearing techniques. Strict gender and generational roles within families are expected.

NATIVE AMERICANS

Approximately 400 Native American tribal and group affiliations exist, many having unique languages and some distinctive cultural elements. Little research has examined the variations among Native Americans with respect to family life or, more specifically, parenting. What is known is that across the groups certain values are largely shared and stressed in child rearing and child development. These include an emphasis on the collective rather than the individual, cooperative and nonconfrontational interpersonal relationships, and a noncompetitive social milieu (Harrison, Pine, Pine, Chan, & Buriel, 1990; Yellowbird & Snipp, 1994). The natural environment and being in harmony with all of life are core values (Carson, Dail, Greely, & Kenote, 1990; Yellowbird & Snipp, 1994), and children are reared into a present time orientation with a focus on current needs. Respect for elders and traditional ways, reverence for life and the land, the centrality of family and tribal life, cooperation, humility, and sharing wealth are emphasized (Garcia Coll et al., 1995, p. 195; Joe & Miller, 1987; Zints, 1970). Avoidance of personal gain or recognition and humility are valued; these sometime conflict with the dominant society's structures and practices of formal education (Carson et al., 1990; London & Devore, 1988).

Strong extended kin networks prevail, and child rearing is shared among numerous caring adults to whom children become closely attached (Carson et al., 1990; London & Devore, 1988). Children are prized and are the beneficiaries of nurturance and adult involvement but are recipients of relatively little interference or direct regulation as children's autonomy is respected (Phillips & Lobar, 1990). Physical punishment is disdained (Carson et al., 1990).

In sum, we will not know the full scope of cultural variations in parenting, or their consequences, until the extremes of economic stratification are eroded and economic hardships and childhood poverty are eradicated. Nor will we understand fully the strengths of relatively distinctive subcultural parenting practices and beliefs until racism and nativism are ended. Major policy reforms and initiatives are needed to empower individual parents and to strengthen families engaged in child rearing. This is so especially given the dynamic relationship between society at large and parenting activities, the scope and power of social problems, and the competing and heavy demands on parents. Martin, pulling together a large array of information, specifies major needs and policy recommendations in the concluding chapter of the book (Chapter 10). In sum, all of us contributing to this book advocate a vigorous and detailed national commitment to the promotion of viable parenting.

Notes

1. Both the psychological and child development literature are replete with discussions of these topics. For comprehensive reviews, see the four-volume set, *Handbook of Parenting*, edited by Bornstein (1995a, 1995b, 1995c, 1995d).
2. Collins (1985), a contemporary sociological theorist, identified three dominant schools in sociology, as did the vast majority of his colleagues: the conflict tradition, the Durkheimian tradition, and the microinteractionist tradition. It is the latter that encompasses the social constructionist perspective.
3. See Bornstein (1995b) for a compilation of well-referenced articles on the biology and ecology of parenting.

References

Abramovitz, M. (1988). *Regulating the lives of women: Social welfare policy from colonial times to the present*. Boston: South End.
Albelda, R., Folbre, N., & Center for Popular Economics. (1996). *The war on the poor: A defense manual*. New York: New Press.
Allen, K. R., & Baber, K. (1992). Starting a revolution in family life education: A feminist vision. *Family Relations, 41*, 378-384.
Ambert, A. M. (1994). An international perspective on parenting: Social change and social constructs. *Journal of Marriage and the Family, 56*, 529-543.

Aravosis, J. (1996, August 8). *Children's Defense Fund: Analysis of welfare bill—"The Personal Responsibility and Work Opportunity Reconciliation Act of 1996."* (Internet: aravosis@tmn.com)

Arendell, T. (1995). *Fathers and divorce.* Thousand Oaks, CA: Sage.

Arendell, T. (1996). *Co-parenting: A review of the literature.* Philadelphia: University of Pennsylvania, National Center on Fathers and Families.

Atwood, J. D., & Ruiz, J. (1993). Social constructivist theory with the elderly. *Journal of Family Psychotherapy, 4*(1), 1-32.

Backett, K. (1982). *Mothers and fathers: Studies of negotiation of parental behavior.* New York: St. Martin's.

Backett, K. (1987). The negotiation of fatherhood. In C. Lewis & M. O'Brien (Eds.), *Reassessing fatherhood* (pp. 74-90). Newbury Park, CA: Sage.

Basow, S. A. (1992). *Gender stereotypes and roles* (3rd ed.). Pacific Grove, CA: Brooks/Cole.

Baumrind, D. (1971). Current patterns of parental authority. *Psychological Developmental Monographs, 4*(1), 1-103.

Baumrind, D. (1972). An exploratory study of socialization effects on black children: Some black-white comparisons. *Child Development, 43,* 261-267.

Baumrind, D. (1978). Parental disciplinary patterns and social competence in children. *Youth & Society, 9,* 239-276.

Baumrind, D. (1993). The average expectable environment is not good enough: A response to Scarr. *Child Development, 64,* 1299-1317.

Bellah, R., Madsen, R., Sullivan, W., Swidler, A., & Tipton, S. (1985). *Habits of the heart: Individualism and commitment in American life.* New York: Harper & Row.

Belsky, J. (1984). The determinants of parenting: A process model. *Child Development, 55,* 83-96.

Belsky, J., Robins, E., & Gamble, W. C. (1984). The determinants of parental competence. In M. Lewis (Ed.), *Beyond the dyad* (pp. 251-279). New York: Plenum.

Berger, B., & Berger, P. (1983). *The war over the family.* Garden City, NY: Doubleday.

Berry, G. L., & Asamen, J. K. (1993). *Children and television: Images in a changing sociocultural world.* Newbury Park, CA: Sage.

Blair, S. L., & Johnson, M. P. (1992). Wives' perceptions of the fairness of the division of labor: The intersection of housework and ideology. *Journal of Marriage and the Family, 54,* 570-582.

Bornstein, M. H. (Ed.). (1995a). *Handbook of parenting,* Vol. 1: *Children and parenting.* Englewood Cliffs, NJ: Lawrence Erlbaum.

Bornstein, M. H. (Ed.). (1995b). *Handbook of parenting,* Vol. 2: *Biology and ecology of parenting.* Englewood Cliffs, NJ: Lawrence Erlbaum.

Bornstein, M. H. (Ed.). (1995c). *Handbook of parenting,* Vol. 3: *Status and social conditions of parenting.* Englewood Cliffs, NJ: Lawrence Erlbaum.

Bornstein, M. H. (Ed.). (1995d). *Handbook of parenting,* Vol. 4: *Applied and practical parenting.* Englewood Cliffs, NJ: Lawrence Erlbaum.

Bould, S. (1993). Familial caretaking: A middle-range definition of family in the context of social policy. *Journal of Family Issues, 14*(1), 133-151.

Bowlby, J. (1969). *Attachment and loss.* New York: Basic Books.

Bretherton, I. (1993). Theoretical contributions from developmental psychology. In P. Boss, R. LaRossa, W. Schumm, & S. Steinmetz (Eds.), *Sourcebook of family theories and methods: A contextual approach* (pp. 275-301). New York: Plenum.

Bronfenbrenner, U. (1985). Summary. In M. Spencer, G. Brookins, & W. Allen (Eds.), *Beginnings: The social and affective development of black children* (pp. 67-73). Hillsdale, NJ: Lawrence Erlbaum.

Brooks, J. B. (1996). *The process of parenting* (4th ed.). Mountain View, CA: Mayfield.

Brooks-Gunn, J. (1995). Strategies for altering the outcomes of poor children and their families. In P. Chase-Lansdale & J. Brooks-Gunn (Eds.), *Escape from poverty: What makes a difference for children?* (pp. 87-117). New York: Cambridge University Press.

Cahill, S. E. (1986). Language practices and self-definition: The case of gender identity acquisition. *Sociological Quarterly, 27,* 295-311.

Cahill, S. E. (1994). And a child shall lead us? Children, gender, and perspectives by incongruity. In N. Herman & L. Reynolds (Eds.), *Symbolic interaction: An introduction to social psychology* (pp. 459-486). Dix Hills, NY: General Hall.

Carlson, L., & Grossbart, S. (1988). Parental style and consumer socialization of children. *Journal of Consumer Research, 15,* 77-94.

Carson, D. K., Dail, P. W., Greely, S., & Kenote, T. (1990). Stresses and strengths of Native American reservation families in poverty. *Family Perspective, 24,* 383-400.

Chao, R. K. (1994). Beyond parental control and authoritarian parenting style: Understanding Chinese parenting through the cultural notion of training. *Child Development, 65,* 1111-1119.

Cheal, D. (1991). *Family and the state of theory.* Toronto: University of Toronto Press.

Cherlin, A. J. (1995). Policy issues of child care. In P. Chase-Lansdale & J. Brooks-Gunn (Eds.), *Escape from poverty: What makes a difference for children?* (pp. 121-137). New York: Cambridge University Press.

Chodorow, N. (1978). *The reproduction of mothering: Psychoanalysis and the sociology of gender.* Berkeley: University of California Press.

Chodorow, N. (1989). *Feminism and psychoanalytic theory.* New Haven, CT: Yale University Press.

Collins, P. H. (1989). The social construction of black feminist thought. *Signs: Journal of Women in Society and Culture, 14,* 745-773.

Collins, R. (1985). *Three sociological traditions.* New York: Oxford University Press.

Condry, J. (1993). Thief of time, unfaithful servant: Television and the American child. *Daedalus, 122*(1), 259-278.

Cowan, C., & Cowan, P. (1985). *Pregnancy, parenthood, and children at three.* Toronto: Society for Research in Child Development.

Cowan, C., & Cowan, P. (1987). Men's involvement in parenthood: Identifying the antecedents and understanding the barriers. In P. Berman & F. Pedersen (Eds.), *Men's transitions to parenthood: Longitudinal studies of early family experience* (pp. 145-174). Hillsdale, NJ: Lawrence Erlbaum.

Cowan, C., & Cowan, P. (1988). Who does what when partners become parents: Implications for men, women and marriage. *Marriage and Family Review, 12*(3-4), 105-131.

Cox, M. S., Owen, M. T., Lewis, J. M., & Henderson, K. V. (1989). Marriage, adult adjustment, and early parenting. *Child Development, 60,* 1015-1024.

Crawley, B. (1988). Black families in a neo-conservative era. *Child Development, 65,* 415-419.

Crnic, K. A., & Booth, C. C. (1991). Mothers' and fathers' perceptions of daily hassles of parenting across early childhood. *Journal of Marriage and the Family, 53,* 1042-1050.

Crockenberg, S. (1987). Predictors and correlates of anger toward and punitive control of toddlers by adolescent mothers. *Child Development, 58,* 964-975.

Crouter, A. C., & McHale, S. M. (1993). The long arm of the job: Influences of parenting work on childrearing. In T. Luster & L. Okagaki (Eds.), *Parenting: An ecological perspective* (pp. 179-202). Hillsdale, NJ: Lawrence Erlbaum.

Dahlstrom, E. (1989). Theories and ideologies of family functions, gender relations, and human reproduction. In M. Bak (Ed.), *Changing patterns of European family life* (pp. 57-78). New York: Routledge.

Demo, D. H. (1992). Parent-child relations: Assessing recent changes. *Journal of Marriage and the Family, 54,* 104-117.

Demo, D. H., & Acock, A. C. (1993). Family diversity and the division of domestic labor: How much have things really changed? *Family Relations, 42,* 323-331.

Demos, J. (1986). *Past, present, and personal: The family and the life course in American history.* New York: Oxford University Press.

Dickerson, B. J. (Ed.). (1995). *African American single mothers: Understanding their lives and families.* Thousand Oaks, CA: Sage.

Dickie, J. R. (1987). Interrelationships within the mother-father-infant triad. In P. Berman & F. Pederson (Eds.), *Men's transitions to parenthood: Longitudinal studies of early family experience* (pp. 113-143). Hillsdale, NJ: Lawrence Erlbaum.

Dizard, J., & Gadlin, H. (1990). *The minimal family.* Amherst: University of Massachusetts Press.

Dodge, K. A., Pettit, G. S., & Bates, J. E. (1994). Socialization mediators of the relation between socioeconomic status and child conduct problems. *Child Development, 65,* 296-318.

Dornbusch, S. M., Ritter, P. L., Lederman, H. P., Roberts, D. F., & Fraleigh, M. J. (1987). The relation of parenting style to adolescent school performance. *Child Development, 58,* 1244-1257.

Dorr, A., & Kunkel, D. (Eds.). (1990). Children in a changing media environment. *Communication Research, 17*(1), 11-23.

Dorr, A., & Rabin, B. E. (1995). Parents, children and television. In M. Bornstein (Ed.), *Handbook of parenting,* Vol 4: *Applied and practical parenting* (pp. 323-352). Englewood Cliffs, NJ: Lawrence Erlbaum.

Douthitt, R. (1988). The division of labor within the home: Have gender roles changed? *Sex Roles, 20,* 693-704.

Engstler, A., & Luscher, K. (1991). *Childhood as a social phenomenon: National report—Switzerland.* Vienna, Austria: European Centre for Social Welfare Policy and Research.

Epstein, S. (1991). Sexuality and identity: The contribution of object relations theory to a constructionist sociology. *Theory and Society, 20,* 825-873.

Feagin, J. R., & Booher Feagin, C. (1996). *Racial and ethnic relations* (5th ed.). Englewood Cliffs, NJ: Prentice Hall.

Ferree, M. M., & Hess, B. B. (1987). Introduction. In B. Hess & M. Ferree (Eds.), *Analyzing gender: A handbook of social science research* (pp. 9-30). Newbury Park, CA: Sage.

Finlay, B., Starnes, C. E., & Alvarez, F. B. (1985). Recent changes in sex-role ideology among divorced men and women: Some possible causes and implications. *Sex Roles, 12,* 637-653.

Finlay, B. (Ed.). (1995). *The state of America's children's yearbook: 1995.* Washington, DC: Children's Defense Fund.

Flax, J. (1987). Postmodernism and gender relations in feminist theory. In M. Maslon, J. O'Barr, S. Westphal-Wihl, & M. Wyer (Eds.), *Feminist theory in practice and process* (pp. 51-74). Chicago: University of Chicago Press.

Folbre, N., & Center for Popular Economics. (1995). *The new field guide to the U.S. economy.* New York: New Press.

Fraser, N. (1989). *Unruly practices: Power, discourse, and gender in contemporary social theory.* Minneapolis: University of Minnesota Press.

Furukawa, S. (1994). The diverse living arrangements of children: Summer 1991. In U.S. Bureau of the Census, *Current population reports* (Series P70, No. 38). Washington, DC: Government Printing Office.

Galinsky, E., Bond, J. T., & Friedman, D. (1993). *The National Study of the Changing Workforce.* New York: Families and Work Institute.

Garcia Coll, C. T., & Meyer, E. C. (1993). The sociocultural context of infant development. In C. Zeanah (Ed.), *Handbook of infant mental health* (pp. 56-69). New York: Guilford.

Garcia Coll, C. T., Meyer, E. T., & Brillon, L. (1995). Ethnic and minority parenting. In M. Bornstein (Ed.), *Handbook of parenting, Vol. 2: Biology and ecology of parenting* (pp. 189-210). Mahwah, NJ: Lawrence Erlbaum.

Garrett, P., Ng'Andu, N., & Ferron, J. (1994). Poverty experiences of young children and the quality of their home environment. *Child Development, 65,* 331-345.

Gergen, M. M., & Gergen, K. J. (1984). The social construction of narrative accounts. In K. Gergen & M. Gergen (Eds.), *Historical social psychology* (pp. 173-189). Hillsdale, NJ: Lawrence Erlbaum.

Gibbs, J. T. (1989). Black American adolescents. In J. Gibbs & L. Huang (Eds.), *Children of color* (pp. 179-223). San Francisco: Jossey-Bass.

Goetting, A. (1986). Parental satisfaction: A review of research. *Journal of Family Issues, 7*(1), 83-109.

Goetting, A. (1994). Do Americans really like children? *Journal of Primary Prevention, 15*(1), 81-92.

Gordon, L. (Ed.). (1990). *Women, the state, and welfare.* Madison: University of Wisconsin Press.

Gordon, M. (Ed.). (1983). *The American family in social-historical perspective* (3rd ed.). New York: St. Martin's.

Graves, S. B. (1993). Television, the portrayal of African Americans, and the development of children's attitudes. In G. Gordon & J. Asamen (Eds.), *Children and television: Images in a changing sociocultural world* (pp. 226-253). Newbury Park, CA: Sage.

Greenberger, E., Goldberg, W., Hamill, S., O'Neil, R., & Payne, C. K. (1989). Contributions of a supportive work environment to parents' well-being and orientation to work. *American Journal of Community Psychology, 17,* 755-783.

Greenberger, E., & O'Neil, R. (1990). Parents' concerns about their child's development: Implications for fathers' and mothers' well-being and attitudes toward work. *Journal of Marriage and the Family, 52,* 621-635.

Gubrium, J., & Holstein, J. (1990). *What is family?* Mountain View, CA: Mayfield.

Hale-Benson, J. E. (1986). *Black children: Their roots, cultures, and learning styles* (rev. ed.). Baltimore, MD: Johns Hopkins University Press.

Hamburg, D. (1990). *A decent start: Promoting healthy child development in the first three years of life* (president's annual essay). New York: Carnegie Corporation of New York.

Hamner, T. J., & Turner, P. H. (1996). *Parenting in contemporary society* (3rd ed.). Boston: Allyn & Bacon.

Hareven, T. K. (1994). Continuity and change in American family life. In A. Skolnick & J. Skolnick (Eds.), *Families in transition: Rethinking marriage, sexuality, child rearing, and family organization* (8th ed., pp. 40-47). New York: HarperCollins.

Harrison, A., Pine, M., Pine, C., Chan, S., & Buriel, R. (1990). Family ecologies of ethnic minority children. *Child Development, 61,* 363-383.

Harwood, R. L. (1992). The influence of culturally derived values on Anglo and Puerto Rican mothers' perceptions of attachment behavior. *Child Development, 63,* 822-839.

Hashima, P. Y., & Amato, P. R. (1994). Poverty, social support, and parental behavior. *Child Development, 65,* 394-403.

Hendrick, H. (1990). Constructions and reconstructions of British childhood: An interpretive survey—1800 to the present. In A. James & A. Prout (Eds.), *Constructing and reconstructing childhood: Contemporary issues in the sociological study of childhood* (pp. 35-59). Bristol, PA: Falmer.

Hetherington, E. M. (1987). Family relations six years after divorce. In K. Pasley & M. Ihinger-Tallman (Eds.), *Remarriage and stepparenting: Current research and theory* (pp. 185-205). New York: Guilford.

Hetherington, E. M. (1993). An overview of the Virginia longitudinal study of divorce and remarriage with a focus on early adolescence. *Journal of Family Psychology, 7,* 39-56.

Hochschild, A., with Machung, A. (1989). *The second shift: Working parents and the revolution at home.* New York: Viking.

Hochschild, A. (1997). *The time bind: When work becomes home and home becomes work.* New York: Metropolitan Books.

Hoff-Ginsberg, E., & Tardiff, T. (1995). Socioeconomic status and parenting. In M. Bornstein (Ed.), *Handbook of parenting,* Vol. 2: *Biology and ecology of parenting* (pp. 161-188). Mahwah, NJ: Lawrence Erlbaum.

Horowitz, J. A. (1993). A conceptualization of parenting: Examining the single parent family. *Marriage and Family Review, 20*(1/2), 43-70.

Horowitz, J. A., Hughes, C. B., & Perdue, B. J. (1982). *Parenting reassessed: A nursing perspective.* Englewood Cliffs, NJ: Prentice Hall.

Joe, J. R., & Miller, D. (1987). *American Indian cultural perspectives on disability.* Tucson: University of Arizona, Native American Research and Training Center.

Kelley, M. L., & Tseng, H.-M. (1992). Cultural differences in childbearing: A comparison of immigrant Chinese and Caucasian American mothers. *Journal of Cross-Cultural Psychology, 23,* 444-445.

Kelley, M. L., Power, T. G., & Wimbush, D. D. (1992). Determinants of disciplinary practices in low-income black mothers. *Child Development, 63,* 573-582.

Keniston, K., & Carnegie Council on Children. (1977). *All our children: The American family under pressure.* New York: Harcourt Brace Jovanovich.

Kohn, M. L. (1979). The effects of social class on parental values and practices. In D. Reiss & H. Hoffman (Eds.), *The American family: Dying or developing* (pp. 45-68). New York: Plenum.

Lamb, M. E., & Oppenheim, D. (1989). Fatherhood and father-child relationships. In S. Cath, A. Gurwitt, & L. Gunsberg (Eds.), *Fathers and their families* (pp. 11-26). Hillsdale, NJ: Analytic Press.

LaRossa, R., & LaRossa, M. M. (1981). *Transition to parenthood: How infants change families.* Beverly Hills, CA: Sage.

LaRossa, R., & LaRossa, M. M. (1989). Baby care: Fathers vs. mothers. In B. Risman & P. Schwartz (Eds.), *Gender in intimate relationships: A microstructural approach* (pp. 138-154). Belmont, CA: Wadsworth.

Lee, M. A., Haught, K., Redlener, I., Fant, A., Fox, E., & Somers, S. A. (1990). Health care for children in homeless families. In P. Brickner, L. Scharer, B. Conanan, M. Savarese, & B. Scanlan (Eds.), *Under the safety net: The health and social welfare of the homeless in the United States* (pp. 119-138). New York: Norton.

LeMasters, E. E., & DeFrain, J. (1989). *Parents in contemporary America: A sympathetic view* (5th ed.). Belmont, CA: Wadsworth.

Lerner, R. M., Castellino, D. R., Terry, P. A., Villarruel, F. A., & McKinney, M. H. (1995). Developmental contextual perspective on parenting. In M. Bornstein (Ed.), *Handbook of parenting,* Vol. 2: *Biology and ecology of parenting* (pp. 285-310). Mahwah, NJ: Lawrence Erlbaum.

LeVine, R. A. (1988). Human parental care: Universal goals, cultural strategies, individual behavior. In R. LeVine, P. Miller, & M. West (Eds.), *Parental behavior in diverse societies* (pp. 3-12). San Francisco: Jossey-Bass.

LeVine, R., & White, M. (1992). The social transformation of childhood. In A. Skolnick & J. Skolnick (Eds.), *Families in transition: Rethinking marriage, sexuality, child rearing, and family organization* (7th ed., pp. 273-293). New York: HarperCollins.

Lin, C.-Y.C., & Fu, V. R. (1990). A comparison of child-rearing practices among Chinese, immigrant Chinese, and Caucasian-American parents. *Child Development, 61,* 429-433.

London, H., & Devore, W. (1988). Layers of understanding: Counseling ethnic minority families. *Family Relations, 37,* 310-314.

Luster, T., & Kain, E. L. (1987). The relation between family context and perceptions of parental efficacy. *Early Child Development and Care, 29,* 301-311.

Luster, T., Rhoades, K., & Haas, B. (1989). The relation between parental values and parenting behavior: A test of the Kohn hypothesis. *Journal of Marriage and the Family, 51,* 139-147.

Maccoby, E. E., & Martin, J. A. (1983). Socialization in the context of the family: Parent-child interaction. In E. Hetherington & P. Mussen (Eds.), *Handbook of child psychology,* Vol. 4: *Socialization, personality and social development* (pp. 1-101). New York: John Wiley.

Maccoby, E. E., & Mnookin, R. H. (1992). *Dividing the child: Social and legal dilemmas of custody.* Cambridge, MA: Harvard University Press.

Martin, G. T., Jr. (1990). *Social policy in the welfare state.* Englewood Cliffs, NJ: Prentice Hall.

Martinez, E. A. (1988). Child behavior in Mexican-American/Chicano families: Maternal teaching and childrearing practices. *Family Relations, 37,* 275-280.

Martinez, E. A. (1993). Parenting young children in Mexican American/Chicano families. In H. McAdoo (Ed.), *Family ethnicity: Strength in diversity* (pp. 184-192). Newbury Park, CA: Sage.

McAdoo, H. P. (1985). Strategies used by black single mothers against stress. *Review of Black Political Economy, 14,* 153-167.

McAdoo, H. P. (1991). Family values and outcomes for children. *Journal of Negro Education, 60,* 361-365.

McAdoo, H. P. (1993). Ethnic families: Strengths that are found in diversity. In H. McAdoo (Ed.), *Family ethnicity: Strength in diversity* (pp. 3-14). Newbury Park, CA: Sage.

McBride, B. A., & Mills, G. (1993). A comparison of mother and father involvement with their preschool age children. *Early Childhood Research Quarterly, 8*, 457-477.

McLanahan, S., & Adams, J. (1987). Parenthood and psychological well-being. *Annual Review of Immunology, 5*, 237-257.

McLoyd, V. C. (1990). The impact of economic hardship on black families and children: Psychological distress, parenting, and socioemotional development. *Child Development, 61*, 311-346.

Mills, C. W. (1959). *The sociological imagination.* New York: Oxford University Press.

Morgan, D. H. (1985). *The family, politics and social theory.* London: Routledge.

Newman, K. S. (1988). *Falling from grace.* New York: Free Press.

Ogbu, J. U. (1981). Origins of human competence: A cultural-ecological perspective. *Child Development, 52*, 413-429.

Ogbu, J. U. (1985). A cultural ecology of competence among inner-city blacks. In M. Spencer, G. Brookings, & W. Allen (Eds.), *Beginnings: The social and affective development of black children* (pp. 45-66). Hillsdale, NJ: Lawrence Erlbaum.

Ogbu, J. U. (1987). Variability in minority school performance: A problem in search of an explanation. *Anthropology and Education Quarterly, 18*, 312-334.

Ogbu, J. U. (1988). Cultural discontinuities and human development. In D. Slaughter (Ed.), *Black children and poverty: A developmental perspective* (pp. 11-28). San Francisco: Jossey-Bass.

Okin Moller, S. (1989). *Justice, gender, and the family.* New York: Basic Books.

Osmond, M. W., & Thorne, B. (1993). Feminist theories: The social construction of gender in families and society. In P. Boss, W. Doherty, R. LaRossa, W. Schumm, & S. Steinmetz (Eds.), *Sourcebook of family theory and methods: A contextual approach* (pp. 591-625). New York: Plenum.

Palermo, G. B. (1995). Adolescent criminal behavior: Is TV violence one of the culprits? *International Journal of Offender Therapy and Comparative Criminology, 39*(1), 11-22.

Parsons, T. (1955). The American family. In T. Parsons & R. Bales (Eds.), *Family, socialization, and interaction process* (pp. 127-211). New York: Free Press.

Parsons, T. (1964). *Social structure and personality.* New York: Free Press.

Patterson, G. R. (1978). *Families: Applications of social learning to family life* (rev. ed.). Champaign, IL: Research Press.

Phillips, S. J., & Lobar, S. L. (1990). Literature summary of some Navajo child health benefits and rearing practices within a transcultural nursing framework. *Journal of Transcultural Nursing, 1*, 13-20.

Pleck, J. H. (1996, June). *Paternal involvement: Levels, sources, and consequences.* Paper presented at the Co-parenting Roundtable of the Fathers and Families Roundtable Series, Philadelphia.

Popenoe, D. (1988). *Disturbing the nest: Family change and decline in modern societies.* New York: Aldine de Gruyter.

Presser, H. B. (1989). Can we make time for children? The economy, work schedules and child care: Population Association of America, 1989 presidential address. *Demography, 26*, 523-543.

Rapp, R. (1982). Family and class in contemporary America: Notes toward an understanding of ideology. In B. Thorne with M. Yalom (Eds.), *Rethinking the family* (pp. 168-187). New York: Longman.

Rashid, H. (1985). Black family research and parent education programs: The need for convergence. *Contemporary Education, 56,* 180-185.

Riessman, C. K. (1990). *Divorce talk: Women and men make sense of personal relationships.* New Brunswick, NJ: Rutgers University Press.

Roland, A. (1988). *In search of self in India and Japan: Towards a cross-cultural psychology.* Princeton, NJ: Princeton University Press.

Rubin, L. (1992). *Worlds of pain.* New York: Basic Books. (Originally published 1976)

Schor, J. B. (1992). *The overworked American: The unexpected decline of leisure.* New York: Basic Books.

Schutze, Y. (1987). The good mother: The history of the normative model of "Mother Love." *Sociological Studies of Child Development, 2,* 39-70.

Schwandt, T. (1994). Constructivist, interpretivist approaches to human inquiry. In N. Denzin & Y. Lincoln (Eds.), *Handbook of qualitative research* (pp. 118-137). Thousand Oaks, CA: Sage.

Schwartz, L. L. (1994). The challenge of raising one's own nonbiological children. *American Journal of Family Therapy, 22,* 195-207.

Scott, J., & Alwain, D. F. (1989). Gender differences in parental strain: Parental role or gender role? *Journal of Family Issues, 10,* 482-503.

Seidler, V. J. (1992). Men, feminism, and power. In L. May & R. Strikwerda (Eds.), *Rethinking masculinity: Philosophical explorations in light of feminism* (pp. 209-220). Lanham, MD: Rowman & Littlefield.

Shon, S. P., & Ja, D. Y. (1992). Asian families. In A. Skolnick & J. Skolnick (Eds.), *Families in transition: Rethinking marriage, sexuality, child rearing, and family organization* (7th ed., pp. 472-489). New York: HarperCollins.

Sidel, R. (1996). *Keeping women and children last.* New York: Penguin Books.

Skolnick, A., & Skolnick, J. (Eds.). (1994). Introduction. In A. Skolnick & J. Skolnick (Eds.), *Families in transition: Rethinking marriage, sexuality, child rearing, and family organization* (8th ed.). New York: HarperCollins.

Small, S. A., & Eastman, G. (1991). Rearing adolescents in contemporary society: A conceptual framework for understanding the responsibilities and needs of parents. *Family Relations, 40,* 455-462.

Stacey, J. (1993). Good riddance to "the family": A response to David Popenoe. *Journal of Marriage and the Family, 55,* 545-547.

Staples, R. (1988). The emerging majority: Resources for nonwhite families in the U.S. *Family Relations, 37,* 348-354.

Steinberg, L., Elmen, J. D., & Mounts, N. S. (1989). Authoritative parenting, psychosocial maturity, and academic success among adolescents. *Child Development, 60,* 1424-1436.

Swidler, A. (1980). Love and adulthood in American culture. In N. Smelser & E. Erikson (Eds.), *Themes of work and love in adulthood* (pp. 120-150). Cambridge, MA: Harvard University Press.

Taylor, R. L. (Ed.). (1994). *Minority families in the United States: A multicultural perspective.* Englewood Cliffs, NJ: Prentice Hall.

Taylor, R. L., Chatters, L., Tucker, M., & Lewis, E. (1990). Developments in research on black families: A decade review. *Journal of Marriage and the Family, 52,* 993-1014.

Therborn, G. (1993, February). *Children's rights and patriarchy.* Lecture, University of Wisconsin, Madison.

Thompson, L., & Walker, A. J. (1995). The place of feminism in family studies. *Journal of Marriage and the Family, 57,* 847-865.

Thorne, B. (1982). Feminist rethinking of the family. In B. Thorne & M. Yalom (Eds.), *Rethinking the family: Some feminist questions* (1st ed., pp. 1-24). New York: Longman.

Thorne, B. (1993). Feminism and the family: Two decades of thought. In B. Thorne & M. Yalom (Eds.), *Rethinking the family: Some feminist questions* (2nd ed., pp. 3-30). New York: Longman.

Tiedje, L. B., & Darling-Fisher, C. S. (1993). Factors that influence fathers' participation in child care. *Health Care for Women International, 14,* 99-107.

Triandis, H. C., Lisansky, J., Setiadi, B., Chang, B. H., Marin, G., & Bentancout, H. (1982). Stereotyping among Hispanics and Anglos: The uniformity, intensity, direction, and quality of auto- and heterostereotypes. *Journal of Cross-Cultural Psychology, 13,* 409-426.

Uhlenberg, P., & Eggebeen, D. (1986). The declining well-being of American adolescents. *Public Interest, 82,* 25-38.

U.S. Bureau of the Census. (1995). *Statistical abstract of the United States.* Washington, DC: Government Printing Office.

U.S. Department of Agriculture. (1995). *Expenditures on children by families: 1995 annual report* (U.S. Department of Agriculture Center for Nutrition Policy and Promotion, Misc. Pub. No. 1528). Washington, DC: Government Printing Office.

U.S. Department of Labor. (1995). *Making work pay: The case for raising the minimum wage* (press release). Washington, DC: Author.

Vega, W. A. (1990). Hispanic families in the 1980s: A decade of research. *Journal of Marriage and the Family, 52,* 1015-1024.

Vega, W. A. (1992). Hispanic families in the 1980s: A decade of research. In A. Skolnick & J. Skolnick (Eds.), *Families in transition: Rethinking marriage, sexuality, child rearing, and family organization* (7th ed., pp. 490-503). New York: HarperCollins.

Vobejda, B. (1995, July 20). Four million U.S. children under 12 go hungry at home, study says. *Washington Post,* p. A4.

Volling, B. L., & Belsky, J. (1991). Multiple determinants of father involvement during infancy in dual-earner and single-earner families. *Journal of Marriage and the Family, 53,* 461-474.

Webster-Stratton, C. (1990). Stress: A potential disrupter of parent perceptions and family interactions. *Journal of Clinical Child Psychology, 19,* 302-312.

Weiss, R. (1990). *Staying the course: The emotional and social lives of men who do well at work.* New York: Free Press.

West, C., & Zimmerman, D. H. (1987). Doing gender. *Gender & Society, 1*(2), 125-151.

Willis, W. (1992). Families with African-American roots. In E. Lynch & M. Hanson (Eds.), *Developing cross-cultural competence: A guide for working with young children and their families* (pp. 121-150). Baltimore, MD: Paul H. Brookes.

Wilson, W. J. (1987). *The truly disadvantaged.* Chicago: University of Chicago Press.

Wilson, W. J. (1996). *When work disappears: The world of the new urban poor.* New York: Random House.

Wolfe, A. (1989). *Whose keeper? Social science and moral obligation.* Berkeley: University of California Press.

Yellowbird, M., & Snipp, M. (1994). American Indian families. In R. Taylor (Ed.), *Minority families in the United States: A multicultural perspective* (pp. 170-201). Englewood Cliffs, NJ: Prentice Hall.

Zaretsky, E. (1976). *Capitalism, the family and personal life.* New York: Harper & Row.

Zelizer, V. A. (1985). *Pricing the priceless child: The changing social value of children.* New York: Basic Books.

Zigler, E. (1995). Foreword. In M. Bornstein (Ed.), *Handbook of parenting* (Vols. 1-4). Mahwah, NJ: Lawrence Erlbaum.

Zill, N., Moore, K. A., Smith, E. W., Steif, T., & Coiro, M. J. (1995). The life circumstances and development of children in welfare families: A profile based on national survey data. In P. Chase-Lansdale & J. Brooks-Gunn (Eds.), *Escape from poverty: What makes a difference for children?* (pp. 38-59). New York: Cambridge University Press.

Zinn, M. B. (1989). Family, feminism, and race in America. *Gender & Society, 4*(1), 68-82.

Zinn, M. B. (1994). Adaptation and continuity in Mexican-origin families. In R. Taylor (Ed.), *Minority families in the United States: A multicultural perspective* (pp. 64-81). Englewood Cliffs, NJ: Prentice Hall.

Zints, M. V. (1970). American Indians. In T. Horn (Ed.), *Reading for the disadvantaged* (pp. 41-48). New York: Harcourt Brace & World.

Zuniga, M. E. (1992). Families with Latino roots. In E. Lynch & M. Hanson (Eds.), *Developing cross-cultural competence: A guide for working with young children and their families* (pp. 151-179). Baltimore, MD: Paul H. Brookes.

2

Parenting in American Society

A Historical Overview of the Colonial Period Through the 19th Century

MARIS A. VINOVSKIS

STEPHEN M. FRANK

Contemporary discussions of parenting often lament recent changes in parent-child relationships, often postulating a mythical "golden age" in the past when parents supposedly raised their children better. Yet these present-day observers usually are unaware of the complex ways in which parents and children actually interacted earlier and fail to appreciate the changing ways in which our ancestors were expected to care for their offspring. Nor have they considered the actual social context in which children were reared historically.

Recent historical scholarship on families and children can provide us with a better understanding of the diverse ways in which parents dealt with their children. As we shall see, however, there still is considerable disagreement among scholars on how children were viewed and treated by parents in the past. Moreover, most of the recent academic analyses are written only from the perspective of the parents rather than of the children because the latter were much less

45

likely to leave behind specific information about their personal experiences.

Our essay focuses on changes in parenting among families in colonial and 19th-century British North America. Although some effort is made to place the American family within its broader European historical context, the main focus is on immigrants to the New World and their descendants. The first three centuries of settlement are particularly interesting from the perspective of parenting because of the major changes in the roles of mothers and fathers in raising their children. This involves looking at not only how parents saw their own roles but also how they conceptualized the nature of childhood. Although at our present state of scholarly work one cannot expect to arrive at any definitive conclusions, we do know enough to raise some intriguing and important speculations about possible changes in parenting over time in early America.

Parenting in Colonial America

Many people today continue to imagine children in the past growing up in large, extended households where grandparents and other relatives were present to help parents raise their offspring. With the disruptive advent of industrialization and urbanization, it is supposed, the extended households made way for smaller nuclear households that were better adapted to the needs of a more mobile and commercialized society. In the process, however, children lost the benefits of living in more multigenerational, more kin-oriented households; simultaneously, the elderly also suffered as their adult sons and daughters in the extended families no longer were there to care for them.

The idea that children in the past grew up in extended households was popular among many earlier scholars (Parsons, 1943; Wirth, 1938). But more recent scholarship has challenged that view. Laslett (1972) and others, using demographic estimates of mean household size, pointed out that most households in preindustrial Europe already were small and nuclear. Although the use of an index of mean household size has been properly criticized because it fails to take into consideration the changes in the size and complexity of individual households over time, most scholars now agree that there were few extended families in Western Europe or colonial America (Berkner, 1973). Interestingly, due to higher fertility and lower mortality in early New England, that region had considerably larger households than did the colonial South or Western Europe, but they still were predominantly nuclear—parents, children, and single servants or lodgers present, but not grandparents or married children (Degler, 1980; Greven, 1972, Vinovskis, 1977, 1987). When couples in early America married, they were expected to set up their own independent households (Demos, 1970; Modell & Hareven, 1973).

If children grew up in smaller, nuclear households in Western Europe, that did not necessarily mean that they were isolated from the influence of friends and neighbors. Indeed, the rather sharp boundary between households and neighbors today did not exist in late medieval England. According to Stone (1977), in 16th-century England, members of the upper classes often were equally oriented to their wider kinship lineage and individuals from the lower classes to their immediate neighbors as to the persons within their own nuclear households. After the mid-17th century, Stone sees the rise of the closed domesticated nuclear family among the bourgeois with the growth of closer and more affectionate ties among family members and the gradual separation between blood-related members of the nuclear family and their servants and lodgers. Again, scholars disagree somewhat on the timing of these changes or the social classes involved, but most concur that English children in the 15th century lived in social settings very different from those of their counterparts 300 or 400 years later (Trumbach, 1978).

The Puritans who migrated to New England in the 17th century brought with them the ideal of a close and loving family. Although the head of the household was expected to rule over the other members, including servants and boarders, there were established expectations and constraints about that role. Unlike the situation that may have existed in medieval England, the boundaries between the colonial household and neighbors already were being more sharply delineated (Demos, 1970; Morgan, 1944/1966; Vinovskis, 1987). Nevertheless, in 17th-century New England, more so than in the Chesapeake (Maryland and Virginia), neighbors and the state often were called on to intervene when households failed to discipline or educate their members (Norton, 1996). By the end of the 18th century, there was a growing differentiation between related members of the nuclear family and the servants or boarders; there also was an increasing sense of privacy and distance between the nuclear family and the other neighbors (Flaherty, 1972).

Just as there have been changes in the nature and functioning of the family over time, there also may have been shifts in how children were treated by their parents. Today we are shocked and distressed whenever we hear of parents abusing or not loving their own children. Therefore, we have difficulty in imaging societies such as ancient Sparta, where parents abandoned their infants to die, or Carthage, where parents sacrificed their own children to the gods (Lancel, 1995; Soren, Khader, & Slim, 1990).

According to many scholars, maternal indifference to infants was common throughout the Middle Ages (Aries, 1962; Stone, 1977). Parents neither paid much attention to their newborn infants nor grieved when they died. Whereas Aries believed that this indifference continued only until the 16th and 17th centuries, Shorter (1975) argued that it persisted among Western European peasants into the 18th and 19th centuries. Moreover, the practice of leaving infants at foundling hospitals or with wet nurses in France as late as the 19th century produced very high mortality rates (Badinter, 1981). Nearly half of all infants born in Paris in the first two decades of the 19th century were placed with wet nurses (Sussman, 1977).

The debate over parental indifference to young children in early modern Europe continues as other scholars challenge the evidence put forth by Aries (1962), Shorter (1975), and Stone (1977). Pollack (1983), for example, pointed to numerous examples of mothers caring for their newborn children and grieving when they died. The decision to abandon an infant to a foundling hospital or to place an infant with a wet nurse often is portrayed as an act of economic desperation, although Shorter (1975) and others reminded us that many of the children were sent to wet nurses by wealthy parents who thought it unfashionable to care for their own young. Even Jacques Rousseau, who is prominently associated with the emerging European romantic view of the child, forced his mistress to give up their own children (Cranston, 1983, 1991).

Whatever the situation in most of Western Europe, infanticide and child abandonment were less prevalent and less tolerated in both England and America (Hoffer & Hull, 1981; Stone, 1977). Authorities in both countries were quicker to prosecute suspected cases of infanticide, and the public was more outraged by such behavior. The use of wet nurses by English upper class mothers quickly became unfashionable in the late 18th century and never was popular in British North America.

A few scholars have argued that early American parents did not grieve when their young children died (Saum, 1974). But other analysts have shown convincingly the affection of parents for their children, including when they had died young (Demos, 1970; Moran & Vinovskis, 1992; Morgan, 1966). Parental love and affection was so commonplace in American homes in the early 19th century that foreign visitors and domestic observers criticized parents for being too child centered (Wishy, 1968). Nevertheless, colonial authorities, especially outside of New England, were reluctant to interfere when parents may have been abusing their children through excessive corporal punishment (Norton, 1996; Wall, 1990). Ironically, efforts to prevent cruelty to animals in Great Britain and the United States in the early 19th century preceded comparable efforts to protect children by nearly 50 years (Behlmer, 1982; Turner, 1980).

Ascertaining how parents perceived their children in the past is more complicated than one might imagine. Rather than using our own views of children as a guide, many historians have argued that parents in the past regarded their children as "miniature adults" rather than as unique and different from adults in all but size. Fleming (1933) stated more than six decades ago that colonial American "children were regarded simply as miniature adults" (p. 60). This important and challenging insight was popularized most effectively by Aries (1962), who claimed that medieval society did not distinguish between children and adults and that the idea of childhood did not even emerge until the 16th and 17th centuries. Since then, several influential American historians (Demos, 1970, 1974; Modell & Goodman, 1990; Trattner, 1989; Zuckerman, 1970) also have argued that colonial Americans perceived and treated their children as "miniature adults."

More recently, European scholars have questioned Aries's (1962) contention that childhood was not perceived as a separate and unique stage of life in medieval and early modern Europe (Hanawalt, 1986, 1993; Kroll, 1977; Schultz, 1995; Shahar, 1990). Similarly, historians of early America have pointed out that Puritans differentiated between children and adults and expected that proper child rearing should be cognizant of individual differences in ability and temperament among children (Axtell, 1974; Kaestle & Vinovskis, 1978, 1980; Moran & Vinovskis, 1986, 1992; Stannard, 1975, 1977).

Although early Americans may have differentiated between children and adults, they did not necessarily view children the same way in which we see them now. Indeed, children in colonial America were seen as much more capable of early intellectual activity than they are today. Puritans believed everyone should be able to read the Bible; hence both men and women were expected to be literate to fulfill their religious duties. Because they also thought that children were likely to die, the Puritans felt it was imperative that young children learn to read as quickly as possible (Slater, 1977; Stannard, 1975, 1977; Vinovskis, 1972, 1976, 1981).

The idea of early childhood learning was reinforced in the early 19th century when infant schools were established in the United States (Kaestle & Vinovskis, 1978, 1980; May & Vinovskis, 1977). Children were encouraged to enter special schools at 2 and 3 years of age. By 1840, about 40% to 50% of all 3-year-olds in Massachusetts were in school.

But attitudes toward the intellectual capabilities of young children are culturally conditioned and can change surprisingly quickly. When Brigham (1833), a prominent physician, announced that premature intellectual activity by children will weaken the minds of children and eventually lead to insanity, educators and parents removed their children from the new infant schools. By the 1850s and 1860s, there were few, if any, 3- or 4-year-olds left in Massachusetts schools (Kaestle & Vinovskis, 1980).

If the images of children in the past and the locations in which they lived varied from those of children today, so did the interaction of parents and children. Today, the mother is seen as the primary and natural caretaker of the child. Historically, the situation was more complex. As we have seen, in Western Europe it was not unusual for children to be nursed by others (Shorter, 1975; Sussman, 1977), and servants or neighbors often provided important care for the young (Aries, 1962; Stone, 1977).

Yet in 17th- and 18th-century England and America, parents were increasingly expected to care for their own children (Morgan, 1966; Stone, 1977). Puritans in particular stressed the importance of parental involvement and preached a division of labor. Whereas the mother saw to the immediate physical needs of the young child, the father, as the head of the household, was responsible as the primary catechizer and educator of that child. If the household failed to educate its children properly, then the state and church often were willing to intervene by moving the young to a more suitable household (Moran & Vinovskis, 1992).

The primacy of the father in educating the child did not last long in the New World. As many New England males stopped joining the church after the mid-17th century, the authorities were in a quandary about who should catechize the children and servants in the households. They explored various alternatives such as using primary school teachers and hiring a second clergyman to catechize children. Eventually, and somewhat reluctantly, they turned to the wives, who continued to join the church in larger numbers than did their husbands. Gradually, the education of young children at home in the 18th century became identified with the mothers so that by the 19th century the mothers were seen as the natural caretakers (Moran & Vinovskis, 1992).

Just as the care and education of children at home shifted toward the mothers, the 18th century also saw the growing willingness of parents to entrust the more formal education of their children to a school. Puritans believed that it was the responsibility of parents to educate their own children, but they did not object when those efforts were complemented by local schoolteachers (Vinovskis, 1995). Over time, families became even more willing to send their children to a neighborhood school, and the number of schools in states such as Massachusetts expanded rapidly in the 18th century. By 1800, nearly all boys and girls in that state attended a public or private school at some point during their lives (Kaestle & Vinovskis, 1980).

Another long-term change in parent-child relationships was the increasing rights of children to control or at least participate in major life course decisions about their marriages and careers. In the 16th and 17th centuries, the heads of the households had unusually strong control over the other members in England and America. Children were expected to follow the advice and guidance of their parents. Yet gradually children were allowed not only to veto marriages to people they disliked but even to select people they loved as mates (Stone, 1977; Trumbach, 1978). Although it is difficult to date precisely the erosion of parental power over the mate selection, it appears that much of this occurred in the late 18th and early 19th centuries in America (Smith, 1973b).

Parenting in 19th-Century America

The apparent timing is significant. Issues of periodization vex the history of parent-child relationships, as the disputed origins of the modern idea of childhood in preindustrial Europe attest. Historians, however, often point to the decades after 1780 as one of the watersheds in the history of American parenting.

We have already noted that patriarchalism diminished and the mother's role expanded in the 18th century, especially in the area of religious instruction. In postrevolutionary America and the early republic, this long-term enhancement of the mother's role became the subject of unprecedented cultural celebration. Writers, clerics, and family advisers trumpeted the ideal of a nurturing motherhood as the essence of femininity, a woman's true and most important calling, even a means to social salvation. Listening to this fanfare for motherhood in the Victorian era, it is easy to imagine that fatherhood lost its meaning in 19th-century households, with maternal nurture crowding fathers to the margins of family life. In point of fact, the expansion of motherhood was something other than a zero-sum game. Later in this section, we see that 19th-century moralists and parents themselves took great pains to maintain a place for fathers at home, notwithstanding the new emphasis on maternalism. First, however, the Victorian fascination with motherhood requires explanation.

A wide array of economic and cultural forces helped to elevate the mother's role at the turn of the 19th century. Under the heading of cultural influence, republican political ideology and softened Christian theology, particularly the growing acceptance among evangelical denominations of childhood conversion, were perhaps the most important vehicles for new modes of parenting.

In the social ferment of the revolutionary era, an outpouring of advice books, philosophical tracts, and novels popularized new ideas about children and the family. Writers in the 18th century, who habitually dramatized issues of political authority in terms of family relationships, came to view patriarchal dominance as a threat not only to the emergent republican social order but also to the well-being of particular families. Unyielding patriarchs, according to the republican view, imperiled the happiness of wives and children as surely as tyrants threatened political liberty (Fliegelman, 1982).

All was not lost, however. Through their capacity for goodness, women in the early republic came to be seen as uplifting influences on their husbands and children, a source of religious values in the home, and a counterforce to the unbridled commercialism and self-interest of the public sphere (Kerber, 1980; Norton, 1980). Although foreshadowed by ideals of maternal tenderness already current in the 18th century (Ulrich, 1982), this reappraisal of women's moral worth gained force under the influence of the Romantic movement. Traits associated with the female character that once were disparaged, such as affection and susceptibility to emotion, now were cast in a more favorable light (Bloch, 1978). These changes often are summarized under the rubric of "republican motherhood," although it is more accurate to speak of the "republican wife." As the historian Lewis (1987) showed, republican moralists focused more on the influence a woman could (and should) have on her husband than on her power to shape her children's lives.

Nonetheless, more favorable assessments of womanhood went hand in hand with new ideas about children and how they should be raised (Degler, 1980). Romantic descriptions of children as naturally innocent, social, and affectionate reshaped parental attitudes by calling for more loving and tender methods of child nurture. Equally important, many Protestant ministers began to question strict Calvinist notions of infant depravity, stressing instead children's redeemability (Wishy, 1968). Belief in redeemable children's susceptibility to maternal influence linked the antipatriarchalism of the 18th century to the domesticity of the 19th century, preparing the way for the exaltation of motherhood and the child-centered private home.

By 1830, a growing consensus of family advice suggested that the object of child rearing was not to break children's will but rather to mold their character. Whereas earlier generations of parents, fearing children's depravity, had stressed the need to conform to external authority, 19th-century parents, less suspicious of children's will, sought instead to build their character and to develop their capacity for self-control. Obedience, it bears emphasizing, remained the primary aim of child rearing, but the means shifted in the antebellum era to stress the internalization of moral prohibitions. The best way in which to mold character, according to 19th-century family advisers, was through emotional nurturance, force of love, and parental example (Kuhn, 1947; Sunley, 1955).

This new emphasis on moral suasion, although prescribed for both parents, tended to enhance the role of the mother. In the 19th century, the ideals of middle-class manhood included the capacity to demonstrate love, kindness, and affection within the family circle (Lystra, 1989). But women were seen as providentially endowed with these emotions, divinely suited to nurture young minds through affection and influence. Accordingly, family advisers and popular domestic writers advanced a conception of motherhood as women's ultimate aim in life and the main standard of 19th-century femininity. For reformers such as Catharine Beecher, motherhood was a means to social salvation. Redeeming the souls of individual family members, Beecher believed, ultimately would lead to creation of a virtuous society (Sklar, 1973). Other advisers, such as Lydia Maria Child, invested motherhood with less moral significance but insisted that a woman's domestic duties had to be performed diligently precisely because they were her duties (Ryan, 1982).

A series of economic and demographic changes affecting the lives of both children and their parents contributed to the new cultural emphasis on feminine domesticity. Under the demographic heading, families became smaller. Although the precise causes of the transition to lower birthrates are controversial, economic change played an important role (Degler, 1980; Vinovskis, 1981). The reduction in fertility reflected, in part, parents' mutual realization that in a commercial-industrial society, children no longer were the economic assets they once had been, either as laborers or for support in old age. Increasingly, parents eager to see their children get ahead in a rapidly changing society felt compelled to keep them in school longer. Smaller families permitted parents to invest more time, energy, and financial resources in each child to prepare sons for respectable careers and daughters for marriage (Kett, 1977). Before the decline in birthrates, which began in some areas of the country in the late 18th century, an average woman bore seven or eight children over the course of her married life. By the end of the 19th century, families had reduced the number of children born to three or four. Although smaller families influenced the parenting of women and men alike, the impact on mothers was most direct. Fewer children meant that women devoted less of their lives to infant care, freeing them to attend to growing children.

Economic change also put a premium on maternal nurture. The vast majority of Americans continued to farm in the first half of the 19th century, but increasingly families used cash from the sale of crops to buy food, clothing, and other necessities that they once had produced themselves (Sellers, 1991). As a commercialized society removed economic production from the home, a new domestic division of labor emerged. Instead of participating in home-based industries, the middle-class wife was expected to devote full-time to keeping house and raising children. At the same time, growing numbers of men shifted their work from farm or workshop to counting houses, mills, factories, and other places of business removed from home. As a consequence, home and work life came to be viewed increasingly as two distinct and separate endeavors (Cott, 1977).

The growing distinction between public and private spheres placed mothers in a position of strategic importance for their developing children. As the economic importance of the household declined, the moral nurture of children was elevated to the center of middle-class family life. Within the ideal home, the more available mother became chiefly responsible for arranging the environment in which the young child would grow up. As a result, mothers came to control their own lives and the lives of their children in ways they had not in earlier periods of American history, a development sometimes described as "domestic feminism" (Smith, 1973a).

The new domestic ideology, and especially growing perceptions of women's expertise in child rearing, registered in legal changes involving child custody and divorce. In early America, the English common law tradition had given fathers almost unlimited custody rights, but by 1820 American courts were placing growing emphasis on the special parenting capabilities of mothers. By looking at the "best interests" of the children and the fitness of the parents, judges began to limit the custody rights of fathers. As early as 1860, a number of states adopted the "tender age" rule, whereby young children were placed in their mothers' care unless the mothers proved unworthy (Grossberg, 1985).

In sum, a series of loosely connected cultural, economic, and demographic developments dramatically expanded the 19th-century mother's role. If that were the entire story, then the last century's legacy to modern parenthood would be unambiguous: a vastly exalted concept of maternal responsibility for the emotional and physical care of children and a shrunken role for the father, one limited primarily to earning the money needed for the family's subsistence. In fact, the story is both more interesting and more complex. Although Victorian Americans were fervent believers in the power of the mother's love, 19th-century parenting abounded in ironies, not least the persistence of paternal domestic authority in the so-called century of the mother. Alongside the venerated mother, Victorian culture placed the responsible family man, a father with vital work to do beyond providing a paycheck.

Although breadwinning became crucial to male identity, fatherly nurture—what 19th-century parents characteristically referred to as a "father's care"—was firmly implanted in new definitions of middle-class masculinity. Beginning in the 1830s and 1840s, Protestant moralists called men home under the banner of "Christian fatherhood." This religiously grounded domestic ideal reverberated as well in secular culture, both early and late in the century.

In its religious variant, proponents of masculine domesticity insisted that "Christian fathers" were jointly responsible with mothers for their children's upbringing. Lamenting the long hours that men were beginning to spend in factories and offices, their excessive involvement in politics, and the leisure time they passed in the company of other men, proponents of Christian fatherhood insisted that good fathers did more than provide for their families. They also exerted themselves on their children's behalf by helping mothers shape their character and by preparing them, especially sons, for adult life. Such men took time to enrich their children's education, to play with them, and to become their companions. These demonstrations of fatherly care, the moralists made clear, not only would redound to the benefit of the children but also would help to invest men's lives with meaning. This moral critique of men's priorities paved the way for a new middle-class male identity: that of a father who recognized his importance at home and refused to cede the domestic space entirely to his spouse—in short, a family man (Frank, 1995).

Throughout the 19th century, a model of domestic paternal authority persisted in religious family culture alongside the rise of the moral mother (McDannell, 1986). In secular guise as well, the evangelical vision of parenting as a moral endeavor uniting the sexes reverberated in 19th-century culture. Themes that emphasized the sanctity of the family and the importance of marriage as a source of masculine joy and fulfillment, for example, filled the pages of popular fiction. Not only female domestic writers but also male authors writing for a male readership depicted men for whom home was an essential ingredient of happiness and a place they sorely missed when deprived of its emotional warmth (McCall, 1991). Similarly, the mid-century vogue of phrenology, a pseudo-scientific but wildly popular account of human nature, posited "philoprogenativeness," or parental love, as a faculty shared by the sexes and indispensable to conjugal happiness. Later in the century, medical writers and scientists emphasized men's biological impact on their children and affirmed that fatherhood was indispensable to true manhood. To fail to become a father struck 19th-century doctors and moral advisers as unnatural, self-indulgent, and immature. Begetting children, they averred, ultimately made men less selfish, more refined, and better disciplined. In this medical view, fatherhood was the crowning reward for the self-restraint, self-culture, and self-mastery central to Victorian conceptions of masculinity (Frank, 1995).

Clearly, then, 19th-century family ideology intended to regulate, rather than subvert, paternal authority, even as it carved out a distinct sphere for women in the home. On one level, of course, the flag-waving for fatherhood was simply an effort to shore up patriarchal power, to insist that men retained their prerogatives as heads and rulers of their households notwithstanding the new importance of mothers. At the same time, the moralists, medical men, and popular writers who invented the 19th-century family man recognized that fathers make vital contributions within families beyond breadwinning and that fathering plays a crucial role in men's lives.

Just as the Victorian mother's role expanded in loose relation to economic change, so was the family man a product of the transition from agriculture to commerce and industry. In the long run, urban-industrial change clearly confirmed that fathers were part-time parents. Breadwinning came first on the list of masculine priorities, with other aspects of fatherly care undertaken as work permitted. But it is by no means clear that paternal availability declined precipitously as a result of the industrial revolution. Many rural fathers left home for long periods of time and thus were less available to their children than were their urban counterparts. So, too, rural youths often left home to attend school or go to work, thereby placing themselves beyond parental reach. Nor were industrial towns necessarily averse to father-child contact. As the historian Hareven (1982) showed, in some factory communities, families worked as a unit and fathers played a decisive role in recruiting their own children as coworkers. In small towns and cities, moreover, shopkeepers and professionals managed to combine home and work through mid-century and, in some cases, well beyond. It is not at all unusual to find in family documents references to fathers whose workdays easily accommodated their presence in and about the home on a variety of errands or to partake of the afternoon meal (Frank, 1995). In short, the separation of home and work wrought by industrialization occurred slowly and unevenly, with significant variation by occupation and class position (Pleck, 1976).

Although its distancing impact on fathers is well known, the 19th century's market revolution produced countervailing tendencies as well. Business life in a commercialized society often fostered the conviction that, outside the family, the world was a selfish and hostile arena full of confidence men and fraught with hypocrisy (Halttunen, 1982). As a consequence, home came to be seen as an oasis from the market, a retreat from the workaday world (Jeffrey, 1972). For many bourgeois men, this idealized home was not just a place to recharge their batteries before reentering the economic fray but was also a source of values opposed to unrestrained capitalism. Families offered men access to a moral life they felt they could not lead on their own. How better to counter unbridled competitiveness and the dissembling of strangers than by cultivating intense familial bonds (Frank, 1995)?

The evidence of diaries and letters suggests that many 19th-century fathers invested considerable time and energy in family life and valued their ties to wives and children. Perhaps as a consequence of diminished availability, the times when fathers were at home in evenings, and especially on Sundays, assumed an almost ritualistic importance in many middle-class homes. At the dinner table or by the fireside, fathers quizzed, played games, or simply talked to their children. Men's diaries and letters demonstrate intense interest in the moral, intellectual, and physical development of both sons and daughters (Frank, 1995).

Such settled domesticity began even before children were born. Examples of men who became increasingly solicitous of their wives during pregnancy are not difficult to find. Men frequently assisted in the birthing chamber, lending practical and moral support to their wives as their children entered the world. When children were young, new understandings of the value of family time vastly expanded the 19th-century father's role as a companion and playmate. References to children having "frolics" with their fathers ring through 19th-century family documents, belying the stereotype of the starched Victorian patriarch.

As children grew older, fathers became less frolicsome and more concerned about securing a place for them in society. In rural communities, fathers guided their sons into farm work or trades at an early age, an obligation that bred both respect and resentment. As occupational transmission became more complicated in cities and towns, pressure mounted on fathers to provide children with extended education. Whereas parents, especially fathers, in rural areas often were reluctant to have children receive more than a basic common school education, a vanguard of urban middle-class parents prided themselves on the sacrifices they made for their children's education. Properly educated children, in fact, became a marker of social class, a sign that parents had taken the time and made the sacrifices needed to secure their children a respectable place in society.

Mounting pressure to provide education coincided with a growing belief that *adolescence,* a term rarely used until the end of the 19th century, was an unsettled time of life. This new conception of youth shaped parental behavior by underscoring the need for close supervision and guidance of sons and daughters to ensure a smooth transition to adulthood (Kett, 1977; Moran & Vinovskis, 1992). Such concerns, coupled with belief in the need for children's prompt and implicit obedience, fostered a controlling, and sometimes imperious, style of parenting that particularly inflected the relationship between fathers and sons (Frank, 1995).

To this point, our discussion of 19th-century parenthood has focused on white, middle-class families. Variations by race, class, ethnicity, and region complicate the story. Although detailed analysis of these differences is beyond the scope of this chapter, a number of generalizations about working-class and immigrant parents are in order. Long after the collective family economy was displaced by the domestic, child-centered, middle-class household, working-class parents and children continued to perceive themselves as a work unit. Labor force participation by women and children posed a critical dilemma for working-class and immigrant families when confronted with middle-class ideals at odds with collective family effort (Hareven, 1991); the employment of working-class women outside the home could create a struggle for power within households when men clung to the sole provider role. Then, too, children who brought language skills learned in school, new perceptions of American behavior, new work habits, and new leisure interests into the home challenged traditional parental authority. Guided by Old World values, different ethnic groups fashioned distinctive family strategies and parental roles. Mothers in Eastern European Jewish households, for instance, were much less likely than their counterparts in other immigrant groups to seek employment in the paid labor force (Glenn, 1990).

Although the variety of ethnic differences cannot be addressed here, the experience of black parents under slavery and freedom was so different from that of whites as to require separate consideration (Stevenson, 1996). Although most slave children lived in stable, two-parent households, the roles played by their parents were distinctive. Recent scholarship dispels the myth of weak ties between slave fathers and their families and has punctured the corresponding stereotype of a prevalent slave "matriarchy." But as the historian Kolchin (1993) showed, slave families typically were less male dominated than 19th-century free families. This was so for at least two reasons. First, because slave families had no legal status, husbands had no more property rights than did their wives. As a consequence, slave husbands lacked the authority over their wives that the legal system bestowed on free men. Second, slave fathers were more likely than mothers to be separated from their children. Men were hired out, were sold off, and ran away more frequently than did women. When parents lived on separate plantations, fathers rather than mothers typically traveled to visit their families on weekends. Accordingly, mother-headed households, although not the norm, were relatively common. In Louisiana, for instance, about one third of slave households were headed by single parents, most often mothers (Kolchin, 1993).

With their parents and older siblings at work, young slave children received relatively little supervision. Until age 7 or 8, most children spent much of their time playing among themselves. Nonetheless, masters interfered in young children's lives in a variety of ways, and slave children soon learned to conform to the wishes of both their parents and their owners. In the words of Kolchin (1993), "Children who saw their parents verbally or physically abused could not fail to draw the appropriate lesson about where real power lay" (p. 142). At the same time, slave parents struggled against the subversion of their authority. Mothers and fathers afforded their children a basic refuge from the horrors of slavery, providing them with love and attention, imparting family customs and religious values, and teaching them the caution needed to survive in a hostile white society (Kolchin, 1993).

In the years following slavery, the vast majority of black children continued to live in two-parent households. As blacks adapted to the vagaries of urban life, the family remained a vibrant institution, with parents rendering vital assistance to children (Gutman, 1976). Nonetheless, cities were especially hard on black parents. The proportion of African American families headed by females in the late 19th and early 20th centuries exceeded that of native-born and immigrant whites. Persistent discrimination, segregation, and under- or unemployment in northern and southern cities undermined the ability of black fathers to support their wives and children. As a result, African American fathers left their families more often than did white fathers (Griswold, 1993).

Conclusion

Distinctive modes of parenting among different social classes and ethnic groups belie easy generalizations about parenthood in the past. Nonetheless, what is most striking about 19th-century parents is not how different they were from their 20th-century counterparts but rather how strikingly "modern" they seem. In large part, the resemblance owes to the consolidation of companionate marriage ideas and, especially, the modern idea of motherhood in the last century. Although the primacy of the mother is discernible earlier in American history and may have its origins in the religious crisis that gripped Puritan New England after the mid-17th century, 19th-century family culture created expectations about who would bring up children and how they would be raised that, until recently, have remained remarkably stable. Especially in the middle class, the pressure on parents to provide children with material and emotional care mounted in the Victorian era. Not far below the surface of the moral mother and the 19th-century family man lay a new anxiety for children's prospects in a rapidly changing society. The flood of Victorian parenting advice both reflected and fed that anxiety. To be sure, 19th-century parents were not all that moralists and family advisers made them out to be or, more precisely, hoped them to be. Some parents always have lacked the playfulness, empathy, and capacity for loving, consistent discipline needed to raise children well. But for men and women alike, those attributes were celebrated in 19th-century culture as the ideal toward which parental behavior should tend.

This is not to postulate a "golden age" or to suggest that 19th-century parents came closer to approximating the ideal than do parents today. Rather, it is to recognize that mothers and fathers in the last century, more so than their 20th-century counterparts, understood parenting to be a moral enterprise and set standards for themselves accordingly.

Industrialization, urbanization, changing images of childhood, and relatively autonomous changes in children's lives, such as the rise and fall of the apprenticeship system and the advent of common schools, redefined the roles of mothers and fathers in the past. Today economic pressure, demographic developments, and the feminist challenge to traditional family roles once again have placed parent-child relationships in transition.

During the past three decades, women, including married women and mothers, have entered the labor force in unprecedented numbers. By the early 1990s, more than half the mothers of children under age 3 were working for wages. Today the typical mother is a working woman, a development that has raised the prospect (so far more in theory than in fact) of greater male commitment to child care.

Spiraling divorce rates also distinguish contemporary parents from their 19th-century counterparts. The divorce rate tripled between 1960 and 1982, and as many as half of the children born in the early 1980s will be children of divorced parents. The increase in single (including never-married) mothers has followed the same steep rise. Today more than 25% of all children are born to mothers who have never been married, and the percentage of such African American children is even higher.

Finally, even parents who benefit from the presence of spouses are coping with external pressures to their 19th-century forebears. Frequently, two-parent families need to accommodate the work schedules of both parents. As a consequence, mundane rituals of 19th-century family life such as regularly sitting down to dinner together are now less common.

In ways large and small, then, recent demographic, socioeconomic, and cultural developments suggest that parenting may have reached another historic watershed, one marked by an accompanying outpouring of scholarly and popular concern about the quality of parent-child relationships. However one assesses the state of contemporary parenthood, that heightened concern contains the possibility at least of recapturing the sense of moral purpose brought to these issues by parents in the past.

References

Aries, P. (1962). *Centuries of childhood: A social history of family life* (R. Baldick, Trans.). New York: Vintage Books.

Axtell, J. (1974). *The school upon a hill: Education and society in colonial New England.* New Haven, CT: Yale University Press.

Badinter, E. (1981). *Motherly love: Myth and reality.* New York: Macmillan.

Behlmer, G. K. (1982). *Child abuse and moral reform in England, 1870-1908.* Stanford, CA: Stanford University Press.

Berkner, L. K. (1973). Recent research on the history of the family in Western Europe. *Journal of Marriage and the Family, 35,* 395-405.

Bloch, R. H. (1978). American feminine ideals in transition: The rise of the moral mother, 1785-1815. *Feminist Studies, 4,* 101-126.

Brigham, A. (1833). *Remarks on the influence of mental cultivation and mental excitement upon health* (2nd ed.). Boston: Marsh, Capen, & Lyon.

Cott, N. F. (1977). *The bonds of womanhood: "Woman's sphere" in New England, 1780-1835.* New Haven, CT: Yale University Press.

Cranston, M. (1983). *Jean-Jacques: The early life and work of Jean-Jacques Rouseau, 1712-1754.* New York: Norton.

Cranston, M. (1991). *The noble savage: Jean-Jacques Rousseau, 1754-1762.* New York: Penguin Books.

Degler, C. N. (1980). *At odds: Women and the family in America from the Revolution to the present.* New York: Oxford University Press.

Demos, J. (1970). *A little commonwealth: Family life in Plymouth colony.* New York: Oxford University Press.

Demos, J. (1974). The American family in past time. *American Scholar, 43,* 422-446.

Flaherty, D. H. (1972). *Privacy in colonial New England.* Charlottesville: University of Virginia Press.

Fleming, S. (1933). *Children and Puritanism: The place of children in the life and thought of New England churches, 1620-1847.* New Haven, CT: Yale University Press.

Fliegelman, J. (1982). *Prodigals and Pilgrims: The American Revolution against patriarchal authority, 1750-1800.* Cambridge, UK: Cambridge University Press.

Frank, S. M. (1995). *Life with father: Parenthood and masculinity in the nineteenth-century American North.* Ph.D. dissertation, Department of Sociology, University of Michigan.

Glenn, S. A. (1990). *Daughters of the Shtetly: Life and labor in the immigrant generation.* Ithaca, NY: Cornell University Press.

Greven, P. J. (1972). The average size of families and households in the province of Massachusetts in 1764 and in the United States in 1790: An overview. In P. Laslett (Ed.), *Household and family in past time* (pp. 545-560). Cambridge, UK: Cambridge University Press.

Griswold, R. L. (1993). *Fatherhood in America: A history.* New York: Basic Books.

Grossberg, M. (1985). *Governing the hearth: Law and the family in nineteenth-century America.* Chapel Hill: University of North Carolina Press.

Gutman, H. G. (1976). *The black family in slavery and freedom, 1750-1925.* New York: Pantheon Books.

Halttunen, K. (1982). *Confidence men and painted women: A study of middle-class culture in America, 1830-1870.* New Haven, CT: Yale University Press.

Hanawalt, B. A. (1986). *The ties that bound: Peasant families in medieval England.* New York: Oxford University Press.

Hanawalt, B. A. (1993). *Growing up in medieval London: The experience of childhood in history.* New York: Oxford University Press.

Hareven, T. K. (1982). *Family time and industrial time: The relationship between family and work in a New England industrial community.* Cambridge, UK: Cambridge University Press.

Hareven, T. K. (1991). The history of the family and the complexity of social change. *American Historical Review, 96,* 95-124.

Hoffer, P. C., & Hull, N. E. H. (1981). *Murdering mothers: Infanticide in England and New England, 1558-1803.* New York: New York University Press.

Jeffrey, K. (1972). The family as utopian retreat from the city. *Soundings, 55,* 21-41.

Kaestle, C. F., & Vinovskis, M. A. (1978). From apron strings to ABCs: Parents, children, and schooling in nineteenth-century Massachusetts. In J. Demos & S. Boocock (Eds.), *Turning points: Historical and sociological essays on the family* (pp. S39-S80). Chicago: University of Chicago Press.

Kaestle, C. F., & Vinovskis, M. A. (1980). *Education and social change in nineteenth-century Massachusetts.* Cambridge, UK: Cambridge University Press.

Kerber, L. K. (1980). *Women of the republic: Intellect and ideology in revolutionary America.* Chapel Hill: University of North Carolina Press.

Kett, J. F. (1977). *Rites of passage: Adolescence in America, 1790 to the present.* New York: Basic Books.

Kolchin, P. (1993). *American slavery, 1619-1877.* New York: Hill & Wang.

Kroll, J. (1977). The concept of childhood in the Middle Ages. *Journal of the History of the Behavioral Sciences, 13,* 384-393.

Kuhn, A. L. (1947). *The mother's role in childhood education: New England concepts, 1830-1860.* New Haven, CT: Yale University Press.

Lancel, S. (1995). *Carthage: A history* (A. Nevill, Trans.). Oxford, UK: Blackwell.

Laslett, P. (Ed.). (1972). *Household and family in past time.* Cambridge, UK: Cambridge University Press.

Lewis, J. (1987). The republican wife: Virtue and seduction in the early republic. *William and Mary Quarterly, 44,* 689-721.

Lystra, K. (1989). *Searching the heart: Women, men, and romantic love in nineteenth-century America.* New York: Oxford University Press.

May, D., & Vinovskis, M. A. (1977). A ray of millennial light: Early education and social reform in the infant school movement in Massachusetts, 1826-1840. In T. Hareven (Ed.), *Family and kin in urban communities, 1700-1930* (pp. 62-99). New York: New Viewpoints.

McCall, L. (1991, November). *Gender in fiction: The creations of literary men and women.* Paper presented at the meeting of the Social Science History Association, New Orleans, LA.

McDannell, C. (1986). *The Christian home in Victorian America, 1840-1900.* Bloomington: Indiana University Press.

Modell, J., & Goodman, M. (1990). Historical perspectives. In S. Feldman & G. Elliott (Eds.), *At the threshold: The developing adolescent* (pp. 93-122). Cambridge, MA: Harvard University Press.

Modell, J., & Hareven, T. K. (1973). Urbanization and the malleable household: An examination of boarding and lodging in American families. *Journal of Marriage and the Family, 35,* 467-479.

Moran, G. F., & Vinovskis, M. A. (1986). The great care of godly parents: Early childhood in Puritan New England. In A. Smuts & J. Hagen (Eds.), *History and research in child development* (pp. 24-37). Chicago: University of Chicago Press.

Moran, G. F., & Vinovskis, M. A. (1992). *Religion, family, and the life course: Explorations in the social history of early America.* Ann Arbor: University of Michigan Press.

Morgan, E. S. (1966). *The Puritan family: Religion and domestic relations in seventeenth-century New England.* New York: Harper & Row. (Originally published 1944)

Norton, M. B. (1980). *Liberty's daughters: The revolutionary experience of American women, 1750-1800.* Boston: Little, Brown.

Norton, M. B. (1996). *Gendered power and the forming of American society.* New York: Knopf.

Parsons, T. (1943). The kinship system of the contemporary United States. *American Anthropologist, 45,* 22-38.

Pleck, E. H. (1976). Two worlds in one: Work and family. *Journal of Social History, 10,* 178-195.

Pollock, L. (1983). *Forgotten children: Parent-child relations from 1500 to 1900.* Cambridge, UK: Cambridge University Press.

Ryan, M. P. (1982). *The empire of the mother: American writing about domesticity, 1830-1860.* New York: Haworth.

Saum, L. O. (1974). Death in the popular mind of pre-Civil War America. *American Quarterly, 26,* 477-495.

Schultz, J. A. (1995). *The knowledge of childhood in the German Middle Ages, 1100-1350.* Philadelphia: University of Pennsylvania Press.

Sellers, C. (1991). *The market revolution: Jacksonian America, 1815-1846.* New York: Oxford University Press.

Shahar, S. (1990). *Childhood in the Middle Ages.* London: Routledge.

Shorter, E. (1975). *The making of the modern family.* New York: Basic Books.

Sklar, K. K. (1973). *Catharine Beecher: A study in American domesticity.* New Haven, CT: Yale University Press.

Slater, P. G. (1977). *Children in the New England mind: In death and in life.* Hamden, CT: Archon Books.

Smith, D. S. (1973a). Family limitation, sexual control, and domestic feminism in Victorian America. *Feminist Studies, 1,* 40-57.

Smith, D. S. (1973b). Parental power and marriage patterns: An analysis of historical trends in Hingham, Massachusetts. *Journal of Marriage and the Family, 35,* 406-418.

Soren, D., Khader, A. B., & Slim, H. (1990). *Carthage: Uncovering the mysteries and splendors of ancient Tunisia.* New York: Simon & Schuster.

Stannard, D. E. (1975). Death and the Puritan child. In D. Stannard (Ed.), *Death in America* (pp. 9-29). Philadelphia: University of Pennsylvania Press.

Stannard, D. E. (1977). *The Puritan way of death: A study of religion, culture, and social change.* New York: Oxford University Press.

Stevenson, B. (1996). *Life in black and white: Family and community in the slave South.* New York: Oxford University Press.

Stone, L. (1977). *The family, sex and marriage in England, 1500-1800.* New York: Harper & Row.

Sunley, R. (1955). Early nineteenth-century American literature on child rearing. In M. Mead & M. Wolfenstein (Eds.), *Childhood in contemporary cultures* (pp. 150-167). Chicago: University of Chicago Press.

Sussman, G. D. (1977). Parisian infants and Norman wet nurses in the early nineteenth century: A statistical study. *Journal of Interdisciplinary History, 7,* 637-654.

Trattner, W. I. (1989). *From poor law to welfare state: A history of social welfare in America* (4th ed.). New York: Free Press.

Trumbach, R. (1978). *The rise of the egalitarian family: Aristocratic kinship and domestic relations in eighteenth-century England.* New York: Academic Press.

Turner, J. (1980). *Reckoning with the beast: Animals, pain, and humanity in the Victorian mind.* Baltimore, MD: Johns Hopkins University Press.

Ulrich, L. T. (1982). *Good wives: Image and reality in the lives of women in northern New England, 1650-1750.* New York: Knopf.

Vinovskis, M. A. (1972). Mortality rates and trends in Massachusetts before 1860. *Journal of Economic History, 32,* 184-213.

Vinovskis, M. A. (1976). Angel heads and weeping willows: Death in early America. *Proceedings of the American Antiquarian Society, 86,* 273-302.

Vinovskis, M. A. (1977). From household size to the life course: Some observations on recent trends in family history. *American Behavioral Scientist, 21,* 263-287.

Vinovskis, M. A. (1981). *Fertility in Massachusetts from the Revolution to the Civil War.* New York: Academic Press.

Vinovskis, M. A. (1987). Historical perspectives on the development of the family and parent-child interactions. In J. Lancaster, J. Altmann, A. Rossi, & L. Sherrod (Eds.), *Parenting across the life-span: Biosocial dimensions* (pp. 295-312). New York: Aldine de Gruyter.

Vinovskis, M. A. (1995). *Education, society, and economic opportunity: A historical perspective on persistent issues.* New Haven, CT: Yale University Press.

Wall, H. M. (1990). *Fierce communion: Family and community in early America.* Cambridge, MA: Harvard University Press.

Wirth, L. (1938). Urbanism as a way of life. *American Journal of Sociology, 44,* 1-24.

Wishy, B. (1968). *The child and the republic: The dawn of modern American child nurture.* Philadelphia: University of Pennsylvania Press.

Zuckerman, M. (1970). *Peaceable kingdoms: New England towns in the eighteenth century.* New York: Knopf.

3

Who's Parenting?

Trends and Patterns

RONALD L. TAYLOR

American family life has undergone significant changes in the past two decades, as have the living arrangements of children. Between 1970 and 1990, for example, the proportion of "traditional" families—nuclear families in which children live with both biological parents—as a percentage of all family groups, declined from 40% to 26%, or by 14 percentage points (U.S. Bureau of the Census, 1991b). By 1991, only one in two children lived in a nuclear family, down from two in three in 1970 and from three in four in 1960 (Hernandez, 1988; U.S. Bureau of the Census, 1994a). Over the same period, the proportion of children in single-parent households increased dramatically, from approximately 12% in 1970 to 27% in 1993 (U.S. Bureau of the Census, 1994b). Most of the increase is accounted for by children living with their mothers, not their fathers. With a growing proportion of women bearing children out of wedlock, together with high divorce rates, more children than ever are spending at least part of their childhoods in single-parent families.

These and related developments are a source of concern among some researchers, policymakers, and other observers with respect to the future of the American family and the well-being of children

(Glenn, 1987; Levitan, Belous, & Gallo, 1988). In his assessment of recent family trends, Popenoe (1993) concluded that changes in the family in the past three decades have transformed the family in ways that threaten its ability to perform its two core functions—child rearing and the provision of affection and companionship to its members. As to the living arrangements of children, Popenoe observed that "a large percentage of children who are born today grow up in a remarkably different family setting than did their forebears of 30 years ago. Major elements of the traditional nuclear family have almost become a thing of the past" (p. 531). Bane and Jargowsky (1988) echoed these sentiments, noting that "the family situations of children have changed dramatically since 1970. The change is astonishing both for its size and for the speed with which it has happened" (p. 222). They argued that the main force accounting for family change since the 1970s has been "a profound change in people's attitudes about marriage and children" (p. 246). Likewise, the final report of the National Commission on Children (1991) concluded,

> For many children and parents, the experiences of family life are different today than a generation ago. Families are smaller. More children live with only one parent, usually their mothers, and many lack consistent involvement and support of their fathers. More mothers as well as fathers hold jobs and go to work each day. Yet children are now the poorest group in America, and if they live only with their mother and she is not employed, they are almost certain to be poor. Moreover, many of the routines of family life have changed; regardless of family income, parents and children spend less time together. (pp. 15-16)

To be sure, there remains considerable disagreement among family researchers as to how best to characterize recent changes in American families and what the long-term implications of these changes are for the status and well-being of children (Glenn, 1993; Kain, 1990; Stacey, 1993). However, it is incontrovertible that major changes in the marital status of the adult population in recent decades, together with other sociodemographic developments, have resulted in dramatic shifts in the parental living arrangements of children and youths. This chapter reviews some of these changes. More specifically, it reviews trends in marriage, divorce, and remarriage and their implications for contemporary parenting. In addition, the chapter identifies some of the most important changes in the parental living arrangements of children that have occurred in recent decades, including the emergence and proliferation of "nontraditional" family forms (Goldscheider & Waite, 1991).

In recent decades, increases in age at first marriage, declining rates of marriage and remarriage, high levels of separation and divorce, and the rising proportion of out-of-wedlock births have contributed to substantial changes in the composition of family households in the United States and in the childbearing and parenting behaviors of Americans. Compared to the case in 1960, fewer marriages are being formed and more individuals are postponing marriage, marrying later, and having fewer children. Moreover, the probability that marriage will end in separation or divorce has increased, as has the probability that a substantial proportion of children will spend some period of their childhoods in single-parent households (Hogan, 1987; Popenoe, 1993). To be sure, several of these trends were in progress well before the 1960s but accelerated or reversed course in the past three decades. These trends signal a demographic revolution that has major implications for the parenting activities of women and men over their life spans (Hogan, 1987).

Marriage, Divorce, and Remarriage

MARRIAGE

Although the median age at first marriage has been rising steadily since the mid-1950s, the past two decades saw a dramatic rise in the proportion of men and women never married. From 1975 to 1993, the median age at first marriage increased by 3 full years for men, from 23.5 to 26.5, and by more than 3 years for women, from 21.1 to 24.5 (U.S. Bureau of the Census, 1994a). Between 1970 and 1993, the proportion who had never married doubled—and in some cases tripled—for men and women in the 25- to 44-year-old age group. In this same period, the proportion of persons ages 30 to 34 who had never been married tripled, rising from 9% to 30% for men and from 6% to 19% for women; among those ages 35 to 39, the proportion more than doubled, from 7.2% to 19.7% for men and from 5.4% to

12.5% for women. With a median age at first marriage of 20.3 for women in 1960, young women in 1993 were marrying more than 4 years later than did their mothers (median age 24.5); young men were marrying nearly 4 years later than did their fathers (U.S. Bureau of the Census, 1993).

There are significant racial differences in the proportion never married by age. Among women under age 30 in 1993, the highest proportion never married was black. At ages 30 to 34 in 1993, 43% of black women had not yet married compared to 16% of white women and 18% of Hispanic women.[1] The racial differential narrows considerably at older ages. At ages 55 to 64, for example, only 9% of blacks had never married by 1993 compared to 4% of whites and 7% of Hispanics (U.S. Bureau of the Census, 1993).

It should be noted that recent increases in the median age at first marriage have returned the never-married population to levels in line with trends of the early 1900s. But the rate of increase in the proportion never married has been greater for specific age groups in recent decades than was experienced before by any successive cohorts born in the 20th century (Cherlin, 1981; Masnick & Bane, 1980). The trend toward older ages at first marriage in recent years, especially for women, is associated with rising levels of educational attainment and higher rates of labor participation. Moreover, improved methods of contraception since the early 1960s, together with the legalization of abortion, have made it possible for unmarried women to reduce the risk of premarital pregnancies that frequently led to marriages in previous birth cohorts. As Hogan (1987) pointed out, "The sexual revolution of the past two decades has coincided with these changes in contraceptive efficacy, allowing men and women to engage in sexual relations outside of marriage without undue fear of an ill-timed pregnancy" (pp. 323-324). In addition, increases in cohabitation may have contributed to delays in marriage, enabling many couples to enjoy some of the benefits of marriage without legal commitments (Bumpass, Sweet, & Cherlin, 1991).

Although older age at first marriage is associated with a lower probability of divorce, delayed marriage also may increase the risk of out-of-wedlock childbearing and single parenting, especially for African American women (Hernandez, 1993; U.S. Bureau of the Census, 1992). In fact, a large proportion of the increase in single-parent households in recent years is accounted for by never-married women maintaining families (U.S. Bureau of the Census, 1990).

The proportion of the population ever married also has declined in recent years, although less dramatically than the proportion never married has increased. Between 1975 and 1990, the percentage of women ever married declined from 63% to 38% for women ages 20 to 24, from 87% to 69% for women ages 25 to 29, and from 93% to 82% for women ages 30 to 34. At ages 40 to 54, the percentage change in marriage rates has been small, with more than 90% recorded as ever being married.

Although overall patterns of change in marriage behavior have been similar for white and black women as well as women of Spanish origin (who may be of any race), there are significant differences by age. The most striking difference among women ever married is the growing differential between black and white women since 1975. Among white women ages 20 to 24 in 1975, nearly two thirds (65%) were ever married compared to 48% of black women (U.S. Bureau of the Census, 1976, 1977). By 1990, the percentage had dropped to 41% for white women and 24% for black women in this age category. This racial differential narrows somewhat over the childbearing years but remains substantial. In 1975, for example, about 94% of white women and 87% of black women ages 30 to 34 had ever been married. By 1990, the percentage for white women had fallen only slightly, to 86%; for black women, however, the percentage fell by a whopping 26 percentage points, to 61%. If current trends continue, it is estimated that fewer than 3 of 4 black women will eventually marry compared to 9 of 10 white women (U.S. Bureau of the Census, 1992).

DIVORCE

The 1960s saw the beginnings of an upward climb in the divorce rate, which rose to 3.2 per 1,000 population by the end of that decade and to 5.2 per 1,000 by 1979. At that time, there was one divorce for every two marriages. The divorce rate remained relatively stable over the 1980s and declined slightly toward the end of that decade. Table 3.1 shows the percentages of women by age in 5-year intervals who were divorced after first marriage for the period 1975 to 1990.

TABLE 3.1 Percentages of Women Whose First Marriages Ended in Divorce, 1975-1990

Age at First Marriage (years)	1975	1980	1985	1990
20-24	11.2	14.2	13.9	12.5
25-29	17.1	20.7	21.0	19.2
30-34	19.8	26.2	29.3	28.1
35-39	21.5	27.2	32.0	34.1
40-44	20.5	26.1	32.1	35.8
45-49	21.0	23.1	29.0	35.2
50-54	18.0	21.8	25.7	29.5

SOURCE: U.S. Bureau of the Census (1976, 1977, 1992).

There were significant increases in divorce after first marriage for women under age 35 between 1975 and 1980 but only one significant increase between 1980 and 1985 or between 1985 and 1990. However, for women age 35 or over, the proportion divorced continued to rise across each 5-year interval from 1975 to 1990. These figures suggest the beginning of stability in the rate of divorce after first marriage for women under age 30 and a greater propensity to divorce among older women. White and black women and women of Spanish origin have followed the same general pattern of divorce after first marriage. However, black women age 34 or under have lower proportions divorced than do white women but have higher proportions at older ages. Women of Spanish origin of all ages (20 to 54) are least likely to have been divorced. Despite evidence of stability and/or decline among women in some age categories, divorce is more prevalent than ever before and "will probably continue to be among the highest recorded in the world" (U.S. Bureau of the Census, 1992, p. 5). If recent trends in divorce continue, it is estimated that between 40% and 60% of first recent marriages to the youngest cohort of women eventually will end in divorce (Bumpass, Sweet, & Martin, 1990).

Numerous explanations have been advanced in the literature for the recent increases in the divorce rate. Among these are greater employment opportunities for women that have made it possible for many wives to terminate marriages that might otherwise remain intact (Hannan, Tuma, & Groeneveld, 1977), increased economic insecurity among families resulting from economic recessions, high unemployment since the mid-1960s that contributed to declines in median family incomes for married-couple families and the increased risk of divorce (Hernandez, 1993), changing attitudes toward marriage and divorce (Norton & Moorman, 1987), and the liberalization of divorce laws (e.g., "no-fault" divorce laws) that made it easier for couples to end their marriages (Jacob, 1988; Sugarman & Kay, 1990). Although it is assumed that the causes are multiple and interrelated (Hogan, 1987; Kain, 1990; Norton & Moorman, 1987; Popenoe, 1993), there is as yet no convincing explanation for the rise in divorce rates.

REMARRIAGE

As divorce has become more common, so too has the proportion of women who have been married more than once. More than 40% of all marriages in the United States involve at least one partner who has been previously married (U.S. National Center for Health Statistics, 1988). Prior to the 1960s, the divorce and remarriage rates rose and fell in tandem. During the 1960s, however, the annual rate of remarriage—the number of remarriages in a given year divided by the number of previously married persons in the population age 15 or older—fell while the divorce rate continued to rise. Remarriage rates, however, have continued to decline since the 1960s. Between 1975 and 1990, for example, the percentage of women remarried after divorce dropped from 48% to 38% for women ages 20 to 24, from 60% to 52% for women ages 25 to 29, from 64% to 60% for women ages 30 to 34, and from 70% to 65% for women ages 35 to 39. Among women ages 40 to 49, the change was less than 4 percentage points. Given these trends, it is estimated that about 2 of 3 separated and divorced women will remarry (Norton & Moorman, 1987; U.S. Bureau of the Census, 1992); for men, the corresponding figure is about 3 of 4 (Sweet & Bumpass, 1987).

The probability of remarriage varies by sociodemographic characteristics. Women who divorce in their teens are more likely to remarry than are women who marry later (Bumpass et al., 1990). Although some studies have shown that the presence or absence of children does not affect remarriage rates appreciably (e.g., Norton & Moorman, 1987), other studies (e.g., Bumpass et al., 1990) have found that women with three or more children have a lower likelihood of remarriage, perhaps because of the difficulty in finding a partner willing to assume the financial responsibility associated with a large family. White women are more likely to remarry after divorce than are black women or women of Spanish origin (U.S. Bureau of the Census, 1992). Based on 1980 census data, Sweet and Bumpass (1987) estimated that about 5 of 10 non-Hispanic white women will remarry within 5 years of their separations compared to about 1 of 3 Mexican American women and 1 of 5 black women. The differential is accounted for, in part, by socioeconomic factors; poor women have a lower remarriage rate than do nonpoor women (Cherlin, 1996). Moreover, for many African American women, the pool of eligible African American males as remarriage partners is severely limited by high rates of male unemployment, mortality, and incarceration (Wilson & Neckerman, 1986).

However, as Cherlin (1996) pointed out, the overall decline in remarriage is somewhat deceptive. He noted the increase in cohabitation among the formerly married between 1970 and 1984 and concluded that during this period "cohabitation had become so widespread among the previously married that its increase had more than compensated for the decrease in remarriage" (p. 385). In sum, a growing number of adults are substituting cohabitation for remarriage, at least in the short term, with some 60% of remarried people living with partners before they remarry (Bumpass & Sweet, 1989; Bumpass et al., 1991).

For some scholars, recent trends in marriage, divorce, and remarriage support the view that a growing number of young adults in society are less enthusiastic about long-term commitments to intimate relationships (Rossi, 1987; Thornton, 1989). Whether the same applies to attitudes toward parenthood is unclear. It is incontrovertible, however, that trends in the nuptial behavior of Americans have had profound consequences for the prevalence and incidence of parenting activities in American society over the past three decades. In consequence of such trends, American children are living in increasingly varied and complex living arrangements.

The Changing Living Arrangements of Children

National studies only recently have become available that focus on children and the wide range of relationships linking them to their families and to society at large (Hernandez, 1993). In 1991, the Bureau of the Census published the first of its findings on the diverse living arrangements of children from the Survey of Income and Program Participants (SIPP). This survey is different from other census reports in that it documents how each person is related to everyone else in the household (U.S. Bureau of the Census, 1994a). It records whether a child lives with his or her biological, step-, foster, or adoptive parents or with a grandparent, an aunt, an uncle, or other relatives. In short, the SIPP provides far more detailed information about the living arrangements of children and family structure than previous census reports. In the discussion to follow, the SIPP is the primary source of data for analysis of trends in the living arrangements of children and changes in the parenting activities of adults over the past two decades.[2] As the SIPP reveals, significant changes have occurred in the proportions of children in nuclear and extended families and single-parent households as well as in the number of children involved in alternative family forms.

THE NUCLEAR FAMILY

The proportion of families with children under age 18 declined over the past two decades. Between 1970 and 1990, more specifically, the number of married-couple families with children dropped by almost 1 million, and their share of all family households declined from 40% to 26% in this period (U.S. Bureau of the Census, 1995b). Not since 1981 has the number of married-couple families with children under age 18 in the home outnumbered those without children. Of the 64.1 million children under age 18 in the United States in 1990, 46.5 million (or 73%) lived with two parents compared to 85% in 1970 and 88% in 1960 (U.S. Bureau of the Census, 1991b). These figures include natural parents and stepparents as well as parents by adoption.

Children in "traditional" nuclear families—that is, families composed solely of both biological parents and full brothers and sisters—

constituted slightly more than one half (51%) of children under age 18 living in such families in 1990, down from 66% in 1970 and 71% in 1960 (Hernandez, 1993). The remaining children lived in households that included single parents, stepparents, grandparents, or other relatives or nonrelatives (U.S. Bureau of the Census, 1994a). Thus the "traditional" nuclear family has become less common as a living arrangement among children today than was the case three decades ago, as more and more children are found in nontraditional households.

Although the majority of children lived in two-parent households in 1991, a significant number did not reside with both biological parents. Table 3.2 shows the numbers and percentage distributions of children by biological, step-, adoptive, and foster parent status in 1991.

As Table 3.2 indicates, in 1991, more than 8 in 10 children in two-parent families lived with both biological parents; 1 in 10 lived with a natural parent and a stepparent, usually the biological mother and stepfather; and fewer than 2% lived with adoptive or foster parents. The proportion of children living with two parents varied by race and ethnicity; in 1991, 79% of white children, 42% of black children, 65% of Hispanic children, and 84% of Asian and Pacific Islander children lived with two parents (U.S. Bureau of the Census, 1992).[3]

BLENDED FAMILIES

In census reports, a child lives in a *blended family* if he or she lives in a household with at least one stepparent, stepsibling, and/or half-sibling (U.S. Bureau of the Census, 1994a). A stepparent is the spouse of the child's natural mother or father but has no biological tie to the child. In 1991, 9.8 million children under age 18 lived in blended families, representing 15% of all children. African American children were somewhat more likely to live in blended families (20%) than were white children (14%) or Hispanic children (14%).[4] It has been estimated that 35% of children born in the early 1980s will spend part of their childhoods living in blended households (Glick, 1984).

The proportion of adopted children under age 18 living in two-parent households can only be estimated given that no comprehensive federal registry exists to provide this information. Based on data from

TABLE 3.2 Children Living With Two Parents, by Biological, Step-, Adoptive, and Foster Parent Status, 1991

Characteristic of Parents	Number (in thousands)	Percentage
Two parents	47,826	100.0
Biological mother and father	40,553	84.8
Biological mother and stepfather	3,672	7.7
Biological father and stepmother	830	1.7
Adoptive mother and father	582	1.2
Foster mother and father[a]	195	—
Other	1,994	4.2

SOURCE: U.S. Bureau of the Census (1991a).
NOTE: Dash (—) represents zero or a number that rounds to zero.
a. Foster relationships only include official placement by a government agency or a representative of a government agency.

the SIPP, it is estimated that 1.1 million children lived with at least one adoptive parent in 1991. Of this number, 581,000 (or 55%) lived with two adoptive parents, 31% lived with one adoptive and one biological parent, and 12% lived with a single parent.

EXTENDED FAMILIES

The *extended family* refers to a family structure that extends beyond the nuclear family and includes other relatives in the household such as a grandparent or an uncle. In census reports, a child is reported to be living in an extended family if at least one parent and someone beyond the nuclear family (related or unrelated to the child) also lives in the household (U.S. Bureau of the Census, 1994b). Economic factors such as poverty, unemployment, and a shortage of affordable housing; social factors such as divorce and remarriage; and cultural factors may influence whether or not a household is extended.

By the census definition, some 8 million children lived in extended families in 1991, representing about 12.5% of all children living with at least one parent. Of all children living with at least one parent, some 6 million (or 9%) lived with extended household members who were relatives only (i.e., grandparents, in-laws, uncles, or aunts). About 3%

of children lived with nonrelatives only, and fewer than 1% lived with both relatives and nonrelatives. The likelihood of living in an extended family is significantly greater for children who live in one-parent households than for children in two-parent families. In 1991, children living with one parent were four times more likely to reside in extended families than were children living with two parents (30% vs. 7%). Only 1% of children living with two parents lived in households extended by nonrelatives compared to 9% of children living with one parent (U.S. Bureau of the Census, 1994a).

The proportion of children living in extended households varies significantly by race and ethnicity. In 1991, black and Hispanic children were twice as likely to live in extended households as were white children (22%, 25%, and 10%, respectively). Household composition is a central factor as well. For example, the proportion of black children living in extended families was three times greater for those living with one parent (32%) compared to those with both parents present (10%). And the proportion of Hispanic children living in extended families with only one parent present was more than double that of those having both parents present (40% vs. 18%) (U.S. Bureau of the Census, 1994a).

Grandparents represent the largest proportion of residential relatives in extended family households, followed by cousins, aunts, and uncles. In 1991, nearly 5 in 10 (46%) children in extended families lived with at least one grandparent, with more than half as many (25%) living with a grandmother only rather than both grandparents (17%). Moreover, children being raised by one parent were more likely to live with a grandparent (46%) than were children being raised with both parents present (31%). With respect to other relatives, nearly equal proportions of children in extended households lived with an aunt (20%), an uncle (19%), or a cousin (22%) in 1991 (U.S. Bureau of the Census, 1994a).

Although the proportion is relatively small, a growing number of children live together with at least one parent in the home of their grandparent(s). An estimated 3.4 million children under age 18 lived in such households in 1993, representing 5% of all children under age 18. This constitutes an increase of only 2% since 1970, when 2.2 million children (or 3%) lived in the home of a grandparent (U.S. Bureau of the Census, 1994b).

Among children living in three-generational extended families with both parents present, more than a third (38%) lived in a grandparent's home. By contrast, 81% of children in three-generational households with only one parent present lived in a grandparent's home. Continuing high rates of divorce and out-of-wedlock childbearing over the past two decades, among other factors, have contributed to the rise in the proportion of children living in the home of a grandparent with a parent present (U.S. Bureau of the Census, 1994a).

In extended households, relatives may assist parents in carrying out parenting tasks—including providing social and emotional support, supervision, and discipline—and teaching skills important in children's development. Especially in some racial and ethnic households, grandparents (usually grandmothers) play a major role in the socialization of children (Wilson, 1987). The greater tendency of blacks, Asians, and Hispanics to live in extended family arrangements relative to whites (Farley & Allen, 1987) increases the opportunity for racial minority and ethnic grandparents to be more involved in the child-rearing process. In their national survey of grandparents, Cherlin and Furstenberg (1992) concluded that African American grandparents are more involved with and exercise more authority in the upbringing of their grandchildren at all income and class levels compared to white grandparents. Such differences may be accounted for, in part, by cultural differences between blacks and whites in the role that grandparents are expected to play (Burton, 1990; Farley & Allen, 1987; Martin & Martin, 1978).

SINGLE-PARENT FAMILIES

As rates of divorce, separation, and out-of-wedlock childbearing have increased over the past two decades, so too has the number of children living in single-parent households. Between 1970 and 1990, the number and proportion of single-parent families increased threefold, from 1 in 10 to 3 in 10. In 1970, there were 3.8 million single-parent families with children under age 18; in 1994, there were 11.4 million (U.S. Bureau of the Census, 1995b).

The vast majority of single-parent households are maintained by women (86% in 1994). But the number of single-parent households headed by men has more than tripled since 1970, rising from 393,000 to 1.5 million in 1994, or from 10% to 14% of the total of all single-parent families in this period.

Single-parent families are created in a number of ways: through divorce, marital separation, out-of-wedlock births, or death of a parent. In 1994, divorce accounted for 38% and never-married parents accounted for roughly the same proportion (38%) of single-parent situations (U.S. Bureau of the Census, 1995b). Marital separation accounted for an additional 20% of single-parent families, whereas 5% were created as a result of the death of a spouse.

The number and proportion of single-parent families vary significantly by race and ethnicity. Of the 11.4 million single-parent families in 1994, about 7.3 million (or 64%) were white, 3.6 million (or 32%) were black, and 1.5 million (or 13%) were of Hispanic origin. Approximately 286,000 (or fewer than 1%) were Asian or Pacific Islander (U.S. Bureau of the Census, 1995a). However, in 1994, single-parent families accounted for a quarter (25%) of all white family groups with children under age 18, almost two thirds (or 65%) of all black family groups, more than a third (36%) of all Hispanic family groups, and about one eighth (14%) of all Asian and Pacific Islander family groups with children (U.S. Bureau of the Census, 1995a). In 1970, the corresponding proportions were 10% for whites and 36% for blacks (U.S. Bureau of the Census, 1995b). (Comparable data for single-parent households of Hispanic origin and for Asians and Pacific Islanders are not available for 1970.)

Although the number of single-parent households has continued to rise over the past two decades, the rates of increase have slowed considerably since 1980. Overall, the average rate of increase in the number of single-parent families declined from 6.0% per year between 1970 and 1980 to 3.4% in 1990 and then rose to 3.9% in 1994. Among whites, the average annual increase in single-parent families declined from 5.7% between 1970 and 1980 to 3.1% in 1990 and then rose to 3.5% in 1994. The corresponding rates among African Americans were an average of 6.1% per year between 1970 and 1980, dropping to 3.8% in 1990 and then increasing to 4.1% in 1994 (U.S. Bureau of the Census, 1995b). Thus, although the number of single-parent families has continued to increase, the rate of increase has been more moderate in recent years relative to that in the 1970s.

Whereas children of divorce made up the largest share of children living with one parent in 1993, the proportion of children living with a never-married parent grew dramatically over the past two decades. Between 1970 and 1981, the proportion of children in single-parent households who lived with a divorced parent increased by 50% (from 30.2% to 43.8%); the proportion living with a never-married parent more than doubled (from 6.8% to 15.2%). Between 1983 and 1993, the proportion of children in one-parent families living with a divorced parent declined from 42% to 37% while the proportion living with a never-married parent rose from 24% to 35%.[5] Thus, whereas a decade ago children in single-parent households were nearly twice as likely to be living with a divorced parent as with a never-married parent, in 1994 single-parent children were only slightly more likely to be living with a divorced parent as with a never-married parent (37% vs. 35%) (U.S. Bureau of the Census, 1995b).

Growth in the proportion of children living with single parents reflects long-term trends in births to unmarried women. Analyzing data for the period 1940 to 1985, Hernandez (1988) found that the ratio of births to unmarried women as a ratio of births to all women rose significantly over this period for both whites and nonwhites.[6] For whites, the ratio rose from about 20 per 1,000 births to 145 per 1,000, an increase of 725% over this 45-year period. For nonwhites, the ratio rose from 168 per 1,000 births to 514 per 1,000, a 306% increase. As these results imply, 14.5% of all white children and 51.4% of all nonwhite children born in 1985 were born to unmarried women (Hernandez, 1988). Over the decade of the 1980s, births to unmarried women increased by 82% and accounted for about 3 of 10 total births in 1991 (U.S. Bureau of the Census, 1994b).

Although much public attention has focused on sharp increases in unwed teenage childbearing in recent years, more than one half of all births to unwed mothers are to women over age 20 (U.S. Bureau of the Census, 1995c). In 1992, nearly a quarter (24%) of single women between ages 18 and 44 had given birth, up from 15% in 1982. Over the decade of the 1980s, the greatest increase in births to single-parent women occurred among affluent, well-educated women and among women in their 30s (U.S. Bureau of the Census, 1992).

For many children living with their mother only, but especially for children living with a never-married mother, a nonparental adult male is available as a potential source of social and emotional support and child care (Hernandez, 1988). More specifically, one in five children (20%) in single-mother families in 1991 lived with at least one adult male in the household, although the proportion was higher for whites (23%) and children of Hispanic origin (21%) than it was for blacks (14%). Of all children living with a single mother, 10% also lived with at least one male relative, 7% with a male nonrelative, and 3% with a male of unknown relation in the household (U.S. Bureau of the Census, 1994a).[7] By comparison, children living with a single father were nearly twice as likely as children living with a single mother to live with an adult of the opposite sex of the parent (37% vs. 20%). Of all children in a father-only household, 19% lived with at least one adult female relative, 13% with an unrelated adult female, and 6% with a female of unknown relation (U.S. Bureau of the Census, 1994a). Most of the unrelated adult males or females living in the households are assumed to be cohabitors or the unmarried partners of single parents (Bumpass et al., 1991).

The rise in the number of single-parent families during the past two decades and the increase in the proportion of never-married, single-parent households suggest that parenthood is less securely connected to marriage than it has been in the past (Popenoe, 1993; Rossi, 1987). Because of the rise in out-of-wedlock births along with continuously high rates of separation and divorce, a majority of children (55% to 60%) born since 1980 are likely to spend some part of their childhoods living with only one parent (Hernandez, 1993).

Para-Parenting

"Para-parenting" arrangements have emerged in recent years as sources of support for a growing number of single parents who are overwhelmed by the stress entailed by the need to balance employment and parenting roles and whose relatives are unavailable for help or support (Schwartz, 1995). These usually are informal arrangements in which a friend or some other unrelated adult or family elects to provide care, supervision, and emotional and material support to a family on a temporary or even permanent basis. Para-parenting relationships have long been a feature of low-income communities (Stack, 1965), where many families have been fragmented and torn apart by economic hardship, drugs, and other problems. But, as Schwartz (1995) observed, such relationships are becoming more common in middle-class families as well. As for low-income, single-mother households, "These para-parenting relationships are not just extras, but crucial to preserving some semblance of a normal childhood" (p. C1).

The dramatic rise over the past two decades in the number of single adults living alone may have contributed to the growing number of para-parenting arrangements in middle- and low-income families. Since 1970, the proportion of single adults ages 25 to 54 living alone increased from 13% to 26% in 1993. For some of these unattached adults, offering parenting assistance in these informal arrangements may fulfill the desire to participate in the lives of children without the formal obligations of marriage and family. Such child care arrangements may represent the emergence of a new form of parenting among Americans in the 1990s (Schwartz, 1995).

LESBIAN AND GAY HOUSEHOLDS

With the emergence of the gay rights movement in the early 1970s, the number of lesbian and gay households with children has been on the rise. An accurate determination of the number of children in such households is difficult because many gay and lesbian parents take pains to conceal their sexual orientation for fear that they may lose child custody rights and/or become the targets of discriminatory treatment (Patterson, 1992). Extrapolating from data derived from several sources, it is estimated that there currently are between 1 million and 5 million lesbian mothers and between 1 million and 3 million gay fathers in the United States (Patterson, 1992; Singer & Deschamps, 1994). Estimates of the number of children of gay and lesbian parents range from 6 million to 14 million. Collins and Coltrane (1991) estimated that approximately 1 in 3 lesbians is a mother and that 1 in 10 gays is a father. (For a more extended discussion of children in gay and lesbian households, see Allen's contribution to this volume [Chapter 8].)

Although the majority of children in gay and lesbian households are children from previous marriages or other heterosexual involvements, a growing number of lesbians and gay men are becoming parents without either. A number of options are available to childless gay men and lesbians including adoption, foster care, surrogate parent-hood, coparenting, artificial insemination, and heterosexual inter-course. According to some reports (Seligmann, 1990; Weston, 1991), lesbian mothers are the fastest growing segment of gay parents, due largely to the availability and popularity of insemination with sperm provided by anonymous donors. In fact, insemination is largely credited for the "lesbian baby boom" on the West Coast in the mid-1970s, which facilitated "biological parenting without requiring marriage, subterfuge, or heterosexual intercourse" (Weston, 1991, p. 169). An estimated 10,000 children are being raised by lesbians who became pregnant through artificial insemination (Singer & Deschamps, 1994). For gay men, surrogacy and donor arrangements with female friends are some alternative options.

The increasing involvement of lesbians and gay men in child rearing must be viewed in the context of other significant developments during the past three decades. As Cherlin (1996) points out, the circumstances that have contributed to the formation of openly gay and lesbian households with children since the 1960s include

> the sharp, post-1960 rise in divorce, which encouraged more homosexual men and women who were in heterosexual marriages (often with children) to end their marriages; the emergence of an openly gay subculture in large cities, which provided a supportive environment for lesbian and gay couples; [and] the greater tolerance of childbearing outside of marriage and single parenting in general. (p. 424)

Despite growing public acceptance of gay and lesbian couples, their parenting and the presence of children in their households remains controversial. Only a handful of states recognize the parental rights of same-sex couples (Singer & Deschamps, 1994).

Summary and Conclusion

As the foregoing discussion makes clear, remarkable changes have occurred in the nuptial behavior and parenting activities of American women and men over the past three decades. These changes have created a wide diversity of living arrangements for children, with one in four living with a single parent. Compared to the case in 1960, more women and men now marry later, are more likely to divorce, and are substantially more likely to live alone or in households with persons other than family members. Although most men and women do eventually marry and become parents, the reduction in the marital fertility rate over the past two decades has resulted in smaller families and fewer children requiring parenting. On the other hand, birthrates among unmarried women have increased dramatically, with the greatest increases occurring among women in their 30s. Although the divorce rate is expected to stabilize during the 1990s, current marriage patterns are expected to continue through the end of the decade, suggesting that single parenthood will become more prevalent throughout the general population.

Although a growing number of single-parent households are headed by men, nearly 9 in 10 single-parent families are headed by women. Mothers continue to assume a much greater share of the responsibility for child rearing and are likely to do so well into the future, often without the support of an extended kin network. As the proportion of households headed by divorced, separated, never-married, or widowed mothers increases, the incidence of poverty among children in these households also is expected to rise (Danziger & Weinberg, 1994). The relationship between female headship and child poverty has been well established. According to Danziger (1995),

> Children in two-parent families have much lower poverty rates than children in mother-only families; children living with never-married mothers have much higher poverty rates than those living with ever-married mothers. Living arrangements are now more important than race when it comes to child poverty—black children in two parent families have a much lower poverty rate than white children living in mother-only families. (p. 97)

The upward trend in single-parent households suggests less overlap between marriage and parenthood today than in the past. The weakening link between marriage and parenthood is evident among all ethnic groups but is most apparent among African Americans. Although the rate of out-of-wedlock births to white women increased dramatically in the past two decades, such births to black women have been consistently higher. As a number of studies have documented (Testa,

Astone, Krogh, & Neckerman, 1989; Tucker & Mitchell-Kernan, 1995; Wilson, 1987), the growing imbalance in the sex ratio among African Americans (created in part by higher mortality and incarceration rates among black males) is a major contributing factor to delayed marriage and the higher rates of out-of-wedlock births, divorce, and singlehood. The number of children present in female-headed households among African Americans is higher on average than the number in white female-headed households. African American children today are three times more likely to live in single-parent homes as are white children. Relatively few of these mother-headed households include grandparents or other related adults. In this sense, African American women have greater parenting and child care responsibilities than do white women (Hogan, 1987).

Growth in the proportion of single-parent households is only one source of the increased diversity and change in the living arrangements of children over the past two decades. The apparent increase in the number of children living with openly gay and lesbian parents represents the expansion of this parenting arrangement, and the growing awareness of such families is helping to force a redefinition of the family and the boundaries of parenthood (Cherlin, 1995). Although the legal system and state regulations governing adoption and foster care have made it difficult for gay men and lesbians to retain custody rights to their children from previous marriages, new birth technologies (e.g., artificial insemination, in vitro fertilization) provide new opportunities for these couples to procreate and raise children.

In sum, remarkable changes have occurred in the parenting activities of Americans in the past two decades. Some of these are extensions of transformations begun earlier in the century, whereas others are a result of more recent social, economic, and political developments. Increasing diversity in living arrangements is likely to be the hallmark of children for some time to come as current patterns of marriage, divorce, remarriage, and nonmarriage result in various forms of blended families and coparenting arrangements. Much of the diversity in children's living arrangements will be linked to issues of race, class, and gender as well as the advantages and disadvantages associated with each, separately and in combination. As the variety of alternative family forms continues to increase, one of the major challenges facing policymakers, now and in the future, is how best to "fashion responses that support and strengthen families as the once and future domain for raising children" (National Commission on Children, 1991, p. 37). Part of the answer lies in a redefinition of *family* and *parenthood*.

Notes

1. Recent national data on household and family characteristics of the Asian and Pacific Islander population are very limited, and the information that is available is not as comprehensive as that reported for the white, African American, and Hispanic populations. The Asian and Pacific Islander population has grown rapidly in the past two decades (at a rate of approximately 4.5% a year), and estimates of its size vary from 7.3 million to 8.8 million. In 1994, the Asian and Pacific Islander population accounted for 3% of the total population in the United States (U.S. Bureau of the Census, 1995a). Where available, data on marital status and living arrangements of the population are included in the text, with the proviso that some of the data reported are not strictly comparable to the distribution of characteristics reported for other populations because of data collection and estimation procedures and sampling errors.

2. The SIPP is based on estimates of children under age 18 inflated to national population controls by age, race, sex, and Spanish origin. According to the report, "Population controls are based on results of the 1980 census carried forward to 1991. The estimates in this report, therefore, may differ from estimates that would have been obtained using 1990 census results brought forward to the survey data" (U.S. Bureau of the Census, 1994a, p. 1).

3. The SIPP and Current Population Survey (CPS) estimates of children living in two-parent families in 1991 differ, with the SIPP estimating more black children living in two-parent families than the CPS (42% vs. 36%). The difference is accounted for by the fact that SIPP and CPS estimates are not based on the same universe of children; the CPS figures exclude children who maintain their own households or family groups.

4. The SIPP does not include data on the proportion of Asian and Pacific Islander children in blended or other nontraditional families.

5. According to Hernandez (1993), estimates of change in the proportion of children living in mother-only families between 1960 and 1988 are rather crude in that new procedures adopted for the CPSs in 1982 and 1983 served to improve the identification of related subfamilies, especially among mother-child families. Therefore, "Some of the increase in mother-only families for 1980 to 1988 actually occurred during the preceding years, especially since 1970, when the largest measured increases in mother-only families occurred among both black and white children" (pp. 76-77).

6. Prior to the 1970s, the term *nonwhite* was a classification of the Bureau of the Census defined to include blacks and Asian American populations. Blacks typically were estimated to constitute more than 95% of persons in this category.

7. These categories are not mutually exclusive. For example, children living with both a relative and a nonrelative were included in both categories.

References

Bane, M. J., & Jargowsky, P. A. (1988). The links between government policy and family structure: What matters and what doesn't. In A. Cherlin (Ed.), *The changing American family and public policy* (pp. 219-255). Washington, DC: Urban Institute Press.

Bumpass, L. L., & Sweet, J. A. (1989). National estimates of cohabitation. *Demography, 26,* 615-625.

Bumpass, L. L., Sweet, J. A., & Cherlin, A. (1991). The role of cohabitation in declining marriage rates. *Journal of Marriage and the Family, 53,* 913-927.

Bumpass, L. L., Sweet, J. A., & Martin, T. C. (1990). Changing patterns of remarriage. *Journal of Marriage and the Family, 52,* 747-756.

Burton, L. M. (1990). Teenage childbearing as an alternative life course strategy in multigenerational black families. *Human Nature, 1,* 123-143.

Cherlin, A. (1981). *Marriage, divorce, and remarriage.* Cambridge, MA: Harvard University Press.

Cherlin, A. (1995). Policy issues of child care. In P. Chase-Lansdale & J. Brooks-Gunn (Eds.), *Escape from poverty* (pp. 121-137). New York: Cambridge University Press.

Cherlin, A. (1996). *Public and private families.* New York: McGraw-Hill.

Cherlin, A., & Furstenberg, F. F. (1992). *The new American grandparent: A place in the family, a life apart.* Cambridge, MA: Harvard University Press.

Collins, R., & Coltrane, S. (1991). *Sociology of marriage and the family* (3rd ed.). Chicago: Nelson-Hall.

Danziger, S. (1995). Commentary. In M. Tucker & C. Mitchell-Kernan (Eds.), *The decline in marriage among African-Americans* (pp. 96-101). New York: Russell Sage.

Danziger, S., & Weinberg, D. (1994). The historical record: Trends in family income, inequality, and poverty. In S. Danziger, G. Sandefur, & D. Weinberg (Eds.), *Confronting poverty: Prescriptions for change* (pp. 18-50). Cambridge, MA: Harvard University Press.

Farley, R., & Allen, W. (1987). *The color line and the quality of life in America.* New York: Russell Sage.

Glenn, N. D. (1987). The state of the American family. *Journal of Family Issues, 8,* 4-27.

Glenn, N. D. (1993). A plea for objective assessment of the notion of family decline. *Journal of Marriage and the Family, 55,* 542-544.

Glick, P. (1984). Marriage, divorce, and living arrangements: A record of social change. *Journal of Family Issues, 5,* 7-26.

Goldscheider, F. K., & Waite, L. J. (1991). *New families, no families? The transformation of the American home.* Berkeley: University of California Press.

Hannan, M. T., Tuma, N. B., & Groeneveld, L. P. (1977). Income and marital events: Evidence from an income-maintenance experiment. *American Journal of Sociology, 82,* 1186-1211.

Hernandez, D. J. (1988). Demographic trends and the living arrangements of children. In E. Hetherington & J. Arasteh (Eds.), *Impact of divorce, single parenting and stepparenting on children* (pp. 3-22). Hillsdale, NJ: Lawrence Erlbaum.

Hernandez, D. J. (1993). *America's children: Resources from family, government and the economy.* New York: Russell Sage.

Hogan, D. P. (1987). Demographic trends in human fertility, and parenting across the life span. In J. Lancaster, J. Altmann, A. Rossi, & L. Sherrod (Eds.), *Parenting across the life span* (pp. 315-349). New York: Aldine de Gruyter.

Jacob, H. (1988). *Silent revolution: The transformation of divorce law in the United States.* Chicago: University of Chicago Press.

Kain, E. L. (1990). *The myth of family decline.* Lexington, MA: D. C. Heath.

Levitan, S. A., Belous, R. S., & Gallo, F. (1988). *What's happening to the American family?* (rev. ed.). Baltimore, MD: Johns Hopkins University Press.

Martin, E. P., & Martin, J. M. (1978). *The black extended family.* Chicago: University of Chicago Press.

Masnick, G., & Bane, M. J. (1980). *The nation's families: 1960-1990.* Boston: Auburn House.

National Commission on Children. (1991). *Beyond rhetoric: A new American agenda for children and families.* Washington, DC: Author.

Norton, A. J., & Moorman, J. E. (1987). Current trends in marriage and divorce among American women. *Journal of Marriage and the Family, 49,* 3-14.

Patterson, C. J. (1992). Children of lesbian and gay parents. *Child Development, 63,* 1025-1042.

Popenoe, D. (1993). American family decline, 1960-1990: A review and appraisal. *Journal of Marriage and the Family, 55,* 527-555.

Rossi, A. (1987). Parenthood in transition: From lineage to child to self-orientation. In J. Lancaster, J. Altmann, A. Rossi, & L. Sherrod (Eds.), *Parenting across the life span* (pp. 31-81). New York: Aldine de Gruyter.

Schwartz, P. (1995, December 4). New bonds: Para-dads, para-moms. *New York Times,* pp. C1, C10.

Seligmann, J. (1990, Winter/Spring). Variations on a theme. *Newsweek* (special edition: The 21st-century family), pp. 38-46.

Singer, B., & Deschamps, D. (Eds.). (1994). *Gay and lesbian stats.* New York: New Press.

Stacey, J. (1993). Good riddance to "the family": A response to David Popenoe. *Journal of Marriage and the Family, 55,* 545-547.

Stack, C. (1965). *All our kin: Strategies for survival in a black community.* New York: Harper & Row.

Sugarman, S., & Kay, H. H. (Eds.). (1990). *Divorce reform at the crossroads.* New Haven, CT: Yale University Press.

Sweet, J. A., & Bumpass, L. L. (1987). *American families and households.* New York: Russell Sage.

Testa, M., Astone, N. M., Krogh, M., & Neckerman, K. (1989). Ethnic variations in employment and marriage among inner-city fathers. *Annals of the American Academy of Political and Social Science, 501,* 79-91.

Thornton, A. (1989). Changing attitudes toward family issues in the United States. *Journal of Marriage and the Family, 51,* 873-893.

Tucker, M. B., & Mitchell-Kernan, C. (Eds.). (1995). *The decline in marriage among African-Americans.* New York: Russell Sage.

U.S. Bureau of the Census. (1976). Number, timing, and duration of marriages: June 1975. In *Current Population Reports* (Series P-20, No. 297). Washington, DC: Government Printing Office.

U.S. Bureau of the Census. (1977). Marriage, divorce, widowhood, and remarriage by family characteristics: June 1975. In *Current Population Reports* (Series P-20, No. 312). Washington, DC: Government Printing Office.

U.S. Bureau of the Census. (1990). Household and family characteristics: March 1990 and 1989. In *Current Population Reports* (Series P-20, No. 447). Washington, DC: Government Printing Office.

U.S. Bureau of the Census. (1991a). The diverse living arrangements of children. In *Current Population Reports* (Series P-70, No. 38). Washington, DC: Government Printing Office.

U.S. Bureau of the Census. (1991b). Marital status and living arrangements: March 1990. In *Current Population Reports* (Series P-20, No. 450). Washington, DC: Government Printing Office.

U.S. Bureau of the Census. (1992). Marriage, divorce, and remarriage in the 1990s. In *Current Population Reports* (Series P-23, No. 180). Washington, DC: Government Printing Office.

U.S. Bureau of the Census. (1993). *Statistical abstract of the United States.* Washington, DC: Government Printing Office.

U.S. Bureau of the Census. (1994a). The diverse living arrangements of children: Summer 1991. In *Current Population Reports* (Series P-70, No. 38). Washington, DC: Government Printing Office.

U.S. Bureau of the Census. (1994b). Marital status and living arrangements: March 1993. In *Current Population Reports* (Series P-20, No. 478). Washington, DC: Government Printing Office.

U.S. Bureau of the Census. (1995a). The Asian and Pacific Islander population: 1994. In *Current Population Reports.* Washington, DC: Government Printing Office. (Internet: http://www.census.gov/population/www/socdemo/race/api.html)

U.S. Bureau of the Census. (1995b). Household and family characteristics: March 1994. In *Current Population Reports* (Series P-20, No. 483). Washington, DC: Government Printing Office.

U.S. Bureau of the Census. (1995c). *Statistical abstract of the United States.* Washington, DC: Government Printing Office.

U.S. National Center for Health Statistics. (1988). *Monthly vital statistics reports,* Vol. 40: *Advanced report of final marriage statistics 1988.* Washington, DC: Government Printing Office.

Weston, K. (1991). *Families we choose: Lesbians, gays, kinship.* New York: Columbia University Press.

Wilson, W. J. (1987). *The truly disadvantaged.* Chicago: University of Chicago Press.

Wilson, W. J., & Neckerman, K. (1986). Poverty and family structure: The widening gap between evidence and public policy issues. In S. Danziger & D. Weinberg (Eds.), *Fighting poverty: What works and what doesn't* (pp. 232-259). Cambridge, MA: Harvard University Press.

4

Doing Parenting

Mothers, Care Work, and Policy

DEMIE KURZ

There is widespread concern in the United States that the family is in crisis. The often-repeated phrase "loss of family values" reflects a range of concerns and anxiety. In public forums and in private homes, people express fears about the high divorce rate and its impact on children, the quality of day care, "latchkey children" unattended after school because their mothers are at work, and the perceived decreased time that family members spend together (Etzioni, 1993; Popenoe, 1988). There is particular concern about single-parent families, which are said to be weak and to produce children who are vulnerable to school failure, crime, and other social problems (Blankenhorn, 1995). These problems are believed by some researchers and policymakers to indicate that there is what they term a "decline" in the family (Popenoe, 1988).

Public discussions about the family have become increasingly acrimonious as commentators and policymakers debate what causes family problems and what measures should be taken to strengthen the family. Increasingly, commentators have blamed mothers for family problems. Common stereotypes portray professional mothers as careerists who are selfishly pursuing their own advancement at the expense of their children, whereas poor mothers are typed as lazy and unwilling to work (Fineman, 1995b; Sidel, 1996). Women on welfare in particular are stereotyped in this way; they are said to raise children who are unable to cope with life and who themselves turn to welfare (Fineman, 1995b; Kurz, 1995).

Unquestionably, families today confront serious problems. Current debates, however, fail to identify what the real problems are. Contemporary family problems do not originate with the behavior of mothers, as is often claimed by the media and by some scholars; rather, they originate with our failure to support the caretaking work that mothers do, which remains virtually unrecognized in our social policies. Nor do problems of the family result from a general process of "family decline." This term can be very misleading. It presumes, for example, that everyone in the family has the same interests. Although it is valuable for some purposes to take the family as a unit of analysis, it is misleading to assume that the family exists predominantly above and beyond the interests of its members. Although men, women, and children frequently act together as a unit in social and family activities, they also have different and potentially conflicting interests.

In this chapter, I examine what I see as the most serious problems facing the contemporary family. My discussion of family problems is informed by a feminist perspective—a perspective that, although it has become increasingly prevalent in family studies in the past decade, is, unfortunately, still at the margins of the field (Thompson & Walker, 1995). Gender and feminist researchers have brought dynamic new approaches to the study of the family. They have challenged the taken-for-granted assumptions about traditional gender roles, the false belief in the separation of public and private life, and the way in which the work that women and mothers do in families is rendered invisible and devalued (Ferree, 1990; Glenn, 1987; Thorne, 1992). Feminist theorists also have documented the power differences between men and women that pervade family life—differences that give men greater resources, give men more power in decision making, and lead some men to use violence to control their partners. Feminist researchers stress that policymakers must attend to the harmful impact social policies can have on women. Finally, feminist scholars increasingly are focusing on questions of race and class, as well as of gender, believing that in defining family problems, and in creating family policy, one must take into account the experiences of families in different race and class groups (Collins, 1991; Dill, 1988; Zinn, 1989).

In this chapter, I discuss what I see as two of the most serious problems of contemporary family life: the failure to support the work of caring for children and other family members, which is done primarily by mothers, and the rise in single-parent families. I focus on mothers' work caring for children. This work is very labor intensive and can be stressful, particularly in combination with the demands of a job. There always have been some mothers, particularly those who are poorer, who have worked both outside and within the home. In recent decades, however, as a result of the dramatic increase in the number of women in the paid labor force, the majority of mothers face the double burden of holding down jobs and returning from work to face a "second shift" (Hochschild & Machung, 1989) of caring for their families. The labor force has made few accommodations to the needs of mothers.

The second major problem for mothers and families is that large and increasing numbers of women are heading families alone. The high divorce rate and the rise in the number of women who bear children out of wedlock have raised the proportion of single-mother families to 27% of all families with children (Saluter, 1994). These mothers face multiple stresses, and many face poverty. The poverty rate for all single mothers with children is astoundingly high—47% (Rotella, 1995). This figure includes never-married and divorced women. The poverty rate for divorced mothers with children also is very high—39% (U.S. Bureau of the Census, 1993). Disproportionate numbers of single mothers who are poor are minority women.

These two problems, the failure to accommodate work and family and the poverty rate of single-mother families, indicate how little value we place on caretaking work and the mothers who do it. Our social policies do not recognize and reward this work (Hochschild, 1995). Arguing that additional social supports will "weaken" the family, policymakers currently are trying to reduce the limited supports that do exist for families. I describe the key crises that confront families (particularly mothers), analyze their causes, and propose strategies for change. I further examine what possibilities exist for supporting care work and strengthening the position of those who do it.

The Failure to Support Mothers and Caretaking

THE BURDENS OF CARE WORK

Currently, mothers face stress due to their dual roles of caring for children and working in the paid labor force. Although 70% of mothers with children under 18 years of age have now entered the labor force (Herz & Wootton, 1996), the previous domain of men, the majority of men have not substantially increased their contribution to household work. Mothers continue to do most of the work of raising children and the bulk of the household labor. Research indicates that wives, including ethnic minority women (Wyche, 1993), still are responsible for two thirds of household work or between 13 and 17 hours more each week of child care and housework than are husbands (Arendell, 1996; Blair & Johnson, 1992). Hochschild and Machung (1989) called this situation a "stalled revolution."

Whereas mothers now are doing a second shift of domestic work (Hochschild & Machung, 1989), it also is the case that there are men who are participating more in families, with some of them sharing equally in child care with their wives. In their samples, Gerson (1993) and Hochschild and Machung (1989) found some men who shared fully in child rearing and believed that fairness demanded that they share housework with their partners. Some researchers argue that since women have entered the workplace in large numbers, fathers' participation in domestic work has increased (Barnett & Rivers, 1996; Coltrane, 1996; Pleck, 1996). Coltrane (1996) claimed that as women's participation in the labor market continues to increase, mothers will demand more of fathers, who will take on more household tasks, particularly child rearing, and will then come to experience more rewards in it. He also cited survey data showing that men in the United States and other industrialized countries now rank fatherhood as more important to them than paid work. Most researchers agree, however, that to date only a relatively small group of men have taken on serious fatherhood and household roles (see Arendell, 1996). Furthermore, Barnett and Rivers (1996) pointed out that women still are responsible for what they call "low-control" jobs, the household jobs that are most stressful because of the constant urgent deadlines including meal preparation, grocery shopping, cleaning up after meals, and doing laundry. Barnett and Rivers contrasted these with the jobs men usually do, "higher control" jobs such as yard work, household repairs, and looking after the car, which are not as stressful because they do not have to be attended to every day and can be done at the discretion of those who do them.

The lack of affordable, quality child care services compounds the problems women face in providing care. Some parents send their children to day care centers, organized and run by individuals and groups in the private sector; some turn to neighborhood day care run out of homes. Programs such as HeadStart provide some day care for poor children. Unfortunately, however, the cost of most child care is high. In 1991, families living below the poverty level spent 27% of their incomes on child care, whereas those with average incomes spent 7% (U.S. Bureau of the Census, 1994, p. 27). The inability to pay for child care is one reason many single mothers must go on welfare (Kurz, 1995). In addition, some mothers, particularly those who are poorer, worry that the facilities of the day care centers their children attend are inadequate.

Several problems result from this lack of father participation and lack of support for doing care work. First, as Hochschild and Machung (1989) and others (Mirowsky & Ross, 1989; Steil, 1994) have suggested, negotiating work and family roles creates significant amounts of stress for mothers. Hochschild and Machung speak of a "speed-up" in family life that has occurred because working mothers now have to accomplish household tasks in much less time than they did when they were housewives. In her survey, Thoits (1986) found that working mothers experienced more anxiety than did any other group surveyed. When fathers do participate in household work, researchers have found that this help is the single most important factor in decreasing stress for working mothers (Hoffman, 1989). Because they rarely have such help, single mothers face even more stress than do married mothers (McLanahan & Adams, 1987).

Second, lack of participation by fathers in family work also creates friction between husbands and wives. Bergmann (1986) and Hochschild and Machung (1989) believe that although women have tried to negotiate for more help from their husbands, there is a limit to how far women will pressure their husbands to take on household work because of their fear that conflict over housework and children could result in divorce and the reduced standard of living it brings for mothers and children. Single mothers receive even less help from fathers with caretaking. According to recent figures from the National Survey of Families and Households, roughly 30% of divorced fathers did not see their children at all in the previous year, 60% saw their children several times or less during the year, and only 25% saw their children weekly (Seltzer, 1991). The more time passes after a divorce, the less fathers see their children (Furstenberg & Cherlin, 1991).

The third problem resulting from the delegation of caretaking work to women is that because they have so many family responsibilities in addition to their job responsibilities, many women find it difficult to advance in the workplace. Promotions require increased commitments of time, a scarce commodity for mothers who return home after work to a second shift of housework and child care. Some mothers remain at lower level jobs where employers are willing to accommodate their need for flexible hours. Others work part-time jobs to have more time to care for their children. Fewer than half of all employed women are full-time, year-round workers (Population Reference Bureau, 1993, p. 85). Part-time work can be particularly important for mothers with very young children or children with special needs. Unfortunately, however, part-time workers typically receive less than proportionate earnings and fringe benefits and also have more difficulty gaining promotions and higher paying jobs (Blau & Ferber, 1992, p. 184).

The gendered division of household labor can have increasing economic costs for women over time. In a marriage, a couple typically invests in the husband's career—he through time in his job, she through time in the family. The result is that the husband's career prospects are enhanced, whereas the wife's are impaired; his earning capacity may grow, whereas hers diminishes. In this way, many women experience the costs associated with combining work and family life, subordinate positions at work and insufficient time at home to be with their families, without as many of the corresponding benefits.

This is not to say that women do not enjoy working or want to work. Barnett and Rivers (1996), in their survey of 300 couples, reported that working women today experience much less anxiety and depression than did housewives of the 1950s, are in better health than were those housewives, and believe they are better off in a two-earner family that can cushion them against economic uncertainty. Significantly, whereas Barnett and Rivers found that women overall are happier than they were in the 1950s, they found that professional women and those with good jobs are the happiest (p. 34). This undoubtedly is because the ability to combine work and home life successfully is strongly related to a family's resources. Families with more income can turn to the market to gain help in balancing work and family responsibilities. Hired help for child care and other household work—such as nannies, housekeepers, housecleaners, and take-out food services—can contribute significantly to lessening the burdens of mothers and can enable some mothers to pursue demanding careers. Because they are so expensive, however, these options are limited to more well-off groups. Furthermore, hired help is not a general solution to the problem of care work because it pits the interests of one group of women, those with enough income to afford such help, against those of lower income, who are disproportionately women of color and who often must turn to low-paying jobs in care work because they have few employment alternatives.

There are other private services that are available to relatively more people, such as housecleaning services and fast-food restaurants. Certainly, many mothers rely on fast-food restaurants to give them a break from cooking or to accommodate a busy schedule of work and caring for children. Although these restaurants are relatively inexpensive, most families cannot afford to eat at them regularly. Furthermore, unlike new gourmet take-out food services, fast-food restaurants do not offer many nutritional benefits.

In a few instances, the marketplace has begun to assume more responsibility for helping with family tasks. A small number of workplaces are experimenting with hiring staff to do errands for workers while the workers are on the job, including shopping for meals and for birthday presents (National Public Radio, 1996). This idea may have some surface appeal because it is workplace policies that can make doing family errands difficult; however, given that company benefits are declining and loyalty to employees is eroding, it is unlikely that many companies would provide such services. Furthermore, some would argue that such a benefit would work to increase families' dependence on the workplace, whereas what is needed is to challenge the many ways in which the workplace controls the conditions of family life.

SINGLE-MOTHER FAMILIES AND THE HIGH POVERTY RATE

A second very serious problem for family life is the poverty that single-mother families face. Two-parent families also can fall into poverty; however, far greater percentages of single-parent families live below the poverty level. As I illustrate in this section, their difficult economic situation highlights the costs of our system of distributing family resources. Although mothers' incomes now are essential to the financial well-being of most families, women still earn substantially less money than do men (Rotella, 1995), both because women's salaries and wages are lower and because many more women than men work part-time. Women of color earn even less money and have fewer family resources to fall back on than do white women, making it that much more difficult for them to live outside of marriage on their own incomes. In the following paragraphs, I describe the situation of divorced and never-married single mothers.

As divorce has become widespread, researchers have documented the difficult economic situation that divorced women face. Nevertheless, many stereotypes of divorced women remain, such as the view that they gain large alimony settlements. In fact, only about one sixth of divorced women receive alimony or spousal maintenance awards, and many mothers face great economic difficulty after divorce (Weitzman, 1985). As noted previously, an astonishing 39% of divorced mothers with children age 18 or under live in poverty (U.S. Bureau of the Census, 1993, p. 79).

The law puts divorced women in a vulnerable and dependent position. Laws regulating the distribution of assets at divorce do not address the fact that women are economically disadvantaged by their participation in marriages that fail. The amounts of money that women receive from marital assets and for child support do not reflect their contributions to their marriages or their needs for themselves and their children after their divorces (Babcock et al., 1996; Kurz, 1995). Only a minority of women receive child support, and amounts are generally low (Garfinkel, 1992; Roberts, 1994).

England and Kilbourne (1990) argued that the reason divorce is so economically disastrous for women is that the tasks in which they have invested so much time, child rearing and housekeeping, are not transferable when a marriage dissolves, unlike the job skills in which men have invested. At divorce, women receive no benefits or compensation for all of the caretaking work they have done. Furthermore, the fact that career assets are not recognized as marital property means that the primary wage earner, generally the husband, is permitted to keep most of the assets accumulated during marriage (Arendell, 1986; Babcock et al., 1996; Weitzman, 1985). Thus the husband does not suffer financially at divorce, whereas the wife, who has invested in her family and in her husband's career, is deprived of a return on her marital investment and must support herself and her children by working at wages that are not sufficient to support them at an adequate standard of living. The decline in the standard of living that divorced mothers face takes a severe toll on their lives (Arendell, 1986; Kurz, 1995), pushing some of them toward permanent downward mobility or even into poverty. Their children, whose well-being is tied to that of their mothers, suffer a similar fate.

Single mothers face even greater economic difficulties than do divorced mothers, and single mothers' poverty rate is even higher. Many single mothers must go on welfare to support themselves and their children because they cannot get jobs that pay living wages or offer health benefits or child care (Sidel, 1996). Supporting children on welfare, however, is very difficult because welfare payments are below the poverty level in every state. Furthermore, new "welfare reform" legislation not only limits the benefits women receive but also ends the entitlement of poor women to government assistance and mandates that they be dropped from welfare programs after specified periods of time.

Our social policies, based on stereotypes of single mothers as social parasites, penalize those single mothers who go on welfare. Traditionally, the welfare system prevented women from working and deducted money from their welfare checks if they did. In a radical change, recent legislation has required women on welfare to work as a condition of receiving benefits (Abramowitz, 1988; Gordon, 1994). Certainly, gaining money and experience in the paid labor force is very important for poor mothers. Welfare regulations, however, are punitive. Although welfare now has strict work requirements, it typically does not provide sufficient funds for day care. Furthermore, welfare policies ignore the need of women on welfare to care for their children, a necessity if women are to find work. Whereas middle-class career women are said to be harming their children by going to work (Barnett & Rivers, 1996), it is as if welfare women, viewed as lazy and shiftless, do not have any child care responsibilities. Antiwelfare rhetoric renders invisible the difficulties of raising children in poverty and ignores the critical fact that women with less education cannot find jobs that will support them and their children or that provide health care benefits.

Because of this failure to support mothers with children outside of marriage, increasing numbers of the poor are women and children. This phenomenon has been referred to as the "feminization of poverty" (Pearce, 1993). Mothers of all backgrounds can be at risk of poverty. It is very important to underscore, however, that because they have lower salaries and fewer job prospects than do white women (Malveaux, 1985; U.S. Department of Labor, 1989), disproportionate numbers of women of color are poor, particularly minority single mothers. Therefore, the feminization of poverty cannot be viewed apart from the "racialization of poverty" (Wilkerson & Gresham, 1993).

Causes of the Failure to Provide Care

It is critical to examine the causes of these two serious problems of family life and to understand them within a framework that addresses issues of gender, race, and class. Too frequently, family problems have been analyzed within a framework that looks to the loss of values as the cause of family problems or, as noted earlier, vague concepts of "family decline." Such frameworks lead to policies, based on the model of the traditional family, that fail to reflect the new realities of the entry of women into the workplace and the rise of single-mother families and that do not address the crises of care work or the rise in female poverty. The United States has no national child care policy, and there is little attempt by employers to give supports and benefits to part-time work. Those mothers who live outside of marriages or partnerships with men who contribute family income are not able to support themselves and their children at an adequate standard of living. As noted earlier, we provide these women with only meager help through a punitive welfare system.

Powerful material and ideological factors underlie the failure to provide assistance for families. Current economic interests contribute to the support of the traditional family as the preferred family form. As Marxist-, socialist-, and other types of feminists have noted, those owning and making profits in business and industry benefit incalculably from the unpaid domestic labor of mothers and other caretakers, particularly women of color (Glazer, 1987; Hartmann, 1981; Luxton, 1980; Smith, 1987); indeed, their profits depend on it. Business and industry make few attempts to support domestic life; rather, they contribute to the stress of family life by failing to make any significant accommodations to it. Many business groups lobbied against passage of the Family and Medical Leave Act, a bill that ultimately did pass but that provides less leave time to care for children and other family members than do bills in other industrialized countries (Reskin & Padavic, 1994) and that, unlike bills in other countries, provides no stipend for caretakers taking a family leave (Kittay, 1995).

In popular and policy circles, the ideal of the traditional family, based on deeply held ideologies about gender roles and the nature of male and female identities, also continues to be the model for family life. Traditional family ideology promotes the traditional role of women as the nurturers of children and other family members who need care. Men, still designated as breadwinners, are to be "independent" and free of caretaking responsibilities. Government policies always have assumed that mothers will be available at any time to take care of children (Abramowitz, 1988; Gordon, 1994). Although only a minority of families now take the form of the traditional family, it continues to be the predominant model of the ideal family, to the serious disadvantage of women. Some even want to make this family form a reality again. Politicians on the right, as well as some conservative and neoconservative thinkers (Blankenhorn, 1995; Murray,

1993; Popenoe, 1988), urge a return to "the true American family" to reinstate traditional marriage as the "cure" for family problems and "family decline." In addition, norms of male dominance dictate that women should live in relationships with men. Punitive policies toward single-mother families, and recent proposals by conservative policymakers and politicians to make it more difficult for couples to divorce, reflect the belief that women should not live independently of men. Such views deny the hardships of marriage and the roles of poverty, domestic violence, and other structural factors in causing divorce or the breakup of male-female unions (Kurz, 1995).

The ideology of the traditional family also promotes the stigmatization of single mothers. Although single mothers always have been stigmatized, they have been increasingly blamed for a whole host of social problems. The animosity toward single mothers is particularly evident in welfare debates and policies. Some commentators (Roberts, 1995; Sidel, 1996) believe that the demonization of single mothers is especially serious because we associate single motherhood with being black, another stigmatized status. Roberts (1995) believes that the myth of the black matriarch, the domineering female head of the black family, fuels the stigmatization of black single women. Although there is a stereotype that single mothers are black, in fact the rate of increase in single motherhood is greater among white women than among black women (U.S. Bureau of the Census, 1995). Thus, although racist beliefs and stereotypes are particularly harmful to women of color, they are in fact harmful to most other women as well because they obscure the need of many mothers for help with caretaking work.

Strategies for Change:
Coparenting and the Role of Fathers

The lack of support for the care work that mothers do and the high poverty rate of single mothers clearly demonstrate that the current system of addressing dependency needs and providing care, based on the policy of relying on a male wage earner to support a traditional family structure, is deeply flawed. Given that the preferred traditional family form is inadequate to the task of providing care in an equitable manner, what alternative possibilities exist for the provision of the physical, financial, and social care of children? The strategy most often suggested is to increase fathers' involvement in family life. Support for this strategy is widespread and has come from many quarters: Feminists have long proposed that fathers share care work (Fineman, 1995b; Silverstein, 1996); a new neoconservative movement, led by David Blankenhorn, has undertaken a public campaign to encourage fathers to spend more time with families (Blankenhorn, 1995); and the right has increasingly promoted father involvement as the solution to family problems (Fineman, 1995b).

For several decades, the women's movement has promoted shared housework and coparenting as major strategies for achieving equality in marriage, one of the most important goals of the movement (Fineman, 1995b; Silverstein, 1996). In addition to promoting the ideal of equality, the women's movement views the goal of equality as having practical benefits. Many in the feminist movement hoped and still hope for an increase in shared parenting so that the burden of managing the household can be shared and mothers can experience less stress while taking care of their children, as well as more flexibility to negotiate for rewards in their work situations. Shared parenting has the potential to allow mothers to make more serious investments in careers and offers the promise of increased well-being for fathers and children.

Although in theory shared parenting would seem to be the ideal means of providing family care, as already discussed, equal participation by fathers has proven difficult to achieve, both within and outside of marriage. A variety of researchers have tried to determine what keeps fathers from becoming seriously involved in the lives of their children. A study of Swedish fathers indicates some of the obstacles to father participation in the care of children (Sandquist, 1987). Despite generous national legislation in Sweden promoting paternity leaves, fathers generally have not taken advantage of these leaves. Fathers in the Swedish study gave two major reasons for their reluctance to take paternity leaves. First, they felt no support from their workplaces for taking leaves to care for children. Second, when they did take on increased child care responsibilities at home, they felt isolated.

The problem of fathers' feelings of isolation may be difficult to surmount. These data suggest, however, that more supportive, flexible workplace policies could increase father participation. It is not clear, however, that such policies are forthcoming in the United States. In this era of downsizing, employers may be even less willing to grant "flex-time," or family leave time. Furthermore, both mothers and fathers may have to work longer hours at less pay. Thus, even in families where fathers are participating more, families will not experience less stress.

A shared parenting model is even more difficult to achieve in single-parent families. Divorced and single fathers typically have spent little time with their children. To encourage more father involvement with children after divorce, policymakers recently have promoted the use of mandatory joint custody laws to encourage fathers to take more social and financial responsibility for their children (Fineman, 1991, 1995b). Many policymakers are responsive to pressures from fathers' rights groups, which have lobbied for mandatory joint custody laws and argue that mothers are denying fathers adequate time with their children and are blocking fathers' participation in decision making about their children's lives (Arendell, 1995). Some women's rights advocates also believe that mandatory joint custody laws are useful in promoting the involvement of fathers with children and that single mothers urgently need the help taking care of children that fathers could provide (Bartlett & Stack, 1986).

Others, however, see mandatory joint custody as a dangerous trend. They believe that mandatory joint custody uses the rhetoric of equality against women, that because mothers have done the work of child rearing, joint custody gives fathers control they have not earned (Becker, 1992; Fineman, 1995b). These critics also point to the fact that although mandatory joint custody laws are supposed to increase father participation in families, evidence indicates that when they have been enacted, father participation in families has not increased (Maccoby & Mnookin, 1992).[1]

The reports of the mothers in my own study, based on a random sample of divorced women with children, reflect these concerns about father participation after divorce (Kurz, 1995). Mothers reported two completely different sets of experiences with custody and visitation. Fully 42% of mothers who reported that visitation took place reported that fathers' lack of involvement in the family after divorce was a serious problem for them. These mothers spent a lot of time trying to involve fathers in children's sports and school activities. Some had to convince fathers that their participation in their children's lives was important. Furstenberg and Cherlin (1991) believe that the kind of father detachment these and other mothers report results from a process of "drift," that playing the ambiguous role of part-time father becomes increasingly difficult because the authority of the role depends on knowing what one's children are doing on a daily basis—a difficult task for fathers who are not living with their children. Remarriage and a new set of children may complete the process of disconnection. Arendell (1995) argued that some fathers distance themselves from their children to avoid the pain they feel at being separated from them.

Addressing this problem of lack of father involvement, Czapanskiy (1989) claimed that new custody laws do not treat mothers fairly. She argued that although joint custody statutes give fathers new rights and powers, they do not require fathers to participate in the activities that are the basis for joint decision making. They require no new duties or responsibilities. Thus, according to Czapanskiy, these statutes enable fathers to realize the promise of joint custody while mothers do not. Women must share control of decision making about their children with fathers while not necessarily receiving any help from fathers in the raising of the children.

There are other problems with policies that try to increase father visitation. In my study, a second group of mothers reported that they wanted less, not more, visitation. Of those mothers who reported that visitation took place, 29% reported a great deal of conflict with fathers. Many of these women believed that fathers were using visitation as a way in which to check up on and control them, and some were afraid of their ex-husbands. A number of them reported that their husbands had been violent during their marriages, and some after the separations, and many of these women were afraid of their ex-husbands. Fully 50% of the women in the sample had experienced violence during their marriages, and some of these women also experienced violence during the separations. Women's fears and their experiences of violence point to the fact that mandatory joint custody can be harmful in some situations by making these mothers vulnerable to violence again. Arendell's (1995) study confirmed that some divorced fathers use visitation as a way in which to try to gain control over their former wives.

In addition to trying to increase fathers' participation in the social lives of their children, policymakers also have tried to make fathers more financially responsible for their children after divorce. They have done this by developing much stricter child support systems. Interest in child support enforcement has grown, in part because it is seen as a way in which to keep women off of welfare (Fineman, 1995b; Kurz, 1995). As a result of the increased attention to child support, there is widespread resentment of fathers who do not support their children—"deadbeat dads" who father children and disappear. The most effective system of child support that has been developed is wage withholding, in which the wages of the noncustodial parent, usually the father, are automatically deducted from his or her paycheck and sent to the custodial parent, usually the mother (U.S. Department of Health and Human Services, 1994, p. 20). Automatic wage withholding, mandated by the Family Support Act to be implemented by 1994, will substantially increase the amount of child support that mothers receive (Garfinkel, 1992).

Unfortunately, however, implementation of wage withholding will take some time. Furthermore, even when wage withholding is implemented, 23% to 35% of mothers never will receive child support (Garfinkel, 1992). Based on reports from the women in my study, there are several factors that will prevent mothers from getting the child support they are due. First, some fathers still will be able to evade payment, particularly by working "under the table." Second, some mothers, particularly those who experienced domestic violence during their marriages, will not apply for child support because they fear their ex-husbands will be violent toward them if they do. Finally, as others have argued (Roberts, 1994), some fathers cannot afford to pay child support. These circumstances demonstrate that a number of women will not be able to count on child support from fathers to provide them with an adequate standard of living.

To increase fathers' financial participation, states have begun to require mothers to locate and identify the fathers of their children to obtain child support, a procedure called *paternity establishment.* Requiring mothers to identify fathers to get child support is part of a general trend to try to make fathers take more financial responsibility for their children. Some states also now require mothers to find and identify fathers as a condition of receiving welfare benefits. Wisconsin, for example, makes full cooperation in paternity determinations of "nonmarital" children a condition of eligibility for receiving assistance (Fineman, 1996). Failure to cooperate disqualifies the caretaker for assistance, and "protective payments" for the child will be paid to "a person other than the person charged with the care of the dependent child" (Fineman, 1996).

Laws such as these can put an undue burden on mothers who have serious conflicts with their former partners, especially those who have suffered physical abuse. At this time, federal law requiring welfare mothers to identify fathers provides for a "good cause" exemption from naming the fathers. However, a determination of good cause is based on the needs of the child, rather than the mother, and is said to exist if the child is at risk of physical or emotional harm from the father or if the mother will suffer such harm from the father that she will be unable to adequately care for the child. These policies will put some mothers at risk. In a high percentage of cases, women seeking welfare have been physically abused and may be at further risk of abuse at the hands of the fathers (Raphael, 1995). Recent research has demonstrated that many women remain at risk of experiencing violence after separations (Kurz, 1996).

Although there are serious obstacles to shared parenting, there also are, of course, many benefits to shared parenting for mothers, fathers, and children, and it remains an important goal for many feminists and women's rights activists (Silverstein, 1996). When fathers coparent, mothers can spend more time in their workplaces, the lives of fathers are enriched, and children benefit not only from increased time with their fathers but also from seeing new models of fatherhood. Encouraging fathers to become involved in parenting should be a high societal priority.

The ideal of equal participation by fathers in child rearing in the immediate future, however, seems elusive. Furthermore, as just noted, in the case of some divorce policies such as mandatory joint custody, the idea of equality can be turned against women. Thus at the present time we cannot rely on father participation to solve the problems of mothers burdened with a "double shift" or the general need for more caretaking time in families. We must find other strategies for supporting mothers and care work. As noted earlier, in the absence of father participation in caretaking, many mothers have relied on those child care, food, and housekeeping services that are available on the market. The ability to use private solutions to meet caretaking needs, however, is dependent on a woman's social class, with lower income women unable to afford much of what is available.

Unfortunately, lawmakers and politicians from both political parties, particularly Republicans, recently have favored turning to "private" strategies to solve the problems of poor single mothers and eliminating almost all public social supports for these women and their families. Viewing the market as the solution to problems of poverty, they have abolished Aid to Families with Dependent Children (AFDC), which for 60 years has provided limited—but guaranteed—financial support to the poorest women and their children. Believing that women are on welfare because they will not work, many politicians claim that leaving them to fend in the marketplace will strengthen their characters and enable them to secure jobs. This strategy not only is completely misguided but is harmful, overlooking how difficult it can be to find a job, how many jobs in the low-wage sector do not pay a living wage, how many low-wage jobs do not provide health benefits, and the high cost of child care. Tragically, the new welfare "reform" bill did not provide adequate funds for day care, health care benefits, or job training; as a result, this reform will push even greater numbers of women and children into poverty. Although the current welfare system has many serious flaws, as will be discussed in the next subsection, there are ways in which it can be reformed.

It is clear that much more government support is required to ease the burdens of mothers and families and to keep them out of poverty. Although such a position goes against prevailing views that favor reducing or even dismantling state support for entitlements and social programs, there is no other way in which to improve and promote greater quality of life in families or to reduce the poverty of single-parent families. We must invest in policies and programs that support the care of children and families. Such policies should benefit all families and help integrate them into the mainstream, unlike current policies that isolate and stigmatize the poor.

THE ROLE OF THE STATE AND THE
AMERICAN RESPONSE TO CARE WORK

A variety of measures are required to support mothers and care work. First, the government must provide better family leave policies. Fortunately, in 1993 the United States passed its first family leave bill guaranteeing mothers and fathers 12 weeks of leave to care for newborns or sick family members. The family leave policy in the United States, however, has many shortcomings such as the fact, noted earlier, that it provides less time for family leave than similar bills in other industrialized countries and no pay for workers during their leaves. Kittay (1995) noted three additional limitations of the family leave bill that are particularly serious: the fact that leaves are unpaid; that they are available only to traditional husband-wife families, not nonmarried cohabiting adults, gay or lesbian families, or extended families; and that employers with fewer than 50 employees are not obligated to provide family leaves. A more extended, comprehensive family leave bill is critical to the future of families.

Second, families need subsidized day care to reduce family stress and so that women can find and keep suitable jobs. Based on a comparative study of the United States, with its limited day care policies, and other countries that have more comprehensive ones, Bergmann (1994) argued that a large government role in the provision of child care and after-school care would go a long way toward eliminating child poverty. Third, to enable all families, especially single-mother families, to maintain an adequate standard of living, women need higher wages. Women's low pay fails to keep large numbers of women above the poverty level and keeps others far below the median income level. Government policies also must provide better benefits for those mothers who work part-time to care for their children. Other economic reforms also are necessary including increasing the minimum wage, regulating wages and benefits in part-time and contingent work, and adopting policies of equal pay for work of comparable worth. For single mothers not to fall into poverty, the government also must provide additional income support, such as unemployment insurance and temporary disability insurance, that provides coverage for the types of earning losses common to single mothers, who sometimes must take time off from work to care for children or other family members. According to Spalter-Roth and

Hartmann (1994), such strategies could mean that a larger number of women would qualify for earned income credit benefits and for unemployment insurance.

Because women generally have low wages, and because many must work part-time to care for their children, many mothers, particularly single mothers, need to have their incomes from paid work supplemented by basic income guarantees. Family allowances, for example, would reduce the inordinately high levels of child poverty found in the United States (Bergmann, 1994). Many other democracies provide support through universal governmental transfers such as child allowances or basic income guarantees. Spalter-Roth and Hartmann (1994) favor a strategy of "income packaging" for single mothers, which would help mothers combine income sources from work, from ex-husbands or ex-partners, and from the state. Finally, mothers need health care for themselves and their children because many jobs do not offer health care benefits, a situation that leaves some women and children vulnerable to the high cost of medical care and, as noted earlier, forces others to turn to welfare, now itself increasingly unreliable.

Those who do not favor state support of families will find many grounds on which to oppose these proposals. First, such reforms are costly. While refusing to support care work and the needs of single mothers, opponents of increased government support for families fail to acknowledge that middle-class families receive many direct and indirect government subsidies that remain hidden from view such as marriage and inheritance laws, insurance and benefit regulations, probate laws, and zoning ordinances (Coontz, 1992). Middle-class families also benefit from tax deductions for children that are worth much more than the child allowances given to mothers on welfare who have more children (Fineman, 1995a). Furthermore, middle-class taxpayers benefit from deductions such as interest paid on mortgage debt and some child care expenses and from the fact that employer contributions to health and life insurance policies frequently are not counted as income (Fineman, 1995b).

Those with business interests also undoubtedly would object to more generous family benefits and would see family leave, higher wages, and greater support for part-time work as unjustifiably cutting into their profits. Thus the reforms just proposed will not be easy to achieve and will only be enacted after considerable political struggle. Despite the denials of those who oppose social supports for families, however, our society does have the money to fund generous social welfare programs. According to Coontz (1992),

> Redistributing just 1 percent of the income of America's richest 5 percent would lift one million people above the poverty line. A 1 percent tax on the net wealth of the richest 2 percent of American families would allow us to double federal spending on education and still have almost $20 billion left to spend somewhere else. . . . One commission has recently suggested that it would be possible to restructure the military to transfer $125 billion a year to other uses over the next ten years. (p. 286)

In addition to objections to cost, some, especially supporters of the traditional family, will oppose reforms that support the family because they fear that increased wages for women, as well as increased support for family health care and day care, will enable women to live more easily outside of marriage (Popenoe, 1988). This may well be true. We must question why we designate the marital unit as the primary site for distributing family resources, however, and consider other ways in which to distribute these resources. In our social policies, we should consider privileging relationships that care for and sustain dependents and distributing benefits through such relationships. This will require developing new models for providing care and resources to families.

Many writers have examined our current conceptions of care and have pointed to their failure to acknowledge that dependency is a permanent feature of life for everyone, whether during childhood, old age, or periods of illness—not an aberrant, deviant condition (DeVault, 1991; Fraser & Gordon, 1994; Hochschild, 1995). Fineman (1995b) and Kittay (1995) argued that there is an additional kind of dependency that affects a major sector of the population: the dependency that results when one is responsible for the care of others. Fineman made a distinction between what she calls "inevitable dependency," the dependency that results from not being able to take care of oneself, and "derivative dependency," the dependency that results from taking care of others. Fineman argued that derivative dependency needs must be given social support. Similarly, Kittay referred to the need to "care for those who care" and urges that our social institutions be responsive both to dependents and to those who attend to dependents (Kittay, 1995).

We must rethink our current ideas about what is "private" and what is "public" and acknowledge that what we currently think of as private often has very public dimensions. For example, Kittay (1995) pointed out that even though we think of many dependency decisions, such as marital decisions, as private, in fact we grant many social privileges on the basis of marriage and we require employers, landlords, hospitals, insurance agencies, and the Internal Revenue Service, for example, to take certain actions on behalf of married people. She argued that, similarly, the private decision to take on the work of dependency and to support a dependent outside of marriage also should include third-party obligations to support the dependency worker. To avoid overinstitutionalizing or overprivatizing family care, Hochschild (1995) called for a balanced sharing of public and private responsibility for care work.

Conclusion

Viewing the family from a feminist perspective, I have identified what I see as two of the major problems of the contemporary family: the double burden faced by mothers who do the majority of family care work while also working in the paid economy, and the poverty and stress faced by single-mother heads of household and their children. Many scholars and other analysts have failed to see these problems because they have not understood how inequities based on gender and race bias are built into the structure of the family. Policymakers similarly fail to take into account factors of gender and race when making family policy. For example, one of the primary solutions proposed to address the current crises of the family has been to promote greater father participation in family life to do caretaking work and provide more financial assistance for single-mother families. Although father involvement should be seriously promoted, and at some point in the future there may be equitable father participation in the social and financial lives of all families, for the time being father participation is not a solution to family problems. Furthermore, in some cases, such as when fathers have been violent, great care must be taken to determine whether fathers should participate in family life. What is required is for our society to assume more collective social responsibility for families through stronger social supports.

Current government policies toward the family are inadequate and flawed. Although there have been government initiatives in the provision of day care and family leave, the government's approach to supporting families continues to assign priority to the traditional nuclear family model. We persist in viewing the welfare state, increasingly associated with AFDC (or welfare), with *dependency*, a stigmatizing and derogatory term (Fraser & Gordon, 1994). Our culture, looking to eradicate dependency, identifies the problems of poverty and hardship as rooted in the characteristics of vulnerable groups such as women, particularly minority women. Racism feeds this tendency to view any kind of family help as dependency. Instead of passing the legislation necessary to reduce poverty, legislators have rushed to restrict benefits for women on AFDC.

We must replace this reliance on outdated views with new thinking about the concepts of *dependency* and *independence*. Our social policies must reflect the reality that family members all are highly interdependent and that all families require social supports. We need to provide all types of families with many more universal, non-means-tested, nonstigmatizing benefits including day care and health care. These measures are necessary for women but also for their children. We need a new model of social welfare that includes not handouts but rather universal benefits for all such as the right to shelter, income supports for working parents, an expanded earned income tax program, and family allowances. The goal of such benefits would be to integrate beneficiaries into the social mainstream, unlike current social welfare programs, which segregate them.

Note

1. There are two types of joint custody: legal, in which a parent has the right to share in important decisions about a child's life (e.g., educational and religious training), and physical, in which the child resides with a parent. Research shows that the enactment of laws creating joint legal custody does not lead to increased contact between a father and his children.

References

Abramowitz, M. (1988). *Regulating the lives of women: Social welfare policy from colonial times to the present.* Boston: South End.

Arendell, T. (1986). *Mothers and divorce: Legal, economic, and social dilemmas.* Berkeley: University of California Press.

Arendell, T. (1995). *Fathers and divorce.* Thousand Oaks: Sage.

Arendell, T. (1996, January). *Co-parenting: A review of the literature.* Unpublished manuscript commissioned by the National Center on Fathers and Families, Philadelphia.

Babcock, B. A., Copelon, R., Freedman, A., Norton, E. H., Ross, S., Taub, N., & Williams, W. (1996). *Sex discrimination and the law: Causes and remedies* (2nd ed.). Boston: Little, Brown.

Barnett, R. C., & Rivers, C. (1996). *She works, he works: How two-income families are happier, healthier, and better-off.* San Francisco: Harper.

Bartlett, K. T., & Stack, C. (1986). Joint custody, feminism, and the dependency dilemma. *Berkeley Women's Law Journal, 2,* 9-41.

Becker, M. (1992). Maternal feelings: Myth, taboo, and child custody. *Review of Law and Women's Studies, 1,* 133-224.

Bergmann, B. (1986). *The economic emergence of women.* New York: Basic Books.

Bergmann, B. (1994, May). *Child care: The key to ending child poverty.* Paper presented at the Conference on Social Policies for Children, Princeton, NJ.

Blair, S., & Johnson, M. (1992). Wives' perceptions of the fairness of the division of labor: The intersection of housework and ideology. *Journal of Marriage and the Family, 5,* 570-582.

Blankenhorn, D. (1995). *Fatherless America: Confronting our most urgent social problem.* New York: Basic Books.

Blau, F. D., & Ferber, M. A. (1992). *The economics of women, men, and work.* Englewood Cliffs, NJ: Prentice Hall.

Collins, P. H. (1991). *Black feminist thought.* New York: Routledge.

Coltrane, S. (1996). *Family man: Fatherhood, housework, and gender equity.* New York: Oxford University Press.

Coontz, S. (1992). *The way we never were.* New York: Basic Books.

Czapanskiy, K. (1989). Child support and visitation: Rethinking the connections. *Rutger's Law Journal, 20,* 619-665.

DeVault, M. L. (1991). *Feeding the family: The social organization of caring as gendered work.* Chicago: University of Chicago Press.

Dill, B. T. (1988). Our mother's grief: Racial ethnic women and the maintenance of families. *Journal of Family History, 13,* 415-431.

England, P., & Kilbourne, B. S. (1990). Markets, marriages, and other mates: The problem of power. In R. Friedland & S. Robertson (Eds.), *Beyond the marketplace: Rethinking society and economy* (pp. 1163-1188). New York: Aldine de Gruyter.

Etzioni, A. (1993). *The spirit of community.* New York: Crown.

Ferree, M. M. (1990). Beyond separate spheres: Feminism and family research. *Journal of Marriage and the Family, 52,* 886-894.

Fineman, M. A. (1991). *The illusion of equality: The rhetoric and reality of divorce reform.* Chicago: University of Chicago Press.

Fineman, M. A. (1995a). Masking dependency: The political role of family rhetoric. *Virginia Law Review, 81,* 501-534.

Fineman, M. A. (1995b). *The neutered mother, the sexual family and other twentieth century tragedies.* New York: Routledge.

Fineman, M. A. (1996). The nature of dependencies and welfare "reform." *Santa Clara Law Review, 36,* 1401-1425.

Fraser, N., & Gordon, L. (1994). "Dependency" demystified: Inscriptions of power in a keyword of the welfare state. *Social Politics, 1*(1), 4-31.

Furstenberg, F. F., Jr., & Cherlin, A. (1991). *Divided families.* Cambridge, MA: Harvard University Press.

Garfinkel, I. (1992). *Assuring child support: An extension of social security.* New York: Russell Sage.

Gerson, K. (1993). *No man's land: Men's changing commitments to family and work.* New York: Basic Books.

Glazer, N. (1987). Servants to capital: Unpaid domestic labor and paid work. In N. Gerstel & H. Gross (Eds.), *Families and work: Towards reconceptualization* (pp. 236-255). Philadelphia: Temple University Press.

Glenn, E. N. (1987). Gender and the family. In B. Hess & M. Ferree (Eds.), *Analyzing gender: A handbook of social science research* (pp. 348-360). Newbury Park, CA: Sage.

Gordon, L. (1994). *Pitied but not entitled: Single mothers and the history of welfare, 1890-1935.* New York: Free Press.

Hartmann, H. (1981). The family as the locus of gender, class, and political struggle: The example of housework. *Signs: Journal of Women in Society and Culture, 6,* 366-394.

Herz, D. E., & Wootton, B. H. (1996). Women in the workforce: An overview. In C. Costello & B. Krimgold (Eds.), *The American woman 1996-97* (pp. 44-78). New York: Norton.

Hochschild, A. (1995). The culture of politics: Traditional, postmodern, cold-modern, and warm-modern ideals of care. *Social Politics, 2,* 331-346.

Hochschild, A., with Machung, A. (1989). *The second shift: Working parents and the revolution at home.* New York: Viking.

Hoffman, L. W. (1989). Effects of maternal employment in the two-parent family. *American Psychologist, 44,* 283-292.

Kittay, E. F. (1995). Taking dependency seriously: The Family and Medical Leave Act considered in light of the social organization of dependency work and gender equality. *Hypatia, 10*(1), 7-29.

Kurz, D. (1995). *For richer, for poorer: Mothers confront divorce.* New York: Routledge.

Kurz, D. (1996). Separation, divorce, and woman abuse. *Violence Against Women, 2*(1), 63-81.

Luxton, M. (1980). *More than a labour of love: Three generations of women's work in the home.* Toronto: Women's Press.

Maccoby, E. E., & Mnookin, R. H. (1992). *Dividing the child: Social and legal dilemmas of custody.* Cambridge, MA: Harvard University Press.

Malveaux, J. (1985). The economic interests of black and white women: Are they similar? *Review of Black Political Economy, 14,* 5-27.

McLanahan, S., & Adams, J. (1987). Parenthood and psychological well-being. *Annual Review of Sociology, 13,* 237-257.

Mirowsky, J., & Ross, C. E. (1989). *Social causes of psychological distress.* New York: Aldine de Gruyter.

Murray, C. (1993, October 29). The coming white underclass. *Wall Street Journal,* p. A14.

National Public Radio. (1996, April 8). Commentary on "Marketplace." Washington, DC: Author.

Pearce, D. (1993). The feminization of poverty: Update. In A. Jaggar & P. Rothenberg (Eds.), *Feminist frameworks* (3rd ed., pp. 290-296). New York: McGraw-Hill.

Pleck, J. H. (1996, June). *Paternal involvement: Levels, sources, and consequences.* Paper presented at the Co-Parenting Roundtable of the Fathers and Families Roundtable Series sponsored by the National Center on Fathers and Families, Philadelphia.

Popenoe, David. (1988). *Disturbing the nest: Family change and decline in modern societies.* New York: Aldine de Gruyter.

Population Reference Bureau. (1993). *What the 1990 census tells us about women: A state factbook* (Vol. 20). Washington, DC: Author.

Raphael, J. (1995). Domestic violence and welfare reform. *Poverty and Race, 4*(1), 19-29.

Reskin, B., & Padavic, I. (1994). *Women and men at work.* Thousand Oaks, CA: Pine Forge.

Roberts, D. (1995). Racism and patriarchy in the meaning of motherhood. In M. Fineman & I. Karpin (Eds.), *Mothers in law* (pp. 224-249). New York: Columbia University Press.

Roberts, P. G. (1994). *Ending poverty as we know it: The case for child support enforcement and assurance.* Washington, DC: Center for Law and Social Policy.

Rotella, E. (1995). Women and the American economy. In S. Ruth (Ed.), *Issues in feminism* (pp. 320-333). Mountain View, CA: Mayfield.

Saluter, A. F. (1994). Status and marital living arrangements: March 1993. In U.S. Bureau of the Census, *Current population reports* (Series P20, No. 478). Washington, DC: Government Printing Office.

Sandquist, K. (1987). Swedish family policy and the attempt to change paternal roles. In C. O'Brien & M. O'Brien (Eds.), *Reassessing fatherhood* (pp. 1444-1460). London: Sage.

Seltzer, J. (1991). Relationships between fathers and children who live apart: The father's role after separation. *Journal of Marriage and the Family, 53,* 79-101.

Sidel, R. (1996). *Keeping women and children last.* New York: Penguin Books.

Silverstein, L. B. (1996). Fathering is a feminist issue. *Psychology of Women Quarterly, 20,* 3-37.

Smith, D. (1987). Women's inequality and the family. In N. Gerstl & H. Gross (Eds.), *Families and work* (pp. 23-54). Philadelphia: Temple University Press.

Spalter-Roth, R. M., & Hartmann, H. (1994). AFDC recipients as care-givers and workers: A feminist approach to income security policy for American women. *Social Politics, 1,* 190-210.

Steil, J. M. (1994). Equality and entitlement in marriage. In M. Lerner & G. Mikula (Eds.), *Entitlement and the affectional bond: Justice in close relationships* (pp. 229-258). New York: Plenum.

Thoits, P. (1986). Multiple identities: Examining gender and marital status differences in distress. *American Sociological Review, 51,* 259-272.

Thompson, L., & Walker, A. J. (1995). The place of feminism in family studies. *Journal of Marriage and the Family, 57,* 847-865.

Thorne, B. (1992). Feminism and the family: Two decades of thought. In B. Thorne & M. Yalom (Eds.), *Rethinking the family* (pp. 3-30). Boston: Northeastern University Press.

U.S. Bureau of the Census. (1993). Poverty in the United States: 1992. In *Current Population Reports* (Series P60, No. 185). Washington, DC: Government Printing Office.

U.S. Bureau of the Census. (1994). Who's minding the kids? Child care arrangements: Fall 1991. In *Current Population Reports* (Series P70, No. 36). Washington, DC: Government Printing Office.

U.S. Bureau of the Census. (1995). Dynamics of economic well-being: Program participation 1990-1992. In *Current Population Reports* (Series P70, No. 41). Washington, DC: Government Printing Office.

U.S. Department of Health and Human Services, Administration of Children and Families, Office of Child Support Enforcement. (1994). *Seventeenth annual report to Congress*. Washington, DC: Government Printing Office.

U.S. Department of Labor, Bureau of Labor Statistics. (1989). Labor force statistics 1948-1987. In *Current Population Survey* (Bulletin 22307). Washington, DC: Government Printing Office.

Weitzman, L. J. (1985). *The divorce revolution*. New York: Free Press.

Wilkerson, M. B., & Gresham, J. H. (1993). The racialization of poverty. In A. Jagger & P. Rothberg (Eds.), *Feminist frameworks: Alternative theoretical relations between men and women* (3rd ed., pp. 297-303). New York: McGraw-Hill.

Wyche, K. F. (1993). Psychology and African-American women: Findings from applied research. *Applied and Preventive Psychology, 2,* 115-121.

Zinn, M. B. (1989). Family, race, and poverty in the eighties. *Signs: Journal of Women in Society and Culture, 14,* 856-874.

5

The Social Construction
of Fatherhood

KATHLEEN GERSON

Not long ago, the term *father* conveyed a clear and unambiguous meaning. A "good father" worked hard, provided his children with an economically secure home, and offered committed but distant guidance. Although he relied on a nurturing woman to meet his children's daily needs for emotional and physical sustenance, he compensated for his aloofness by winning the bread that mothers baked. This notion of the "good providing" father never accurately captured the full range of fathering behavior, but it dominated as a cultural ideal and reflected the reality in most American households.

How strangely out of date that once unquestioned image seems today! Instead of a dominant view, we now face an array of diverse and contending patterns. In one scenario, American fathers are sharing the burdens of breadwinning with equally hard-working wives, but they are refusing to assume their fair share of work in the home. In these families, the gender revolution has stalled at the domestic doorway, where men resist entering the domain of housework and child care (Hochschild with Machung, 1989).

Another scenario focuses on an even more disturbing development: the growth of "male rebels" and "deadbeat dads." From this vantage point, a growing group of men are eschewing even minimal responsibility for children. In the wake of higher rates of divorce, postponed

119

marriage, and out-of-wedlock births, rising numbers of children are growing up with little economic or emotional support from their fathers. Their mothers must struggle to support and care for them with little in the way of paternal contributions.

Both of these views offer disheartening images of men as fathers, suggesting that social change has freed men of their historic obligations without holding them responsible for new ones. These developments have endangered the well-being of children and added to the responsibilities of mothers. However, a third image provides a more optimistic view of the changing contours of fatherhood as we approach a new century. This perspective focuses on the rise of "nurturing fathers," who are participating in the full range of child-rearing joys and burdens, from diaper changing and midnight feedings to playground supervision and doctor visits. Rather than rejecting responsibility for the care of children, these "new fathers" are sharing the care of their offspring to an unprecedented extent.

These images offer conflicting views of fathers in the wake of rapid social change in gender relations and family patterns. They also stand in stark contrast to the dominant assumptions about fathering that prevailed several decades ago, when breadwinning husbands and homemaking wives accounted for nearly two thirds of all American households. Since that time, men have undergone a quiet revolution. With less fanfare than women, but with no less significance, they have developed new and more diverse patterns of commitment to women, children, and families.

Although a minority of men still maintain the good provider pattern once so prevalent, a growing number have chosen or been forced to reject that path. Some have opted to avoid ties to family or children altogether, preferring to pursue freedom and autonomy instead of marital commitment. Others have become deeply involved in caring for their children in ways that extend well beyond the economic support that traditional breadwinners provide. Most of these nurturing fathers resist full domestic equality, but a significant minority are moving in that direction. Change has led in several directions at the same time. If the future remains uncertain, it is nevertheless clear that there will be no return to the brief period in American history when most fathers assumed the responsibilities and could claim the privileges of being their families' sole or primary breadwinners.[1]

Studying Fatherhood in Changing Times

To better understand the causes and consequences of men's changing commitments, we need to take a close look at the group most
affected by and most responsible for current trends—men who came
of age during the recent period of rapid change in family life, work
organization, and the relations between the sexes. Their lives reveal
the historical forces that are promoting—and limiting—family and
gender change. Their responses to new freedoms and new constraints
have challenged some long-standing beliefs about the nature and
experience of fatherhood. Understanding their lives provides a rare
opportunity to chart the processes of change and uncover the hidden
causes of men's behavior. It also provides clues to understanding the
more general processes by which men develop, or fail to develop,
strong commitments to children and family life.

By comparing men who came of age during this period but had
different experiences and made different choices, it is possible to
discover the social foundations of men's commitments. I thus conducted in-depth, life history interviews with a strategic sampling of
this group, including men who had become fathers, men who planned
to become fathers, and men who hoped to avoid fatherhood. The
sample consists of 138 men from diverse social and economic backgrounds. All of the men were between the ages of 28 and 45 years at
the time they were interviewed, and 96% were above the age of 30.[2]
As young and middle-aged adults, they were in the family- and
career-building stages of their lives—old enough to be facing consequential life decisions about work, marriage, and parenthood, yet
young enough to be directly affected by the gender revolution of the
past several decades. They were well situated to illumine the diverse
paths men are taking. Their lives offer a lens through which to view
the dynamics of change.

Emerging Patterns of Male Commitment

Three general patterns emerged among the men who were interviewed. The men in the first group (who accounted for about 36% of
all those who were interviewed) viewed fatherhood in primarily

economic terms. Although many of these men were involved with women who held paid jobs, they saw themselves as the *primary* earners in their families. These men held tightly to a "breadwinning" definition of fatherhood despite the changes they observed in other men's lives.

Another group of men (who made up about 30% of those I interviewed) decided to avoid fatherhood and to distance themselves from family commitments. Some of these men opted not to have any children, whereas others became estranged from the children they had fathered in the wake of marital breakups. All of these men developed an "autonomous" orientation in which they sought freedom and eschewed family obligations.

A third group of men (accounting for the remaining 33% of the sample) moved in a more auspicious direction. These men developed an ethic of "involved fatherhood." In contrast to the other two groups, they concluded that "good fathering" included extensive involvement in the daily tasks of child rearing and nurturing. Although only a minority of these "involved fathers" shared equally or assumed primary responsibility for their children's care, all became (or planned to become) substantially more involved than their breadwinning and autonomous counterparts.

Taken together, these men forged a range of strategies that correspond to national trends. Those who held tightly to a primary breadwinning ethic, even when their wives were employed, reflect the "stalled revolution" in which men remain aloof from domestic work even as women become increasingly committed to paid work. Those who avoided any fathering ties represent the male rebels and deadbeat dads who have left increasing numbers of women and children in the lurch. Those who became involved fathers represent the small but growing group of men who have become more integrated into domestic life.

Why did some men opt for breadwinning, others distance themselves from children, and still others become involved fathers? These divergent paths are not an artifact of class differences. Although college-educated men were slightly more likely to develop an involved outlook and working-class men were somewhat more likely to become breadwinners or to avoid fatherhood, the variety within each class and the similarities between them are much greater than the differences.[3] Middle-class men have no monopoly on nurturance, and working-class and poorer men are not the only ones with reservations about assuming the responsibilities of breadwinning.

As important, the paths these men traveled do not reflect the unfolding of "natural inclinations" or early childhood experiences. As children, these men held a wide array of outlooks and expectations about the future. While about half expected to become primary breadwinners when they grew up, the other half wished to avoid that fate. These men looked to marriage, fatherhood, and breadwinning with uncertainty, ambivalence, and apprehension. Although a small number (about 9%) hoped to establish egalitarian work and family commitments, most were either averse to becoming breadwinners or loath to think about the future at all. They viewed family responsibilities and steady jobs as traps to avoid. Many did not explicitly reject breadwinning, but they refused to plan for futures that appeared dangerous and beyond their control. Surprisingly, working-class men were not the only ones to view the future with skepticism, since 45% of the middle-class men were also suspicious in their youth about becoming breadwinners.

Whatever the view from childhood, most men did not sustain their early outlooks. Only 38% of those who hoped to become breadwinners maintained that view in adulthood, whereas only about 29% of those who hoped to avoid traditional fatherhood actually did so as adults. As the men aged and confronted unexpected constraints and opportunities, the majority changed direction and altered their outlooks on fatherhood.

The Social Foundations of Change

Why did most men undergo some kind of change while others remained true to childhood hopes and dreams? What explains why some men became traditional breadwinners while others moved toward more innovative patterns of fatherhood? And why did some nontraditional men reject fathering ties while others became deeply involved, nurturing fathers? The answers to these questions lie in understanding two important aspects of social change.

First, the social foundations of fatherhood are changing. As social change has eroded men's breadwinning abilities and sent legions of women into the workplace, men have had to develop new responses to the historic tensions between freedom and sharing, independence and interdependence, and privilege and equality. Second, because men possess different resources and occupy varied social positions, they have experienced and interpreted change in different ways. Some have been relatively insulated from the changes taking place around them, but most have had to develop new outlooks and strategies in the face of unexpected options and pressures.

Some men were able to sustain their early outlooks over time, but most had to reassess and realign their commitments. As a group, they developed a diverse range of fathering strategies. Whatever path men followed, their choices emerged from differing exposures to a *mix* of unforeseen freedoms and losses. And while their strategies diverge, the interplay between social and personal change provides a uniting thread.

PATHS TOWARD BREADWINNING

Breadwinning fathers traveled a path that moved against the tide of social change. Their choices underscore the persisting power of traditional incentives, even as social forces undermine this option for other men. Unlike their nontraditional peers, breadwinners encountered few threats to workplace success and few pressures to transform their domestic involvement.

First, breadwinning fathers were able to obtain good jobs with steady incomes. Many were surprised to find that it took little effort to move ahead in the workplace. With little awareness of the structural advantages men enjoy in the labor force, they attributed their unexpected success to "good luck." These felicitous experiences led breadwinning fathers to discard earlier fears about joining the "rat race" and to embrace demanding jobs that left little room for domestic involvement.

In addition to finding good jobs, breadwinning fathers also established lasting commitments to women who were willing and able to relieve them of domestic responsibilities. Some breadwinners actively sought domestically oriented partners, but others became involved with women who turned toward domesticity only after encountering roadblocks of their own at work. In these cases, the structure of male advantage pushed breadwinning men out of the home even as it pulled their wives into it.

For breadwinning fathers, unexpected success at work and commitment to domestically oriented women converged to support a view of fatherhood that stresses economic contributions. These men felt committed to having and supporting children, but they downplayed the importance of participating in child care. They became traditional fathers, even when they had originally hoped to avoid such a fate.

PATHS TOWARD AUTONOMY

While breadwinning fathers relinquished dreams of freedom for more settled lives, autonomous men forsook traditional aspirations to pursue freedom from fatherhood. The experiences that propelled them down this path contrast vividly with those encountered by their breadwinning peers.

Autonomous men were more likely to encounter blocked opportunities at work and to become disillusioned by dead-end jobs. They responded by renouncing the ideal of a stable work career. In its place, they sought freedom from work or freedom to pursue personally fulfilling but less secure work. This emphasis on autonomy took many forms, from accepting the risks of self-employment, to changing jobs frequently, to rejecting work and advancement opportunities. Whatever the strategy, it produced the same outcome—a growing aversion to becoming a father or assuming the economic responsibilities of fatherhood.

These men also were more likely to encounter difficulties in their relationships with women. In the wake of dissatisfying, sometimes embittering experiences, they became wary of commitment and developed more open-ended stances toward intimate relationships. These men also were more likely to have dissatisfying experiences with children. Some decided to remain childless after observing the problems other fathers faced. Others developed an emotional and economic distance from their own children in the wake of family breakups.

Autonomous men thus encountered different opportunities and constraints than did their breadwinning counterparts. Instead of finding satisfaction in stable, secure jobs, they felt stifled by the rat race and sought other avenues of fulfillment. Rather than establishing committed bonds with women prepared to feather shared domestic nests, they moved toward more tenuous, discretionary personal relationships. And instead of being pulled toward economic responsibility for children, they sought to limit their parental commitments.

PATHS TOWARD INVOLVED FATHERHOOD

While autonomous men moved away from family commitment in response to declining supports for breadwinning, involved fathers took a very different path. These men encountered a quite different mix of opportunities and constraints. Unlike breadwinners, they faced incentives to change their orientations at work. Unlike autonomous men, they faced convincing reasons to forge committed relationships with women and children. A unique combination of pushes and pulls prompted involved fathers to develop orientations toward fathering that are hard to distinguish from mothering.

Involved fathers also encountered unexpected roadblocks or changes of direction at work. Middle-class fathers were more likely to opt out of "fast-track" traditional careers in favor of more intrinsically satisfying but less economically rewarding occupations such as social work, teaching, and freelance employment. Working-class fathers were more likely to find themselves in jobs where expected promotions and other opportunities never materialized. For these men, once promising careers became "just jobs." Whether they chose new career paths or became disenchanted with old ones, these men made room in their work lives for other pursuits.

Nurturing fathers, like autonomous men, developed looser ties to work than did breadwinners. Yet these men became more rather than less involved in family life. They crafted different responses to similar work situations because of crucial differences in their relationships with women and experiences with children. Most involved fathers built relationships with women who became committed to pursuing work careers. Choosing work-committed partners relieved these men of sole or primary responsibility for supporting families, and it also gave their female partners an increased desire and ability to secure male participation in child rearing. Experiences with children also kindled the desire to be involved. Unlike both autonomous men and breadwinners, involved fathers found unexpected pleasure in caring for their own children or others' children.

This special mix of domestic and workplace experiences inspired involved fathers to discover and develop nurturing capacities. Yet these men faced many obstacles, and most resisted genuine parenting equality. Only a minority of these men (about a third) became equal or primary parents, and they did so in the face of unusual circumstances. Fathers whose work offered a high level of control and flexibility (especially compared to that of their partners) were able to participate equally. Men whose partners enjoyed better long-term prospects at work concluded that parenting equality made the most sense. And involved fathers who found themselves without women to depend on, due to either death or divorce, became equal or primary parents to their children. These social contexts, which reverse the usual balance of incentives between fathers and mothers, are rare. Equal fathering thus remains a strategic choice for only a small group of men.

In sum, differences in exposure to new opportunities and con-straints—at the workplace, in relationships with women, and in experiences with children—combined in different ways to promote divergent fathering patterns. These varied experiences led men to confront different options and to develop diverse fathering strategies.

THE EXPERIENCE OF FATHERING CHANGE

Men are traveling not only diverse paths but also fragile and ambiguous ones. As they face trade-offs among domestic work, paid work, and leisure, the chosen balance can vary not only among men but also over the course of any individual's life. Indeed, vacillation and change are likely responses to changes in life circumstances. Increasingly, men (and women) move in and out of different family forms over the course of their lives, altering their domestic and work commitments along the way. Over time, any individual man may find himself moving from one pattern to another in unexpected ways. These instances are especially instructive, for they illustrate the im-portance of social circumstance in shaping men's fathering commit-ments.

Several men did not participate in rearing the children born in first marriages but became intimately involved in caring for the children of second marriages. In these cases, divorce and remarriage created contrasting contexts for decision making. Joe, a construction worker and aspiring actor, moved from avoidance to involvement when he entered a new relationship. A contentious divorce left him estranged from a son, and subsequent commitment to a professional dancer brought him deeply into the process of rearing their young daughter. His newfound joy in nurturing his new child left him longing for what he had missed—and could never retrieve—with his 12-year-old son:

> When I see her going through new stages, it reminds me of him—being cheated at not having him at the breakfast table or helping him out. . . . It's sad that there will never be a way to repay him for any of the pain of the separation and that sort of thing.

For Max, a gardening supervisor, the hope of a better experience with another child in a happier marriage provided a way of "making up" for his earlier "sins of omission":

> I was separated and divorced at an early age [for the kids]—ages of 4 and 5 [years]. That's a big loss, a big void in my life. Because of my absence, it bothers me. . . . So this would be a way of making up for that.

Not surprisingly, the emerging desire to nurture prompted discomforting feelings about the past. Joe struggled to remain philosophical and to ward off guilt. He told himself that despite the harm he had caused, divorce had offered the only route to a happier life:

> I'd feel so guilty that somewhere was this little kid growing, and I could be a part of it. . . . There's a part of me that says you should have just knuckled under and pumped gas or whatever for the rest of your life. And I was thinking, "No, God damn it. As much as he has a life I'm responsible for, I've got my own life that I'm responsible for." Fortunately, he's a great guy and has come through it all right.

In a world where divorce and remarriage are common, men who become estranged from the offspring of first marriages but involved with the offspring of subsequent ones comprise a fast-growing group (see Furstenberg, 1988). Yet it also is possible to be more involved in rearing children from a first marriage than those from a second marriage, especially if the original conditions fostering involvement undergo change.

For Tom, an editor, a change in job situation—more than a change in his marital partner—was decisive. When his son was born, he was a graduate student who stayed home while his first wife went to work. Years later, as he and his second wife planned for a child, he could not hope to duplicate this experience. Instead, his "9-to-5" job demanded his daily absence while his new wife, a freelancer, planned to stay home:

> She works at home, so she's the one who's going to be with the child each day. Not as a housewife, but more of the day-to-day responsibility. Even if I do go to another job, I'll still go off to the office each day. So it's not likely to be the way it was with my son. And it's too bad.

These "mixed" cases provide powerful evidence that men's parental choices are neither innate nor unalterable. Situational opportunities and constraints play a vital role, and different contexts can evoke or suppress different capacities. Circumstantial changes in marriage or at work can prompt changes in parental involvement. Uncertain change leaves men confronting unpredictable options, which often produce unexpected responses. It is thus hardly surprising that many men feel confused, wary, and ambivalent. Having experienced unforeseen turns in their lives, they recognize the possibility of future change as well. Sandy, a physical therapist, explained,

> Sometimes I question where I should be at a certain stage in life because my priorities vacillate. Sometimes the job is not that important and the family is. But sometimes when the family becomes so important, the job does too because you want to do more for your family.

Explaining New Patterns of Fatherhood

The growing diversity in men's lives undermines many of our most cherished assumptions about men as fathers. Whether flattering or critical, traditional paradigms stress men's lack of interest in child care and nurturance and their stronger desire to pursue achievement in the public world of work. Thus psychological approaches view fathering as the expression of men's "masculine personalities," whereas cultural approaches stress the importance of a "culture of masculinity" and structural approaches posit "male dominance" as the prime cause of men's fathering behavior. Although these varied frameworks focus on different causes, they all posit some key factor that binds men together and separates them from women.

The complicated paths men are forging pose a challenge to prevailing theories of fatherhood. Because these theories tend to view men as a homogeneous group that shares certain psychological capacities, cultural values, and/or common interests, they are not well equipped to account for the rise of new and increasingly diverse patterns of fatherhood. These important social changes in fathering practices offer an ideal opportunity to reexamine and expand our customary ways of making sense of men's lives. They direct us toward a closer look at the *social factors* that are transforming men's commitments as fathers, husbands, and workers.

PSYCHOLOGICAL DIVERSITY AMONG MEN

Perhaps the most widely accepted approach to explaining fathering emphasizes how processes of childhood socialization create adult men with muted desires and limited capacities to develop close, nurturing relationships with children. Although important differences exist between classical socialization theories and more recent feminist revisions, these approaches make similar assumptions about the nature and causes of men's fathering attachments. They argue that, whether through role learning or unconscious psychodynamic processes of attachment and separation, boys develop masculine personalities that favor instrumental goals over interpersonal intimacy. Once created, this complex of psychological predispositions prompts adult men to avoid strong emotional attachments and to turn toward accomplishment in the wider world of work. Men's childhood experiences, especially in the family, are seen as crucial determinants of their adult choices. Men make similar work and family choices, which are reproduced across generations via the socialization process.[4]

Yet we have seen that contemporary men do not appear to share a common set of psychological traits or a uniform outlook on fathering. Moreover, I found that men's childhood experiences bear a complex and weak relationship to their adult choices. These men developed varied and ambiguous relationships with their fathers, mothers, and other influential figures. The contexts of childhood produced ambivalent and changing reactions in sons. While some adopted the values espoused in their cultural milieus, others rebelled against them. Over time, most men encountered complex and surprising adult worlds that forced reassessments of the meanings of their parents' lives and their own early outlooks.

Childhood provides a point of departure from which men's life trajectories develop, but it does not and cannot determine the twists and turns of adulthood. In a rapidly changing world, early aspirations can turn out to be difficult, or even impossible, to achieve. Childhood experiences can and often do leave men ill prepared for the future, but adulthood can offer opportunities as well as dangers. In the process of adjusting to changing options and circumstances, men can develop or discover new emotional resources.

Even among those who do not experience significant changes, the adult context matters. It can support stability in some lives while forcing change in others. Ultimately, adult opportunities and constraints will shape how men evaluate, respond to, and resolve the conflicts and ambiguities of their childhoods.[5]

The notion of a masculine personality underestimates the rich variety of men's outlooks, motives, and choices. Although a minority of men do fit the stereotype of the distant, work-obsessed father, this image does not capture the range or complexity of men's fathering capacities. As a group, men display a wide variety of parenting orientations including those typically considered the purview of "mothering." Thus a notable number of men are rejecting the supreme value of work achievement and looking for gratification in intimate parenting bonds. Michael, a therapist and custodial single father, discovered the following:

> I'm very sensitive to what may not be being said in the interaction between people. And I'm very empathic. I was told when I was in analytic training that I was extremely empathic, and I was very much able to tune in to the underlying feeling in another person.

Carlos, an engaged social worker, agreed:

I'm a very nurturing person, but I don't think it's specifically geared toward a child because I respond that way to adults also. I maintain long-term relationships. I have a lot of friendships that are in double-digit figures in terms of years. They're long-term, and there's a lot of emotional interaction between us. I have a friendship that is now 25 years old, and we're still extremely close. And so it's not something that's just oriented toward children.

Although some men conform to the masculine stereotype of distant and unattached fathers, other men are willing and able to establish intimate, deeply bonded relationships with children. A full account of the changing patterns of fatherhood needs to acknowledge and explain the expanding range of psychological patterns and emotional possibilities for men. As diversity in men's temperaments, outlooks, and life choices grows, we will stand on safer ground by rejecting stereotypes of masculinity (just as we now understand that classical notions of *femininity* are misleading and oversimplified) and recognizing that large numbers of men do not fit the assumptions of a masculine personality. Then we will be better able to discover the social conditions that either enable or suppress close bonds between fathers and children.[6]

THE AMBIGUITY OF MASCULINE CULTURE

Another approach to explaining fatherhood emphasizes the role of "masculine culture." The meaning of manliness varies with different theories, but it usually encompasses notions such as independence, aggressiveness, physical or emotional strength (often defined as "inexpressiveness"), and violence. Regardless of which masculine value is stressed, these approaches argue that cultural values and expectations produce male behavior and that cultural change precedes change in behavior.[7]

A culture of masculinity also has a limited ability to explain men's diverse paths and strategies. First, the values, norms, and beliefs concerning manhood have deeper historical roots than the current trends. The cultural tradition that idealizes male flight from commitment extends back at least to the period of the frontier and manifest destiny. Our literary tradition is replete with male cultural "heroes" (such as Huckleberry Finn, Captain Ahab, and even the Lone Ranger) who earn and maintain their manhoods by escaping the bonds of domesticity and the responsibilities of fatherhood (Fiedler, 1966). Because these values emerged long before the contemporary period, they cannot explain why dramatic changes in behavior are occurring now.

Second, the cultural tradition of masculinity is too complex to provide a simple blueprint for individual behavior. Men are exposed to a paradoxical cultural legacy that stresses conflicting values. American culture idealizes both the responsible good provider and the man alone, freed of obligations to children and family. Because these cultural ideals are ambiguous and contradictory, it is impossible for any one man to live up to all of them. Note, for example, the competing ideals proposed by breadwinners and their less traditional counterparts. Kevin, a breadwinner, declared,

> Being a man, to me, is living up to my age-old responsibilities that we've been handed from father to son since the cave dwellers—taking care of my family.

Marshall, also a breadwinner, came to a similar conclusion:

> A man takes care of what he's responsible for first. He makes sure those people he cares about or is close to are taken care of. A good man is responsible for himself, is a good provider, is solid and always there for the people who need him.

The ideals espoused by those who avoided or rejected parenthood provide a noticeable contrast. Bart, a divorced father of two, thus concluded,

> I believe if you don't like what you're doing, you can get out and go do something else.

Arnold, who is married and childless, agreed:

> Some people are happy just surviving. I think there's more to life than just surviving. A lot of people do without for the kids. I don't want to do without nothing.

Stan, a single mechanic, added,

> Guys at work—they're hustling, looking to get overtime all the time, complaining that [they've] got to do this, got to do that. More times than not, people have told me that I had it made. I can come and go as I please.

These conflicting cultural traditions oblige men to choose between opposing ideals as they endeavor to develop their own definitions of maturity. The prevailing culture may exert pressure, but it does not provide clear-cut guidelines for behavior.[8] Moreover, new visions have arisen to compete with the long-standing cultural ambivalence about freedom and commitment. Alongside the breadwinner ethic and the ideal of the unfettered loner, a new model of manhood stresses interdependence and mutual vulnerability (Cancian, 1987). Howard, a financial manager, declared that "real men" are defined not by their emotional aloofness but by their commitment to caring and emotional openness:

> A real man is someone who understands what it is to give and take in a relationship, has compassion not only for the person he has the relationship with but people in general. He is close to his family and has a desire not only to achieve for himself but to make the world a little bit nicer. That's basically what a real man is.

This new vision contrasts with the cultural tradition that poses freedom and responsibility as competing masculine ideals. It rejects the view that *masculine* is the opposite of *feminine* and does not make rigid distinctions between *fathering* and *mothering*.[9] Rather, this new cultural ideal stresses the similarities between men and women and asserts that gender differences are smaller, more malleable, and less desirable than traditional views suggest. Edward, a single physician, argued that perceived gender differences are socially constructed and reflect social evaluations of behavior rather than essential, sex-related characteristics:

> To me, the key to being a man, the same thing as being a woman, is being a good human being. There's nothing that really defines being a man. It doesn't mean you can't cry. I could stay at home and be happy and have a lot of what would be, quote, feminine characteristics. In some situa-

tions, it helps to be macho, but a lot of that just reflects stereotypes. If it's a guy, he's aggressive; if it's a woman, she's a ball buster. And it can be the same behavior. Sometimes I wish it [were] a little clearer, but basically you've got to say, "What are you as an individual?"

Despite his working in the psychoanalytic tradition, which stresses essential gender differences, Eliot, a single psychiatrist, agreed:

I have some feelings about human beings being a lot more amorphous [and] androgynous. And I think this caretaking experience, if men get more involved, is going to bring out their more feminine feelings and will help men to relate better. I think it's very positive. Maybe it wasn't meant to be that way, [but] I can't see why not.

Older ideals, such as good providing and male independence, persist even as new ones, such as involved fathering, emerge alongside them. The cultural constructs of masculinity, like the patterns of men's lives, are diversifying. The emergence of new cultural visions raises questions about how new values and beliefs are created and how they affect behavior. Recent changes in masculine beliefs and ideals reflect men's efforts to cope with fundamental social-structural changes in the economy, the workplace, and the home. The erosion of social supports for male primary breadwinning has prompted a growing debate over the appropriate role of fathers. Cultural confusion and disagreement are more a result than a cause of this change. As Scott, a medical technician, explained, changes in his options produced changes in his outlook, not the reverse:

Back in my father's time, being a man was being the supermacho image, but macho doesn't fit anymore. Being a man means the male partner in this family, being the procreator, but it has no real delineation as to being the breadwinner anymore because we share it equally.

Finally, there is rarely a simple causal relationship between what people value and what they choose. More often, men face a wide discrepancy between their preferred ideals and their actual choices. Some may face circumstances that allow them to enact their highest ideals, whereas others may change their ideals to more closely fit their circumstances. But many face circumstances that leave them coping with gaps between options and ideals, between what they do and what they feel they *should* do.

The disparity between values and behavior can take a variety of forms. The cultural tradition of masculine independence, for example, does not necessarily produce male flight. More often, it provides an "escape fantasy" for those leading more mundane lives. Jesse, a construction worker with a family to support, felt nostalgia for what he imagined to be a freer way of life:

> If I were ever to have a wish of going back in time, or ahead in time, it would be the early 1800s in the West. I would be a little more comfortable there—and it may sound strange—to wear a six-gun on your side. You come home and someone is messing with your wife, and you go "boom," get it over with, and bury him in a cornfield. At that point in time, society wouldn't consider you an outcast.

On the other hand, Oliver, a lawyer, idealized a more involved kind of fathering:

> One of the friends I admire most has radical feelings on child rearing, which includes much more sharing and acting as the nurturing father for his two daughters. He does probably 50% of the work. He has more flexibility in his work schedule, and he's just someone who seems to have manufactured more hours out of the day than I can get by on. And that does bring out feelings in me that, yeah, he's doing it better than I'm doing it, because he seems to have it all and I'm clearly aware of my limitations.

So did Glen, a businessman:

> It would be ideal if I could go to work half the time and Gloria could go to work half the time. Then each of us would be home half the time. I think it would be great for us. I think it would be great for Aaron. But society isn't organized that way. Society just said, "No, it wouldn't be great for society." So it just isn't going to happen.

In sum, life choices need to be distinguished from fantasies. Cultural ideals neither cause nor reflect behavior in a simple, direct way. Competing, fluctuating values are more likely to produce ambivalence and confusion than strict adherence to cultural injunctions. Mixed emotions and guarded flexibility are common no matter what the choice. Arthur, a sewage worker in a dual-earner marriage, asserted,

> I generally like to see the wife be able to stay home and take care of the children [and] the man be able to make enough money to get proper support. But in today's society, you don't know when it's going to break. The man may be out of work, and the woman will have to go to work. You have to be flexible.

Morrie, a recreation supervisor who had never married, admitted,

> When I see men that have wives and children, I have mixed feelings. I feel that life has treated them good, things are going well. But the other side is that they are put in the position to have to work more than one job. They're very tired; everything they do today is a struggle, and it's all to support their families. You have to weigh things like that and understand that has its setbacks.

Masculine culture thus provides a contradictory context for decision making, and most choices require giving up some ideals to attain others. Men either sustain old ideals or invent new ones to make sense of actions that emerge from socially structured options and dilemmas. They use, create, and selectively call on culture in the process of crafting fathering strategies in response to social change (Swidler, 1986).

THE EROSION OF MALE DOMINANCE

A third approach stresses the role of male dominance, or patriarchy, in shaping fatherhood. These theories focus not on psychology or culture but rather on how institutional arrangements bestow power and privilege on men, who in turn act to perpetuate these advantages. In the public sphere, men enjoy economic and occupational advantages; in the domestic sphere, they are excused from the least pleasant and most time-consuming tasks of parenthood. Their advantages in one sphere contribute to their advantages in the other. Workplace advantages give men the economic and social power to avoid domestic work, and the avoidance of domestic work gives men advantages in a competitive marketplace. Male power and privilege are thus recreated via a mutually reinforcing and self-sustaining cycle (Hartmann, 1976; Polatnik, 1973; Reskin, 1988).

The patterns of men's lives have taken a more varied and complex form, however. Although men continue to enjoy social, political, and economic advantages because they are men, the closing decades of the 20th century have witnessed important changes in both the degree and nature of male advantage. The decline of primary breadwinning and the expansion of women's legal and economic rights have eroded traditional bases of patriarchal control. Male privilege persists, but it faces increasing assault. The historic advantages men once took for granted are now open to debate and challenge.[10] Even the most traditional men confront new pressures to change and new challenges to their authority. This context has given male privilege a double-edged quality in which it continues to offer considerable rewards but also entails new costs. Contemporary men are torn between the historic benefits of dominance and the price that it exacts.

What's more, beyond the group advantages all men possess lie important variations. Male power "is not spread in an even blanket" across all men or "every department of social life" (Connell, 1987, p. 109). These differences among men matter. Because men have encountered different occupational and family opportunities, they have developed different views about where their best interests lie.

Breadwinners, for example, have good reasons to defend male privilege in the face of increasing opposition. As women have fought for equal rights and other men have moved away from family patterns that emphasize male breadwinning, those who remain committed to the good provider ethic feel embattled and threatened. They fear the erosion of advantages that their fathers could take for granted. It is thus no surprise that these men have concluded that male control in marriage and male distance from child rearing are not only justified but also in everyone's best interest. Jacob, a single businessman frustrated by the difficulty in finding an "old-fashioned" woman, declared that marriage was no place to consider equality:

> I think somebody should be more or less in control in the marriage. I don't think you can have a democracy sort of thing—clashing all the time. You obviously have to make compromises, but somebody should

be a little bit in control. You can't say, "What do you want to do?" It's not gonna work. And it won't set a good example for the children.

George, a married park worker who provided the sole support for his wife and two children, deplored the decline of paternal authority and the rise of fathering as a nurturing activity:

> My father ruled the house. He wouldn't touch a diaper; he wouldn't touch a dish. He supported the family and that was it. He was very good to my mother and to us—no abuse like there is today—but you knew he was the father and you didn't bother your father. When he finished supper, he walked with his friends and they read the newspaper and talked sports and nobody bothered them. Mama didn't ask where he was going [or] when he was coming home. My father answered to no one. The men were men in those days. Today, it's not that way. I don't think it's good. I'm not a male chauvinist, but I think years ago, compared to today, people were happier.

In contrast to these defenses of patriarchy and disengaged fatherhood, those who have rejected breadwinning hold very different stances toward male dominance. Whether they have avoided parenthood or become involved fathers, nontraditional men see little advantage and much disadvantage to authoritarian control over wives and girlfriends. Not only does it produce economically dependent wives, it also subverts the chances for an emotionally satisfying relationship. The desire for personal freedom and mutual support makes dominance seem, at least to some extent, counterproductive. Joel, a childless carpenter married to a librarian, explained how little he stood to gain, both emotionally and economically, from trying to dominate his very independent wife:

> I don't want to stifle her. I have friends like that. I thought these people were reasonably enlightened. The guy's bright, well educated, [and] won't let his wife out to work. He's crazy. No wonder they don't get along. The thought of trying to control someone like that is horrifying. I couldn't go for that.

Hank, a paramedic married to a hospital administrator, added that his wife's economic attainments provided benefits to him as well:

Who should have primary responsibility for providing the family income? Whoever's better at it. I'd let Connie do all of it. She takes the checkbook. I make a joke out of it, but the bills get paid and I don't have to worry. She can do anything I can do, and she can do a lot of things better than I can do. She should have full rights, equal pay, [and be] treated as an individual, a unit, a person to respect—not because of gender, hair color, or skin color.

Those who reject breadwinning may still enjoy male advantages, but they are also more likely to question its legitimacy. There are differences, however, between those who wish to avoid parenthood and those who would prefer to be involved fathers. Although both groups support equality in the public sphere, they do not agree about private commitments.

Autonomous men support women's economic self-sufficiency because it enhances their own ability to remain independent, free of the obligations that accompany breadwinning. Chuck, a systems analyst who had never married, declared,

I'm not really big on women who stay home and just raise kids. I think everybody should be a fully functioning, self-supporting adult, and certainly economically that's a necessity now. In terms of women's issues, if [women] prepared themselves for the idea that they have to assume their financial burdens and responsibilities, they won't have to be emotional hostages to toxic relationships. And men won't either.

However, for men hoping to avoid fatherhood, this vision of economic and social equality does not extend to the domestic sphere. Equal responsibility for earning a living is not the same as equal responsibility for rearing a child. Their own desire for personal freedom produces an ideological paradox. They espouse the equal right to be free while resisting the equal responsibility of domestic work. Even though he upheld a woman's right to work, Mark, an environmental adviser, rejected sharing at home:

When you see someone who's splitting the child care equally with his wife, that turns me off. I've run into that kind of thing, especially where guys would do the cooking and cleaning and stuff. That really doesn't sit right. I like to cook every once in a while for the enjoyment of actually doing it, but to actually do it day in and day out—I don't know.

This separation of public rights and private obligations explicitly rejects a traditional ideology of dominance, but it replaces it with a less overt form. Because dominance via primary breadwinning entails too many economic obligations, this strategy replaces overt male control with a more subtle form of power: male indifference. These men argue that they will neither stand in a woman's way *nor* offer her any help. Women thus have the right, if they choose, to be "super-women" who work and take care of their homes. As Jay, a gardener, put it,

> I guess an ideal woman would be one who could hold a job and could raise a family and could cook and do all the things.

Involved fathers, by contrast, are discomfited by male dominance both in the home and in the workplace. They may not always live up to their ideals, but they have concluded that men and children as well as women benefit from more equal sharing. Hank explained,

> The full-time breadwinner—that's not the ideal for me. He's missing a lot. I know exactly what happens Saturday and Sunday if he works Monday through Friday. Saturday he's probably with the beers, and Sunday he's watching football or something until the kids get old enough. And by that time it's too late. You've got to start when they're 3 months old, not when they're able to pick up a football.

Because men enjoy different opportunities and face diverse constraints, they have developed different outlooks on dominance and control. Breadwinners have good reasons to hold tight to traditional views that justify and enhance male dominance. Those who have rejected breadwinning have equally good reasons to replace these beliefs with visions that stress either freedom or sharing. Separated by different life experiences, men have constructed contrasting interests in the process of reaching different conclusions about the benefits and costs of dominance itself.

EXPANDING PREVAILING PARADIGMS

Psychological processes, cultural values, and male power all play important roles in shaping men's commitments to children and families. Yet we need to expand our understanding of *how* these factors affect men's lives. Men's diverse patterns of fatherhood do not, and cannot, emerge from forces that unite all men or reproduce social patterns in an unchanging way. Rather, men, no less so than women, form a diverse group of socially situated actors. Changing social structures have offered men new freedoms but also have imposed new constraints, forcing them to respond in creative ways. To make sense of the diverse pathways men are forging, we need a framework that focuses on the contours of large-scale institutional change, the different ways in which men are exposed to change, and the diverse coping strategies they are developing in response to new options and pressures.

The Changing Structures of Fatherhood

Deeply rooted and widespread change has undermined male breadwinning and promoted the growth of new patterns of fatherhood. These social shifts include a decline in men's economic entitlement, a rise in women's attachment to paid work, an expansion of alternatives to permanent marriage, and a growing separation between marriage and parenthood. These institutional changes, which are interrelated and mutually reinforcing, have transformed men's options and evoked varied reactions.

THE EROSION OF MALE
ECONOMIC ENTITLEMENT

As a group, men continue to enjoy significant economic advantages including higher average wages, superior access to the most prestigious jobs, and limited responsibility for domestic tasks. Nevertheless, changes in the economy and the occupational structure have eroded many men's economic security. Although male executives and professionals have enjoyed rising incomes, the vast majority of male workers have experienced stagnating earnings and contracting prospects for secure, highly rewarded jobs.

Since the early 1970s, when the United States emerged from the burst of post–World War II economic expansion, American workers have faced a lower rate of economic growth. With the exception of men in the upper 10% of the wage ladder, male workers across the wage hierarchy have suffered declining or stagnant earnings. Although less educated men have suffered the steepest declines, all but the best educated and most highly paid workers have lost ground. Between 1973 and 1988, the entire bottom 75% of the male workforce experienced wage reductions (Mishel & Frankel, 1991, pp. 78-79). Men under age 45 working year-round full-time, as well as white males serving as their families' only breadwinners, have been especially hard hit. The median inflation-adjusted income for men who were sole breadwinners fell 22% between 1976 and 1984 (Kosters & Ross, 1988, p. 11; Phillips, 1990, p. 18).

The decline in men's wages is linked to changes in the number and types of jobs available to men. Over this same period, the percentage of jobs in highly rewarded, male-dominated economic sectors such as industrial production has declined while the share of jobs in less rewarded and secure economic sectors such as service work has grown. Because jobs in manufacturing and related sectors provide higher earnings on average than do jobs in the expanding service sector, the transfer of jobs from the former to the latter has contributed significantly to the overall decline in men's earnings (Uchitelle, 1990).

These economic setbacks have not been confined to the poor or to racial minorities, nor do they show any signs of abating. Because they are based on structural changes in the economy over which individual men have little control, they are likely to continue for the foreseeable future. Mishel and Frankel (1991) thus concluded that

> despite the widely held assumption that higher-paying white-collar jobs are the wave of the future, there is little evidence that the deterioration of job quality and wages that took place in the 1980s will be reversed in the 1990s. . . . It is unlikely that wages will be greater in the year 2000 than they were in 1980. (pp. 119, 125, 127)

The stagnation of wages and the decline in job security have eroded men's ability to earn family or living wages on a consistent, predictable basis. Despite the persistence of occupational sex segregation and a gender gap in wages, changes in the occupational structure have undermined men's economic dominance along with their role as family breadwinners. The economic support of wives and children has become more difficult and less attractive to a growing proportion of men.

THE RISE OF COMMITTED
EMPLOYMENT AMONG WOMEN

The erosion of economic security among men has been accompanied by the rise of committed employment among women. As men's labor force participation has dropped below 80%, women's has risen above 60% (Schor, 1992). Among women between the ages of 25 and 44, the age range in which women once dropped out of the workforce to bear and rear children full-time, that rate has climbed to around 75% (U.S. Department of Labor, 1991). More important, women have become more committed to full-time, long-term work outside the home. In 1990, only 23% of employed women worked part-time (up from 63% in 1960), and about 6% of these part-time workers would have preferred full-time work if they could find it (Mishel & Frankel, 1991, p. 43; U.S. Department of Labor, 1991). Among full-time employed women, 46% asserted that they thought of their work as careers rather than as jobs (Belkin, 1989).

Women are joining the paid workforce for many reasons including the enticements of expanding opportunities and the pressures created by eroding male incomes and high divorce rates.[11] Whatever the causes, women's growing commitment to paid work has given them increased economic independence and a growing incentive to challenge men's privileges at work and in the home.

Certainly, women's growing determination to build full-time work careers has challenged men's access to the best jobs. Men must now vie with committed women workers for employment rewards; they also face new pressures to share more equally at home. The push for workplace equity undermines the legitimacy, if not the reality, of male privilege. Legal challenges, such as affirmative action, comparable worth, and sexual harassment initiatives, are only the tip of the iceberg. Discrimination in pay and employment persists, but modest improvements have taken place in women's average earnings and access to better jobs. Thus, between 1979 and 1991, when men's average wages were falling, women's were rising an average of 7.8%

(Uchitelle, 1992). The pay gap between women and men persists, to be sure, but it narrowed from about 63% in 1979 to about 72% in 1990.[12] And although most women continue to work in lower paying, female-dominated jobs, a notable proportion have made inroads into professional and managerial positions dominated by men (Jacobs, 1991).

These trends appear to be "solid and enduring" (Nasar, 1992). As younger generations of women enter the labor force, their stronger work commitment is likely to push the gains for women higher. For example, in 1979, 74% of young women reported that they expected to be in the labor force when they were 35 years of age. In 1988, 53% of all B.A. degrees, 52% of all M.A. degrees, 37% of all Ph.D.'s, and 36% of all professional degrees were awarded to women. These younger cohorts of women appear to be keeping pace with their male counterparts. In 1987, the work experience of women in their 30s showed 90% equivalence to the work experience of comparable men (Nasar, 1992).

Women's expanded ability to survive on their own is as important as their labor marker gains. Employment gives women independent incomes, even if they are likely to be lower than men's. Most women thus no longer have to marry for economic reasons; if they do marry, they are more likely to make important contributions to their families' economic welfare. Indeed, as men's average earnings have fallen, women's earnings have provided the means by which the average family income has remained stable over the past two decades (Kilborn, 1992). Women's growing commitment to paid work has thus given them increasing economic clout, expanding their options regarding marriage and making their families more dependent on them (see Bergmann, 1986; Fuchs, 1989).

This fundamental change in women's situation has important but paradoxical implications for men. On the one hand, women's growing economic independence has given men greater freedom to avoid commitment or to leave relationships without feeling economically responsible for the people left behind. On the other hand, independent sources of income give women more leverage in relationships. They, too, possess the option to leave. If they stay, they bring more resources to the process of domestic bargaining. As women become less dependent on men, men are both less and more constrained. They are freer to leave, but they also face new pressures to become more equal partners if they stay.

THE RISE OF ALTERNATIVES TO
PERMANENT MARRIAGE

New forms of sexual and marital partnerships also have implications for men's choices. Since the 1950s, more flexible and less binding forms of commitment have grown in acceptance and popularity. High divorce rates are the most obvious indicators of this trend. The divorce rate peaked in 1979 and 1981 and then decreased slightly, but it has remained stable since 1986 (Barringer, 1989). As the divorce rate has stabilized, the rates of people living alone and cohabiting outside of marriage have grown. By 1991, 10% of American households consisted of men living alone and 15% consisted of women living alone, up from 5.6% and 11.5%, respectively, in 1970. An additional 5% of households were made up of unrelated adults living together (without children), up from about 2% in 1970 (U.S. Bureau of the Census, 1992). A 1988 survey found that more than 40% of heterosexuals between the ages of 25 and 39 had lived with persons of the opposite sex outside of marriage (Barringer, 1989; Bumpass, 1990). Legal marriage clearly has become more discretionary, one of a number of alternatives for living, sharing intimacy, and meeting sexual needs. Not only are more adults living outside of marriage, but more adults are moving in and out of different family and household arrangements over the course of their lives.[13]

The expansion of legitimate alternatives to permanent marriage, like the rise in women's economic resources, has given men new choices and new constraints. Men are freed from the obligation to maintain lifelong economic and emotional commitments to one woman (and her children). However, men also must cope with women who have more discretion about when and whether to marry or stay married. The transformation of heterosexual commitment from a permanent bond to a changeable one has left men in an ambiguous position. They are freer to escape a relationship, but they also are less able to impose their will on partners or to force them to stay if they wish to leave.

THE SEPARATION OF MARRIAGE
AND PARENTHOOD

As marriage has become less secure and more optional, parental ties have become increasingly distinct from marital bonds. The rise in divorce and out-of-wedlock births has loosened the connection between childbearing and child rearing—especially for men. Although a growing number of divorced fathers retain some form of legal or physical custody of their children, the overwhelming majority of children remain with their mothers in the event of divorce or an out-of-wedlock birth. Whereas about 17% of one-parent white families and about 7% of one-parent black families are headed by fathers, the remaining one-parent families are headed by divorced, separated, or never-married women.[14] Thus 21% of all families with children were headed by women in 1988, up from about 9% in 1960. In 1987, 17% of white mothers and 50% of black mothers with children under age 18 were not living with husbands (up from about 6% and 22%, respectively, in 1960) (Jencks, 1992, p. 195). Under current conditions, half or more of all American children will likely spend at least part of their childhoods in a single-parent family, most likely headed by a woman (Bumpass, 1990; Luker, 1991).

A growing proportion of men now find parental ties, like marriage itself, voluntary and discretionary. Fatherhood as an economic, social, and emotional institution is increasingly based on what men want and find meaningful rather than on what they are constrained—by women and society—to do. The implications are, again, ambiguous. Certainly, the rise of divorce and out-of-wedlock childbearing make it easier for men to avoid parental responsibilities if they prefer. On the other hand, biological fatherhood no longer confers automatic power over or access to offspring. Fathers who wish to sustain strong attachments to their children may find that they have to work harder than they anticipated to keep their children in their lives.

UNEVEN EXPOSURE AND DIVERGENT
RESPONSES TO CHANGE

These institutional and economic shifts are widespread, interrelated, and beyond the capacity of any individual or group to prevent. Although their combined effect is to reduce the supports for traditional fatherhood, it is less clear what types of fathering patterns are likely to take its place. The long-range prospects for fatherhood are uncertain for several reasons.

First, changes in the organization of work, marriage, and the economy are ambiguous, leading in different directions at the same time. They offer men more freedom to escape the responsibilities of the good provider ethic, and they make it more difficult to achieve. However, they also replace these historic constraints and insecurities with newer ones. Men possess expanded freedom to avoid commitment, but they also face growing pressure to share more equally. These changes have uncertain effects, offering men new options but creating new dilemmas as well. These institutional changes have compelled men to respond in new ways to the attractions and disadvantages of fatherhood.

In addition, men's exposure to institutional change is uneven, leaving some searching for new ways of life and others defending older ones. Institutional change has affected different groups of men in different ways. Some have been able to retain patriarchal control in so-called traditional households, but others have found their range of control over women and children diminished. They have faced good reasons to relinquish some control in exchange for either greater freedom or more sharing. Differences in men's exposure to change have promoted differences in their strategies for coping with these new dilemmas. Because social change has different consequences for different groups of men, their fathering strategies are increasingly diverse and even opposed.

The Social Transformation of Fatherhood

A range of social shifts has changed the context in which men make fathering choices and has transformed the patterns of fatherhood in America. Men's divergent choices are reasonable, if often unexpected and unconscious, reactions to these institutional changes. As the social supports for primary breadwinning continue to erode, men face a choice between maintaining their historic privileges and easing their historic burdens. Will they resist the pressures for change in an attempt to preserve these privileges or, instead, embrace the expanded opportunity to ease or escape the burdens that traditional fatherhood entails? And how will they cope with the costs of each strategy? Whether they choose breadwinning, autonomy, or involved fatherhood, they have little choice but to develop new ways in which to negotiate the uncharted territories of change.

If institutional change requires individual change, then individual change adds another element of uncertainty to social change. Eroding economic opportunities, for example, may spark diverse reactions. Those who are able to forge stable marriages with domestic women may decide to work harder to bolster their positions as family breadwinners. Those who become committed or attracted to a work-committed woman may opt to share breadwinning and caretaking. Those whose intimate relationships with women or children have been unfulfilling and painful may decide to go it alone and keep their earnings to themselves.

The crosscutting pressures on men thus provide the underpinnings for many different futures. While some men may continue to find well-rewarded, secure jobs, a growing group will not. While some men will marry early and stay married to the same partners for life, others will postpone marriage, get divorced, or stay single. While some men will marry women who are willing and able to do the bulk of domestic work whether or not they hold paid jobs, a growing group will find that the women they meet and become involved with are committed to working outside the home and unwilling to perform two jobs while their partners only perform one. In the face of these changes, some men will find that equality and sharing offer compensations to offset their loss of power and privilege, but others are likely to conclude that maintaining power or avoiding commitment are more attractive alternatives. We are living through a protracted period when no one pattern predominates and no one set of values is shared by all. Indeed, diversity in men's fathering choices is here to stay.

Although the future can take many forms, it is clear that some sort of change is inevitable. Closing our eyes, wishing it were not so, or proclaiming it wrong will not make change reverse or disappear. These changes present opportunity and risk. They offer the hope of greater equality between fathers and mothers as well as closer ties between fathers and children. However, they also pose the danger that a gulf between men, many of whom feel estranged from family life, and women and children, many of whom are left to fend for themselves with diminishing resources, will continue to grow. If we wish to nourish a more nurturant and equal vision of fatherhood, then we will have to create more social supports for involved fatherhood. The ultimate outcome remains open because it depends on how we, as individuals and as a society, respond to the inescapable but still uncertain transformation of fatherhood in America.

Notes

1. In 1990, only 32.7% of American men were married and living with nonemployed spouses. Even more striking, only 19.5% of men were actually breadwinners, given that the remaining 13.2% were not employed (U.S. Bureau of the Census, 1991).

2. See Gerson (1993) for a full description of the sampling procedures and study findings.

3. For example, 36% of the college-educated group and 31% of the working-class group became involved fathers. Furthermore, 32% of the college-educated group and 29% of the working-class group avoided parenthood.

4. Classical "sex-role identity" theories argue that boys "learn" to be men by identifying with their fathers and other male "role models." They also stress the role of rewards and punishments in inducing boys to behave in appropriately masculine ways (see Maccoby & Jacklin, 1974; Weitzman, 1984). Feminist revisions of psychodynamic and moral development theories point to the importance of unconscious dynamics between parents, especially mothers, and children during the earliest years of life. This perspective argues that developmental processes in childhood lead boys to develop "rigid ego boundaries" and to stress an "ethic of rights" rather than an "ethic of care" (see Chodorow, 1978; Gilligan, 1983). Classical and feminist socialization theories reach similar conclusions about the nature of male psychology, but they place different values on the desirability and inevitability of gender socialization processes. Classical theories argue that these processes are natural, healthy, and inevitable. They imply that when deviations occur, the consequences will be unpleasant (and even dire) for men, women, and children. By contrast, feminist theories argue that gender socialization processes are socially constructed and organized to confer power and privilege on men. They argue that more equal child-rearing practices, which can diminish the differences between men and women, are both possible and socially desirable. Wrong (1961) presented a classic and still peerless critique of the "oversocialized" view of human action. Pleck (1981) offered an insightful critique of the "myth of masculinity."

5. A rich literature on human development over the life course shows how changes in adult opportunities produce changes in the process of adult development. See, for example, Buchman (1989), Elder (1978), and Gerth and Mills (1953).

6. In studying widowers who became single fathers, Risman (1986) found that structural conditions, rather than socialization, created intimate relationships between fathers and their children.

7. Ehrenreich (1983) used a cultural explanation to explain the decline of the male breadwinner in postwar America. She argued that popular culture has promoted men's flight from commitment by making singlehood and the pursuit of leisure socially legitimate choices for men. A "male revolt" against the family thus preceded the rise of modern feminism. This argument is compelling, but it ignores the fact that the cultural tradition extolling male flight from domestic obligations began long before the current trends emerged. It also ignores the fact that, along with a rise in male family abandonment, we also have witnessed the rise of cultural ideals that extol the sensitive man and the nurturing father. Other cultural arguments focus on the significance of men's "inexpressiveness" (see Balswick, 1979). Willis (1977) analyzed how working-class masculine culture, which stresses rebellion against authority and the superiority of physical prowess to mental prowess, actually serves to keep working-class boys at the bottom of the class hierarchy.

8. Swidler (1980) discussed how the American cultural tradition stresses both freedom and commitment as competing definitions of maturity. Komarovsky (1976) analyzed the dilemmas and contradictions of the "male role."

9. Kimmel (1987) and Jardine and Smith (1987) provided ample evidence that there is a historical tradition of support for feminism among men.

10. It is important to distinguish between the degree of change and the direction of change. Although inequality persists, the long-term historical trend is in the direction of declining patriarchal control. Collins (1971) thus argued that advanced market economies, which are marked by high female labor force participation rates and strong state structures, provide women with sufficient economic resources and legal protections to challenge male control. Men often resort to extreme means to retain power, but these efforts meet increasing opposition from women and the state. For example, men continue to use violence and physical force to enforce their will, but it is no longer deemed a legitimate use of patriarchal authority.

11. Most women do not view these choices as either voluntary or involuntary. Rather, both preference *and* necessity have prompted them to join the labor force. See Gerson (1985) for a fuller consideration of the multiple pushes and pulls that have sent a growing number of women into the workplace in late 20th-century America.

12. See U.S. Department of Labor (1991). Mishel and Frankel (1991) reported that "48 percent of the reduction in inequality is due to falling real wages among men and 52 percent is due to rising real wages among women" (p. 81).

13. For overviews of changes in patterns of marriage, divorce, and cohabitation, see Bumpass (1990), Cherlin (1992), Espenshade (1985), and Furstenberg (1990).

14. Among whites, about 60% of one-parent families are headed by divorced or separated women. Among blacks, more than 50% of one-parent families are headed by never-married women (Suro, 1992).

References

Balswick, J. O. (1979, July). The inexpressive male: Functional, conflict and role theory as competing explanations. *The Family Coordinator,* pp. 331-335.

Barringer, F. (1989, June 9). Divorce data stir doubt on trial marriage. *New York Times,* pp. A1, A28.

Belkin, L. (1989, August 20). Bars to equality of the sexes seen as eroding slowly. *New York Times*, pp. A1, A26.

Bergmann, B. (1986). *The economic emergence of women*. New York: Basic Books.

Buchman, M. (1989). *The script of life in modern society: Entry into adulthood in a changing world*. Chicago: University of Chicago Press.

Bumpass, L. L. (1990). What's happening to the family? Interactions between demographic and institutional change. *Demography, 27*, 483-490.

Cancian, F. M. (1987). *Love in America: Gender and self-development*. New York: Cambridge University Press.

Cherlin, A. J. (1992). *Marriage, divorce, remarriage* (rev. ed.). Cambridge, MA: Harvard University Press.

Chodorow, N. (1978). *Reproduction of mothering: Psychoanalysis and the sociology of gender*. Berkeley: University of California Press.

Collins, R. (1971). A conflict theory of sexual stratification. *Social Problems, 19*, 3-21.

Connell, R. W. (1987). *Gender and power*. Stanford, CA: Stanford University Press.

Ehrenreich, B. (1983). *The hearts of men: American dreams and the flight from commitment*. New York: Anchor Doubleday.

Elder, G. H., Jr. (1978). Approaches to social change and the family. In J. Demos & S. Boocock (Eds.), *Turning points: Historical and sociological essays on the family* (pp. 1-38). Chicago: University of Chicago Press.

Espenshade, T. J. (1985). Marriage trends in America: Estimates, implications, and underlying causes. *Population and Development Review, 11*, 193-245.

Fiedler, L. (1966). *Love and death in the American novel* (rev. ed.). New York: Stein & Day.

Fuchs, V. R. (1989). *Women's quest for economic equality*. Cambridge, MA: Harvard University Press.

Furstenberg, F. F., Jr. (1988). Good dads/bad dads: Two faces of fatherhood. In A. Cherlin (Ed.), *The changing American family and public policy* (pp. 193-215). Washington, DC: Urban Institute Press.

Furstenberg, F. F., Jr. (1990). Divorce and the American family. *Annual Review of Sociology, 16*, 379-403.

Gerson, K. (1985). *Hard choices: How women decide about work, career, and motherhood*. Berkeley: University of California Press.

Gerson, K. (1993). *No man's land: Men's changing commitments to family and work*. New York: Basic Books.

Gerth, H., & Mills, C. W. (1953). *Character and social structure*. New York: Harcourt, Brace, & World.

Gilligan, C. (1983). *In a different voice: Psychological theory and women's development*. Cambridge, MA: Harvard University Press.

Hartmann, H. (1976). Capitalism, patriarchy, and job segregation by sex. In M. Blaxall & B. Reagan (Eds.), *Women and the workplace* (pp. 137-170). Chicago: University of Chicago Press.

Hochschild, A., with Machung, A. (1989). *The second shift: Working parents and the revolution at home*. New York: Viking.

Jacobs, J. A. (1991). *Women's entry into management: Trends, authority, and values among salaried managers*. Unpublished manuscript, Department of Sociology, University of Pennsylvania.

Jardine, A., & Smith, P. (1987). *Men in feminism*. New York: Methuen.

Jencks, C. (1992). *Rethinking social policy*. Cambridge, MA: Harvard University Press.

Kilborn, P. T. (1992, January 2). The middle class feels betrayed, but not enough to rebel. *New York Times,* section 4, pp. 1-2.

Kimmel, M. S. (1987). Men's responses to feminism at the turn of the century. *Gender & Society, 1,* 261-283.

Komarovsky, M. (1976). *Dilemmas of masculinity.* New York: Norton.

Kosters, M. H., & Ross, M. N. (1988, Winter). A shrinking middle class? *The Public Interest,* pp. 3-27.

Luker, K. (1991, Spring). Dubious conceptions: The controversy over teen pregnancy. *The American Prospect,* pp. 73-83.

Maccoby, E., & Jacklin, C. N. (1974). *The psychology of sex differences.* Stanford, CA: Stanford University Press.

Mishel, L., & Frankel, D. M. (1991). *The state of working America.* Armonk, NY: M. E. Sharpe.

Nasar, S. (1992, October 18). Women's progress stalled? It just isn't so. *New York Times,* section 3, pp. 1, 10.

Phillips, R. (1990). *Putting asunder: A history of divorce in Western society.* Cambridge, UK: Cambridge University Press.

Pleck, J. (1981). *The myth of masculinity.* Cambridge, MA: MIT Press.

Polatnik, M. (1973). Why men don't rear children. *Berkeley Journal of Sociology, 18,* 45-86.

Reskin, B. F. (1988). Bringing men back in: Sex differentiation and the devaluation of women's work. *Gender & Society, 2,* 58-81.

Risman, B. J. (1986). Can men "mother"? Life as a single father. *Family Relations, 35,* 95-102.

Schor, J. (1992). *The overworked American.* New York: Basic Books.

Suro, R. (1992, December 29). For women, varied reasons for single motherhood. *New York Times,* section 4, p. 2.

Swidler, A. (1980). Love and adulthood in American culture. In N. Smelser & E. Erikson (Eds.), *Themes of work and love in adulthood* (pp. 120-147). Cambridge, MA: Harvard University Press.

Swidler, A. (1986). Culture in action: Symbols and strategies. *American Sociological Review, 51,* 273-286.

Uchitelle, L. (1990, December 16). Not getting ahead? Better get used to it. *New York Times,* section 4, pp. 1, 6.

Uchitelle, L. (1992, May 14). Pay of college graduates is outpaced by inflation. *New York Times,* pp. A1, B12.

U.S. Bureau of the Census. (1991). *Current population reports* (Series P23, No. 173). Washington, DC: Government Printing Office.

U.S. Bureau of the Census. (1992). *Current population reports* (Series P20, No. 458). Washington, DC: Government Printing Office.

U.S. Department of Labor. (1991). *Working women: A chartbook* (Bulletin 2385). Washington, DC: Government Printing Office.

Weitzman, L. J. (1984). Sex-role socialization. In J. Freeman (Ed.), *Women: A feminist perspective* (3rd ed., pp. 157-237). Palo Alto, CA: Mayfield.

Willis, P. (1977). *Learning to labor: How working class kids get working class jobs.* New York: Columbia University Press.

Wrong, D. H. (1961). The oversocialized conception of man in modern sociology. *American Sociological Review, 26,* 183-193.

6

Divorce and Remarriage

TERRY ARENDELL

Divorce and remarriage appear here to stay, to paraphrase Bane's (1976) earlier assertion about marriage. Both single-parent families and stepfamilies are common arrangements for rearing children. Marital separation and divorce continue to be the primary events leading to one-parent households, although the number and proportion of those headed by never-married mothers is rising steadily (U.S. Bureau of the Census, 1995b).[1] Remarriage of a divorced parent is the principal source of stepparent family formation. Although all families continuously experience various changes to which they must adjust and adapt, including the ongoing developmental ones (especially children's), marital dissolution and remarriage present numerous challenges. Family members must negotiate and work out residential arrangements and relationships, including parent-child ones, in the altered family situations. Also subject to change are parenting approaches and activities.

Until recently, more was known about the structures in which children lived than was known about what actually occurred within families as they managed day-to-day activities and functions as well as confronted the unusual and unexpected. The approach to families undergoing divorce or remarriage was one that assumed family dysfunction, and child outcomes were found to be adverse. More specifically, earlier research and discussion of parenting in divorced and remarried families focused on family composition and examined the effects, often assumed to be dire, of the absence of a parent, usually the father.

Particularly because of the common tendency not to distinguish divorced families from those headed by never-married mothers, especially low-income or poor unmarried teen mothers who typically have an array of unique problems facing them, single-parent families still are discussed as if they are inadequate family environments for children. Indeed, studies that do not carefully disaggregate types of single-parent families obtain findings that show that children being reared in these families have diminished well-being (e.g., Blankenhorn, 1995; McLanahan & Sandefur, 1994; Popenoe, 1988). This continues to impede our approach to and understanding of the effects of divorce and remarriage on parenting and children's development. Nonetheless, a growing body of research findings indicates that although the consequences of divorce are diverse, with some being far from optimal, for the most part "life goes on in a fairly normal fashion in the households of divorced families" (Maccoby & Mnookin, 1992, p. 296). The same can be said for many stepparent families.

Increasingly common in the study of parenting in divorce and remarriage is attention to family interactional processes and variations in experiences and outcomes (e.g., Arditti, 1995; Booth & Dunn, 1994; Hetherington, 1993). Outcomes no longer are assumed to be dire and problematic. Research more commonly now draws on, and contributes to the development of, conceptual frameworks that view the family as dynamic and emergent in character. Family units are seen to adjust and adapt. Diversity is acknowledged, and scholars advocate greater attention to this because "it is the diversity rather than the inevitability of outcomes that is notable in response to divorce and remarriage" (Hetherington, 1993, p. 55). Already, differences in experiences and outcomes by gender—the "hers" and "his" of marriage and divorce—are recognized and studied (e.g., Arendell, 1986, 1995; Kitson & Holmes, 1992; Riessman, 1990), as are, by some, the variations in other family members' experiences within particular units (e.g., Thorne, 1993). Still, many questions remain unanswered. For instance, how do well-adjusted and functioning divorced or remarried families differ from each other? How do race, ethnicity, socioeconomic status, religion, and geographical region affect family transitions and adjustments? These have received scant research attention to date.[2]

Specifically, the family systems paradigm, and variations on it, frame much of the current research and theorizing on marital disruptions and family formations and dynamics. For example, describing the Virginia Longitudinal Study of Divorce and Remarriage and its underlying conceptual framework, Hetherington (1992) observed,

> We see divorce and remarriage not as single events but as part of a series of changes in family organization, functioning, and life experiences, and we expect the factors that promote psychological well-being or problems in family members and relationships to vary over time. Each family member is viewed as part of an interactional, interdependent system in which the behavior of each individual or subsystem, such as the marital, parent-child, or sibling subsystem, modifies that of other subsystems. Thus, individuals and subsystems are linked in a network of feedback loops, and a change in one leads to changes in the others. (p. 13)

This chapter provides an overview of the current research findings on parenting in divorced and remarried families that result from the marriages of divorced parents. Covered initially (and briefly because these were addressed in detail in Chapter 3) are the demographic patterns in marital dissolution and remarriage. Next is a consideration of postdivorce parenting; specifically addressed are the effects of divorce on parenting quality, custody arrangements, and economic support. Next reviewed is primary parenting—custodial mothers, custodial fathers, and cocustodial or dual-custody parents. An overview of involvement by noncustodial parents—both noncustodial mothers and noncustodial fathers—and issues pertaining to visitation follows. Child outcomes in divorce are considered, in part in relationship to postdivorce parenting approaches and styles as well as to intraparental conflict and its effects on parenting and children's well-being. Then discussed are remarriage and parenting in families having a stepparent or stepparents. Stepparent relationships and roles and child outcomes in stepparent families also are reviewed in this final section.

Demographic Patterns in
Marital Dissolution and Remarriage

The divorce rate more than doubled between the early 1960s and mid-1970s. Despite some fluctuations in the annual divorce rates, more than 1 million marriages still are dissolved each year. If trends continue as anticipated, as many as three in five first marriages will end in legal dissolution, as they have since 1980. Second marriages have a somewhat higher termination rate (Gottman, 1994; Kitson & Holmes, 1992; Martin & Bumpass, 1989).

Most likely to divorce are younger adults in shorter term marriages with dependent children. Indeed, children are involved in approximately two thirds of all divorces (U.S. Bureau of the Census, 1995a), and more than half of all children experience their parents' divorces before they reach 18 years of age (Cherlin & Furstenberg, 1994; Furstenberg & Cherlin, 1991; Martin & Bumpass, 1989). Nearly twice as many black children as white children born to married parents will experience parental divorce if trends persist as expected (Amato & Keith, 1991). Marital separation and dissolution rates among parents in other racial and ethnic groups, which generally have been lower than those among whites and blacks, also are increasing (U.S. Bureau of the Census, 1995b). Children who experience divorce spend an average of 5 years in single-parent homes (Glick & Lin, 1986); even among those whose custodial mothers remarry, about half spend 5 years with their mothers alone (Furstenberg, 1990).

Separation and divorce are not the only transitions in parents' marital status and household arrangements experienced by children. Even though remarriage rates are declining, with only about two thirds of separated or divorced women and about three fourths of men likely to remarry compared to three fourths and four fifths, respectively, in the 1960s, more than one third of adults currently in first marriages will divorce and remarry before their youngest children reach age 18. Thus a high proportion of children will experience the remarriage of one parent, if not both, and the formation of a stepfamily or stepfamilies. Moreover, many children will experience the dissolution of a stepfamily when a parent and stepparent divorce. About one in six children will experience two divorces of the custodial parent before the child reaches age 18 (Furstenberg & Cherlin, 1991). Additionally, increasing numbers of adults, including those who are custodial parents of minor children, are cohabiting. Whether they eventually will marry remains to be seen (see Cherlin & Furstenberg, 1994).

Approximately 1 in 10 children in 1992 lived with a biological parent and a stepparent, and this proportion is expected to increase. About 15% of all children lived in blended families—homes in which children lived with at least one stepparent, stepsibling, or half-sibling. More children lived with at least one half-brother or half-sister than with a stepparent or with at least one stepsibling (Furukawa, 1994).[3] Because the practice of cohabitation, or sharing domestic life and intimacy without legal marriage, is increasing steadily, the number of children who reside with a custodial parent and her or his adult partner, who presumably functions, at least to some extent, as a stepparent—a *quasi-stepparent*—probably is much higher than the official numbers indicate (Cherlin & Furstenberg, 1994, pp. 363-365). Because the large majority of children whose parents divorce live with their mothers, most residential stepparents and quasi-stepparents are men. Census data for 1991 show that among children in single-mother families (which includes never-married as well as divorced), 20% also lived with an adult male (related or unrelated) present in the household. About 37% of children living with a single father also lived with an adult female (related or unrelated) (Furukawa, 1994, pp. 1-2).

Irrespective of family form, child rearing involves an array of interrelated tasks and functions. Sahler (1983) defined parenting as a special category of child rearing that "is the art of overseeing a child's growth and development" (p. 219). Adult roles in families with children can be characterized, to paraphrase Cowan and Cowan (1988), as those of parenting, providing, and partnering. A spouse, in her or his partnering, also contributes to parenting by providing support to the other parent in her or his parenting (e.g., Crnic &

Booth, 1991; May & Strikwerda, 1992a). Partnering is ended with divorce, as is, to varying degrees, the providing of parenting support to the other parent. But what happens to parenting and providing in divorce?

Divorce

POSTDIVORCE PARENTING

With respect to family functioning, marital dissolution can be a lengthy process, often underway years before the actual spousal separation occurs. Children show the effects of marital dissension and discontent long before divorce (e.g., Amato & Booth, 1996; Block, Block, & Gjerde, 1986, 1988; Shaw, Emery, & Tuer, 1993). Adjustment to the changes wrought by divorce itself can be a gradual and lengthy process, and many parents and children enter a "crisis" period after the marital separation that can last for several years (e.g., Chase-Lansdale & Hetherington, 1990; Hetherington, 1987, 1988; Morrison & Cherlin, 1995). Maccoby and Mnookin (1992), in the Stanford Custody Project, concluded that

> divorcing parents find it difficult to take the time and trouble required to negotiate with children over task assignments and joint plans. Under these conditions of diminished parenting, children tend to become bored, moody, and restless and to feel misunderstood; these reactions lead to an increase in behaviors that irritate their parents, and mutually coercive cycles ensue. (pp. 204-205)

A related phenomenon is single parents' lesser ability to make control demands on their children. Examining data from the National Survey of Families and Households, Thomson, McLanahan, and Curtin (1992) found that single parents of both sexes seem to be "structurally limited" in their ability to control and make demands on a child without the presence of another adult.

The extent and duration of uneven parenting, however, varies by families, with some family units adapting fairly rapidly to their altered circumstances and arrangements, achieving stable and healthy family functioning rather soon after divorce. Some units take much longer to find an equilibrium. Others have a delayed reaction, functioning well initially and then encountering adjustment difficulties (e.g., Kitson & Holmes, 1992). In addition, "some show intense and enduring deleterious outcomes" (Hetherington, 1993, p. 40). Whatever the pattern, parental functioning usually recovers over time, returning nearly to the level found in intact families (Hetherington, 1988; Hetherington, Cox, & Cox, 1982). That is, most family units formed by divorce establish workable and functional interactional processes (Maccoby & Mnookin, 1992; Wallerstein & Blakeslee, 1989).

One of the first major tasks facing parents in divorce is that of determining children's living arrangements as family members separate into two households. Most custody decisions occur with little discussion between the parents, and relatively few custody allocations are actually litigated. Yet the working out of parenting and parental relationships after divorce, including children's access to and involvement with the nonresidential parent if parenting is not shared, can be complicated and difficult, involving various changes and intraparental conflicts. Of the four relationships between married persons that must be altered in divorce—parental, economic, spousal, and legal (Maccoby & Mnookin, 1992)—the parental divorce is perhaps the most difficult to achieve (Ahrons & Wallisch, 1987a, p. 228; see also Bohannon, 1970).

CUSTODY ARRANGEMENTS FOR
MINOR CHILDREN

Three residential patterns are available for children in divorce: maternal, paternal, and dual. Primary physical custody, maternal or paternal, is the situation in which children spend more than 10 overnights in a 2-week period with a particular parent (Mnookin, Maccoby, Albiston, & Depner, 1990, pp. 40-41). Dual or shared custody is defined as the situation in which "the children spend at least a third of their time in each household" (Maccoby & Mnookin, 1992, p. 203).[4] Shared custody is unusual. Even in California, where dual custody probably is more common than anywhere else, only about one in six children actually lives in a shared custody situation. And in these circumstances, "more often than not" mothers handle the bulk of the managerial aspects of child rearing (Maccoby & Mnookin, 1992, p. 269).

As has been the case for most of this century, maternal custody is predominant; more than 85% of children whose parents are divorced are in the custody of their mothers (U.S. Bureau of the Census, 1995a). A somewhat higher proportion of offspring actually reside with their mothers because, in legally mandated dual-custody situations, children often spend relatively little time with their fathers (e.g., Maccoby & Mnookin, 1992; Seltzer, 1991; Seltzer & Bianchi, 1988). Overwhelmingly, then, it is mothers who become the primary parents in divorce.

The pattern of mothers being the primary parents, irrespective of marital transitions or even official custody allocations, is consistent with the division of labor in intact married families. Mothers perform most parenting tasks before divorce; caring for children remains a gendered activity defined as women's work (Tiedje & Darling-Fisher, 1993; Fish, New, & Van Cleave, 1992), even though some increases in men's involvement in parenting activities in intact marriages has occurred over the past three decades. These increases, although moderate, are both proportional (in comparison with levels of involvement by mothers) and absolute (in terms of greater numbers of hours) (Pleck, 1996).

ECONOMIC SUPPORT OF CHILDREN

Although the preseparation parenting division of labor persists after divorce with mothers doing most of the parenting, what does change is the economic providing for minor children. Whereas men's earned incomes provide the larger share of the economic resources available to intact married families, divorced custodial women assume most financial responsibilities for their offspring. The overwhelming body of scholarly research and governmental and other policy studies shows that fathers' contributions to the economic support of their children are much reduced after marital dissolution (e.g., Kellan, 1995; Maccoby & Mnookin, 1992) despite many men's claims to the contrary (e.g., Arendell, 1995). Approximately three fourths of divorced mothers have child support agreements, but only about half of those women receive the full amounts ordered in the agreements

(Holden & Smock, 1991; Scoon-Rogers & Lester, 1995). One fourth receive no payment whatsoever, and the other one fourth receive irregular payments in amounts less than those ordered. According to the Congressional Research Service, only about $13 billion of the $34 billion in outstanding support orders was collected in 1993 (Kellan, 1995, p. 27). Moreover, child support payments amounted to only about 16% of the incomes of divorced mothers and their children in 1991. The average monthly child support paid by divorced fathers contributing economic support in 1991 was $302, amounting to $3,623 for the year (Scoon-Rogers & Lester, 1995). Fathers' limited or lack of financial contributions to the support of their children not residing with them is not offset by other kinds of assistance (Teachman, 1991, p. 360).

As a group, women's incomes drop more than 30% following divorce. About 40% of divorcing women lose more than half of their family incomes, whereas fewer than 17% of men experience this large a drop (Hoffman & Duncan, 1988). Men, in general, experience an increase in their incomes—an average of 15%—partially because they share less of their incomes with their children (Furstenberg & Cherlin, 1991; Kitson & Holmes, 1992; Maccoby & Mnookin, 1992). For many women, the financial hardships accompanying divorce become the overriding experience, affecting psychological well-being and parenting as well as dictating decisions such as where to live, what type of child care to use, and whether or not to obtain health care (Arendell, 1986; Kurz, 1995).

Children's economic well-being after divorce is directly related to their mothers' economic situations. Those living with single mothers are far more likely to be poor than are children in other living arrangements; families headed by single mothers are nearly six times as likely to be impoverished as are families having both parents present (U.S. Bureau of the Census, 1995a). This is not the experience of children being raised by single fathers because men's wages are higher than women's (Holden & Smock, 1991; Scoon-Rogers & Lester, 1995; Seltzer & Garfinkel, 1990); about one eighth of custodial fathers, compared to nearly two fifths of divorced custodial mothers, are poor (Scoon-Rogers & Lester, 1995). Divorced women and their children do not regain their predivorce standards of living until 5 years after the marital breakups. Women's decisions to remarry often involve economic considerations; the surest route to financial well-being for many women is remarriage, not their employment, even when it is full-time (Furstenberg & Cherlin, 1991; Kitson & Morgan, 1990).

Primary Parenting:
Custodial Mothers and Fathers

Both mothers and fathers can and generally do parent effectively as single parents (e.g., Greif, 1987; Greif & DeMaris, 1990; Risman, 1989). Yet mothers' parenting after divorce conforms in large measure to that done before divorce, whereas fathers' parenting is not so predictable, due largely to their relative inexperience in child rearing. "Fathers, as single parents, or even as visiting parents, typically have more to learn than single mothers do" (Maccoby & Mnookin, 1992, p. 35). One divorced custodial father put it this way:

> It was terrifying at first, just terrifying. . . . I didn't know what parenting was about, really. I mean, who teaches us how to parent? I really didn't know how to ask for help. I don't truly remember the first year. It was day by day by day. After about a year, I managed to figure out that I had my act together. But it goes deeper than all of that. I had to learn to relate to them, relate to them as people. (quoted in Arendell, 1995, pp. 220-221)

Men and women apparently encounter somewhat different parental challenges when they become single custodial parents, and they seem to have somewhat different strengths and weaknesses (Maccoby & Mnookin, 1992, p. 203). Residential fathers encounter more difficulty in keeping track of their children's school progress, whereabouts, and friends and interests than do mothers; this pattern also is evident among nonresidential fathers in comparison to nonresidential mothers. Custodial mothers, as well as noncustodial mothers, report more difficulty in remaining firm and patient. These differences are not accounted for by children's sexes or ages.

Comparisons between custodial parents, however, warrant several caveats. The first came from Maccoby and Mnookin (1992) and addressed divorced custodial parents specifically: "Residential parents are not exactly comparable with respect to the amount of time they have with their children. For residential fathers, the children are away (at the mother's house) more often" (p. 208). That is, mothers, whether residential or not, spend more time with their offspring and engage in more parenting work than do fathers. Moreover, children view a mother's involvement as a kind of basic right in contrast to a father's parenting involvement, which they see as more exemplary and generous, mirroring the persistent cultural double standard about parenting as a gendered activity (Furstenberg & Cherlin, 1991).

The second caveat to making direct comparisons between custodial mothers and fathers is that they differ demographically. Custodial fathers are more likely to be currently married than are divorced mothers (46% vs. 27%). Custodial fathers typically are older than custodial mothers, with about half of fathers being at least age 40 and only 11% under age 30. Only 24% of custodial mothers are over age 40, whereas 31% are under age 30. Additionally, custodial fathers are more highly educated than mothers; fathers are twice as likely to have at least a bachelor's degree (19% vs. 10%). So, too, are they less likely to have only a high school diploma or less (56% vs. 64%) (Scoon-Rogers & Lester, 1995, pp. 2-3).

CUSTODIAL MOTHERS

For mothers, the move to single parenting often is not a major one in that they were the primary parents while married. Both the principal emotional parent-child bond and parenting activities carry over into the postdivorce situation. The quality of a mother's parenting after divorce can be fairly well predicted from her earlier parenting (Maccoby & Mnookin, 1992, p. 35; Hetherington et al., 1982). Even so, many newly divorced mothers experience role overload in and anxiety with respect to parenting alone. They must confront the emotional effects of the ending of their marriages, even as they try to cope with greater economic demands and fewer financial resources. Often divorced mothers increase their hours of paid employment in an attempt to make ends meet, and this means a reduction in time spent with their children. Also, they must adjust to not being able to call on the other parent for assistance with routine family tasks such as providing supervision and transportation for children, even if this had been done during marriage by the husband only in a pinch. Newly divorced mothers must attend to and facilitate children's adjustments to the family and economic changes as well as meet their developmental needs. Many single mothers feel isolated and alone in their parenting. Social lives often are highly restricted by the lack of both time and economic resources as well as by child care needs. Also, when dating is pursued, provisions for children and decisions about time must be made (e.g., Arendell, 1995; Kurz, 1995).

The women in my study of 60 divorced California mothers (Arendell, 1986), none of whom had remarried and all of whom were living alone with their children, who found it easiest to adjust to single parenting had the following circumstances:

> Their children were of elementary school age or older. They received regular financial assistance in supporting their children. They worked fewer hours than the average workweek. And they had parenting help— from their own parents and relatives, or from the children's father. (pp. 80-81)

Few of the women, however, had all of these advantages (see also Weitzman, 1985). Little has changed in this regard; in her recent research conducted nearly a decade later, Kurz (1995) found much the same thing.

Despite the numerous challenges they face, a majority of mothers say that their experiences during and after their divorces have brought them closer to their children. They feel they are more open and direct, and some deliberately change patterns of communication with their children, becoming more like a team having a senior partner and a junior partner(s) (Arendell, 1986, p. 82). Many, even most, custodial mothers are satisfied, even pleased, with the quality of their parenting after divorce (e.g., Kurz, 1995; Maccoby & Mnookin, 1992). Remarking on the discovery of her many skills, one mother said,

> I think single parenting makes you really strong, very creative and resourceful. You know the saying, "Necessity is the mother of invention"? Well, you find out how strong you really are and just what you can do. It's amazing. (quoted in Arendell, 1986, p. 84)

CUSTODIAL FATHERS

Custodial fathers often also experience role overload. In contrast to the counterpart mothers, however, fathers receive offers of assistance from relatives and have more discretionary income with which to purchase some services, including babysitting, to pursue independent social lives (Arendell, 1995). Nonetheless, custodial fathers express many of the concerns conveyed by single mothers: too little time and money as well as restricted social lives. Some feel uncertainty about the effectiveness of their parenting and their children's well-being (e.g., Greif & DeMaris, 1990). Custodial fathers, like mothers, lament the constraints imposed by single parenting and full-time employment that limit their participation in leisure and play activities with their children. They too feel socially isolated as custodial parents. One custodial father, for example, said,

> I think it's the biggest drawback, the terrible loneliness of being a single parent. Terribly lonely. You're not only physically by yourself, but you feel isolated; you feel like you're in a cement box sometimes. There's no one, you know, I mean, whoever taught us how to raise kids? It's got to be tough enough with two parents. But at least then you have somebody, at least creative debate, you know: "Well, that was stupid and you should try this." Instead, it's been making every decision. So there was none of that, and that really, really is tough. (quoted in Arendell, 1995, p. 242)

Many custodial fathers believe that they are far more involved in child rearing than they would have been had they remained married.

COCUSTODIAL PARENTS OR DUAL CUSTODY

Unusual in divorce is the practice in which both parents consistently share and equitably divide parenting tasks and responsibilities. Actual coparenting, or shared parenting or dual residence, is done by probably fewer than 10% of divorced families in the nation (Maccoby & Mnookin, 1992). Such coparenting involves a range of activities: sharing both major and day-to-day decisions as well as child-rearing and coparenting difficulties; discussing children's personal problems; sharing children's school and medical problems; planning special events in children's lives; discussing children's adjustments to divorce, progress, and accomplishments; and examining and planning child-related finances (Ahrons & Wallisch, 1987b; Arendell, 1995, pp. 202-203, 1996). How individual parents actually work out, structure, and manage coparenting subsequent to divorce is largely unknown (e.g., Arendell, 1996; Maccoby, Depner, & Mnookin, 1990, p. 142).

Shared parenting seems to require certain conditions and is not suitable for all divorced parents (Benjamin & Irving, 1990; Donnelly & Finkelhor, 1992, 1993). One conducive factor is flexible employment so that schedules, both each other's and their children's, can be accommodated. Another is adequate incomes given that shared custody can be a costly enterprise with the need to maintain two homes equipped for children. Transportation needs typically are greater in the shared parenting arrangement.

Parents must be motivated not only to handle the logistics and planning required in coparenting, which can be extensive and demanding, but also to attempt to relate to each other in cooperative and collaborative fashion (Ahrons & Wallisch, 1987b; Donnelly & Finkelhor, 1993). Negotiations about child care issues are crucial in the coparenting relationship (Fishel & Scanzoni, 1989), and regular discussions centered on planning and scheduling enhance the workability of coparenting (e.g., Arendell, 1995). Conflict between divorced coparents, however, is not uncommon, even in shared custody arrangements. Maccoby and associates (1990) found that

> dual-residence parents talked to each other somewhat more frequently and in general maintained a higher level of cooperative communication. However, they did not experience less discord, and the prevalence of the conflicted pattern was as great in the dual-residence families as in the primary-residence ones. (pp. 152-153)

Parents who voluntarily enter into and maintain shared residential custody arrangements find them to be satisfying and believe the arrangements are beneficial to their children (e.g., Ahrons & Wallisch, 1987b; Ambert, 1988; Benjamin & Irving, 1990). At the same time, there is evidence that women and men have different experiences in and varied levels of satisfaction with these custody arrangements, with fathers typically being more satisfied than mothers (Ahrons, 1983; Benjamin & Irving, 1990; Emery, 1988). One reason may be the persistent inequitable division of labor. "Parents agree that in dual-residence families, mothers are more likely than fathers to take major responsibility for each of the [parenting] functions, although fathers frequently say that *both* parents are involved" (Maccoby & Mnookin, 1992, p. 212; emphasis in original).

Parenting Involvement by Noncustodial Parents

Most divorced parents do not share parenting equally; one typically continues handling most parenting responsibilities or, less commonly, is assigned custody and assumes these tasks, whereas the other (noncustodial) parent is granted visitation. These parents must maintain some contact if they are both to be involved with their children, especially when their children are quite young. Yet many divorced parents distrust and seek to avoid each other, and few actively collaborate in parenting. Numerous divorced parents insist they would have no contact whatsoever with their former spouses if they did not share children (e.g., Ahrons & Wallisch, 1987b).

Many divorced parents have little to do with each other, even with respect to child-rearing issues. Seltzer (1991), analyzing nationally representative survey data, found that fewer than one third of divorced parents discuss their children with each other during a 12-month period and that just over 20% talk with each other about their children at least weekly. Even among those parents, the level of noncustodial fathers' participation in decision making is limited; only 17% have a great deal of influence on decisions about important aspects of children's rearing such as regarding health care matters, education, or religious teaching (see also Furstenberg & Cherlin, 1991). Most divorced parents engage in *parallel parenting*; they "maintain separate and segregated relations with each of their children and have a tacit agreement not to interfere in each other's lives" (Furstenberg & Cherlin, 1991, pp. 39-40). Children probably benefit when parents who are in conflict shift to disengaged parallel parenting (Maccoby & Mnookin, 1992).

Parenting by nonresidential parents varies enormously, from very active, regular, and frequent levels of involvement to complete disengagement and absence. To be an engaged, noncustodial parent is fraught with challenges. Custodial parents also find the visitation situations difficult; indeed, overall, they report more logistical problems over visitation than do noncustodial parents. A primary complaint is that of last-minute changes in plans involving their children by the nonresidential parents (Maccoby et al., 1990).

NONCUSTODIAL MOTHERS

Relatively little research has been directed at noncustodial divorced mothers, partly because they constitute a small proportion of nonresidential parents. Evidence to date, however, is consistent in the finding that noncustodial mothers remain active in their children's lives to a much greater extent than do noncustodial fathers (e.g., Greif, 1987, 1990; Maccoby & Mnookin, 1992). One study, which focused specifically on nonresidential mothers who had lived apart from their children for an average of 5 years, found that nearly 97% had ongoing relationships with their children. More specifically,

> Slightly more than 26 percent of the women reported spending time with their children on a weekly basis. Additionally, 24.6 percent of the respondents saw their children on a monthly basis, which means that one half of the mothers interact with their children fairly frequently. Another 36.2 percent asserted visiting their children on a quarterly basis. While annual visits were the rule for 7.7 percent of the respondents and their children, these more often than not represented two- to three-month summer visits. (Herrerías, 1995, p. 247)

Additionally, the majority (almost 71%) reported being satisfied with their parent-child relationships. Furthermore, 77% described having close and caring relations with their offspring, 11.6% said their relations with their children were somewhat strained, and 9% recounted relational problems with one child but not the rest of their children (p. 248). More than a third reported wanting more contact with their offspring, and the majority of mothers reported two major problems as nonresidential parents: bearing full financial responsibility for children's travel from their primary residence and lacking money for when the children were with them (see also Arditti, 1995).

Children evaluate their relationships with noncustodial mothers more favorably than those with noncustodial fathers, even when the amount of contact is taken into consideration (e.g., Arditti, 1995; Furstenberg, Morgan, & Allison, 1987). Because nonresidential mothers have greater and more regular and sustained contact with their children than do nonresidential fathers,

> mothers do more for children living with their fathers than fathers do for children living with their mothers. Nonresidential mothers continue, in many cases, to actively participate in childrearing despite their separate living arrangements. (Maccoby & Mnookin, 1992, p. 212)

NONCUSTODIAL FATHERS

The picture of parental involvement by noncustodial fathers and their levels of satisfaction is much more mixed than that by noncustodial mothers. With the prevalence of maternal custody, the large majority of divorced fathers fall into the category of nonresidential parents. Overall, noncustodial fathers' involvement with children declines steadily over time. "The pattern of modest initial contact and a sharp drop-off over time is strikingly similar across studies" (Furstenberg & Cherlin, 1991, p. 36; see also Furstenberg et al., 1987; Seltzer, 1991). Based on data from the National Survey of Families and Households, nearly 30% of children whose parents are divorced and who live with their mothers have not seen their fathers at all during the prior year. Less than a third of children who see their fathers have extended periods of time with them. Just under a third visit at least once a week or spend at least 3 weeks a year with their fathers (Seltzer, 1991).

Overall, although handling basic care needs when together with their children, visiting fathers assume little responsibility for and have limited involvement in the larger range of activities involved in primary parenting (e.g., Chambers, 1984; Marsiglio, 1991). Few fathers, irrespective of frequency of contact, assist their children with homework or projects, handle health or dental care appointments, or schedule lessons or other activities. Furstenberg and Cherlin (1991) concluded, "Even in the small number of families where children are seeing their fathers regularly, the dads assume a minimal role in the day-to-day care and supervision of their children" (p. 36).

Men who see their children infrequently have little other contact with them (e.g., Arendell, 1995). National survey data show a relationship between types of contacts:

> Among those who did not visit at all during the past year, only 10 percent had any contact by telephone or mail, and most (77 percent) of those who visited regularly (i.e., at least 1-3 times per month) also maintained regular contact by telephone or mail. . . . Fathers and children who maintain close touch through visiting communicate regularly in other ways as well. (Seltzer, 1991, p. 85)

Nonresidential fathers often find it difficult to be active parents and to construct and maintain meaningful parent-child relationships subsequent to divorce. For many, visitation is awkward and unsatisfactory. Fathers argue that visitation simply reinforces the ambiguity they feel about their roles as parents after divorce (e.g., Emery, 1988). One father, for example, explained,

> Visitation puts you in the position that you're a visitor to your child. The connotation of a visitor is, well, you know how when you go to visit somebody's home, you can't tell somebody in their home what to do? You go visit another country, hey, you have to respect their culture. I'm a visitor in my child's life, so I have no control, I have nothing to say. I'm just there. (quoted in Arendell, 1995, p. 147)

His remarks also point to his understanding, shared by a majority in the study, that being an authority figure is intrinsic to fathering. Yet paternal authority is eroded by the divorced and noncustodial parent situation. Another father who complained about the loss of control also described the turmoil he felt as a result of the limitations of visits with his children:

> Three times out of three, I would be an emotional wreck. It was awful, awful. By the time your coat is off, you're not interacting, you're worrying about when they'll go back. You're tearing your heart and guts out saying, "[I'm] only going to see them for a few hours." . . . It's awful, it's awful. (pp. 154-155)

A frequent argument made by critics of the visitation system is that custodial mothers prevent fathers from seeing their children (e.g.,

Sanderson, 1985; Krause, 1990). Yet most custodial mothers argue that they would prefer their children to have regular contact with their fathers (Arendell, 1986; Furstenberg & Cherlin, 1991; Kurz, 1995), and many divorced fathers choose to see their children far less than the amount of time specified in their custody and visitation agreements (Arendell, 1995; Maccoby & Mnookin, 1992). Men often "lock" themselves out of their nonresidential children's lives as a way to demonstrate their anger at or to exert power over their former wives and blame them for the "necessity" of the men's actions. For example, one of the fathers in my study, who withdrew totally from his children's lives after spending numerous months "unsuccessfully" embroiled in dissension with his former spouse over arrangements for their children, characterized his absence as "a response to the condition of 'forced impotence,' a response to the total denial of my rights" (Arendell, 1995, p. 157). The violation, as he saw it, was maternal custody. Another father, who became an absent father after unsuccessful attempts to obtain shared custody, offered a similar explanation:

> I will not be a visiting uncle. I refuse to let some woman [former wife], judge, attorney, or social worker reduce me to that status. I'm a parent, and parents do not *visit* their children. If I see my child only every other weekend, I become nothing more than a visiting uncle. I am a father in name only at this point. Until and unless I can be a father in every sense, I simply refuse to have any part of this. (quoted in Arendell, 1995, p. 147)

These fathers' remarks were representative of other men's and shed some light on the high levels of parental disengagement by divorced fathers.

Time parameters, role ambiguity, emotional distance, and inexperience all are factors in noncustodial fathers' limited caregiving and nurturing of their children. Many fathers are seemingly ill equipped or unwilling to make the kinds of adjustments that would promote continued and vital father-child relationships in the divorce situation. A large majority of divorced fathers in my study—66 of the 75—engaged in *traditionalization* (LaRossa & LaRossa, 1989) as their primary line of action in their postdivorce parenting. That is, they turned to that which was familiar in their searches for definition and task assignment in the unfamiliar circumstance of divorce. Seeking answers, direction, and affirmation in divorce, they looked to customary views and approaches, acting in largely conventional ways and relying on the practices and tactics of the gender belief system. This resulted in a persistently high level of preoccupation with former wives and a continued perception that they, *as men,* are victimized in divorce. This impeded affirmation of the postdivorce father-child relationship or any movement toward successful parenting activities. Moreover, men found it difficult to disaggregate their former spouses from the children and the spousal relationships and roles from the parental ones (Arendell, 1995). The large majority of fathers in my project typically expressed extensive and overtly hostile feelings toward their former wives and described an array of actions taken to demonstrate those feelings.

Those men who made concerted efforts to avoid or diminish conflict with their former wives were anomalies. Their objective was to protect their relationships with their children, irrespective of custody status, and to work toward creating for their children "best-case scenarios" in divorce. These men—9 of the 75—were active and highly engaged parents. Each was a primary parent, either managing the bulk of child rearing by himself or coparenting with his former wife. These 9 were caught up in both adaptation and creativity; they engaged in the processes of *innovation* (as contrasted with *traditionalization*). They actively rejected what they perceived to be men's standard behaviors in divorce, and they searched out and developed strategies more congruent with their objective to actively parent their children. Child centeredness prevailed in their accounts and actions. They not only expressed affection for their offspring but actively engaged in parenting work, unlike the majority (Arendell, 1995; see also Frey, 1986; May & Strikwerda 1992b; Tronto, 1989).

Parental involvement as a noncustodial parent requires deliberation and intent. Yet most of the nonresidential fathers in my study had developed few, if any, strategies for parenting and relating to their children. This was exacerbated by their former spouses' increasing unwillingness over time to actively facilitate and mediate the father-child relationship. During the time spent with their children, most fathers emphasized entertainment. Pursuing recreational activities inside and outside of the home, watching television or rented videos, and sharing meals, often at fast-food restaurants, dominated the time regularly visiting fathers spent together with their children. Indeed, parenting and parental relations were described repeatedly in terms of the activities shared with children; being a visiting parent was synonymous with sharing in recreational pursuits (Arendell, 1995).

The most satisfied noncustodial parents are those who have contact with their children frequently and regularly and who have found ways in which to have structured family lives when they are together. The advantages of this pattern were summarized by Chase-Lansdale and Hetherington (1990):

> Those few fathers who do see their children regularly and frequently are more likely to develop close relationships with them, especially if they establish a home where the children can visit and stay overnight [Russell, 1983]. This permits the enjoyable quotidian family activities that stand in marked contrast to the superficial, "every day is Christmas" or "tour guide" quality of the short and isolated visits to amusement parks, shopping malls, and restaurants typical of most father-child outings [Hetherington et al., 1982; Hetherington & Hagan, 1986]. (pp. 112-113)

Child Outcomes in Divorce

How children fare with divorce is a crucial question, one intimately related to issues of parenting. The arguments vary, with assertions ranging from children being irreparably damaged to children adapting successfully to divorce. Most research evidence suggests that a large majority of children adjust reasonably well to their parents' marital dissolutions. In examining two rounds of the longitudinal National Survey of Children, Baydar (1988) reported, "The most important result is that the separation of parents does not appear to be detrimental to a child's emotional well-being" (p. 979). Amato and Keith (1991), in examining the results of 92 studies, concluded that the lasting adverse effects are quite weak:

> Our findings, which are based on data from over 13,000 children, confirm that children of divorce experience a lower level of well-being than do children living in continuously intact families. The view that children of divorce adapt readily and reveal no lasting negative consequences is simply not supported by the cumulative data in this area.

However, the effect sizes in this literature are weak rather than strong. The largest reliable mean effect sizes (for conduct and father-child relations) are in the order of one quarter of a standard deviation between intact and divorced groups. The mean effect sizes for psychological well-being, self-concept and social adjustment reflect approximately one-tenth of a standard deviation between groups. Although these latter findings are statistically significant, many people would consider them to be trivial. (p. 30; see also Amato, 1994)

Some argue that the research findings on the effects of divorce on children are not so clear-cut (see, for review, Bolgar, Sweig-Frank, & Paris, 1995). But even those arguments are tempered when large data sets are the bases of analysis, especially those involving longitudinal studies and not just small, nonrepresentative samples (Amato & Booth, 1996). That a majority of children seem to cope with and adapt well to the change in their parents' marital status is particularly salient because many children enter the divorce phase already disadvantaged by exposure, often of long duration, to parental strife and conflict (Block et al., 1986, 1988; Chase-Lansdale & Hetherington, 1990). Furthermore, as numerous scholars point out, children who experience the dissolution of their parents' marriages may well have to cope with multiple adverse circumstances including family events prior to divorce (e.g., Furstenberg & Teitler, 1994). Allen (1993, p. 47), for example, argued that when scholars (and others) uncritically compare divorced families to nondivorced ones, they imply that two-parent intact families inevitably result in positive parenting outcomes. Other events that might be more detrimental than divorce itself, as she notes, are father abandonment; failure to pay child support; neglect; intersection of class, race, and gender with poverty; and women's inequality in traditional families.

Some earlier findings suggested that a child's sex and age mattered in postdivorce adjustment. Hetherington (1993, pp. 48-49), drawing from recent work, concluded that these variables—sex and age—are not pivotal factors in children's divorce responses and adjustments (see also Furstenberg & Teitler, 1994; Garasky, 1995). Sex differences in adverse responses, previously attributed to boys, disappeared in Hetherington's (1993) longitudinal study as children moved into adolescence. Where age mattered, it was for adolescents, all of whom showed somewhat increased problem behaviors. Children with

divorced and remarried parents did show more such problem behaviors than did those whose parents remained married. "Adolescence
often triggered problems in children from divorced and remarried
families who had previously seemed to be coping well" (p. 49).
Furstenberg and Teitler (1994) summarized findings pertaining to
adolescents:

> The findings indicate that certain effects of divorce are quite persistent
> even when we consider a wide range of predivorce conditions. Early
> timing of sexual activity, nonmarital cohabitation, and high school
> dropout do appear to be more frequent for children from divorced
> families. (p. 188)

The researchers note that these outcomes may be a result of growing
up in single-parent homes or witnessing parents' marital transitions,
among other things, not just divorce itself (p. 188).

Also, in contrast to earlier arguments, being reared by same-sex
parents appears not to be inherently beneficial to children (Powell &
Downey, 1995). And, although it may seem counterintuitive,
children's overall well-being in divorce does not seem related to the
extent of involvement or quality of parent-child relationship with the
noncustodial father (e.g., Amato & Keith, 1991; Bolgar et al., 1995;
Furstenberg & Cherlin, 1991).

The quality of the relationship with a custodial parent and that
parent's overall level of functioning is a central factor in children's
adjustment to divorce and the transition to a single-parent family
(Furstenberg & Cherlin, 1991; Emery, 1988; Hetherington, 1987;
Hetherington et al., 1982). Parenting style is much more significant
for children's and adolescents' well-being than is family configuration
(e.g., Ellwood & Stolberg, 1993; McFarlane, Bellissimo, & Norman,
1995; Steinberg, Elmen, & Mounts, 1989). (See Chapter 1 for a fuller
discussion of the three predominant American parenting styles:
authoritarian, permissive, and authoritative.)

PARENTING APPROACHES

Hetherington (1987, p. 197) concluded that a majority of divorced
mothers use the *authoritative* parenting style (Baumrind, 1971), which

involves high levels of warmth, involvement, monitoring, and maturity demands as well as moderately high but responsive control and relatively low conflict. By contrast, divorced fathers vary across the four parenting styles identified: permissive, disengaged, authoritarian, and authoritative (Hetherington, 1987). In another study, divorced fathers were found to be more authoritarian generally in their parenting than were mothers (Kurdek & Fine, 1993). Children found to be maladjusted after divorce (both in single-parent and remarried households) and showing characteristics such as aggression, insecurity, impulsivity, irritability, and being withdrawn seldom were parented with the authoritative style. They were, according to Hetherington (1993),

> more likely to be exposed to neglecting, disengaged, or ineffectively authoritarian parenting styles. One of the most notable characteristics of these children is that they had no relationship with a close, caring adult either within or outside of the home. (p. 52)

Behavioral problems were directly related to parenting approaches and continued conflict between the parents. Hetherington further summarized her findings:

> Generally, from first grade on, an authoritative environment both in the home and in the school was associated with greater achievement and social competence and fewer problem behaviors in children. These effects were most marked for children in divorced and remarried families, for children in nondivorced families with high levels of marital conflict, and for children who reported high levels of negative stressful life events. (pp. 54-55)

Such inadequate and detrimental parenting, of course, is not restricted to divorced and single or divorced and remarried parents.

In one small exploratory study, "successful" single parents were assessed according to Curran's (1983) model of family health. Seven central themes characterized their successful parenting: acceptance of the responsibilities and challenges presented in single-parent families; prioritization of the parental role; employment of consistent, non-punitive discipline; emphasis on open communication; ability to foster individuality within a supportive family unit; recognition of need for self-nurturance; and development and maintenance of family rituals and traditions (Olson & Haynes, 1993). These are consistent with the authoritative parenting style.

INTRAPARENTAL CONFLICT

Persistent conflict between parents undermines the healthy functioning and well-being of children (e.g., Furstenberg & Cherlin, 1991; Hetherington, 1993; Johnston, Kline, & Tschann, 1989). Thus, although divorce poses challenges to parents who want to ensure and enhance children's healthy and positive development and well-being, it can benefit children by removing them "from stressful or acrimonious family relationships" (Hetherington, Stanley-Hagan, & Anderson, 1989, p. 310).

Children who have experienced divorce or divorce and remarriage but relatively little intraparental conflict show higher levels of well-being than do children who have not experienced such marital transitions but have been exposed to family strife. For example, Amato, Loomis, and Booth (1995) noted,

> It is often claimed that children are better off in single-parent families than in two-parent families marked by high levels of discord. Our study provides the strongest evidence yet in support of this notion. Divorce can remove a child from a hostile, dysfunctional, and perhaps abusive environment. (p. 913; see also Amato & Keith, 1991)

Indeed, various researchers conclude that it is intraparental conflict that most adversely affects children in divorce and that to more fully understand the effects of divorce on children will require more systematic attention to the predivorce family (e.g., Amato et al., 1995; Block et al., 1986, 1988). More specifically, Amato and Booth (1996, p. 357) found, in their analysis of longitudinal data from a nationally representative sample, that the *predivorce* quality of the parents' marriage is associated with postdivorce parent-child relationships; parental affection for children, particularly the father's; and children's behavioral problems. As these researchers observed, their findings are consistent with other recent studies (e.g., Block et al., 1988; Cherlin et al., 1991; Furstenberg & Teitler, 1994; Shaw et al., 1993). At the same time, their conclusions have particular value in that the sample population is representative of the national population. These findings "suggest that at least some of the problems in children's behavior and in parent-child relationships observed after divorce are present many years before marital disruption" (Amato & Booth, 1996, p. 363).

Because many marriages that end in dissolutions have high levels of conflict, postdivorce dissension can be an extension of established routines (see Ambert, 1988). Additionally, conflict often is exacerbated initially by separation (Chase-Lansdale & Hetherington, 1990) and not infrequently involves violence (Arendell, 1995; Kurz, 1995; Mahoney, 1991). The persistence of or increase in marital conflict into the postseparation circumstance further undermines the stability of children's situations and impairs their abilities to adapt to family transitions while undermining parenting effectiveness.

Remarriage

Research attention to stepparenting has increased dramatically in the past 15 years as the divorce and remarriage rates have escalated and remain high. For instance, Coleman and Ganong (1990, p. 925) noted that there were only a handful of studies published prior to 1980 but more than 200 during the decade of the 1980s. The increased attention has continued into the 1990s (e.g., see Booth & Dunn, 1994).

The circumstances leading to the formation of stepfamilies vary. They especially include the marriages of formerly unmarried teen mothers, widowed parents, and divorced ones. Prior to the early 1970s, the death of a spouse was the principal prior circumstance leading a parent to remarry, not divorce as is now the case. Even just among those formed by divorced parents, stepparent families are diverse in composition. For instance, Dunn and Booth (1994, p. 220) noted that two scholars, Burgoyne and Clark (1982), had identified 26 different types. Children may reside with either a stepmother or a stepfather, although the latter is far more common given the preponderance of mother custody. Or, children may have a non-residential stepparent. Additionally, children may have stepsiblings and half-siblings with whom they may or may not share residences. More specifically,

> somewhere between two-fifths and half of these children [whose parents remarry] will have a stepsibling, although most will not typically live with him or her. And for more than a quarter, a half-sibling will be born within four years. Thus, about two-thirds of children living in step-families will have either half-siblings or stepsiblings. (Furstenberg, 1990, p. 154)

Depending on their cognitive developmental stage, children construct family relatedness with stepsiblings and half-siblings in various ways, adding to the complexity in understanding family relationships (Bernstein, 1988). Ahrons and Wallisch (1987a) posited a scenario of family complexity:

> Hypothetically, at three years postdivorce, the binuclear family system [that formed by the biological parents having separate residences] could include two parents, two stepparents, four sets of grandparents, and five sets of children (the children of the formerly married pair, each new partner's children from a first marriage [stepsiblings to the biological children], and two sets of new children of the remarried pairs [half-siblings of the biological children]. (p. 231)

The amount of domestic life and parenting shared with nonresidential family members can range greatly between family units and across time for particular children. Variations among stepfamilies occur, moreover, not only in their configurations but also in their functioning.

The remarriage of a divorced parent and creation of a stepfamily entail numerous disruptions and transitions. Altered by the entry of another adult into the family is the family system established by the custodial parent and children following divorce. As Cherlin and Furstenberg (1994) wrote in their recent overview of the stepparenting literature,

> After divorce, single parents and their children establish, often with some difficulty, agreed-upon rules and new daily schedules. They establish ways of relating to each other that may differ from the pre-disruption

days. . . . Put another way, single parents and children create a new family system. Then, into that system, with its shared history, intensive relationships, and agreed-upon roles, walks a stepparent. It can be difficult for the members of the stepfamily household to adjust to his or her presence. (p. 370)

Multiple relationships are at issue when a man marries a divorced mother, even if the new stepfather has no biological offspring of his own. These include the new stepfather's relationship with his wife, hers with her children, his own developing one with her children, the biological father's with his children, and the biological father's with his former wife as well as with the stepfather. If the new stepfather has offspring, the numbers and potential complexities of kin relationships increase dramatically. If he and his wife conceive children of their own, the relationships are further compounded. Adding to the problems of achieving a smoothly functioning stepfamily, a stepparent often enters a family unit expecting to be a "healer," intending to pull the family out of its supposed postdivorce disarray and into harmony and well-being (Papernow, 1988). These intentions, and even the perception of family chaos, often are unrealistic.

Children, and sometimes the custodial parent, often resist a newcomer's efforts to exert authority and alter the existing family dynamics (Hetherington, 1993; Hetherington et al., 1992). Disruption is not limited to the relationship between the stepparent and stepchildren; it can involve the relationship between the custodial parent and children as well. Conflict within the original unit often increases (Brooks-Gunn, 1994, p. 179). Other problems may include a decline in parental supervision and responsibility as the parent divides her time between a new spouse and her children, shifting alliances between family members, and open tension and disputes between children and stepparent and between children of the original unit (e.g., Brooks-Gunn, 1994, p. 170; Hetherington, 1993; Hetherington et al., 1992). Nor are interpersonal tensions and difficulties limited to the residential unit. They may involve the noncustodial parent, his spouse, or other relatives, such as grandparents, aunts, or uncles. Dealing with the larger family context is an ongoing, lengthy, and demanding process (Mills, 1988; more generally, see Beer, 1988).

Some stepparents respond to children's resistance by becoming more authoritarian and dogmatic. Others, on the other hand, withdraw emotionally and cease their attempts to forge intimate relationships. They move to "exhibiting little warmth, control, or monitoring. [These] stepparents are not necessarily negative, they are just distant" (Brooks-Gunn, 1994, p. 179; Hetherington, 1993). Whatever the strategy assumed by stepparents, it has direct impacts on the home ambiance and parent-child relationships. In turn, these all affect the interactional dynamics between spouses; the effects become circular and interactive.

As with other kinds of family transitions, restabilization often follows the initial disequilibrium experienced by the newly formed stepfamily (Ahrons & Wallisch, 1987a; Hetherington, 1993; Hetherington et al., 1992). The successful integration of a stepparent into a family is a gradual process, sometimes taking years (e.g., Papernow, 1988, p. 60). Not all families reach such a level; indeed, a large number of stepfamilies dissolve through divorce long before they ever approach the place of becoming smoothly functioning households.

STEPPARENT RELATIONSHIPS AND ROLES

Few social guidelines are available to help shape the stepparent family or stepparent role (Gross, 1987; Marsiglio, 1992). Cherlin's (1978) earlier characterization of remarriage as an incomplete institution remains relevant with respect to the family created by remarriage.[5] That is, for the most part, persons coming together into a stepfamily situation—bringing with them particular marital and familial histories, resources, relationships, and expectations—must forge their way into largely undefined and unfamiliar territory. Moreover, many of the cultural images of stepfamilies and stepparents are negative. Thus, the newly formed family created by remarriage of one or both adults is truly emergent, dynamic, and processual. The newly married couple is motivated to make a workable family system, but their hopes and intentions sometimes are foisted on recalcitrant or reluctant offspring of one adult or the other (or both). The new family is overlaid onto an earlier one. Spanier (1988) summarized the situation facing newly formed stepfamilies:

Where but in stepfamilies do we find children and adults, once strangers, becoming relatives without the customary trappings of human development? What stepfamilies have in common is the challenge of working as a social system, sometimes against difficult odds, often in the wake of decidedly unpleasant remnants of a previous relationship, usually within a framework of relocation, and almost always without an accepted vocabulary for describing the participants in relation to each other. (p. ix)

The roles and positions of stepparents vary widely. Some stepparents become parent-like figures, establishing and maintaining deep emotional bonds with the children of their spouses. Stepfathers who live with their biological children as well as stepchildren are more likely to report having a consistently positive father-like role with their stepchildren than are those who live only with the latter (Marsiglio, 1992, p. 209). Some stepparents take on the activities and status of more distant relatives such as remote uncles, aunts, or cousins. Adult friends to children, ranging from distant to close, are roles and relationships assumed by some stepparents. Some are like adult boarders in the home with respect to the children, having a relationship (in this case intimate) with the other adult—the spouse—but limited involvement with or affection for the children and assuming basically no responsibility for their care and upbringing (e.g., Ahrons & Wallisch, 1987a; Beer, 1988).

The stepparent's initiation of a positive relationship is crucial. Cherlin and Furstenberg (1994) concluded, from their review of the research, that the primary influence on the character of the stepparent-stepchild relationship is the effort made by the stepparent to forge kin-like relations: "In all cases, how much like a family member a stepparent becomes depends directly on his or her efforts to develop a close relationship with stepchildren" (p. 360). Yet the stepparent role must be negotiated and finessed, all within the context of a preexisting family system and history and the presence and approval or disapproval of the primary parent as well as of the nonresidential parent. The stepparent alone cannot create the kind of familial relationships he or she desires or holds as the ideal.

It appears to be easier to be a stepfather than a stepmother (Ambert, 1989; Cherlin & Furstenberg, 1994, p. 371; White, 1994). Several issues contribute to this difference. One is that children seem more willing to accept substitute fathers than substitute mothers (Furstenberg & Cherlin, 1991), perhaps being influenced by the cultural norms shaping the different statuses and roles for men and women in families. Also, children's attachments to mothers typically are stronger than those to fathers, and so they may feel more loyalty conflicts with respect to the relationship with stepmothers. Women typically are more involved in parenting activities, whether as biological parents or as stepparents, and so are more likely to elicit resistance from stepchildren. Residential stepmothers also are more likely to be in relatively more unique circumstances than are stepfathers because unusual circumstances often are present in paternal custody arrangements. Irrespective of such factors, nonresidential mothers tend to have higher levels of parental involvement than do nonresidential fathers. Thus, residential stepmothers are more likely to have to contend with the continued presence and influence of children's biological mothers as the family context extends dynamically beyond the walls of the immediate residence. Stepfathers, although typically less involved (and perhaps because of this lesser involvement), are more satisfied with their roles overall than are stepmothers (Ahrons & Wallisch, 1987a). Stepparenting is more satisfying with live-in children than with live-out ones. The quality of marriage for stepmothers is more pleasing when the children reside with them and their fathers, but stepchildren's residence is not a factor in marital satisfaction for stepfathers. Stepparenting probably is more detrimental to women than to men because of the inequitable division of domestic labor (Ambert, 1989).

Factors identified as influencing the shape of the evolving stepparent-stepchild relationship include the child's ages, his or her relationship with the nonresidential parent, and the spousal relationship between the stepparent and custodial parent. Apparently not influencing the quality of the stepfather-stepchild relationship, specifically, are the sex of the child, whether or not the mother has actually married her partner, the amount of time that has passed between the wife's (or partner's) previous relationship and theirs, or the length of their relationship (Marsiglio, 1992).

With respect to the significance of the child's age, specifically, the younger the child, the more likely he or she is to consider the stepparent to be a "real" parent (Furstenberg & Teitler, 1994; Marsiglio,

1992). If a stepparent enters the family after the child is beyond preschool age, then the likelihood of the development of strong emotional bonds is relatively low. Additionally, younger children appear to be integrated into and to accept the extended kin networks formed by remarriage. This is not typically the case for adolescents (Furstenberg, 1990). The more frequently the child sees the non-residential parent, the less likely the establishment of a parental-like relationship between child and stepparent.

Another factor in the relationship between stepparent and stepchild is the quality of the spousal relationship. "The more satisfactory that relationship, the more authority the stepparent has to take on a parental role" (Cherlin & Furstenberg, 1994, p. 367). At the same time, "remarriage and stepparenthood are not equivalent" (Brooks-Gunn, 1994, p. 179), and the quality of the marriage is not an independent determinant of the quality of the stepparent-stepchild relationship. Finally, as Cherlin and Furstenberg (1994) reported, there probably is individual variation depending on the child's temperament: "Some children may be more welcoming to new parents than others. So there may be differences in the quality of relationships among children in the same family" (p. 367). Papernow (1988) noted that not all stepparent-stepchild relationships are equal: "Some children may fully engage while others may not" (p. 78; see also Ahrons & Wallisch, 1987a).

Although beneficial to residential family members when step-parents establish warm and close parental-like relationships with the children, the consequences for the father-child relationship are not sanguine. Nonresidential fathers' involvement often decreases when stepfathers live with their children. For example, Seltzer and Bianchi (1988), addressing noncustodial fathers specifically, concluded,

> Our findings suggest that contemporary American society constrains children to two or fewer parents. Even children who live apart from biological parents, and know for certain that their absent parent is still alive, are unlikely to maintain ties with their parent when an alternative step-parent, adoptive parent, or other adult caretaker is available within the child's own household.... Non-custodial parents discard ties to their biological children with divorce, and the ties are replaced through remarriage. Children alternate between having one and two parents. (p. 674; see also Furstenberg & Cherlin, 1991)

Clearly, many fathers' relationships with their children and their levels of parental affection are adversely affected by divorce (e.g., Amato & Booth, 1996; Booth & Amato, 1994; White, 1992, 1994). What is an already tenuous parental relationship for many fathers is exacerbated by a mother's remarriage. Men seem to be engaging in *serial fatherhood*, assuming some parental responsibilities for the children of the women with whom they live and then discontinuing most, if not all, of those activities upon separation, even if those children are their biological offspring (Arendell, 1995; Furstenberg, 1988).

What remains the most viable relationship throughout various parental marital transitions is the bond between children and the primary parent or, in those rare cases in which both parents are integrally involved in parenting, between children and both biological parents. By contrast, the kinship bonds between stepparents and stepchildren are fragile, less enduring, and not as significant (Kurdek & Fine, 1993; White, 1994; see also Cherlin & Furstenberg, 1994, p. 375). Moreover, the emotional bonds between stepparents and stepchildren, for the most part, do not endure when stepchildren become adults as they do between custodial parents and adult children (White, 1994; see also Aquilino, 1994).

CHILD OUTCOMES

Findings regarding the effects of parental remarriage on children are mixed. Some evidence suggests that children in stepfamilies are worse off than children in single-parent families, with both being somewhat worse off than children in intact families as long as they are in low-conflict families (Amato & Keith, 1991, p. 37). Thus, in contrast to earlier arguments, these data suggest that children are not necessarily better off with parental remarriage. The prior argument was based primarily on two issues. One was the probable improvement in overall standard of living upon the mother's remarriage. The second assumption was that the restoration of a two-parent household and the presence of an adult male as a father figure, in and of themselves, enhanced children's well-being. But these changes have not proven to have the inevitable positive effects expected (e.g., Cherlin & Furstenberg, 1994).

Other research concludes that children in stepfamilies are similar to children in single-parent families on all measures of well-being and behavior (e.g., Brooks-Gunn, 1994; Kurdek, 1994). In their review, Cherlin and Furstenberg (1994) asserted,

> Only one finding is well-established concerning the long-term effects on children of having lived in a stepfamily household. Children in stepfamily households—particularly girls—leave their households at an earlier age than do children in single-parent households or in two-parent households. They leave earlier to marry; and they also leave earlier to establish independent households prior to marrying. (p. 374; see also White, 1992, 1994)

By contrast, some data suggest that parental remarriage benefits children in the longer term. "The findings of our study suggest that stable maternal remarriage is positive for both sons and daughters of divorce, but that the benefit becomes apparent only later in life as children of divorce explore young adult relationships" (Bolgar et al., 1995, p. 148).

Parental remarriage initially results in a deterioration of children's emotional well-being, particularly among early adolescents (Hetherington, 1993). Based on data from the National Survey of Children, when children enter stepfamilies, they show a diminished ability to concentrate, become withdrawn, and express unhappiness. Boys exhibit restless behavior (Baydar, 1988, p. 976). Of crucial importance, however, most children's negative responses are temporary (e.g., Chase-Lansdale & Hetherington, 1990; Hetherington, 1993). Furthermore, stepparents can contribute significantly to children's development and well-being, both in their direct relationships with the offspring of their spouses and by providing support to their spouses in their parenting (e.g., Papernow, 1988).

Crucial to children's overall well-being and development in remarriage and stepparent families, as in divorced and intact families as well, is the *quality* of parenting:

> In fact, few differences emerge between children living continuously with both biological parents and either children living with a singly divorced mother or children living in a stepfather family. These findings lead to the plausible conclusion that what negatively affects children's

well-being is not so much the kind of family structure in which they happen to reside, but the history of the quality and consistency of the parenting they receive. (Kurdek, 1994, p. 38)

Growing evidence indicates, not surprisingly, that children are most negatively impacted by multiple divorces. In these situations, again, it is the quality and consistency of parenting that are most significant.

Conclusion

In conclusion, a sizable proportion of American children will experience their parents' divorce. The majority of these children will be parented predominantly by one parent, not by both parents. Many of these children also will experience the formation of a stepparent family when a parent remarries. In many families, both parents will remarry, resulting in situations where children have both a live-in and a live-out stepparent. And numerous children will experience another parental divorce. Children, then, are experiencing multiple transitions in the composition and arrangements of their families. Current evidence indicates that the vast majority of children adjust to these changes successfully. What is most crucial in children's well-being and positive outcomes, according to a growing body of research, is the quality and constancy of the parenting by the primary parent. Experiencing relatively low intraparental and other family conflict is crucial for children's adjustment to changing circumstances and positive development.

Notes

1. Importantly, and often overlooked in the literature, families affected by divorce, and their styles of parenting and the issues confronting them, are distinctive in numerous ways from those of single-parent families in which the parent, usually the mother, is a never-married parent. The focus in this chapter is specifically on the parenting of dependent children in families experiencing divorce and/or remarriage.

2. For an exception, see Kurz (1995). Her study focuses specifically on mothers but involves a representative sample from the Philadelphia area, and she pays particular attention to variations by race and class.

3. See Chapter 3, Taylor's contribution to this volume, for details regarding temporal changes in these patterns and variations by race and ethnicity.

4. *Custodial* and *residential* parent are used interchangeably here, as are *noncustodial* and *nonresidential* parent. See also Maccoby and Mnookin (1992) and Mnookin et al. (1990).

5. Chambers (1984), among others, analyzed the extensive legal ambiguity surrounding stepparents' rights and obligations in American law and culture more broadly.

References

Ahrons, C. R. (1983). Predictors of parental involvement postdivorce: Mothers' and fathers' perceptions. *Journal of Divorce, 6*(3), 55-59.

Ahrons, C. R., & Wallisch, L. (1987a). Parenting in the binuclear family relationships between biological and stepparents. In K. Pasley & M. Ihinger-Tallman (Eds.), *Remarriage and stepparenting: Current research and theory* (pp. 225-256). New York: Guilford.

Ahrons, C. R., & Wallisch, L. (1987b). The relationship between former spouses. In D. Perlman & S. Duck (Eds.), *Intimate relationships: Development, dynamics, and deterioration* (pp. 269-296). Newbury Park, CA: Sage.

Allen, K. R. (1993). The dispassionate discourse of children's adjustment to divorce. *Journal of Marriage and the Family, 55*, 46-50.

Amato, P. R. (1994). Life-span adjustment of children to their parents' divorce. *The Future of Children: Children and Divorce, 4*(1), 143-164.

Amato, P. R., & Booth, A. (1996). A prospective study of divorce and parent-child relationships. *Journal of Marriage and the Family, 58*, 356-365.

Amato, P. R., & Keith, B. (1991). Parental divorce and the well-being of children: A meta-analysis. *Psychological Bulletin, 11*, 26-46.

Amato, P. R., Loomis, L. S., & Booth, A. (1995). Parental divorce, marital conflict, and offspring well-being during early adulthood. *Social Forces, 73*, 895-915.

Ambert, A. M. (1988). Relationship between ex-spouses: Individual and dyadic perspectives. *Journal of Social and Personal Relationships, 5*, 327-346.

Ambert, A.-M. (1989). *Ex-spouses and new spouses: A study of relationships*. Greenwich, CT: JAI.

Aquilino, W. S. (1994). Impact of childhood family disruption on young adults' relationship with parents. *Journal of Marriage and the Family, 56*, 296-315.

Arditti, J. (1995). Noncustodial parents: Emergent issues of diversity and process. *Marriage and Family Review, 20*(1-2), 283-304.

Arendell, T. (1986). *Mothers and divorce: Legal, economic, and social dilemmas*. Berkeley: University of California Press.

Arendell, T. (1995). *Fathers and divorce*. Thousand Oaks, CA: Sage.

Arendell, T. (1996). *Co-parenting: A review of the literature*. Unpublished manuscript, National Center on Fathers and Families, Philadelphia.

Bane, M. J. (1976). *Here to stay: American families in the twentieth century*. New York: Basic Books.

Baumrind, D. (1971). Current patterns of parental authority. *Developmental Psychology Monographs, 4*, 1-103.

Baydar, N. (1988). Effects of parental separation and reentry into union on the emotional well-being of children. *Journal of Marriage and the Family, 50,* 967-981.

Beer, W. R. (Ed.). (1988). *Relative strangers: Studies of stepfamilies processes.* Totowa, NJ: Rowman & Littlefield.

Benjamin, M., & Irving, H. H. (1990). Comparison of the experience of satisfied and dissatisfied shared parents. *Journal of Divorce and Remarriage, 14,* 43-61.

Bernstein, A. C. (1988). Unraveling the tangles: Children's understanding of stepfamily kinship. In W. Beer (Ed.), *Relative strangers* (pp. 83-111). Totowa, NJ: Rowman & Littlefield.

Blankenhorn, D. (1995). *Fatherless America: Confronting our most urgent social problem.* New York: Basic Books.

Block, J. H., Block, J., & Gjerde, P. F. (1986). Personality of children prior to divorce: A prospective study. *Child Development, 57,* 827-840.

Block, J. H., Block, J., & Gjerde, P. F. (1988). Parental functioning and the home environment in families of divorce: Prospective and concurrent analyses. *Journal of American Academy of Child and Adolescent Psychiatry, 27,* 207-213.

Bohannon, P. (1970). *Divorce and after.* Garden City, NY: Doubleday.

Bolgar, R., Sweig-Frank, H., & Paris, J. (1995). Childhood antecedents of interpersonal problems in young adult children of divorce. *Journal of the American Academy of Child and Adolescent Psychiatry, 34*(2), 143-150.

Booth, A., & Amato, P. R. (1994). Parental marital quality, divorce and relations with offspring in young adulthood. *Journal of Marriage and the Family, 56,* 21-34.

Booth, A., & Dunn, J. (Eds.). (1994). *Stepfamilies: Who benefits? Who does not?* Mahwah, NJ: Lawrence Erlbaum.

Brooks-Gunn, J. (1994). Research on stepparenting families: Integrating disciplinary approaches and informing policy. In A. Booth & J. Dunn (Eds.), *Stepfamilies: Who benefits? Who does not?* (pp. 167-204). Mahwah, NJ: Lawrence Erlbaum.

Burgoyne, J., & Clark, D. (1982). Parenting in stepfamilies. In R. Chester, P. Diggory, & M. Sutherland (Eds.), *Changing patterns of child-bearing and child-rearing* (pp. 133-147). London: Academic Press.

Chambers, D. (1984). Rethinking the substantive rules for custody disputes in divorce. *Michigan Law Review, 88,* 477-569.

Chase-Lansdale, P. L., & Hetherington, E. M. (1990). The impact of divorce on life-span development: Short and long term effects. In D. Featherman & R. Lerner (Eds.), *Life span development and behavior* (Vol. 10, pp. 105-150). Hillsdale, NJ: Lawrence Erlbaum.

Cherlin, A. (1978). Remarriage: An incomplete institution. *American Journal of Sociology, 84,* 634-650.

Cherlin, A. J., & Furstenberg, F. F., Jr. (1994). Stepfamilies in the United States: A reconsideration. *Annual Review of Sociology, 20,* 359-381.

Cherlin, A. J., Furstenberg, F. F., Chase-Lansdale, P. L., Kiernan, K. E., Robins, P. K., Morrison, D. R., & Teitler, J. O. (1991). Longitudinal studies of effects of divorce on children in Great Britian and the United States. *Science, 252,* 1386-1389.

Coleman, M., & Ganong, L. H. (1990). Remarriage and stepfamily research in the 1980s: Increased interest in an old family form. *Journal of Marriage and the Family, 52,* 925-940.

Cowan, C., & Cowan, P. (1988). Who does what when partners become parents: Implications for men, women and marriage. *Marriage and Family Review, 12*(3-4), 105-131.

Crnic, K. A., & Booth, C. C. (1991). Mothers' and fathers' perceptions of daily hassles of parenting across early childhood. *Journal of Marriage and the Family, 53,* 1042-1050.

Curran, D. J. (1983). *Traits of a healthy family.* New York: Ballantine Books.

Donnelly, D., & Finkelhor, D. (1992). Does equality in custody arrangement improve the parent-child relationship? *Journal of Marriage and the Family, 54,* 837-845.

Donnelly, D., & Finkelhor, D. (1993). Who has joint custody? Class differences in the determination of custody arrangements. *Family Relations, 42,* 57-60.

Dunn, J., & Booth, A. (1994). Stepfamilies: An overview. In A. Booth & J. Dunn (Eds.), *Stepfamilies: Who benefits? Who does not?* (pp. 217-224). Mahwah, NJ: Lawrence Erlbaum.

Ellwood, M. S., & Stolberg, A. L. (1993). The effects of family composition, family health, parenting behavior and environmental stress on children's divorce adjustment. *Journal of Child and Family Studies, 2*(1), 23-36.

Emery, R. (1988). *Marriage, divorce, and children's adjustment.* Newbury Park, CA: Sage.

Fish, L. S., New, R. S., & Van Cleave, N. J. (1992). Shared parenting in dual-income families. *American Journal of Orthopsychiatry, 62,* 83-92.

Fishel, A. H., & Scanzoni, J. (1989). An exploratory study of the post-divorce coparental relationship. *Journal of Divorce, 13*(2), 95-119.

Frey, R. G. (1986). Being a divorced father as primary parent: A phenomenological investigation. *Conciliation Courts Review, 24*(1), 71-78.

Furstenberg, F. F. (1988). Good dads—bad dads: Two faces of fatherhood. In A. Cherlin (Ed.), *The changing American family and public policy* (pp. 193-209). Washington, DC: Urban Institute.

Furstenberg, F. F. (1990). Coming of age in a changing family system. In S. Feldman & G. Elliot (Eds.), *At the threshold: The developing adolescent* (pp. 147-170). Cambridge, MA: Harvard University Press.

Furstenberg, F. F., & Cherlin, A. (1991). *Divided families: What happens to children when parents part.* Cambridge, MA: Harvard University Press.

Furstenberg, F. F., Morgan, S. P., & Allison, P. (1987). Parental participation and children's well-being after marital dissolution. *American Sociological Review, 52,* 695- 701.

Furstenberg, F., & Teitler, J. O. (1994). Reconsidering the effects of marital disruption: What happens to the children of divorce in early adulthood. *Journal of Family Issues, 15,* 173-190.

Furukawa, S. (1994). The diverse living arrangements of children: Summer 1991. In U.S. Bureau of the Census, *Current Population Reports* (Series P70-38). Washington, DC: Government Printing Office.

Garasky, S. (1995). The effects of family structure on educational attainment: Do the effects vary by the age of the child? *American Journal of Economics and Sociology, 54*(1), 89-106.

Glick, P. C., & Lin, S.-L. (1986). Recent changes in divorce and remarriage. *Journal of Marriage and the Family, 48,* 737-747.

Gottman, J. M. (1994). *What predicts divorce? The relationship between marital processes and marital outcomes.* Hillsdale, NJ: Lawrence Erlbaum.

Greif, G. (1987). Single fathers and noncustodial mothers: The social worker's helping role. *Journal of Independent Social Work, 1*(3), 59-69.

Greif, G. (1990). Split custody: A beginning understanding. *Journal of Divorce, 13*(3), 15-26.

Greif, G. L., & DeMaris, A. (1990). Single fathers with custody. *Families in Society,* *71*(5), 259-266.

Gross, P. (1987). Defining post-divorce remarriage families: A typology based on the subjective perceptions of children. *Journal of Divorce, 10,* 205-217.

Herrerías, C. (1995). Noncustodial mothers following divorce. *Marriage and Family Review, 20*(1/2), 233-255.

Hetherington, E. M. (1987). Family relations six years after divorce. In K. Pasley & M. Ihinger-Tallman (Eds.), *Remarriage and stepparenting: Current research and theory* (pp. 185-205). New York: Guilford.

Hetherington, E. M. (1988). Parents, children, and siblings six years after divorce. In R. Hinde & J. Stevenson-Hinde (Eds.), *Relationships within families* (pp. 311-331). Cambridge, UK: Clarendon.

Hetherington, E. M. (1992). Coping with marital transitions: A family systems perspective. *Monographs of the Society for Research in Child Development, 57*(2-3, Serial No. 227), 1-14.

Hetherington, E. M. (1993). An overview of the Virginia Longitudinal Study of Divorce and Remarriage with a focus on early adolescence. *Journal of Family Psychology, 7,* 39-56.

Hetherington, E. M., & Clingempeel, W. G., with Anderson, E., Deal, J., Hagan, M. S., Hollier, A., & Lindner, M. (1992). Coping with marital transitions: A family systems perspective. *Monographs of the Society for Research in Child Development, 57*(2-3, Serial No. 227), 1-14.

Hetherington, E., Cox, M., & Cox, R. (1982). Effects of parents and children. In M. Lamb (Ed.), *Nontraditional families: Parenting and child development* (pp. 233-288). Hillsdale, NJ: Lawrence Erlbaum.

Hetherington, E. M., & Hagan, M. S. (1986). Divorced fathers: Stress, coping and adjustment. In M. E. Lamb (Ed.), *The father's role: Applied perspectives* (pp. 103-134). New York: John Wiley.

Hetherington, E. M., Stanley-Hagan, M., & Anderson, E. R. (1989). Marital transitions: A child's perspective. *American Psychologist, 44,* 303-312.

Hoffman, S. D., & Duncan, G. D. (1988). What are the consequences of divorce? *Demography, 23,* 641-645.

Holden, K., & Smock, P. J. (1991). The economic costs of marital dissolution: Why do women bear a disproportionate cost? *Annual Review of Sociology, 17,* 51-78.

Johnston, J. R., Kline, M., & Tschann, J. M. (1989). Ongoing postdivorce conflict in families contesting custody: Do joint custody and frequent access help? *American Journal of Orthopsychiatry, 59,* 576-592.

Kellan, S. (1995). Child custody and support. *Congressional Quarterly Researcher, 5*(2), 25-48.

Kitson, G. C., with Holmes, W. M. (1992). *Portrait of divorce: Adjustment to marital breakdown.* New York: Guilford.

Kitson, G., & Morgan, L. (1990). The multiple consequences of divorce: A decade review. *Journal of Marriage and the Family, 52,* 913-924.

Krause, H. D. (1990). Child support reassessed: Limits of private responsibility and the public interest. In S. Sugarman & H. Kay (Eds.), *Divorce reform at the crossroads* (pp. 166-190). New Haven, CT: Yale University Press.

Kurdek, L. A. (1994). Remarriages and stepfamilies are not inherently problematic. In A. Booth & J. Dunn (Eds.), *Stepfamilies: Who benefits? Who does not?* (pp. 37-44). Mahwah, NJ: Lawrence Erlbaum.

Kurdek, L. A., & Fine, M. A. (1993). The relation between family structure and young adolescents' appraisals of family climate and parenting behavior. *Journal of Family Issues, 14*, 279-290.

Kurz, D. (1995). *For better or for worse: Mothers confront divorce.* New York: Routledge.

LaRossa, R., & LaRossa, M. M. (1989). Baby care: Fathers vs. mothers. In B. Risman & P. Schwartz (Eds.), *Gender in intimate relationships: A microstructural approach* (pp. 138-154). Belmont, CA: Wadsworth.

Maccoby, E. E., Depner, C. E., & Mnookin, R. H. (1990). Coparenting in the second year after divorce. In J. Folberg (Ed.), *Joint custody and shared parenting* (pp. 132-155). New York: Guilford.

Maccoby, E. E., & Mnookin, R. H. (1992). *Dividing the child: Social and legal dilemnas of custody.* Cambridge, MA: Harvard University Press.

Mahoney, M. R. (1991). Legal images of battered women: Redefining the issue of separation. *Michigan Law Review, 90*(1), 1-89.

Marsiglio, W. (1991). Paternal engagement activities with minor children. *Journal of Marriage and the Family, 53*, 973-986.

Marsiglio, W. (1992). Stepfathers with minor children living at home. *Journal of Family Issues, 13*, 195-214.

Martin, T. C., & Bumpass, L. L. (1989). Recent trends in marital disruption. *Demography, 26*(1), 37-51.

May, L., & Strikwerda, R. (1992a). Fatherhood and nurturance. In L. May & R. Strikwerda (Eds.), *Rethinking masculinity: Philosophical explorations in light of feminism* (pp. 75-92). Lanham, MD: Rowman & Littlefield.

May, L., & Strikwerda, R. (Eds.). (1992b). *Rethinking masculinity: Philosophical explorations in light of feminism.* Lanham, MD: Rowman & Littlefield.

McFarlane, A. H., Bellissimo, A., & Norman, G. R. (1995). Family structure, family functioning and adolescent well-being: The transcendent influence of parental style. *Journal of Child Psychology and Psychiatry and Allied Disciplines, 36*, 847-864.

McLanahan, S., & Sandefur, G. (1994). *Growing up with a single parent: What hurts, what helps.* Cambridge, MA: Harvard University Press.

Mills, D. M. (1988). Stepfamilies in context. In W. Beer (Ed.), *Relative strangers* (pp. 1-29). Totowa, NJ: Rowman & Littlefield.

Mnookin, R., Maccoby, E. E., Albiston, C. R., & Depner, C. E. (1990). Private ordering revisited: What custodial arrangements are parents negotiating? In S. Sugarman & H. H. Kay (Eds.), *Divorce reform at the crossroads* (pp. 37-74). New Haven, CT: Yale University Press.

Morrison, D. R., & Cherlin, A. J. (1995). The divorce process and young children's well-being: A prospective analysis. *Journal of Marriage and the Family, 57*, 800-812.

Olson, M., & Haynes, J. (1993). Successful single parents. *Families in Society: The Journal of Contemporary Human Services, 74*(5), 259-267.

Papernow, P. L. (1988). Stepparent role development: From outsider to intimate. In W. Beer (Ed.), *Relative strangers* (pp. 54-82). Totowa, NJ: Rowman & Littlefield.

Pleck, J. H. (1996, June). *Paternal involvement: Levels, sources, and consequences.* Paper presented at the Co-Parenting Roundtable of the Fathers and Families Roundtable Series sponsored by the National Center on Fathers and Families, Philadelphia.

Popenoe, D. (1988). *Disturbing the nest: Family change and decline in modern societies.* New York: Aldine de Gruyter.

Powell, B., & Downey, D. B. (1995, August). *Well-being of adolescents in single-parent households: The case of the same-sex hypothesis.* Paper presented at the annual meeting of the American Sociological Association, Washington, DC.

Riessman, C. K. (1990). *Divorce talk: Women and men make sense of personal relationships.* New Brunswick, NJ: Rutgers University Press.

Risman, B. (1989). Can men "mother"? Life as a single father. In B. Risman & P. Schwartz (Eds.), *Gender in intimate relationships* (pp. 155-164). Belmont, CA: Wadsworth.

Russell, G. (1983). *The changing roles of fathers.* St. Lucia, Queensland: University of Queensland Press.

Sahler, O. J. (1983). Adolescent mothers: How nurturant is their parenting? In E. McAnarney (Ed.), *Premature adolescent pregnancy and parenthood* (pp. 219-230). New York: Grune & Stratton.

Sanderson, J. (1985). When daddy can't be daddy anymore. In F. Baumli (Ed.), *Men freeing men* (pp. 163-202). Jersey City, NJ: New Atlantis.

Scoon-Rogers, L., & Lester, G. H. (1995). Child support for custodial mothers and fathers: 1991. In U.S. Bureau of the Census, *Current population reports* (Series P60-187). Washington, DC: Government Printing Office.

Seltzer, J. A. (1991). Relationships between fathers and children who live apart: The father's role after separation. *Journal of Marriage and the Family, 53,* 79-101.

Seltzer, J. A., & Bianchi, S. M. (1988). Children's contact with absent parents. *Journal of Marriage and the Family, 50,* 663-677.

Seltzer, J. A., & Garfinkel, I. (1990). Inequality in divorce settlements: An investigation of property settlements and child support awards. *Social Science Research, 19,* 82-111.

Shaw, D. S., Emery, R. E., & Tuer, M. D. (1993). Parental functioning and children's adjustment in families of divorce: A prospective study. *Journal of Abnormal Child Psychology, 21,* 119-134.

Spanier, G. (1988). Foreword. In W. Beer (Ed.), *Relative strangers* (pp. ix-xi). Totowa, NJ: Rowman & Littlefield.

Steinberg, L., Elmen, J. D., & Mounts, N. S. (1989). Authoritative parenting, psychosocial maturity, and academic success among adolescents. *Child Development, 60,* 1424-1436.

Teachman, J. (1991). Contributions to children by divorced fathers. *Social Problems, 38,* 358-371.

Thomson, E., McLanahan, S. S., & Curtin, R. B. (1992). Family structure, gender, and parental socialization. *Journal of Marriage and the Family, 54,* 368-378.

Thorne, B. (1993). Feminism and the family: Two decades of thought. In B. Thorne & M. Yalom (Eds.), *Rethinking the family: Some feminist questions* (2nd ed., pp. 3-30). New York: Longman.

Tronto, J. (1989). Women and caring: What can feminists learn about morality from caring? In A. Jaggar & S. Bordo (Eds.), *Gender/body/knowledge: Feminist reconstructions of being and knowing* (pp. 172-187). New Brunswick, NJ: Rutgers University Press.

U.S. Bureau of the Census. (1995a). Child support for custodial mothers and fathers: 1991. In *Current population reports* (Series P60-187). Washington, DC: Government Printing Office.

U.S. Bureau of the Census. (1995b). *Statistical abstract of the United States, 1994.* Washington, DC: Government Printing Office.

Wallerstein, J., & Blakeslee, S. (1989). *Second chances: Men, women, and children a decade after divorce*. New York: Ticknor & Fields.

Weitzman, L. (1985). *The divorce revolution: The unexpected social and economic consequences for women and children in America*. New York: Free Press.

White, L. K. (1992). The effect of parental divorce and remarriage on parental support for adult children. *Journal of Family Issues, 13*, 234-250.

White, L. K. (1994). Coresidence and leaving home: Young adults and their parents. *Annual Review of Sociology, 20*, 81-102.

7

Lesbian and Gay Families

KATHERINE R. ALLEN

*Lesbian and gay parents essentially reinvent the family as a plu-
ralistic phenomenon. They self-consciously build from the ground
up a variety of family types that don't conform to the traditional
structure. In so doing, they encourage society to ask, "What is a
family?" The question has profound meaning in both the culture at
large and the very heart of each of our intimate lives. It is like a tree
trunk from which many branches extend. What is a mother, a
father, a parent, a sibling? Can a child have two or more mothers or
fathers? Is one more "real" by virtue of biological or legal parent
status? How does society's recognition (or its absence) foster or
impede parent-child relationships? To what extent does the state
shape family life? To what extent can nontraditional families alter
the state's definition of family?* (Benkov, 1994, p. 142)

The families formed by lesbians and gay men provide a unique
opportunity to understand how individuals of all backgrounds
shape and are shaped by the social and historical processes in which
they live. As parents, lesbians and gay men can take little for granted
in their family circumstances because they are constricted legally from
protecting and maintaining their family ties. All their actions on behalf
of family formation and extension must be deliberate.

AUTHOR'S NOTE: I thank Terry Arendell, Judith Stacey, and Tamara J. Stone for their
insightful comments.

At the heart of the matter about lesbian and gay parenting is concern over child outcomes. Until recently, most of the research on this issue has questioned how children will turn out if they have lesbian or gay parents. Despite public and judicial prejudice regarding the potential experience of children reared by lesbian or gay parents, researchers have found that there are no observable negative effects on children. In a review of 12 studies comparing children of lesbian or gay parents to children of heterosexual parents on the issues of gender identity, gender role behavior, and sexual orientation, Patterson (1992) concluded that children's development was not compromised in lesbian or gay families and that children in those families did not differ from children of heterosexual parents. Regarding other child outcomes, empirical research suggests that "children of lesbian and gay parents have normal relationships with peers and that their relationships with adults of both sexes are also satisfactory" (p. 1034).

Instead of such negative outcomes predicted by public sentiment, comparisons between parents who are heterosexual and parents who are gay, as well as ethnographic studies of parenting in lesbian and gay households, suggest more affirmative ways in which to view the effects of being reared by lesbian or gay parents. Researchers cite at least four potential benefits to children reared by lesbian or gay parents. First, children learn to respect, empathize with, and tolerate the multicultural environments in which others live (Laird, 1993; Patterson, 1992; Rafkin, 1990). Second, they have the opportunity to experience flexible interpretations of gendered behavior and the freedom to engage in egalitarian roles in personal and intimate relationships (Blumstein & Schwartz, 1983). Third, they come to understand that families are based not only on biological relationships but, perhaps more so, on love, self-definition, and choice (Cunningham, 1992; Laird, 1993; Weston, 1991). Fourth, with the emergence of intentional and visible gay cultural activities in recent decades, children of lesbian and gay parents observe and experience strong ties in the gay community that have the potential to support and enhance their family relationships (Herdt, 1992; Weston, 1991).

In this chapter, I address the context and experience of parenting in families headed by lesbian or gay adults. This examination is guided by a synthesis of feminist, life course, and postmodern perspectives. These perspectives, taken together, aid in the understanding of parenting as a socially constructed phenomenon. Because of the legal, social, and historical challenges faced by lesbian and gay parents, the families they form call into question the "edifice constructed upon the model of a mother, father, and 2.4 children" (Rubenstein, 1996, p. 340). Lesbian and gay parents challenge the primacy enjoyed by "traditional" heterosexual marriage and parenthood. They reveal, by their innovation in creating and maintaining families that thrive even in a hostile social environment, that parenting is not an essentialistic or inherently natural experience. Lesbian and gay parents exemplify that families are constructed by a variety of biological, adoptive, and chosen kin ties.

Theoretical Perspective

A synthesis of core assumptions from three theoretical frameworks used in family studies guides this examination: feminism, life course, and postmodernism.

A FEMINIST PERSPECTIVE

A feminist perspective sensitizes awareness of the power that exists in social relations and demonstrates how inequities are distributed throughout society according to gender, race, and class (Osmond & Thorne, 1993). Recent analyses reveal that sexual orientation must be considered as another major axis of social stratification. Not just a subset of gender issues, sexual orientation brings unique considerations to the understanding of how individual lives intersect with social-historical processes and structures (Demo & Allen, 1996). For example, Brown (1989) integrated sexual orientation with a feminist perspective on gender, race, and class, thereby proposing a new synthesis of feminist ideas about family diversity.

Brown (1989) identified three aspects of lesbian and gay experience shared by this most diverse of all minority groups: biculturalism, marginality, and normative creativity. First, biculturalism refers to the fact that lesbians and gay men simultaneously live in a heterosexual and gay world. Many gay people have identified as heterosexual or behaved heterosexually at some times in their lives. Like biracial individuals, lesbians and gay men "develop ways to live within this matrix of complexity, to balance and value the differences that lie within" (p. 449). Furthermore, biculturalism is a concept that links gay people to members of other oppressed groups. Peters (1988) described, for example, the dual socialization that black parents provide their children to help them confront institutionalized racism and, at the same time, to become self-sufficient, competent adults.

Second, marginality refers to the awareness of "otherness" experienced by people who are positioned as different from the norm of heterosexuality (Brown, 1989). As described by black and feminist standpoint theorists (see Collins, 1990; Smith, 1987), being an "other" provides a double vision of reality—the capacity to see what is invisible to those with more power in the social system. The norm of heterosexuality is supported by an institutionalized system of oppression—heterosexism—that functions like racism and sexism to provide disproportionate rewards to those who conform to the privileged status of being "white, thin, male, young, heterosexual, christian, and financially secure" (Lorde, 1984, p. 116).

Third, normative creativity refers to the innovative possibilities that derive from being different. "By lacking clear rules about how to be lesbian and gay in the world, we have made up the rules as we go along" (Brown, 1989, p. 451). Laird (1993) observed the creative responses to lacking clear role models in either the gay community or society at large: "Gay and lesbian families may be more free to choose from the best of both the straight and gay worlds, innovating in those areas where neither community practices nor family traditions meet their visions" (p. 293).

A LIFE COURSE PERSPECTIVE

A life course perspective sheds light on the normative and nonnormative transitions that accompany roles and relationships as individuals and families change over time (Bengtson & Allen, 1993). Many aspects of life experience are predictable, such as getting married and having children, but most people have little anticipatory socialization for claiming a gay identity or incorporating a gay relative into the family. A life course perspective provides a way in which to describe individual experience within the context of changing social and historical processes over time. It allows us to grasp the diversity and complexity in family life (Elder, 1981). The attention to transactions among individuals, families, and society avoids the tendency to view families through a unitary lens as a series of orderly stages simply marked by changes in marital and parental roles. The life course perspective critiques traditional developmental theory, pointing out that the notion of set stages reifies family experience by establishing a false dichotomy about what is normal and what is not. The families of lesbians and gay men challenge this normative view and encourage new ideas to explain diverse family structures and processes (Demo & Allen, 1996).

One example of the kind of diversity introduced by lesbian and gay parents is the impact of children on a couple's relationship satisfaction. The transition to parenthood, more so than the transition to marriage, has been shown to strain marriage relationships for men and women. Adding a new and dependent member to a family brings stress to parents given the demands for constant care and attention required by infants and young children. These new demands have greater impact on women in a heterosexual partnership, as marriage tends to become more traditional and patriarchal following the birth of a child (LaRossa & LaRossa, 1981). Yet research on lesbian mother families, who comprise most of the knowledge base about lesbian and gay parenting, suggests a different dynamic may be operating for lesbian mothers in intimate relationships. Koepke, Hare, and Moran (1992) found that having children increases lesbian couple satisfaction. Studies of heterosexually married couples, by contrast, consistently find that the presence of children decreases marital satisfaction (White & Booth, 1985).

A POSTMODERN PERSPECTIVE

Finally, a postmodern perspective expands on earlier under-standings that reality is socially constructed and that social experience cannot be taken as natural, at face value, or in any fixed way (Lather, 1991). Rather than the search for universals, multiple truths in human experience are expected and embraced (Hewitt, 1992). Using this perspective, there can be no singular description of a "lesbian or gay family experience" and no prototype or blueprint to represent all gay parents and their children. In contrast to the positivist search for a singular truth or type, a postmodern perspective is sensitive to the differences across individuals. It recognizes the tensions and contradictions that are perceived and experienced in family life. *Women and family* historically have been viewed as synonymous. A feminist postmodern perspective, however, uncovers the contradictions in women's experiences within families. This view allows us to see ways in which women are supported and limited in their care for families. They receive little societal compensation or recognition yet are expected to shoulder most of the responsibility (Baber & Allen, 1992).

The combination of core elements of these three perspectives is informed by the use of an additional idea: reflexivity. Fonow and Cook (1991) defined reflexivity as the tendency "to reflect upon, examine critically, and explore analytically the nature of the research process" (p. 2), particularly as filtered through the researcher's own experience in constructing knowledge. In an attempt to situate the researcher's allegiances and to deconstruct the potential biases that go unnamed in typical research reports, feminists and other scholars who promote multiple perspectives acknowledge the potential impact of an author's personal life experience on the research process. Reflexive insight from lived experience is used to increase the trustworthiness of the ideas presented (Lather, 1991).

Relevant to the theoretical and empirical perspectives presented in this chapter is my lived experience as a lesbian mother. By making the connection between my personal experience and intellectual accounts of knowledge transparent, the theoretical synthesis I present offers a constant reminder of the tentative nature of knowledge. I name my private experience as a lesbian mother as a way in which to intensify the validity of the knowledge I present. Without such reflexive sensitivity, the ideas would be just one more story written as a singular truth. Instead, there are multiple truths and countless perspectives that could be combined to describe parenting in lesbian and gay families in the late 20th century. For example, several scholars have reviewed and evaluated the literature on outcomes for children of lesbian and gay parents (see Bozett, 1987; Gottman, 1990; Patterson, 1992; Victor & Fish, 1995). In this chapter, I am concerned with the varying intersections of gender, generation, and sexual orientation as filtered through a feminist, life course, and postmodern perspective on family diversity.

The synthesis I present is helpful in understanding the particular contradictions posed by lesbian and gay parenting. There are numerous ironies—many of them cruel and unnecessary, yet others refreshing and hopeful—that accompany such parenting. The experience of lesbian motherhood, for example, is both constricting and liberating. On the one hand, coming out as a lesbian mother is not embraced by heterosexual society. Unlike heterosexually married mothers, whose parenting is deemed appropriate, lesbians are stigmatized for having children (DiLapi, 1989). Because the lesbian community historically has not been child centered (Slater & Mencher, 1991, p. 376), having a child may decrease the support a lesbian receives from peers (Lewin, 1993). On the other hand, becoming a mother may give a lesbian social acceptance from her family, even if the family disapproves of her lesbian identity, because motherhood is a "crucial female rite of passage" (Rohrbaugh, 1992, p. 471) that renders a woman an adult when she becomes a mother (Lewin, 1993). Lesbian motherhood, then, is characterized by claims of "passing" in a traditional way as an acceptable woman in the wider society and, ironically, by claims that a lesbian who becomes a mother is truly revolutionary for daring to parent without the obvious support or involvement of a husband/father. To handle these challenges to traditional conceptualizations of family, it is necessary to use a synthesis of sociological perspectives that allows for complexity, diversity, and difference.

Lesbian and Gay Parenting
in Historical Perspective

Although lesbians and gay men always have been parents, the social and political climate of the late 20th century has changed the degree to which they can be open about their parenting. Today, there is a greater self-consciousness among lesbian and gay people regarding their advocacy and action on behalf of equal participation and protection in the wider society. Homoerotic behavior has ancient roots, but a gay identity and consciousness is a 20th-century phenomenon (Duberman, Vicinus, & Chauncey, 1989). The term *homosexual* was not coined until the late 19th century, and the identity of contemporary lesbians and gay men has emerged with the civil rights and social movements of the late 20th century (Faderman, 1991; Herdt, 1992).

EMERGENCE OF GAY IDENTITY, CULTURE, AND CIVIL RIGHTS

On June 27, 1969, the Stonewall Inn Riot in New York City initiated the beginning of the contemporary civil rights movement for gay men, lesbians, and bisexual and transgendered people. The riot followed the burial of gay icon Judy Garland, an entertainer revered by drag performers in gay bars and clubs (Editors of the *Harvard Law Review*, 1990). Continually harassed by police, bar patrons fought the arbitrary abuse of power against their right to congregate in public places. Stonewall became a defining moment in which decades of quiet gay activism among working-class, middle-class, and upper class "homosexuals" converged into a unifying social movement (D'Emilio & Freedman, 1988). Stonewall occurred at the end of the 1960s, a watershed for black civil rights and the women's liberation movement. This event launched a new generation of lesbians and gay men, the "Stonewall generation," who introduced gay pride into the wider culture (Herrell, 1992, p. 229).

In addition to the emergence of a gay identity and the accompanying gay cultural systems that supported having a gay identity, other social-historical factors brought more gay people out in the open. Lesbians and gay men increasingly moved to urban centers, generating new markets for gay newspapers, community centers, and neighborhood services (Faderman, 1991; Herdt & Boxer, 1992). Important events that have shaped the growing possibility of living an openly gay life included the American Psychiatric Association's removal of homosexuality from its list of mental disorders in 1974, the American Psychological Association's removal of such stigmatized language in 1975, the U.S. Civil Service Commission's ending of the ban against employing gay men and lesbians in 1975, and Harvey Milk's election as the city of San Francisco's first openly gay supervisor in 1977 (Burke, 1993; D'Emilio & Freedman, 1988; Herek, Kimmel, Amaro, & Melton, 1991).

LESBIAN AND GAY PARENTS
AND THE LAW

Challenges to state sodomy laws are an important milestone in the improvement of civil rights for lesbians and gay men as individuals, partners, and parents. Sodomy laws, originally designed to regulate sexual relations as appropriate for procreation only, have been the primary barrier to ensuring civil rights for lesbians and gay men. Rubenstein (1996) reported that in 1961, every state in the United States had a sodomy law barring oral and anal sexual relations between homosexuals and heterosexuals alike. However, these laws, unevenly and infrequently applied, have been used disproportionately against homosexual acts. In the 1970s, 26 states eliminated their sodomy statutes through legislative action in an attempt to modernize their penal codes (D'Emilio & Freedman, 1988, p. 324). Ironically, some state legislatures "added new laws barring only homosexual sodomy" (Rubenstein, 1996, p. 333). In 1993, Nevada and the District of Columbia repealed their sodomy laws (p. 334). States that still have gay-only sodomy laws are Arkansas, Kansas, Kentucky, Missouri, Montana, and Texas. The other states with sodomy laws are Alabama, Arizona, Florida, Idaho, Louisiana, Maryland, Michigan, Minnesota, Mississippi, North Carolina, Oklahoma, Rhode Island, South Carolina, Tennessee, Utah, and Virginia (Editors of the *Harvard Law Review*, 1990, p. 10).

Because of the existence of sodomy laws and the lack of legal protection given to lesbians and gay men, openness about a gay sexual orientation has been cause for a parent to jeopardize her or his parental rights (Zicklin, 1995, p. 57). In a review of legal cases related to gay family relationships, Zicklin (1995) demonstrated that judicial decisions regarding child custody have been characterized by "arbitrarity" (p. 68). On the one hand, sodomy laws rarely are applied, and several lower courts in states in which sodomy statutes continue to exist have declared them unconstitutional. On the other hand, their continued appearance in states' penal codes allows them to be used prejudicially as a basis to discriminate against or prosecute lesbian and gay people. In the 1986 case of *Bowers v. Hardwick*, the U.S. Supreme Court ruled 5 to 4 against a gay man's charge that his arrest under Georgia's sodomy law was unconstitutional (Editors of the *Harvard Law Review*, 1990, p. 8).

Judicial misconceptions and prejudices regarding sexual orientation continue to find their way into legal decisions, demonstrating that barriers to equal treatment under the law are cultural, not in the law itself (Zicklin, 1995, p. 58). Falk (1989) cited several myths that were found to influence judges' decisions to deny custody of their children to lesbian mothers. The body of legal decisions related to lesbian mothers reflects myths about women as lesbians, primarily that lesbians are emotionally unstable or unable to act in a maternal way. Additional myths reflect assumptions about the harm done to children if lesbian parents were allowed to raise them. Myths related to child outcomes include the assumptions that children would be harmed emotionally, molested, and unable to assume an appropriate gender role and that they would become homosexual themselves. A final category of myths that impacts judicial decisions is the widespread belief that children of lesbian mothers will be "traumatized or stigmatized by society or their peers" (Falk, 1989, p. 943). A large body of social science research on the mental health of lesbian women, the parenting ability of lesbian mothers, and outcomes for children reared in lesbian families disputes all of these myths (Falk, 1989). Yet court rulings continue to be illogical and prejudicial when the sexual orientation of a parent is an issue (Zicklin, 1995).

Until recently, then, sexual orientation per se has been used as a reason to deprive a parent of custody or visitation with her or his biological child or children, based on the automatic assumption that children are harmed by having a lesbian or gay parent (Rubenstein, 1996, p. 339). Although lesbians and gay men still are treated with extreme inequity in our legal system, there are cases in which the civil rights of lesbians and gay men are supported. For example, the 1989 case of *Braschi v. Stahl* eventually was decided in favor of a gay man who argued that he should be able to inherit his deceased partner's lease to a rent-controlled apartment (Zicklin, 1995, p. 63). This case set a precedent on which the gay community could argue that "gays form the functional equivalent of marriage and that their relationships should be treated as such" (p. 63). The *Braschi* case paves the way for the current situation in Hawaii, where a group of lesbian and gay couples argued that "denying same-sex couples the opportunity to marry was discrimination on the basis of gender" (quoted in Rubenstein, 1996, p. 338). This argument states that if a man has the right to marry a woman, then it is gender discrimination for a woman not to have the right to marry a woman. As Hawaii debates the possibility of legalizing same-sex marriages, many states have proposed legislation to prohibit their states from being forced to recognize marriages taking place in Hawaii. The Defense of Marriage Act (DOMA), recently signed into law, bans federal recognition of same-sex marriages. This act was supported by the president of the United States and by many citizens, revealing the politicized nature of the quest for legal recognition of gay partnerships (Gallagher, 1996). DOMA defines marriage as a union only between one man and one woman. Many commentators have observed that although the gay marriage controversy is a sign of the backlash against lesbians and gays, its visibility in the media and in politics exemplifies the importance of gay civil rights at the national level (Stacey, 1996).

THE NEED FOR PARTNERSHIP RIGHTS AND RECOGNITION

The events of the 1960s and 1970s were important markers in the development of gay identity, gay cultural systems, and gay civil rights, but it was not until the 1980s that the families of lesbians and gay men became more public (Pies, 1988). Two important developments in the 1980s, the Sharon Kowalski case and the AIDS epidemic (Rubenstein, 1996), brought increasing visibility to what had previously had been considered an oxymoron: the families of lesbians and gay men. Prior to the 1980s, lesbians and gay men were treated merely as individuals, and gay rights were fought mainly on the basis of privacy and freedom of speech, as guaranteed by the First Amendment (Rubenstein, 1996).

Regarding the first issue, Karen Thompson fought her partner's parents in a legal battle for 9 years to gain the right to guardianship after her partner, Sharon Kowalski, was physically and mentally disabled in a car accident (see Laird, 1993; Rubenstein, 1996; Thompson & Andrzejewski, 1988). Second, the AIDS epidemic had far-reaching consequences for the families of gay men and lesbians. The existence of AIDS in this country was first made public in 1981; by 1987, there were more than 45,000 cases in the nation and more than 4,400 in

San Francisco alone. The deaths of thousands of gay men and the public apathy and resistance toward finding a cure mobilized gay activists more than had any previous issue (D'Emilio, 1989). With the complications arising from many gay men dying and their partners unable to claim the normative rights associated with spousal illness or widowhood, gay men, lesbians, and their supporters mobilized around the need for partnership rights (Rubenstein, 1996). The AIDS crisis and its corresponding reminder of the lack of legal recognition of gay and lesbian partners led to a major event in the gay civil rights movement. On October 11, 1987, 600,000 people participated in the March on Washington to protest governmental indifference to AIDS (D'Emilio, 1989). National Coming Out Day was established in 1988 to commemorate this event and to promote the visibility of lesbian and gay people worldwide (Marcus, 1993).

At issue for gay couples is the fundamental right to marry (Editors of the *Harvard Law Review*, 1990). The quest for legal recognition of gay partnerships is intensifying as the expectation to be treated with equality and civility among gay people increases (Eskridge, 1996). Marriage brings many advantages, such as social and emotional support, but only heterosexual couples have the right to expect and enjoy its material and legal advantages. Zicklin (1995) summarized the benefits of a legal spouse as follows:

> the right to inherit from a spouse who dies without a will; the right to consult with doctors and make crucial medical decisions in the event of a spouse's critical illness or mental incompetence; immunity from having to testify against a spouse in a criminal proceeding; the right of residency for a foreign spouse of a U.S. citizen; the right to sue for emotional harm from wrongful damage sustained by one's spouse; the right to visit one's spouse in government-run institutions, such as prisons and hospitals; the right to Social Security survivor's benefits; the right of an employee to include a legally married spouse on his or her health insurance coverage; the option to reduce the couple's tax liability by filing joint returns; other organizational benefits such as married student housing, reduced tuition fees, and access to an organization's facilities. (pp. 55-56)

If a couple has children, the marginality of a lesbian or gay relationship also prohibits or jeopardizes the legal status of the nonbiological parent to the child. As of 1992, about 200 second-parent adoptions had been permitted in seven states and the District of Columbia ("NCLR to Come Out," 1992). Otherwise, the nonlegal parent, or coparent, is a legal stranger to the child. The child is ineligible for medical or social security benefits the nonlegal parent may have, the child does not inherit automatically if that parent should die, and the nonlegal parent has no legal recourse if the couple's relationship ends (Zicklin, 1995).

THE POLITICS OF COMING OUT IN THE 1990s

As the legal situation of gay individuals in general improves, so too does the openness with which they are coming out about their family statuses (Zicklin, 1995). Being out, which refers to a person's open identification as lesbian, gay, or bisexual, is an important family issue. Secrecy about a couple's sexual orientation can interfere with parenting functions and roles (Rohrbaugh, 1992, p. 470). In addition, the degree to which a parent is out to members of the wider community, such as a child's teacher and school administrators, is an important factor in lesbian and gay families because openness directly relates to the child's experience in school (Casper & Schultz, 1996). When administrators and teachers in school environments communicate acceptance, verbally and structurally, toward heterogeneous family circumstances, parents are freer to disclose their family compositions and children experience support for their particular family arrangements (Casper, Schultz, & Wickens, 1994).

Lesbian and gay parents face an unprecedented time in the 1990s. On the one hand, there is a growing and visible movement to legitimate gay families and to secure the same protections given to traditional nuclear families. On the other hand, there is an increasing backlash against gay people and their right to parent, to have partnership benefits, and to have the legal protections taken for granted by heterosexuals. The situation of Sharon Bottoms in Virginia reflects this contradiction. In 1993, she lost custody of her biological child to her own mother. Under any other circumstances, a grandparent is considered a legal stranger, yet the sexual orientation of the parent was the primary factor in the judge's ruling. The case was appealed to the Virginia Supreme Court, and the ruling was upheld.

The 1990s is a battleground for gay civil rights because this issue has replaced abortion rights as the mobilizing force of the radical right (Rubenstein, 1996, p. 336). Florida and New Hampshire are two states that already ban adoption by lesbian or gay couples. The National Center for Lesbian Rights reported that pressure from far right legislators led to antilesbian and gay family legislation or policies being introduced in 11 more states; legislation was introduced in Washington and Oklahoma, for example, to ban lesbians and gay men from adopting children, and legislation was introduced in Oregon to deny unmarried women access to artificial insemination. The other 8 states in which similar legislation was introduced, as of 1995, are California, Maine, Missouri, Montana, Nebraska, South Carolina, South Dakota, and Utah ("The Homefront Battle," 1995). On the other hand, 3 states give the right to adopt children to lesbian and gay couples; New York recently joined Vermont and Massachusetts in allowing gay parent adoption.

Although the current decade has been called "the gay nineties" by popular culture magazines such as the September 8, 1995 issue of *Entertainment Weekly*, it also is a time in which hate crimes and physical violence against gay people are increasing (Herrell, 1992). One measure of societal indifference and outright hostility toward gay people can be seen in the treatment of gay and lesbian youths. The lack of societal support for this population is cited as a cause of the alarming fact that gay and lesbian youths comprise 30% of all adolescent suicides (Savin-Williams & Cohen, 1996, p. 191).

Despite the lack of social and legal support, lesbians and gay men are becoming parents and openly creating families in new ways. Their growing visibility is a sign that they are willing to take the risks involved in coming out to demonstrate their basic civil rights to live, parent, and couple just as any other member of society. Lesbian and gay parents remain politically vulnerable given the barriers to full legal protection. Because the law tends to conserve rather than change society, it is unlikely that full equality will be given to lesbian and gay parents until public acceptance of lesbian and gay individuals has increased (Eskridge, 1996). In concluding his study of the illogical legal decisions regarding lesbian and gay family relationships, Zicklin (1995) stated, "The task for the gay community is what it was in 1969: to convince the rest of society of the moral nature of same-sex attraction and of the human relationships that flow from it. Favorable legal decisions will follow" (p. 72).

Prevalence and Diversity
of Lesbian and Gay Families

Accurate estimates of the number of lesbian and gay people or parents are virtually impossible given the various definitions of sexual orientation used in empirical research, the failure to ask questions relevant to sexual orientation, and the exclusion of lesbians, gay men, and bisexuals from most investigations (Allen & Demo, 1995). Despite these limitations, estimates of the substantial number of lesbian and gay people and their families are reported in the literature. Parents, Families, and Friends of Lesbians and Gays, the largest organization devoted to the families of lesbian and gay people, estimates that one out of every four families has a gay member (Goodman, 1991). This figure is based on the quotation by Kinsey and associates (Kinsey, Pomeroy, & Martin, 1948; Kinsey, Pomeroy, Martin, & Gebhard, 1953) that 10% of the population is lesbian or gay. The Kinsey Institute arrived at the 10% figure by averaging the 7 percent of women and 13 percent of men who report having "*predominantly* homosexual experiences (4s, 5s and 6s on the Kinsey scale)" (Voeller, 1990, p. 33; emphasis in original). This figure was reconfirmed in the 1970s in response to challenges of its accuracy (Voeller, 1990).

Later studies continued to question the Kinsey Institute's figures. Fay, Turner, Klassen, and Gagnon (1989) summarized data on adult men and reported a lower percentage—between 3% and 6% of the adult male population—as exclusively homosexual. Still, they also stated that these lower figures are underreported given the societal intolerance of same gender sexuality.

Identifying the number of lesbians and gay men who are parents is even more difficult. The editors of the *Harvard Law Review* (1990) reported that "approximately three million gay men and lesbians in the United States are parents, and between eight and ten million children are raised in gay or lesbian households" (p. 119).

Most gay and lesbian adults have become parents through previous heterosexual marriages. Approximately one fifth of gay men and one third of lesbians have been in heterosexual marriages (Harry, 1983). About half of these marriages resulted in at least one biological child (Bell & Weinberg, 1978). Estimates of lesbian and gay parenting also are underreported due to the increasingly diverse ways in which they become parents. Bozett (1989) estimated that between 1 million and 3 million gay men are fathers of biological children, but he recognized that this is a conservative figure because it excludes gay men with adopted children, foster children, or stepchildren and those who have become fathers by donating sperm. Falk (1989) cited a range of 1.5 to 5.0 million lesbians living with their children, but this figure is increasing given the number of women becoming mothers through donor insemination. Indeed, there is evidence of a "baby boom" among women having children in the context of lesbian partnerships (Patterson, 1995; Weston, 1991). In 1990, it was estimated that between 5,000 and 10,000 lesbians had borne children after coming out, and many more have become mothers through adoption (Flaks, Ficher, Masterpasqua, & Joseph, 1995).

DEFINING LESBIAN AND GAY FAMILIES OF CHOICE

Defining the families of lesbians and gay men also is a challenging, yet instructive, task. Numerous definitions have been suggested as a way in which to characterize the diversity, multiplicity, and uniqueness of the families created or headed by lesbians or gay men. In attempting to navigate the complexity of describing lesbian and gay families, Allen and Demo (1995) offered a definition that accounts for partnerships and parenthood: "Lesbian and gay families are defined by the presence of two or more people who share a same-sex orientation (e.g., a couple) or by the presence of at least one lesbian or gay adult rearing a child" (p. 113).

Patterson (1994) suggested that "lesbian and gay families" also be used to refer to any family constellation that includes at least one gay or lesbian member. She argued that many of the issues lesbian and gay members face are sufficiently different to warrant a term that identifies the additional complexities in their experience. Laird (1993) suggested the term "dual-orientation families" to signal the broader kinship system of which sexual orientation diversity is only one factor. Dual orientation, for example, would apply to lesbian parents with a heterosexual teenage son.

Rohrbaugh (1992) described three varieties of lesbian family structure: blended families, single parents, and couples having children together. Her categories are instructive for the present discussion. Blended families probably are the most common type of lesbian or gay family structure given the fact that, in the past, most lesbians and gay men became parents in the context of heterosexual marriages. The families they created after coming out would be more likely characterized as stepfamilies or blended families in which a gay or lesbian parent and his or her children joined in a new household with another gay or lesbian adult who was not the children's biological parent (Rohrbaugh, 1992). Most gay male stepfamilies are noncustodial households given the intersection of gender and sexual orientation that makes it unlikely for a gay man to gain custody of his children (Crosbie-Burnett & Helmbrecht, 1993).

Today, more lesbians are using alternative insemination to have children outside of heterosexual marriage or intercourse. Donor insemination, primarily by using the sperm of gay men, was hailed in the 1980s as the unprecedented resolution to the fertility problem of two lesbians or two gay men. Initially, critical considerations regarding the choice of donor involved whether to use a known or an unknown donor and the extent of involvement of the nonbiological comother (see Pies, 1988, for a history of the lesbian and gay parenting movement). With the widespread influence of AIDS, the initial enthusiasm with which lesbians and gay men embraced alternative insemination has been reconsidered. After conducting a study of insemination cases in San Francisco, Pies (1988) reported that alternative fertilization, although rare, could be a mode of transmission for the AIDS virus. The lesbian and gay parenting movement, primarily a self-help community, responded to this concern with increasing knowledge and sophistication about safe insemination practices (see Benkov, 1994; Martin, 1993; Pies, 1988).

Lesbian and gay parenting in the 1990s brings new definitions, structures, and processes to mainstream society. Language characterizing these brave new families includes "planned lesbian mother families" (Flaks et al., 1995, p. 105) and "the reinvented family" (Benkov, 1994, p. 142). This language emphasizes the deliberateness and intentionality in constructing kin ties that are characterized more by emotional and social commitments than by genetics (Stacey, 1996). As Weston's (1991) study of kinship within a gay community demonstrated, lesbians and gay men redefine families as units of choice, not biology.

As important as it is for scholars to provide shared understanding of the phenomena they study, attempts to define complex, pluralistic experiences do not match the shifting landscape of postmodern family arrangements. It is difficult to define my own family of choice using kinship terminology or the preceding expanded descriptions. My partner and our children fit with portions of these definitions, but there are unique aspects to our history that render a common definition inadequate. Perhaps our experience is relevant to others in that any definition of family, to be accurate, should accommodate the unique connections between parents and children as they change over time.

My partner and I live with our two sons. Our older son was conceived in my former heterosexual marriage. At first, our blended family consisted of a lesbian couple and a child from one partner's previous marriage. After several years, our circumstances changed. My brother's life partner became the donor and father to our second son, who is my partner's biological child. My partner and I draw a boundary around our lesbian-headed family in which we share a household consisting of two moms and two sons, but our extended family consists of additional kin groups. For example, my former husband and his wife have an infant son, who is my biological son's second brother. All four sets of grandparents and extended kin related to our sons' biological parents are involved in all our lives to varying degrees. These kin comprise a diversity of heterosexual and gay identities as well as long-term married, ever-single, and divorced individuals.

Regarding the legal and social circumstances of our family, I sometimes am considered a single head of household; other times, I am considered the main breadwinner of a family of four. I cannot claim my partner or nonbiological son on my health insurance, but I was able to purchase life insurance under a domestic partnership clause through my retirement fund. Several years ago, my partner and I had a public celebration to share our commitment to each other with our extended network of family and friends. In the absence of language for this event, I have heard others refer to it variously as a marriage, a commitment ceremony, a lesbian wedding, and "that day in your backyard."

Lesbian and Gay Parents as Innovators

Against the backdrop of a history of legal restriction and second-class status, lesbian and gay parents demonstrate remarkable strength and resiliency (Demo & Allen, 1996). These families develop coping strategies that challenge societal norms, assert their human rights, and support their identities (Levy, 1992). Reflecting on the negative societal discourse about lesbian families, Laird (1994) concluded that lesbians and their children "have not been broken by society's words about them" (p. 123). They have tailored their lives to better suit their lived experiences and the realities facing families today. Given the intersection of gender and sexual orientation in the families they create, lesbian and gay parents challenge the presumed normality of traditional gender roles. They pioneer new ways of living in families and prompt scholars to sharpen and expand our definitions of family structure and process (Allen & Demo, 1995; Stacey, 1996).

The lesbian and gay parenting movement is evidence of the urgency felt by people whose right to raise children is challenged by the very institutions that are supposed to support families. Developments over the past three decades have brought many lesbian and gay parents out into the open. They have become proactive, making use of publishing venues and other media to share their knowledge about creating and maintaining families—from how to obtain sperm for donor insemination to how to prepare wills in the absence of the legal protection of marriage. Lesbians and gay men also are becoming the lawyers, judges, teachers, social workers, and citizens who are working to secure equal rights for their families. They are using normative creativity (Brown, 1989) to validate their own families and advocate on behalf of the social change necessary to respect and honor diversity.

References

Allen, K. R., & Demo, D. H. (1995). The families of lesbians and gay men: A new frontier in family research. *Journal of Marriage and the Family, 57,* 111-127.

Baber, K. M., & Allen, K. R. (1992). *Women and families: Feminist reconstructions.* New York: Guilford.

Bell, A. P., & Weinberg, M. S. (1978). *Homosexualities: A study of diversity among men and women.* New York: Simon & Schuster.

Bengtson, V. L., & Allen, K. R. (1993). The life course perspective applied to families over time. In P. Boss, W. Doherty, R. LaRossa, W. Schumm, & S. Steinmetz (Eds.), *Sourcebook of family theories and methods: A contextual approach* (pp. 469-499). New York: Plenum.

Benkov, L. (1994). *Reinventing the family: The emerging story of lesbian and gay parents.* New York: Crown.

Blumstein, P., & Schwartz, P. (1983). *American couples: Money, work, sex.* New York: William Morrow.

Bozett, F. W. (1987). Children of gay fathers. In F. Bozett (Ed.), *Gay and lesbian parents* (pp. 39-57). New York: Praeger.

Bozett, F. W. (1989). Gay fathers: A review of the literature. In F. Bozett (Ed.), *Homosexuality and the family* (pp. 137-162). New York: Harrington Park.

Brown, L. S. (1989). New voices, new visions: Toward a lesbian/gay paradigm for psychology. *Psychology of Women Quarterly, 13,* 445-458.

Burke, P. (1993). *Family values: Two moms and their son.* New York: Random House.

Casper, V., & Schultz, S. (1996). Lesbian and gay parents encounter educators: Initiating conversations. In R. Savin-Williams & K. Cohen (Eds.), *The lives of lesbians, gays, and bisexuals* (pp. 305-330). Fort Worth, TX: Harcourt Brace.

Casper, V., Schultz, S., & Wickens, E. (1994). Breaking the silences: Lesbian and gay parents and the schools. *Teachers College Record, 94,* 109-135.

Collins, P. H. (1990). *Black feminist thought.* Boston: Unwin Hyman.

Crosbie-Burnett, M., & Helmbrecht, L. (1993). A descriptive empirical study of gay male stepfamilies. *Family Relations, 42,* 256-262.

Cunningham, A. (1992, September 27). Ozzie and Ozzie: What America can learn from gay families. *Washington Post,* pp. C1, C3.

D'Emilio, J. (1989). Gay politics and community in San Francisco since World War II. In M. Duberman, M. Vicinus, & G. Chauncey (Eds.), *Hidden from history: Reclaiming the gay and lesbian past* (pp. 456-473). New York: NAL Books.

D'Emilio, J., & Freedman, E. B. (1988). *Intimate matters: A history of sexuality in America.* New York: Harper & Row.

Demo, D. H., & Allen, K. R. (1996). Diversity within lesbian and gay families: Challenges and implications for family theory and research. *Journal of Social and Personal Relationships, 13,* 417-436.

DiLapi, E. M. (1989). Lesbian mothers and the motherhood hierarchy. In F. Bozett (Ed.), *Homosexuality and the family* (pp. 101-121). New York: Harrington Park.

Duberman, M. B., Vicinus, M., & Chauncey, G., Jr. (Eds.). (1989). *Hidden from history: Reclaiming the gay and lesbian past.* New York: NAL Books.

Editors of the *Harvard Law Review.* (1990). *Sexual orientation and the law.* Cambridge, MA: Harvard University Press.

Elder, G. H., Jr. (1981). History and the family: The discovery of complexity. *Journal of Marriage and the Family, 43,* 489-519.

Eskridge, W. N., Jr. (1996). *The case for same-sex marriage: From sexual liberty to civilized commitment.* New York: Free Press.

Faderman, L. (1991). *Odd girls and twilight lovers: A history of lesbian life in twentieth-century America.* New York: Penguin Books.

Falk, P. J. (1989). Lesbian mothers: Psychosocial assumptions in family law. *American Psychologist, 44,* 941-947.

Fay, R. E., Turner, C. F., Klassen, A. D., & Gagnon, J. H. (1989). Prevalence and patterns of same-gender sexual contact among men. *Science, 243,* 338-348.

Flaks, D. K., Ficher, I., Masterpasqua, F., & Joseph, G. (1995). Lesbians choosing motherhood: A comparative study of lesbian and heterosexual parents and their children. *Developmental Psychology, 31,* 105-114.

Fonow, M. M., & Cook, J. A. (1991). Back to the future: A look at the second wave of feminist epistemology and methodology. In M. Fonow & J. Cook (Eds.), *Beyond methodology: Feminist scholarship as lived research* (pp. 1-15). Bloomington: Indiana University Press.

Gallagher, J. (1996, July 23). Love and war. *The Advocate: The National Gay and Lesbian Newsmagazine,* pp. 22-28.

Goodman, P. (1991, May). *Supporting our gay loved ones: A parents FLAG perspective.* Paper presented at the annual meeting of the American Psychiatric Association, New Orleans, LA.

Gottman, J. S. (1990). Children of gay and lesbian parents. In F. Bozett & M. Sussman (Eds.), *Homosexuality and family relations* (pp. 175-196). New York: Harrington Park.

Harry, J. (1983). Gay male and lesbian relationships. In E. Macklin & R. Rubin (Eds.), *Contemporary families and alternative lifestyles* (pp. 216-234). Beverly Hills, CA: Sage.

Herdt, G. (Ed.). (1992). *Gay culture in America.* Boston: Beacon.

Herdt, G., & Boxer, A. (1992). Introduction: Culture, history, and life course of gay men. In G. Herdt (Ed.), *Gay culture in America* (pp. 1-28). Boston: Beacon.

Herek, G. M., Kimmel, D. C., Amaro, H., & Melton, G. B. (1991). Avoiding heterosexist bias in psychological research. *American Psychologist, 46,* 957-963.

Herrell, R. K. (1992). The symbolic strategies of Chicago's Gay and Lesbian Pride Day Parade. In G. Herdt (Ed.), *Gay culture in America* (pp. 225-252). Boston: Beacon.

Hewitt, N. A. (1992). *Multiple truths: The personal, the political, and the postmodernist in contemporary feminist scholarship.* Working Paper No. 5, Center for Research on Women, Memphis State University.

The homefront battle: The radical right's assault on lesbian and gay families. (1995, Spring). *National Center for Lesbian Rights Newsletter,* pp. 1, 10.

Kinsey, A. C., Pomeroy, W. B., & Martin, C. E. (1948). *Sexual behavior in the human male.* Philadelphia: W. B. Saunders.

Kinsey, A. C., Pomeroy, W. B., Martin, C. E., & Gebhard, P. H. (1953). *Sexual behavior in the human female.* Philadelphia: W. B. Saunders.

Koepke, L., Hare, J., & Moran, P. B. (1992). Relationship quality in a sample of lesbian couples with children and child-free lesbian couples. *Family Relations, 41,* 224-229.

Laird, J. (1993). Lesbian and gay families. In F. Walsh (Ed.), *Normal family processes* (2nd ed., pp. 282-328). New York: Guilford.

Laird, J. (1994). Lesbian families: A cultural perspective. In M. Mirkin (Ed.), *Women in context* (pp. 118-148). New York: Guilford.

LaRossa, R., & LaRossa, M. M. (1981). *Transition to parenthood: How infants change families*. Beverly Hills, CA: Sage.

Lather, P. (1991). *Getting smart: Feminist research and pedagogy with/in the postmodern*. New York: Routledge.

Levy, E. F. (1992). Strengthening the coping resources of lesbian families. *Families in Society, 73*, 23-31.

Lewin, E. (1993). *Lesbian mothers: Accounts of gender in American culture*. Ithaca, NY: Cornell University Press.

Lorde, A. (1984). *Sister outsider*. Freedom, CA: Crossing.

Marcus, E. (1993). *Is it a choice? Answers to 300 of the most frequently asked questions about gays and lesbians*. New York: HarperCollins.

Martin, A. (1993). *The lesbian and gay parenting handbook: Creating and raising our families*. New York: HarperPerennial.

NCLR to come out boldly for second-parent adoptions. (1992, Spring). *National Center for Lesbian Rights Newsletter*, pp. 1, 8-9.

Osmond, M. W., & Thorne, B. (1993). Feminist theories: The social construction of gender in families and society. In P. Boss, W. Doherty, R. LaRossa, W. Schumm, & S. Steinmetz (Eds.), *Sourcebook of family theories and methods* (pp. 591-623). New York: Plenum.

Patterson, C. J. (1992). Children of lesbian and gay parents. *Child Development, 63*, 1025-1042.

Patterson, C. J. (1994). Lesbian and gay families. *Current Directions in Psychological Science, 3*, 62-64.

Patterson, C. J. (1995). Families of the lesbian baby boom: Parents' division of labor and children's adjustment. *Developmental Psychology, 31*, 115-123.

Peters, M. F. (1988). Parenting in black families with young children: A historical perspective. In H. McAdoo (Ed.), *Black families* (2nd ed., pp. 228-241). Newbury Park, CA: Sage.

Pies, C. (1988). *Considering parenthood* (2nd ed.). San Francisco: Spinsters/Aunt Lute.

Rafkin, L. (Ed.). (1990). *Different mothers: Sons and daughters of lesbians talk about their lives*. Pittsburgh, PA: Cleis.

Rohrbaugh, J. B. (1992). Lesbian families: Clinical issues and theoretical implications. *Professional Psychology: Research and Practice, 23*, 467-473.

Rubenstein, W. B. (1996). Lesbians, gay men, and the law. In R. Savin-Williams & K. Cohen (Eds.), *The lives of lesbians, gays, and bisexuals* (pp. 331-344). Fort Worth, TX: Harcourt Brace.

Savin-Williams, R. C., & Cohen, K. M. (1996). Psychosocial outcomes of verbal and physical abuse among lesbian, gay, and bisexual youths. In R. Savin-Williams & K. Cohen (Eds.), *The lives of lesbians, gays, and bisexuals* (pp. 181-200). Fort Worth, TX: Harcourt Brace.

Slater, S., & Mencher, J. (1991). The lesbian family life cycle: A contextual approach. *American Journal of Orthopsychiatry, 61*, 372-382.

Smith, D. E. (1987). *The everyday world as problematic: A feminist sociology*. Boston: Northeastern University Press.

Stacey, J. (1996). *In the name of the family: Rethinking family values in the postmodern age*. Boston: Beacon.

Thompson, K., & Andrzejewski, J. (1988). *Why can't Sharon Kowalski come home?* San Francisco: Spinsters/Aunt Lute.

Victor, S. B., & Fish, M. C. (1995). Lesbian mothers and their children: A review for school psychologists. *School Psychology Review, 24,* 456-479.

Voeller, B. (1990). Some uses and abuses of the Kinsey Scale. In D. McWhirter, S. Sanders, & J. Reinisch (Eds.), *Homosexuality/heterosexuality: Concepts of sexual orientation* (pp. 32-38). New York: Oxford University Press.

Weston, K. (1991). *Families we choose: Lesbians, gays, kinship.* New York: Columbia University Press.

White, L. K., & Booth, A. (1985). The transition to parenthood and marital quality. *Journal of Family Issues, 6,* 435-449.

Zicklin, G. (1995). Deconstructing legal rationality: The case of lesbian and gay family relationships. *Marriage and Family Review, 21,* 55-76.

8

Children and Gender

SCOTT COLTRANE

MICHELE ADAMS

Most people assume that gender flows naturally from sex. We divide the world into women and men based on their possession of different biological equipment. But in a world where that equipment is generally hidden from sight, gender provides the visible social equivalent. Goffman (1977) told us that "it is for membership sorting that biology provides a neat and tidy device; the contingencies and response that seem so naturally to follow along the same lines are a consequence of social organization" (p. 330). Where biology gives us sex, social organization gives us gender; the catch is that the two, although often congruent, do not necessarily have to match. Because sex and gender are neither always the same nor always different, and because sex usually (although not invariably) is biologically determined, any discussion of gender must take into account its social origins and subsequent transmission across generations.

As a socially constructed process, gender is emergent, dynamic, and varying; as a social construction, gender reflects an underlying sense of the way in which society sees itself at any given historical moment.

AUTHOR'S NOTE: The analysis presented in this chapter is based on material included in Coltrane's *Gender and Families* (Pine Forge, 1997).

Gender identity is one of the links between the self and society, and transmission of gender begs the question of how society is instilled in the individual. Our task in this chapter is to explore that link. Generally, we ask the question: How do children acquire their gender identities? Specifically, we ask this question within the framework of the family: What part do parents play in engendering their children?

Because of the importance of family in gender socialization, we begin our exploration by looking at the involvement of the family, and particularly parents, in the engendering process. We then move on to a review of various historical and contemporary theories of gender development, ending the theoretical section with an "interactionist synthesis" incorporating elements from several well-known theorists. From this conceptual discussion, we progress to a summary of relevant research on childhood gender socialization, describing how parents treat boys and girls differently from the time they are infants until they become young adults. We then summarize what social scientists have concluded about how this influences child development and social interaction. We conclude with a brief discussion of the feminist critique of current gender socialization practices and potential avenues for altering the gender development status quo.

Sex Versus Gender

Although historically the terms *sex* and *gender* have been used interchangeably, more recently the two have come to be understood as distinct notions, with *sex* (or *sex class*) taking on a biological connotation and *gender* a cultural implication. In this way, gender generally is understood to be socially constructed. We "do gender" in everyday interaction in the sense that our actions signal an underlying masculine or feminine nature (West & Zimmerman, 1987). This process produces taken-for-granted differences between girls and boys and between women and men, but these differences are not fundamentally natural, essential, or biological. One is not automatically classified as a male or female on the basis of observed biological sex but rather on the basis of appearance and behavior in everyday social interaction (Coltrane, 1996, p. 50). In fact, recent research on sex and gender suggests that the relationship between the two is far more complicated than was previously assumed by more biologically based models of human behavior (for reviews, see Bem, 1993; Bleier, 1984; Butler, 1990; Epstein, 1988; Lorber, 1994; but cf. Rossi, 1977).

By doing gender, individuals attempt to pass themselves off as either masculine or feminine through the use of props and behaviors that are "understood" to be associated with one or the other of the sex classes. Goffman (1959) referred to this type of activity as "impression management," alluding to "techniques employed to safeguard the impression fostered by an individual during his presence before others" (p. 14). Although children also do gender, their social knowledge, behavioral repertoires, and stocks of available props usually are less sophisticated than those available to adults. In fact, until children reach the age when they are able to perform adequately their own gender impression management, thus supporting their own gender identities, their parents (and, less frequently, other interested adults) tend to perform this function on their behalf. Consequently, we see parents "color-coding" their newborns in either pink or blue, dressing them "in miniaturized versions of adults' sex class associated costumes, and sometimes even tap[ing] bows to female infants' hairless heads" (Cahill, 1989, p. 284).

Families as Primary Socializing Agents

Childhood development of gender identity (or sex identity) was once thought to be relatively unproblematic. There was little, if any, discussion of its purposes, variations, or implications. Generally speaking, most people assumed that gender and sexual identity naturally unfolded as children matured. Consequently, before mid-century, little attention was given to documenting how and why children developed specific gender-linked traits and behaviors (Maccoby, 1992).

As gender came to be understood as the cultural equivalent of sex, researchers began to devote more study to those factors that were implicated in shaping a child's gender identity. In today's society, numerous agents in a variety of different settings—including parents, teachers, and peers at home, at school, and at play—are seen as affecting children's gender role socialization (Etaugh & Liss, 1992).

Even the media are involved, to a greater or lesser extent, in forming a child's gender identity.

However, although the process of socialization occurs in many different contexts, it generally is assumed that the most important aspects of socialization take place within the family (see Coltrane, 1997). This reflects the idea that even though people continue to change and learn throughout life, it is during childhood that they acquire enduring personality characteristics, interpersonal skills, and social values (Maccoby, 1992). The family acts as a microcosm of society; here a child is first exposed to culture. The simple occurrence of being born into a certain family provides a particular set of socialization experiences including where one lives, what one eats and wears, who one sees, what kind of education or medical care one gets, what kind of work one does, and numerous other things, both small and large. Such characteristics, summarized in terms of social class, ethnicity, religion, and family composition, will, to a large extent, control what a child's living conditions and life chances will be as they grow up (Collins & Coltrane, 1995; Peterson & Rollins, 1987).

Families also are important because they provide children's first exposure to interaction with others. Compared to other animals, all human beings are born "premature" with awkwardly functioning bodies and brains that are only partially developed. Consequently, to survive, human newborns need substantial care and attention. Many other animals learn how to survive in the world in a relatively short period of time, but human babies need to grow and develop over many years before they can become self-sufficient and able to assume their places in society. Different cultures have different expectations of variously aged children; however, no human child can survive without the care of his or her parents or other adults for the first few years of the child's life. The child's extreme dependence on others makes the socialization that occurs in families particularly salient; it also is one of the major reasons that adult-child relationships remain emotionally charged well into adult life (Maccoby, 1992).

In all known societies, children grow and mature physically, emotionally, and intellectually in families. All families, of course, are not alike; families in most other societies generally have been larger and less isolated than our current American version, typically living in much smaller dwellings. Children have, in fact, usually grown up interacting with more people and observing more adults than they do in contemporary America. Regardless of the diverse living arrangements, however, babies routinely have developed the capacity to roll over, sit up, crawl, walk, and run in family settings. Similarly, each child learns how to recognize faces, make gestures, and eventually talk by interacting with family members and other people in the immediate family household. Not only do most developmental processes unfold in such family contexts, but the child also first learns the meaning of authority and gains awareness of what is acceptable and unacceptable behavior within the family. As the child matures, the importance of the family decreases somewhat, with an associated increase in the importance of the peer group, schools, and other socializing agents. Most researchers agree, however, that the family remains the primary socializing agent for the child at least until the teenage years (Maccoby, 1992; Peterson & Rollins, 1987).

Perception of the direction of influence has changed, however. Originally, most theories of childhood socialization advocated a one-way, "top-down" socialization model in which parents were understood to be the teachers and children the "empty vessels who were gradually filled up with the necessary social repertoires" (Maccoby, 1992, p. 1007). Society was understood to shape parents, and parents were understood to shape children (see, e.g., Inkeles, 1968; Parsons & Bales, 1955). More recent socialization theories, however, tend to promote the idea of reciprocal influence between parent and child, where socialization is both an ongoing and an interactive process. Children increasingly are seen as active participants in their own socialization, acting back on their environments, socializing those around them (including their own parents), even as they themselves are socialized (Corsaro, 1997; Maccoby, 1992; Peterson & Rollins, 1987).

PARENTS' TRADITIONAL ROLE
IN ENGENDERING CHILDREN

Because during the early part of the 20th century most people considered gender identity to be a natural by-product of childhood maturation, researchers gave scant attention to studying how and why children developed specific gender-linked traits and behaviors. It was not until the 1950s and 1960s that social scientists began to pay more attention to parents' role in forming childhood gender, but even then they were mostly concerned with maintaining the status quo. Researchers, doctors, social workers, religious leaders, and parents wanted to make sure that boys turned out "masculine" and girls turned out "feminine." In general, there was a consensus among the "experts" that boys and girls should be treated differently and that this differential treatment was both normal and beneficial for the entire society.

The civil rights and women's movements of the 1960s and 1970s introduced new ideas about gender into popular and scientific debates over how children should be raised. As a result of the change in consciousness engendered by these social movements, people began to ask whether child-rearing techniques might not actually be promoting prejudice and perpetuating inequality. Rather than being advantageous, rigid and polarized stereotypes might be preventing boys and girls from developing their full human potential. This view represented a radical change from the earlier insistence that boys needed manly role models and girls required stay-at-home moms to forestall their becoming social misfits. Thus a new ideal of more gender-neutral child rearing emerged, continuing to gain in popularity through the 1970s and 1980s and into the 1990s.

Theories of Gender Development

Once researchers began questioning the origins of gender identity in children, various theories surfaced to attempt to explain how gender was acquired. Around the turn of the century, Freud (1905, 1924) suggested that, rather than gender naturally evolving as a child matured, a mother's relationship to her infant instead formed the basis for the development of a normal adult sexual identity. Freud did not assume, for example, that a male infant would automatically develop a male sexual identity just because he had a penis. According to Freud, the interplay of sexual attractions between a child and his or her mother fashioned the child's sexual identity, which unfolded through various stages, each of which required its own successful resolution.

Freud suggested that children had innate sexual urges that they learned to direct, at an unconscious level, toward "appropriate" others in the context of family interactions. His theories assumed that the most important interactions took place early in the child's life, shaping the child's gender identity and setting the emotional tone of psychological dilemmas that he or she would later encounter as an adult. According to Freud, because the individual's self is at first merged with the mother, an infant does not have a firm sense of separateness. Infants of both sexes are cared for by mothers; therefore, "mother" is symbolically and unconsciously incorporated into both boys' and girls' psyches. As the primary caregiver, the mother also is the first erotic love object for both sexes. For the child to develop in sexually appropriate ways, according to Freud, this early erotic attachment to the mother must be broken and directed outward. Although many of the specifics of Freud's developmental framework have been disputed over the years, his basic insights about the unconscious mind and sexual or erotic impulses have become part of our cultural stock of knowledge, used by many theorists to try to understand the psychology of sex and gender (Erikson, 1950; Mitchell, 1974).

Another individualized model of childhood socialization was developed in the early part of the 20th century by Piaget. Although somewhat different from Freud's psychoanalysis, Piaget's theory also was both social and biological, incorporating the basic idea that a child advances through a series of predetermined stages of increasing competence and self-regulation. Piaget (1926, 1932), in producing one of the first cognitive versions of ages and stages, concentrated on the child's interaction with and adaptation to his or her environment. Such interaction thus allowed the child to become an active participant in his or her own development process.

Piaget (1932) and later Kohlberg (1966, 1969) challenged the supposition that children are docile recipients of knowledge who learn by passively absorbing information from parents and other adults around them. Instead, these theorists assumed that children are active cognitive beings themselves, seeking information from their environments and organizing it in predictable ways as they try to make sense of the world and their places within it. Even if their minds can only grasp certain concepts at specified ages, children constantly are involved in seeking patterns and figuring out categories. Consequently, children construct a sense of self and learn about social rules as they develop cognitive capacities. For Kohlberg, both the nature of children's cognitive processing and the natural perceptual salience of the male-female dichotomy lead children to choose gender as a major organizing principle for social rules. For Piaget (and other theorists), it is the childhood "preoperational" stage that leads children to think that same-sex behavior is morally required and rigidly fixed (Bem, 1983; Kohlberg, 1966; Maccoby, 1992; Martin, 1993; Piaget, 1932). More recently, however, cognitive psychologists have determined that gender development is more complex and variable than Kohlberg and others had originally thought and that it must be understood within a cultural context.

Whereas Freud and Piaget focused on individualized models of the child's socialization processes, more "social" theories also were developed, concentrating on how the structure and functioning of society are maintained as the child comes to internalize common social norms regulating thought and behavior. For Durkheim, writing at the turn of the century, these communal norms took the form of the "collective conscience," which perpetuated social order as it was internalized by the child. Somewhat later, Mead (1912/1982, 1934/1967) created a model of childhood socialization that centered on the child's formation of a "self" through social interaction and internal conversations. For Mead, the child's route to development of self advanced through several progressively more complex stages, culminating in internalization of the "generalized other" or community of attitudes.

At about this time, Vygotsky (1934/1962), a contemporary of Mead, elaborated the concept of the "zone of proximal development." According to Vygotsky, the zone of proximal development represents that level of accomplishment, just beyond the immediate potential of the child, that an adult caregiver facilitates to draw the child developmentally forward. Later, Bruner (1986) emphasized "scaffolding," which extended Vygotsky's zone of proximal development by envisioning the adult as supporting the activities of the child until the child could perform those activities independently (Winter & Goldfield, 1991).

CONTEMPORARY PSYCHOANALYTIC
THEORIES OF GENDER

Freudian psychoanalytic theory subsequently was expanded by Chodorow (1976, 1978, 1985) and certain feminist theorists

(Dinnerstein, 1976; Johnson, 1988; Mitchell, 1974) who, although considering additional social factors, placed more emphasis on early infancy and corrected for Freud's relative neglect of girls' psychological development. Chodorow's theory presents a social explanation of why men and women seem so different in a deep psychological sense, based on who does the work of parenting (Chodorow, 1978). Stereotypically, men prefer "things" rather than people, a preference that appears deeply ingrained. Stereotypical women, on the other hand, seem to focus on people and emotions. They are more "relational," with fluid ego boundaries and a greater capacity to merge with those around them. In personal relationships, they prefer intimacy and warmth. Their identity is based more on how they are received by the group than on their solitary pursuits or accomplishments. This "feminine" temperament is perceived as being deep-seated and resistant to change, providing, according to Chodorow (1978), a good explanation for why women continue to take primary responsibility for raising children.

Possessing the same biological sex as her mother, it is not necessary for a girl, unlike a boy, to sever the deep primary maternal attachment, Chodorow maintains. For a much longer time than a boy, therefore, a girl is allowed to remain emotionally and physically close to her mother because her identity does not depend on being different or separate. Consequently, a girl can form a self without radically separating from either her mother or the internalized unconscious image of her mother. As a result, a girl tends to develop a "feminine" personality that allows her to intuitively experience the world in connection with others, thus retaining more of the sense of merging with the world that an infant experiences in the original love relationship with the mother.

Although also raised by a mother, a boy, unlike a girl, must reject his mother in the normal course of establishing a sense of self. The result is that a boy develops a "masculine" personality that is more disconnected and independent than that of a girl. A male infant, realizing that he is not like the mother, conceives an identity based on this difference. A boy, having internalized the mother in early infancy and experienced her as the first erotic love object, must distance himself not only from his physical mother but also from a deep part of his own psyche. Consequently, boys and men are predisposed to experience the world as fundamentally separate from other people, developing more rigid ego boundaries and tending to be distant from others. There is a tendency for men to be relatively unconcerned with their own or others' emotions, and they are therefore more prone than women to be instrumental and domineering (Chodorow, 1976). Chodorow's theory is thus a very general view of, among other things, how parenting practices perpetuate personality differences based on gender.

GENDER AND SOCIAL LEARNING THEORY

Early behaviorist theories of childhood socialization assumed that children's behaviors were learned through the administration of rewards and punishments. Parents, as the teachers, dispensed these rewards and punishments to reinforce the desired behavior of their children, who were the learners (Maccoby, 1992; Peterson & Rollins, 1987). Social learning theorists, recognizing that reinforcement alone failed to adequately explain how children acquire such particulars as attitudes, later expanded the behaviorist model to incorporate an emphasis on observation and imitation of adult and peer models as well as self-reinforcement (Bandura, 1962). According to social learning theory, besides "concrete" models including parents, teachers, siblings, and peers, "symbolic presentations" such as those introduced in the media can affect the acquisition of gender-stereotypical behavior. Social learning theorists also argue that "internalizing gender attitudes and identity occurs because one has already engaged in gender-typed behavior" (Losh-Hesselbart, 1988, p. 547). In other words, according to this theory, gender is enacted before it is internalized; thus observation and imitation of the gender model will lead to children's developing attitudes that will consummate their internal gender identification.

COGNITIVE-DEVELOPMENTAL
THEORIES OF GENDER

Within the past few decades, the cognitive developmental approach to socialization, which was initiated by Piaget and Mead earlier in the century, has expanded dramatically. Instead of assuming that all children everywhere go through the same developmental stages, researchers have begun to recognize complex reciprocal effects between children and their environments. Recent research provides fascinating insights into socialization processes occurring in a variety of contexts and involving complex correlations between social settings, cognitive structures, and emotions (see Cahill, 1986; Goodman, 1985; Maccoby, 1992; Power, 1986). In general, cognitive theories have focused on how developing children perceive the world, process information, and develop the capacity for rational thought. Although variants of cognitive development theories and studies associated with them are too numerous to summarize in this chapter, here we review one important version of the cognitive approach to gender, identified as gender schema theory (Bem, 1983). Gender, according to Bem, is not something that is naturally produced in the minds of children but instead reflects the gender polarization prevalent in the larger culture. Although it rejects the narrow ages and stages view of Piaget and Kohlberg, Bem's theory retains an emphasis on how children process information about the world as they develop increasingly complex cognitive and reasoning skills.

The core of Bem's theory is a cognitive structure called a schema, which is a way of organizing information in the mind. A schema, Bem (1983) said, is "a network of associations" that "functions as an anticipatory structure, a readiness to search for and to assimilate incoming information in schema-relevant terms" (p. 603). Although it allows individuals to impose structure and meaning onto a broad array of incoming stimuli, a schema also is highly selective (Bem, 1983). In this regard, Bem (1993) suggested that gender "schematicity" is

the imposition of a gender-based classification on social reality, the sorting of persons, attributes, behaviors, and other things on the basis of the polarized definitions of masculinity and femininity that prevail in the culture, rather than on the basis of other dimensions that could serve equally well. (p. 125)

A kind of perceptual lens, a gender schema predisposes us to see the world in terms of two clearly defined "opposites"—male and female, masculine and feminine.

According to this theory, children become gender schematic without even realizing it when the culture in which they live is stereotyped according to gender. Developing networks of associations that guide their perceptions, children come to see the world in gender-polarized ways. Because a gender schema channels our thinking along gender predefined paths, the gender categories it creates can incorporate a wide variety of information while at the same time implicitly forcing us to ignore other ways of categorizing people or things. Therefore, Bem (1983) suggested that, like schema theories in general, gender schema theory "construes perception as a constructive process in which the interaction between incoming information and an individual's preexisting schema determines what is perceived" (p. 604).

Bem's theory establishes connections between gender polarization in the larger culture, the organization of everyday life, and children's developing views of the world. From the moment they are born, children's lives are organized according to culturally driven gender-polarized patterns, from color-coded receiving blankets to sex-specific toys. The different ways in which parents talk to boys and girls, the different social experiences they provide, and the different expectations they have for them all communicate to children the ultimate importance of the male-female distinction. In this way, children learn that everything in their world can and should be classified according to gender. According to Bem, a gender schema is a culturally mandated way in which to view the world, not something over which we have either choice or control. Because it is interjected into our basic ways of perceiving and thinking, gender is rendered both unavoidable and unconscious (for related views, see Kessler & McKenna, 1985; West & Zimmerman, 1987).

The effects of gender polarization extend deeper than different color schemes for boys and girls. All children eventually learn to relate gender schematicity to the self. Children assess their own thoughts, feelings, and behaviors relative to the gender polarization they observe in the culture and come to view themselves in accordance with its unyielding either/or dichotomy. They tend to favor those traits and behaviors that presumably conform to the gender schema while avoiding those that do not. Learning, for example, that it is inappropriate for girls to desire power or for boys to desire intimacy, they enact these stereotypical scripts in their daily lives. Thus, according to Bem's cognitive approach, children's self-concepts also become gender stereotyped and "the two sexes become, in their own eyes, not only different in degree, but different in kind" (Bem, 1983, p. 604).

The notion of a gender schema that organizes our world and guides our perceptions is an intriguing one, and much research supports the idea that children generate cognitive frameworks and gender scripts that reflect cultural values and shape future behavior (Martin, 1993; Signorella, Bigler, & Liben, 1993). Individuals with polarized gender schemata are more likely than others to notice and pay attention to details that conform to the schemata and to quickly store that information in memory according to its link with gender. People with polarized gender schemata also are substantially faster than others at endorsing gender-appropriate attributes and rejecting those that are gender inappropriate. Bem also noted that individuals who describe themselves as more gender stereotyped tend to sort information into categories on the basis of gender even when there are other categories more appropriate for sorting the information, leading such people to exaggerate gender differences and to ignore the similarities between men and women (Bem, 1983).

Bem's work on gender schema has been confirmed and extended by other researchers who have evaluated how children create gender "scripts" (Levy & Fivush, 1993). Even very young children organize their knowledge of the world in terms of time-ordered routines that they regularly observe and in which they participate. There are, for instance, scripts for changing a diaper, going to bed, and eating dinner. Scripts furnish children with expectations about what to anticipate from different people in particular situations. Operating similar to schemata, scripts organize perceptions and permit children to understand, process, and predict events and related information. Children employ scripts to help them acquire language, develop cognitive categories, and learn logical reasoning (Nelson, 1986). Gender scripts are especially significant for the thought processes of developing children. For younger children, in particular, an occurrence that is inconsistent with a gender script is apt to be ignored, not remembered, or to be distorted in memory to conform to the script (Levy & Fivush, 1993). Gender scripts, similar to gender schemata, teach children that boys and girls are different, dispensing prescriptions and proscriptions for their respective behaviors. Early research indicates that preschool children attend more to scripts for their own sex; some studies find that boys have more elaborate scripts and are more concerned with following them than are girls (Fagot, 1985; Levy & Fivush, 1993).

INTERACTIONIST THEORIES OF GENDER

Interactionist theories, as the name implies, focus on how individuals create shared meanings through social interaction. According to Mead, on whose theoretical formulations most contemporary interactionist theories are based, the hostility of the natural environment coupled with the relative vulnerability of human beings necessitates that people cooperate to survive. Cooperation requires communication, and communication requires that people interact. Interactionist theories are grounded in the assumption that a person communicates in interaction by taking into account the actions of the coacting "other," a phenomenon also known as role-taking. Childhood socialization, for Mead, thus involves acquiring the ability to role-take. According to Mead, a child progresses through three distinct stages in which he or she gradually comes to incorporate first one and then many others into the range of his or her role-taking capabilities. A fully developed self is realized when the child finally is able to internalize the relevant social norms, or community of attitudes, which Mead refers to as the "generalized other."

Although interactionist theories have undergone revision and expansion since Mead's time, the basic idea that the individual must incorporate shared social norms and attitudes to effectively interact has been retained. Social interaction and collective tasks can be performed only if societal members "organize their experience and behavior in terms of shared rules of interpretation and conduct" (Cahill, 1986, p. 163). The object of childhood socialization, then, is to produce children who internalize these social rules, thus becoming "self-regulating participants in social encounters" (Goffman, 1967, p. 44).

Similarly, the goal of childhood gender socialization is to produce societal members who have the ability to regulate their own gender presentations in accordance with socially accepted patterns that typically are dichotomized in terms of masculine or feminine. One important interactionist model of gender identity socialization was suggested by Cahill (1986), who saw "the gender development process [as] the process whereby societal initiates are recruited into self-regulated participation in the interactional achievement of normally sexed identities" (p. 167). Although noting that "childhood socialization does not consist of empirically discrete, easily identifiable stages" (p. 170), Cahill nevertheless recognized certain phases through which the child is likely to pass in becoming a gender-self-regulating participant in social interaction. Although part of a continuous process of socialization, the "sequential pattern" of these phases can be characterized, according to Cahill, in terms of the nature of the child's participation as he or she interacts with the social environment that includes parents, other significant adults, and peers.

Cahill identifies these interactional stages as acquiescent participation, unwitting participation, exploratory participation, apprentice participation, and bona fide participation. He notes, furthermore, that with each passing stage, the child becomes more of an active agent in regulating his or her own gender performance relative to the participation of parents and others. As an acquiescent participant, the child simply accepts the gender investiture made by parents and other significant adults on the basis of the child's biological sex class. With continued exposure to gender-differential treatment and social bestowal of "gender-appropriate" traits, the child begins, unwittingly, to respond behaviorally in a gender-differentiated way. Acquiring the use of language and greater agency with age and maturity, the child then begins to explore various gender identity options. At this stage, however, the child finds, through both direct and indirect approbation and censure, that the alternatives are limited to either the derogatory category of "baby" or the alternate positive category of "big girl" or "big boy." Beginning to comprehend the boundaries of appropriate gender behavior that will lead to a favorable categorization, the child typically starts to incorporate a commitment to socially "correct" gender behavior that corresponds to his or her sex class. Thus "by the end of the preschool age years . . . children are self-regulating participants in the interactional achievement of their own normally sexed identities" (Cahill, 1986, p. 177). Nevertheless, although the child has reached this stage of gender self-regulation, it remains for society to recognize and honor his or her gender identification, which generally is achieved sometime after the biological stages that we call *preadoles-cence* and *adolescence*. In continuing to prepare for socially recognized (i.e., bona fide) participation in society's exacting system of gender interaction, the child acts as an apprentice participant, honing his or her gender presentation skills first in the context of same-sex friendships and later in the context of opposite-sex, or heterosocial, interaction. Finally, having attained the confidence of society that he or she is capable of "not only interactionally reproduc[ing] the natural and moral order of normally sexed persons but also transmit[ting] that disciplined system of social interaction to successive generations" (p. 180), the child becomes accepted as a bona fide participant in society's gender interaction order.

Cahill's model offers a persuasive interactionist perspective on how children participate in developing their own gendered identities. The agency of children in the process is both typical of interactionist theories and atypical of previous theories of childhood socialization, most of which portray top-down, parent-to-child socialization processes. Interactionist models such as Cahill's tend to "organize their insights around the theme of children's active participation in processes of socialization" (Thorne, 1987, p. 94), relatively deemphasizing the parents', and ultimately the society's, part in children's gender development. Recent research has largely supported a focus on children's agency in their own socialization processes, complemented by the idea of reciprocal socialization of parents and children (Boulding, 1980). However, to a greater or lesser extent, research also has continued to support the implications of parental involvement in children's socialization as well as social circumscription of the environments in which children are socialized. Although parental involvement in children's gender socialization may derive from the power that inheres in the parent-child relationship itself, it also may be less overtly an expression of dominance than an expression of guidance, direction, and encouragement.

TOWARD AN INTERACTIONIST SYNTHESIS OF GENDER SOCIALIZATION

We propose an interactionist synthesis of childhood gender socialization, supplementing Cahill's model by emphasizing the role of parents and cultural stereotypes as suggested in the work of Vygotsky, Bruner, Bem, and others. A child is born into a gendered universe that, for better or worse, currently uses sex class distinctions as a fundamental tool for simplifying the complexities of modern life. Thus, from the moment a child is born, his or her world is essentially circumscribed by a predefined gender schema, a "generalized readiness . . . to encode and to organize information . . . according to the culture's definitions of maleness and femaleness" that is "derived from the sex-differentiated practices of the social community" (Bem, 1983, p. 603). Although Bem suggests that this gender schema is "mediated by the child's own cognitive processing" (p. 603), nevertheless, it also operates to structure the child's world in gender-differentiated ways.

While organizing the world of the child, a separate, individually mediated framework of gender schematicity also serves to organize the world of the child's parent. This parent-mediated gender schema is indirectly transmitted to the child during the child's initial involvement as an acquiescent participant in the gender development process. As the child acquires increasing agency in the process, the elements of the gender schema that he or she cognitively interprets and subsequently internalizes will include not only the parentally mediated gender schema but also the experiences acquired in the succeeding phases of the child's "recruitment into self-regulated participation" in the society's system of gendered interaction. As a kind of cognitive frame, the gender schema acts for the individual, whether adult or child, as a link between the society's gender polarization and the way in which he or she orders everyday life. Thus this comparatively flexible cognitive frame of gender schematicity forms the backdrop against which the child's interaction with his or her parents takes place.

The childhood gender socialization process, as portrayed in Cahill's interactionist model, is a recruitment process designed to bring the child into self-regulating participation in a disciplined system of social interaction (Cahill, 1986, p. 167). In general terms, there is an implicit inverse relation between the active participation of the child and that of the environment that includes his or her parents. In other words, as the child moves from acquiescent to bona fide (i.e., legitimated) participation in the recruitment process, his or her engagement in the interaction becomes progressively more active. Conversely, parental participation initially is quite dynamic and then decreases as the child begins to be more actively involved in his or her own gender development.

During the child's acquiescent participant stage, the parent is the "investing" participant, actively imbuing the child with gendered characteristics drawn from the parent's cognitively mediated gender schema. For example, in one study (Rubin, Provenzano, & Luria, 1974), when parents were asked to rate their newborns shortly after birth having only the infants' sex class information available, girls were judged to be littler, softer, finer featured, and more inattentive than boys, although in reality the infants did not differ on any objective measure (Stern & Karraker, 1989, p. 502).

It is during the child's unwitting participation stage of gender development that we can begin to integrate Vygotsky's zone of proximal development and Bruner's concept of scaffolding into the interactionist model. At this stage, the parent (or significant adult other) provides reinforcement for the child's inadvertent performance of sex-differentiated behavior that generally has followed from exposure to sex-differential treatment in the initial phases of gender development. Vygotsky's zone of proximal development and Bruner's scaffolding both are conceptual tools that attempt to explain the manner in which the parent attempts to provide support for the child while drawing him or her forward developmentally beyond his or her actual developmental level. In this way, the parent's overt reinforcement and support of the child "perpetuates the interactional achievement of societal initiates' normally sexed identities and, by implication, propels the gender development process" (Cahill, 1986, p. 171).

As the child's more assertive explorations of gender identities emerge in what Cahill refers to as the exploratory participation stage, the parental scaffolding stage of interactional participation takes on greater salience, with scaffolding itself representing less active and concomitantly more supportive participation on the part of the parent. Here the parent continues to "entice" the child into achieving a more developmentally sophisticated gender identity, dispensing gender-appropriate props that encourage the child to explore mainly that gender identity which is considered to be socially correct. Toys, for instance, allow the parent to provide direction to the child, who at this point is beginning to "try on" various gender identities. Studies have shown, for example, that, during preschool and kindergarten years, parents give their children even more gender-stereotyped toys and furnishings than they gave them as infants. Boys' rooms accommodate more vehicles, sports equipment, animals, machines, and military toys; by contrast, girls' rooms house more dolls, dollhouses, and domestic toys (Bradbard, 1985; Etaugh and Liss, 1992; Pomerleau, Bolduc, Malcuit, & Cossette, 1990; Rheingold & Cook, 1975). Furthermore, when preschool children request certain toys, parents are much more willing to provide them if they are gender-stereotypically "correct" (Robinson & Morris, 1986).

In addition, as the child acquires more mature interaction skills and becomes a more active interactant with others in the social world, the child begins to develop and internalize his or her own gender schemata, further decreasing the amount of either active or supportive gender interaction needed from the parent. Although parent-child interaction relating to the gender socialization process generally is sustained for some additional length of time, parental participation in the child's recruitment process continues to gradually decrease until the child has acquired "both the complex knowledge and intricate skills which underlie bona fide societal members' actions and interactions" (Cahill, 1986, p. 164), that is, until the child has become a legitimate member of the gendered adult community.

Empirical Research on Childhood Gender Socialization

Although the relative participation of parents and children in the child's gender socialization process may vary depending on the interactional skills of the child, it is clear that the process itself begins immediately after the child's birth when the parents announce their new baby to the world in gender-coded colors and with sex-typical adjectives. At first, parents tend to invest their children with different gender characteristics based on stereotypic sex class expectations; later, children themselves take up the gauntlet and actively enact stereotyped gender roles as they begin to incorporate their own "appropriate" gender schemata. Numerous studies have documented various aspects of the gender socialization process including the respective roles of parents and the child in the proceedings and the degree to which sex-differential treatment is conferred on the child. In the following, we discuss some of the most relevant recent studies on childhood gender socialization processes.

Most adults go to great lengths to make male and female infants appear different although they are, in fact, very similar to one another. As soon as an infant's sex is known, parents and other adults begin gender-differential treatment toward the child. As already noted, color-coded blankets and identification bracelets generally are provided by the newborn nursery, with pink identifying girls and blue distinguishing boys. Gifts are selected for newborns depending on their sex; girls generally receive pastel outfits, often with ruffles, whereas boys are given tiny jeans and bright, bold-colored outfits (Fagot & Leinbach, 1993). So that other people can readily identify their infants' sex class, parents habitually dress them in sex-appropriate clothes and endeavor to style their infants' hair in stereotyped ways (Shakin, Shakin, & Sternglanz, 1985). Even the bedrooms of infants are decorated and arranged based on gender stereotypes; girls' rooms typically are painted pink and populated with dolls, whereas boys' rooms are painted blue, red, or white and contain an abundance of vehicles and sports gear (Pomerleau et al., 1990).

In one type of labeling study, people are exposed to a baby and then asked questions about the baby's personality traits or behaviors. Dressed in gender-neutral clothes, the baby is labeled "male" for some people and "female" for others. Other than the sex of the baby, people typically are given very little, if any, information about the infant. Because the baby's true sex always is the same, these studies can effectively isolate the impact of calling the baby a boy or a girl. Roughly two dozen such studies have been conducted; although their specific results vary, in general they show that the actual sex of the baby makes little difference because people rely on gender stereotypes to rate the infant. Interestingly, when the people doing the rating are children, this becomes especially true (Cowan & Hoffman, 1986; Stern & Karraker, 1989). For example, in studies using child raters, boy babies typically were seen as bigger, stronger, and noisier; often as faster, meaner, and harder; and sometimes as angrier and smarter than girl babies (Stern & Karraker, 1989).

In several studies looking at how adults interacted with infants, babies labeled "girls" were given more verbalization, interpersonal stimulation, and nurturance play. Conversely, more encouragement of activity and more whole-body stimulation were given to those labeled "boys." This pattern also has been noted for parents (particularly fathers) with their own children (Cherry & Lewis, 1976; Fagot, 1974, 1978; Fagot & Leinbach, 1993; Stern & Karraker, 1989).

Some of the labeling studies analyzed adults' choice of toys for babies to evaluate whether they were using gender stereotypes in interacting with infants. Approximately half of the studies indicated no differences, presumably because most of the toys were inappropriate for infants. Nevertheless, in general, dolls more often were given to baby girls and footballs or hammers more often were provided to baby boys, lending support to the idea that adults encourage play with gender-specific toys, even in infants under 1 year of age (Stern & Karraker, 1989).

Although not always the case, the general conclusion that can be drawn from these laboratory experiments with infants is that people have a tendency to treat boy and girl babies differently. Knowing an infant's sex is most likely to influence adults' evaluation of the infant if there is little other information available or if the infant's behavior is ambiguous. In addition, most of these studies have been conducted on college campuses with well-educated subjects who probably were trying to avoid acting in rigidly gender-stereotyped ways (Stern & Karraker, 1989). Most gender stereotyping, however, is perpetuated by parents in their own homes interacting with their own babies, although it is more difficult to draw statistical conclusions from such studies. Such research suggests that even with infants under 1 year of age, parents' expectations are different for girls and boys. Parents tend to construct the infants' environments in different ways, treat them differently, and in many subtle ways guide them toward gender-appropriate behavior (Deaux, 1984; Fagot, Leinbach, & O'Boyle, 1992; Huston, 1983).

Parents' attitudes and behaviors tend to have a substantial impact on the gender development of infants and toddlers, who develop gender schemata and gender scripts based on what they are exposed to in their immediate environments. In fact, infants are actively engaged in processing information from their earliest days, and they are exposed to gender-relevant messages from their births. By the time they are 7 months old, infants can discriminate between men's and women's voices and generalize this capability to strangers. Infants under 1 year of age also can differentiate individual male and female faces. Even before they are verbal, although they have not yet developed gender schemata, young children are developing gender categories and making generalizations about people and objects in their environments (Fagot & Leinbach, 1993).

Although they cannot always link gender to anatomical sex, preschool children between 2 and 4 years of age usually are able to perceive gender labels for themselves and other children (Fagot & Leinbach, 1993). By the time they are 2 years old, roughly 80% of American children can distinguish males from females on the basis of social cues such as hairstyle and clothing, but only half of 3- and 4-year-olds can distinguish males from females if all they have to go on are biologically natural cues such as genitalia and body physique (Bem, 1989; 1993, p. 114). In other words, preschool children in the United States learn that the cultural accoutrements of gender are more significant than the underlying physical differences between boys and girls.

Additionally, children quickly incorporate new information into their developing gender schemata. Before they are 5 years old, American children have learned to allocate bears, fire, and "something rough" to boys and men, whereas they connect butterflies, hearts, and flowers with girls and women (Leinbach & Hort, 1989). Although they are not directly taught to relate bears to men, by this age children are able to categorize using a gender schema that connects qualities such as strength and dangerousness with males. In the same way, flowers and butterflies become associated with being female through a metaphorical cognitive process that identifies women with gentleness (Fagot & Leinbach, 1993, p. 220).

As mentioned previously, during the preschool and kindergarten years, parents tend to give children even greater numbers of gender-stereotyped toys than they gave them as infants. Because different kinds of toys and furnishings promote different activities, they tend, in turn, to reinforce rigid gender schemata and scripts. "Masculine" toys such as trucks and balls foster independent or competitive activities necessitating little verbal interaction, whereas "feminine" toys such as dolls favor quiet, nurturing interaction with other playmates, encouraging physical closeness and verbal communication (Wood, 1994).

Not only do parents provide gender-stereotyped environments, but they also interact with preschool- and school-aged children in sex-differential ways, often rewarding gender-typical play and punishing gender-atypical play (Huston, 1983; Jacklin, DiPietro, & Maccoby, 1984; Lytton & Romney, 1991). In this way, boys are deterred from playing house and girls are dissuaded from engaging in vigorous competitive sports or games. Additionally, essentially all studies looking at preschool- and school-aged children find that parents engage boys in physical play more often than they do girls (Lytton & Romney, 1991; Maccoby & Jacklin, 1974).

Another area in which parents exhibit sex-differentiated treatment of their children is household tasks, where studies show that parents consistently assign boys and girls gender-segregated chores. Household responsibilities such as cooking and cleaning usually are allotted to girls, whereas more active duties such as lawn mowing typically are assigned to boys (Goodnow, 1988; McHale, Bartko, Crouter, & Perry-Jenkins, 1990). As with toys, performing different chores promotes specific perspectives on experiencing and understanding the world. Girls' chores usually take place inside the home, emphasizing nurturing activities and taking care of other people, whereas boys' chores usually take place outside the home, emphasizing the maintenance of things.

In other areas, gender socialization studies report more mixed results. Although some studies indicate that parents display more emotional warmth toward girls and encourage more emotional dependence in them, others find little difference in parents' tolerance of boys' and girls' proximity and comfort seeking (Fagot, 1978; Lytton & Romney, 1991; Maccoby & Jacklin, 1974). Although differences generally are small, research shows that parents more frequently encourage achievement in boys, discourage aggression in girls, and use more physical discipline with boys (Lytton & Romney, 1991). Researchers also report that these patterns can vary by ethnic or cultural group, with African American boys and girls socialized more equally toward both autonomy and nurturing than white children

(Albert and Porter 1988; Bardwell, Cochran, & Walker, 1986; Hale-Benson, 1986).

Results of Childhood Gender Socialization

Socialization helps nonmembers learn how to fit into the existing order of the world (Wentworth, 1980, p. 85). Gender prescriptions and proscriptions, even as they are socially constructed, can be viewed as one aspect of that existing world. Because children are socialized into existing gender arrangements, they tend to reproduce these arrangements as adults, assuming, to an appreciable degree, the masculine or feminine characteristics to which they have been exposed (Thorne, 1993). Thus, in a circular pattern, as gendered arrangements are socially reproduced, sex-typed socialization results, and as sex-typed socialization is enacted, gendered arrangements are socially reproduced.

Research into gender socialization processes has shown that because boys and girls are treated differently and put into different learning environments, they develop different needs, wants, desires, skills, and temperaments. In short, boys and girls evolve into different kinds of adults—men and women—who barely question how or why they end up with such dissimilar attitudes and tendencies. Although the causal process presently is the subject of debate, the basic underlying model reflects the operation of a self-fulfilling prophecy (Bem, 1993; Merton, 1948; Rosenthal & Jacobson, 1968). Assuming that boys and girls are supposed to be different, people treat them differently and subsequently provide them with different developmental opportunities. This differential treatment promotes certain self-concepts and behaviors that then tend to re-create the preconceived cultural stereotypes about gender. Thus a kind of social illusion is created, for, as the process repeats itself across generations, gender stereotypes come to be seen as natural and impervious to change in spite of the fact that such gender stereotypes are constantly re-created and modified in interaction.

Although the self-fulfilling prophecy concept actually is somewhat more complicated than this suggests, the basic idea is that if we treat boys and girls differently, they will develop in dissimilar ways. From a social constructionist framework, we can see that it is not just that boys and girls are fundamentally and unalterably different. Instead, they must learn how to fit in as appropriately gendered individuals to be considered competent members of society. This is a mandatory process; because of the importance of gender to the adults in our society, children are called on to conform to the gender standards currently in vogue. A large part of children's identity development involves forming their gender identities, and they must work very hard to make their actions and thoughts conform to the expectations of the people around them. In the process of interacting with adults and their peers, children literally "claim" their gender identities (Cahill, 1986). By applying the concept of "doing gender" not only to adults but to children as well, we can see that gender is not something innate but rather something that is re-created on a continual basis (Kessler & McKenna, 1985; West & Fenstermaker, 1993; West & Zimmerman, 1987).

In spite of the presumption that gender is socially constructed, most people do not believe they have choices about it; generally, they give gender very little thought at all. Rarely, in fact, do parents question how their own identities are interlaced with the meaning of gender, and most of them are unaware of how gender shapes expectations for their children. But in countless little ways, beginning before babies are even born, gender is rendered so important that it is impossible for children to ignore. For example, medical tests currently allow a pregnant woman to resolve the gender of her unborn child. Knowing the sex class of the child allows parents to decorate the nursery in gender-correct colors and permits well-wishers to buy gender-appropriate clothes and accessories, all long before the baby's anticipated arrival. Although some couples still prefer to be "surprised" by the sex of their babies, many take advantage of the opportunity to save time in the future by prepurchasing gender-relevant attire and, in effect, readying the gender stereotypes into which they subsequently will introduce their children.

Of course, once children are born, gender prescriptions and proscriptions (what boys/girls should do and should not do, respectively) become so much a matter of habit that parents rarely are even aware of them. Thus gender takes on a static quality in spite of the fact that "doing gender" is in reality a constant, ongoing process. The sense of gender is so ingrained in daily activities that it appears to take on a life of its own. In a very basic sense, gender becomes a lens through which the world is viewed. And this gender lens subsequently is transmitted to children without even a conscious awareness of the gender transmission process.

Socialization, of course, is not limited to childhood. In many ways, socialization never stops, given that adults continue to be faced with social pressures to adopt appropriate behaviors and thoughts. As pointed out previously, recent research provides evidence of reciprocal socialization effects between parents and children, with children contributing significantly to their own parents' socialization processes. Still, the dependence of children on adults, and their need to develop a sense of self in interaction with others, makes them especially likely to internalize messages about gender from the larger culture.

Intergenerational Transmission of Gender Stereotypes

In general, fathers enforce gender stereotypes more than do mothers, especially in sons. This tendency extends across types of activities including toy preferences, play styles, chores, discipline, interaction, and personality assessments (Caldera, Huston, & O'Brien, 1989; Fagot & Leinbach, 1993; Lytton & Romney, 1991). In spite of the fact that both boys and girls receive gender messages from their parents, boys nevertheless are encouraged to conform to culturally valued masculine ideals more than girls are encouraged to conform to lower status feminine ideals. Boys also receive more rewards for gender conformity (Wood, 1994). Because society places greater emphasis on men's gender identity than on women's, there is a tendency for more attention to be paid to boys, reflecting an androcentric cultural bias that values masculine traits over feminine ones (Bem, 1993; Broverman, Broverman, Clarkson, Rosenkrantz, & Vogel, 1970; Lorber, 1994).

Masculine gender identity also is considered to be more fragile than feminine gender identity (Bem, 1993; Chodorow, 1978; Dinnerstein, 1976; Mead, 1949) and takes more psychic effort because it requires suppressing human feelings of vulnerability and denying emotional connection (Chodorow, 1978; Maccoby & Jacklin, 1974). Thus boys are given less gender latitude than are girls, and fathers are more intent than mothers on making sure that their sons do not become "sissies." Later, as a result, these boys-turned-men will tend to spend considerable amounts of time and energy maintaining gender boundaries and denigrating women and gays (Connell, 1995; Kimmel & Messner, 1994).

Nonetheless, fathers' role in sustaining gender difference is neither fixed nor inevitable. Mothers' relatively lax enforcement of gender stereotypes relates to the amount of time they spend with children. Because they perform most of the child care, mothers tend to be more pragmatic about the similarities and dissimilarities between children, and their perceptions of an individual child's abilities are, therefore, somewhat less likely to be influenced by preconceived gender stereotypes. Similarly, when men are single parents or actively coparent, they behave more like conventional mothers than like standard fathers (Coltrane, 1996; Risman, 1989). Involved fathers, like mothers, encourage sons and daughters equally, using similar interaction and play styles for both. They also tend to avoid both rigid gender stereotypes and the single-minded emphasis on rough-and-tumble play that are customary among traditional fathers (Coltrane, 1989; Parke, 1996). As a result, boys hold less stereotyped gender attitudes as teenagers and young adults when fathers exhibit close, nurturing, ongoing relationships with them as preschool- or school-aged children (Hardesty, Wenk, & Morgan, 1995; Williams, Radin, & Allegro, 1992).

The bottom line illustrated by recent research shows that parents tend to establish different learning environments for boys and girls and expect them to do different things, although these patterns are beginning to weaken slightly. Girls are given dolls and tea sets to play with while being encouraged to cuddle, clean house, and take care of others. Boys are supplied with balls and trucks, are actively engaged in rough-and-tumble play, and are required to take out the trash. Generally speaking, girls are expected to be kind and caring, whereas boys are presumed to be independent and aggressive.

Importantly, differences in the ways in which parents act toward boys and girls perpetuate separate spheres for men and women. Parents promote nurturing behaviors for girls and autonomy for boys by creating different social environments and holding different expectations for them. In this way, parents promote the formation of gender schemata, gendered personalities, and taken-for-granted gender scripts that make gender differences seem natural and inescapable (Crouter, McHale, & Bartko, 1993; Eccles, Jacobs, & Harold, 1990; Etaugh & Liss, 1992; Thompson & Walker, 1989). Most girls, for example, grow up with an interest in babies. They also are more responsive to infants and take more responsibility for them than do boys (Ullian, 1984). Experiencing more contact with young children, girls also have more opportunities to develop nurturing capacities, and by the time they reach childbearing age they are predisposed to want to bear children and to take primary responsibility for their care (Bem, 1993; Chodorow, 1978). Boys, on the other hand, are likely to be unemotional, competitive, and individualistic, developing into young adult men who are relatively uninterested in babies and unprepared to care for the emotional needs of others.

In addition, because of these gender ideals, young men tend to grow up feeling entitled to the domestic services of women. Preoccupied with reaffirming their masculinity, men also are prone to use violence when they feel threatened (Connell, 1995; Kaufman, 1993; Kimmel & Messner, 1994). These individual gender attributes and parenting preferences, in turn, help reproduce cultural gender differences and perpetuate gender inequality in the larger society (Chafetz, 1990; Coltrane, 1988; Hartsock, 1983). Clearly, by raising children to be "proper" boys and girls, parents prepare the next generation to occupy unequal positions in a system of gender hierarchy.

Feminist Critique of Childhood Socialization

Historically, largely through the perpetuation and internalization of gender differences, women's identification with motherhood, and thereby with children, has come to describe their femininity in some essential way. As the parent who bears and nurses the infant, the mother is "naturally" assumed to have a closer, more symbiotic relationship with her child than is the child's father. This assumed symbiosis has, in fact, often worked to the detriment of both mother and child, as patriarchal cultures have tended to define the mother by her relationship to her child, whereas by association the child remains tied to the culture's ideological derogation of women. Even men are ultimate victims of a system that perpetuates a masculinity that essentially dehumanizes them both through an absence of emotion and, ultimately, through violence.

Feminists have, therefore, been among the forerunners in attempting to change the traditional patriarchal family structure and the system of childhood gender socialization, both of which have contributed to reproduction of the existing gender hierarchy. In the past several decades, due, among other reasons, to women's dramatic increase in participation in the paid workforce and to the ideological changes wrought by the current women's movement, changes are beginning to be noted in the traditional family structure. We currently are seeing the rise of alternative family forms that include increases in single-parent families, gay and lesbian households, stepparenting situations, and cohabiting couples both with and without children. Gender socialization practices appear, however, to be somewhat more resistant and slower to change because, perhaps, as Alanen (1990) suggested, the "*new* family arrangements are evaluated against the *accepted* knowledge of childhood and socialization, that is, knowledge based on observations of a particular version of the family" (p. 15; emphases added).

Feminists contend that in past forms of social organization, neither women nor children have been considered active participants in the public sphere. Only in recent times, largely through the efforts of the contemporary wave of the women's movement, have women begun to be "re-visioned as active, speaking subjects" (Thorne, 1987, p. 88). Children, however, continue to be marginalized; unless identified as a social problem by adult society, children remain on the fringes of the public adult world (Denzin, 1973; Thorne, 1987). Childhood socialization practices are, in effect, aimed at reproducing adults, and the child "remains *negatively defined*: defined not by what the child *is* but by what he or she is *not* but is subsequently going to be" (Alanen, 1990, p. 16; emphases in original).

What suggestions do feminists make for changing the existing process of childhood gender socialization? The theorist and ethnographer Thorne (1993) suggested that we cannot continue to view childhood socialization as a process leading to the end result of grown adults; instead, we must view children interacting as an end in itself. The typical view of socialization is an adult-centered view in which the power and authority of grown-ups is taken for granted. It does not allow for questions about social control, status inequities, or children's rights to self-determination (Alanen, 1990; Speier, 1976). We ought to be moving toward theories and research agendas that minimize the elitism of the adult-centered worldview and begin to acknowledge children as agents in their own socialization processes. If we can incorporate images of children as agents in our models, we will come closer to seeing socialization as a socially constructed process rather than as a process of simple internalization.

Deconstructing the family into diverse types and experiences of families has been one goal of feminist family studies. Granting agency and autonomy to both women and children is another. As Thorne (1987, p. 97) noted, women and children repeatedly have been defined in terms of one another. More thorough study of children, in all their diversity and in varied institutional contexts, will provide an important corrective for past socialization research and will strengthen feminist visions of and strategies for social change (p. 104).

Conclusion

The family is considered to be the most important primary socializing agent for the child, the context in which he or she learns to be not only an adult but an adult with a masculine or feminine gender identity. Historical theories of socialization that viewed the process as a top-down model transmitting social values from society to parent to child recently have been challenged to reflect more reciprocal socialization effects between parents and child. Nevertheless, the power and dependency structure of the parent-child relationship still is reflected in the transmission of gender schemata and gender scripts to children. In effect, we see that current patterns of gender socialization tend to reflect a kind of self-fulfilling prophecy in which the parents treat their child differently and harbor differential expectations for gender-appropriate behavior based on his or her sex class. This differential treatment is then internalized as part and parcel of the child's gender identity, which then reasserts the existing gender order as the child reaches adulthood and begins to interact with children of his or her own. The results tend to reproduce patterns of males as unemotional, nonnurturing, sometimes violent men and females as nurturing, emotional, dependent women.

We also see that the current patterns of childhood socialization can change. The traditional father, as we have noted, tends to be the parent most actively involved in perpetuating rigid gender stereotypes in his children. However, we also have observed that as fathers become more actively involved in parenting, their rigid gender stereotypes tend to soften; here, then, is one avenue for change. Similarly, feminists are actively championing acknowledgment of children's agency in socialization processes, hoping that strengthening children's voices will promote deconstruction of the patriarchal edifice that historically has engulfed both women and children.

References

Alanen, L. (1990). Rethinking socialization, the family, and childhood. *Sociological Studies of Child Development, 3,* 13-28.

Albert, A. A., & Porter, J. R. (1988). Children's gender-role stereotypes: A sociological investigation of psychological models. *Sociological Forum, 3,* 184-210.

Bandura, A. (1962). Social learning through imitation. In M. Jones (Ed.), *Nebraska Symposium on Motivation* (pp. 211-274). Lincoln: University of Nebraska Press.

Bardwell, J. R., Cochran, S. W., & Walker, S. (1986). Relationship of parental education, race, and gender to sex role stereotyping in 5-year-old kindergartners. *Sex Roles, 15,* 275-281.

Bem, S. L. (1983). Gender schema theory and its implications for child development: Raising gender-aschematic children in a gender-schematic society. *Signs: Journal of Women in Society and Culture, 8,* 598-616.

Bem, S. L. (1989). Genital knowledge and constancy in preschool children. *Child Development, 60,* 649-662.

Bem, S. L. (1993). *The lenses of gender.* New Haven, CT: Yale University Press.

Bleier, R. (1984). *Science and gender.* New York: Pergamon.

Boulding, E. (1980). The nurture of adults by children in family settings. *Research in the Interweave of Social Roles: Women and Men, 1,* 167-189.

Bradbard, M. R. (1985). Sex differences in adults' gifts and children's toy requests at Christmas. *Psychological Reports, 56,* 969-970.

Broverman, I., Broverman, D. M., Clarkson, F. E., Rosenkrantz, P. S., & Vogel, S. R. (1970). Sex-role stereotypes and clinical judgments of mental health. *Journal of Consulting and Clinical Psychology, 34,* 1-7.

Bruner, J. S. (1986). *Actual minds, possible worlds.* Cambridge, MA: Harvard University Press.

Butler, J. P. (1990). *Gender trouble: Feminism and the subversion of identity*. New York: Routledge.

Cahill, S. E. (1986). Childhood socialization as a recruitment process: Some lessons from the study of gender development. *Sociological Studies of Child Development, 1*, 163-186.

Cahill, S. E. (1989). Fashioning males and females: Appearance management and the social reproduction of gender. *Symbolic Interaction, 12*, 281-298.

Caldera, Y. M., Huston, A. C., & O'Brien, M. (1989). Social interactions and play patterns of parents and toddlers with feminine, masculine, and neutral toys. *Child Development. 60*, 70-76.

Chafetz, J. S. (1990). *Gender equity: An integrated theory of stability and change*. Newbury Park, CA: Sage.

Cherry, L., & Lewis, M. (1976). Mothers and two-year-olds: A study of sex-differentiated aspects of verbal interaction. *Developmental Psychology, 12*, 278-282.

Chodorow, N. (1976). Oedipal asymmetries and heterosexual knots. *Social Problems, 23*, 454-467.

Chodorow, N. (1978). *The reproduction of mothering: Psychoanalysis and the sociology of gender*. Berkeley: University of California Press.

Chodorow, N. (1985). Beyond drive theory: Object relations and the limits of radical individualism. *Theory and Society, 14*, 271-319.

Collins, R., & Coltrane, S. (1995). *Sociology of marriage and the family* (4th ed.). Chicago: Nelson-Hall.

Coltrane, S. (1988). Father-child relationships and the status of women. *American Journal of Sociology, 93*, 1060-1095.

Coltrane, S. (1989). Household labor and the routine production of gender. *Social Problems, 36*, 473-490.

Coltrane, S. (1996). *Family man: Fatherhood, housework, and gender equity*. New York: Oxford University Press.

Coltrane, S. (1997). *Gender and families*. Thousand Oaks, CA: Pine Forge.

Connell, R. W. (1995). *Masculinities*. Berkeley: University of California Press.

Corsaro, W. A. (1997). *The sociology of childhood*. Thousand Oaks, CA: Pine Forge.

Cowan, G., & Hoffman, C. D. (1986). Gender stereotyping in young children: Evidence to support a concept-learning model. *Sex Roles, 14*, 211-224.

Crouter, A. C., McHale, S. M., & Bartko, W. T. (1993). Gender as an organizing feature in parent-child relationships. *Journal of Social Issues, 49*, 161-174.

Deaux, K. (1984). From individual differences to social categories: Analysis of a decade's research on gender. *American Psychologist, 39*, 105-116.

Denzin, N. K. (Ed.). (1973). *Children and their caretakers*. New Brunswick, NJ: Transaction Books.

Dinnerstein, D. (1976). *The mermaid and the minotaur: Sexual arrangements and sexual malaise*. New York: Harper & Row.

Eccles, J. S., Jacobs, J. E., & Harold, R. D. (1990). Gender role stereotypes, expectancy effects, and parents' socialization of gender differences. *Journal of Social Issues, 46*, 183-201.

Epstein, C. F. (1988). *Deceptive distinctions: Sex, gender, and the social order*. New Haven, CT: Yale University Press.

Erikson, E. H. (1950). *Childhood and society*. New York: Norton.

Etaugh, C., & Liss, M. B. (1992). Home, school, and playroom: Training grounds for adult gender roles. *Sex Roles, 26*, 129-147.

Fagot, B. I. (1974). Sex differences in toddlers' behavior and parental reaction. *Developmental Psychology, 10,* 554-558.

Fagot, B. I. (1978). The influence of sex of child on parental reactions to toddler children. *Child Development, 49,* 459-465.

Fagot, B. I. (1985). Changes in thinking about early gender-role development. *Developmental Review, 5,* 83-96.

Fagot, B. I., & Leinbach, M. D. (1993). Gender-role development in young children: From discrimination to labeling. *Developmental Review, 13,* 205-224.

Fagot, B. I., Leinbach, M. D., & O'Boyle, C. (1992). Gender labeling, gender stereotyping, and parenting behaviors. *Developmental Psychology, 28,* 225-230.

Freud, S. (1905). Three contributions to the theory of sex. In A. Brill (Ed.), *The basic writings of Sigmund Freud* (pp. 553-629). New York: Random House.

Freud, S. (1924). *A general introduction to psychoanalysis.* New York: Boni & Liveright.

Goffman, E. (1959). *The presentation of self in everyday life.* New York: Anchor Books.

Goffman, E. (1967). *Interaction ritual: Essays on face-to-face behavior.* New York: Pantheon Books.

Goffman, E. (1977). The arrangement between the sexes. *Theory and Society, 4,* 301-331.

Goodman, N. (1985). Socialization I: A sociological overview. In H. Farberman & R. Perinbanayagam (Eds.), *Foundations of interpretive sociology: Original essays in interaction* (pp. 73-94). Greenwich, CT: JAI.

Goodnow, J. J. (1988). Children's housework: Its nature and functions. *Psychological Bulletin, 103,* 5-26.

Hale-Benson, J. E. (1986). *Black children: Their roots, culture, and learning styles.* Provo, UT: Brigham Young University Press.

Hardesty, C., Wenk, D., & Morgan, C. S. (1995). Paternal involvement and the development of gender expectations in sons and daughters. *Youth & Society, 26,* 283-297.

Hartsock, N. C. M. (1983). *Money, sex, and power.* New York: Longman.

Huston, A. C. (1983). Sex-typing. In E. Hetherington & P. Mussen (Eds.), *Handbook of child psychology* (Vol. 4, pp. 387-467). New York: John Wiley.

Inkeles, A. (1968). Society, social structure and child socialization. In J. Clausen (Ed.), *Socialization and society* (pp. 73-129). Boston: Little, Brown.

Jacklin, C. N., DiPietro, J. A., & Maccoby, E. E. (1984). Sex-typing behavior and sex-typing pressure in child/parent interaction. *Archives of Sexual Behavior, 13,* 413-425.

Johnson, M. M. (1988). *Strong mothers, weak wives.* Berkeley: University of California Press.

Kaufman, M. (1993). *Cracking the armour: Power, pain, and the lives of men.* Toronto: Viking.

Kessler, S. J., & McKenna, W. (1985). *Gender: An ethnomethodological approach* (2nd ed.). Chicago: University of Chicago Press.

Kimmel, M. S., & Messner, M. A. (Eds.). (1994). *Men's lives.* New York: Macmillan.

Kohlberg, L. (1966). A cognitive-developmental analysis of children's sex-role concepts and attitudes. In E. Maccoby (Ed.), *The development of sex differences* (pp. 82-173). Stanford, CA: Stanford University Press.

Kohlberg, L. (1969). Stage and sequence: The cognitive developmental approach to socialization. In D. Goslin (Ed.), *Handbook of socialization theory and research* (pp. 347-480). Chicago: Rand McNally.

Leinbach, M. D., & Hort, B. (1989, April). *Bears are for boys: "Metaphorical" associations in the young child's gender schema.* Paper presented at the Biennial Conference of the Society for Research in Child Development, Kansas City, MO.

Levy, G. D., & Fivush, R. (1993). Scripts and gender: A new approach for examining gender role development. *Developmental Review, 13,* 126-146.

Lorber, J. (1994). *Paradoxes of gender.* New Haven, CT: Yale University Press.

Losh-Hesselbart, S. (1988). Development of gender roles. In M. Sussman & S. Steinmetz (Eds.), *Handbook of marriage and the family* (pp. 535-563). New York: Plenum.

Lytton, H., & Romney, D. M. (1991). Parents' differential socialization of boys and girls: A meta-analysis. *Psychological Bulletin, 109,* 267-296.

Maccoby, E. E. (1992). The role of parents in the socialization of children: An historical overview. *Developmental Psychology, 28,* 1006-1017.

Maccoby, E. E., & Jacklin, C. N. (1974). *The psychology of sex differences.* Stanford, CA: Stanford University Press.

Martin, C. L. (1993). New directions for investigating children's gender knowledge. *Developmental Review, 13,* 184-204.

McHale, S. M., Bartko, W. T., Crouter, A. C., & Perry-Jenkins, M. (1990). Children's housework and psychosocial functioning: The mediating effects of parents' sex-role behaviors and attitudes. *Child Development, 61,* 1413-1426.

Mead, G. H. (1967). *Mind, self, and society.* Chicago: University of Chicago Press. (Originally published 1934)

Mead, G. H. (1982). *The individual and the social self: Unpublished works of George Herbert Mead* (D. Miller, Ed.). Chicago: University of Chicago Press. (Originally published 1912)

Mead, M. (1949). *Male and female.* New York: William Morrow.

Merton, R. K. (1948). The self-fulfilling prophecy. *Antioch Review, 8,* 193-210.

Mitchell, J. (1974). *Psychoanalysis and feminism: Freud, Reich, Laing and women.* New York: Random House.

Nelson, K. (1986). *Event knowledge: Structure and function in development.* Hillsdale, NJ: Lawrence Erlbaum.

Parke, R. (1996). *Fathers.* Cambridge, MA: Harvard University Press.

Parsons, T., & Bales, R. F. (1955). *Family socialization and interaction process.* Glencoe, IL: Free Press.

Peterson, G. W., & Rollins, B. C. (1987). Parent-child socialization. In M. Sussman & S. Steinmetz (Eds.), *Handbook of marriage and the family* (pp. 471-507). New York: Plenum.

Piaget, J. (1926). *The language and thought of the child.* New York: Harcourt, Brace.

Piaget, J. (1932). *The moral judgment of the child.* London: Kegan Paul.

Pomerleau, A., Bolduc, D., Malcuit, G., & Cossette, L. (1990). Pink or blue: Environmental stereotypes in the first two years of life. *Sex Roles, 22,* 359-367.

Power, M. B. (1986). Socializing of emotionality in early childhood. *Sociological Studies of Child Development, 1,* 259-282.

Rheingold, H. L., & Cook, K. V. (1975). The contents of boys' and girls' rooms as an index of parents' behavior. *Child Development, 46,* 459-463.

Risman, B. J. (1989). Can men mother? Life as a single father. In B. Risman & P. Schwartz (Eds.), *Gender in intimate relationships* (pp. 155-164). Belmont, CA: Wadsworth.

Robinson, C. C., & Morris, J. T. (1986). The gender-stereotyped nature of Christmas toys received by 36-, 48-, and 60-month-old children: A comparison between nonrequested vs. requested toys. *Sex Roles, 15,* 21-32.

Rosenthal, R., & Jacobson, L. (1968). *Pygmalion in the classroom: Teacher expectations and pupils' intellectual development*. New York: Holt.

Rossi, A. S. (1977). A biosocial perspective on parenting. *Daedalus, 106*(2), 1-31.

Rubin, J. Z., Provenzano, F. J., & Luria, Z. (1974). The eye of the beholder: Parents' views on sex of newborns. *American Journal of Orthopsychiatry, 44,* 512-519.

Shakin, M., Shakin, D., & Sternglanz, S. H. (1985). Infant clothing: Sex labeling for strangers. *Sex Roles, 12,* 955-963.

Signorella, M. L., Bigler, R. S., & Liben, L. S. (1993). Developmental differences in children's gender schemata about others: A meta-analytic review. *Developmental Review, 13,* 147-183.

Speier, M. (1976). The adult ideological viewpoint in studies of childhood. In A. Skolnick (Ed.), *Rethinking childhood* (pp. 168-186). Boston: Little, Brown.

Stern, M., & Karraker, K. H. (1989). Sex stereotyping of infants: A review of gender labeling studies. *Sex Roles, 20,* 501-522.

Thompson, L., & Walker, A. J. (1989). Gender in families: Women and men in marriage, work, and parenthood. *Journal of Marriage and the Family, 51,* 845-871.

Thorne, B. (1987). Re-visioning women and social change: Where are the children? *Gender & Society, 1,* 85-109.

Thorne, B. (1993). *Gender play: Girls and boys in school*. New Brunswick, NJ: Rutgers University Press.

Ullian, D. (1984). Why girls are good: A constructivist view. *Sex Roles, 11,* 241-256.

Vygotsky, L. S. (1962). *Language and thought* (E. Hanfmann & G. Vakar, Trans.). Cambridge, MA: MIT Press. (Originally published 1934)

Wentworth, W. M. (1980). *Context and understanding: An inquiry into socialization theory*. New York: Elsevier.

West, C., & Fenstermaker, S. (1993). Power, inequality and the accomplishment of gender: An ethnomethodological view. In P. England (Ed.), *Theory on gender/feminism on theory* (pp. 151-174). New York: Aldine de Gruyter.

West, C., & Zimmerman, D. H. (1987). Doing gender. *Gender & Society, 1,* 125-151.

Williams, E., Radin, N., & Allegro, T. (1992). Sex role attitudes of adolescents reared primarily by their fathers: An eleven year follow-up. *Merrill-Palmer Quarterly, 37,* 457-476.

Winter, J. A., & Goldfield, E. C. (1991). Caregiver-child interaction in the development of self: The contributions of Vygotsky, Bruner, and Kaye to Mead's theory. *Symbolic Interaction, 14,* 433-447.

Wood, J. T. (1994). *Gendered lives: Communication, gender, and culture*. Belmont, CA: Wadsworth.

9

Employment and Child Care

JENNIFER GLASS

SARAH BETH ESTES

Until fairly recently, family historians agree, the provisioning activities of adult men and women complemented their child-rearing activities because both types of work were located and controlled within the family household (Bernard, 1981; Degler, 1980; Hareven, 1982; Lasch, 1977; Laslett, 1983). One of the most consequential of the massive social transformations associated with industrialization in the 19th and 20th centuries has been the separation of workplace from household and the breakdown of the prior symbiosis between production and reproduction. This problematic relationship between employment and child care has been the subject of various "stopgap" solutions since the mid-19th century—child labor, industrial homework, household extension, the ideology of separate spheres, and the fight for a masculine "family wage" among them (Amott & Matthaei, 1991; Brenner & Ramas, 1984; Kessler-Harris, 1982). Our current preoccupation with work-family conflict is merely the most recent incarnation of this seemingly intractable problem.

From the myopic viewpoint of the late 20th century, the problem seems to lie with the unwillingness of mothers to stay home with their children or the unwillingness of employers to provide family-responsive workplace policies, depending on one's political viewpoint. We argue, by contrast, that the underlying problem is neither with women's life choices nor with employers' intransigence but rather lies in the fundamental incompatibility of family time and industrial time, in the words of Hareven (1982). The remainder of this chapter is divided into three sections. In the first, we provide a historical and conceptual framework for understanding the rise in mothers' breadwinning responsibilities and our current child care predicament, in the second, we review the contemporary struggle to make workplaces family responsive and the extent of the child care problem in the United States. In the third, we summarize the negative effects of the current state of affairs on children and families. We conclude by offering an analysis of the individual and collective obstacles and incentives to change the current imbalance between employers' and children's claims on parents' time.

Historical Framework

It now seems clear that the agrarian household economy prior to industrialization, despite its inequalities and uncertainties in the provision of subsistence, did enable parents to blend child-rearing and productive economic activity. Indeed, the extensive use of children as household workers, apprentices, and servants in adjacent households shows that children were viewed as essential sources of labor in the household economy (whose contributions, of course, grew more valuable as they got older). The ability to use offspring as sources of wealth and old age support, when combined with high mortality rates in infancy and childhood, encouraged high fertility among adult men and women. This pattern has persisted in much of the world even to the present day.

Scholarship has shown us that this pattern of high fertility and child labor continued into the early period of industrialization in Western Europe and the United States (Brenner & Ramas, 1984). Early factories sometimes were filled with entire families laboring at the same location but at different tasks (Hareven, 1982). But this pattern did not persist into the 20th century because the increasingly onerous demands placed on workers undermined the health and well-being of mothers and children while the supply of male labor grew concomitantly larger as the need for agricultural labor declined. Immigration and continued rural-to-urban migration encouraged the formation of predominantly male labor unions that fought to "protect" women and children from the harshness of factory work by excluding them from collective bargaining and employment outside the home (Brenner & Ramas, 1984; Hartmann, 1981). In theory, at least, the productivity gains of industrialization would free women and children from the labor force, directing their energies instead to full-time domesticity for women and increased schooling for older children. Whether women wanted such a transformation in their social role and whether parents wanted the prohibition on child labor in favor of compulsory schooling are matters of historical debate, but the outcomes of the transition to industrialization are not. By the beginning of World War I, the ideology of separate spheres for men and women had long been established, child labor had been abolished, and a long-term decline in fertility had begun (Davis, 1989). Children had begun the transformation from being economic assets to being economic liabilities for their parents, and discrimination against women in the labor force had been not only institutionalized but also justified on the grounds that men earned a "family wage" to support wives and children in their new social roles.

More important than the historical details of this transformation, however, is the fact that it fundamentally altered the social contracts between husbands and wives and between employers and employees as well as the relationship between personal and collective well-being. Husbands and wives no longer jointly produced children and reared them together; fathers' responsibilities to educate and discipline their children waned as child rearing became an exclusively feminine preoccupation (Furstenberg, 1988). Once excused from the greater part of child rearing, men were more easily coerced into long hours of labor. Work away from home became the means through which men expressed their devotion to their families. The breadwinner role became men's family role, even if it meant taking two or three jobs to support their families and spending relatively little time interacting with family members (Bernard, 1981).

In such a normative family/gender system, employers were free to indulge their preferences for longer hours of work as a way in which to minimize training and turnover costs. Although work hours declined from the late 19th century until the 1930s, the movement for shorter work hours then came to a grinding halt at 40 hours per week with allowable overtime at higher pay. By the onset of World War II, organized labor had capitulated to a bargaining relationship in which hours and working conditions were set by management, whereas only wages and job security were negotiable (Hunnicutt, 1988). The significance of this newly institutionalized employment contract cannot be overstated; it forms the basis for the contemporary view that employers are entitled to establish workloads that require extensive overtime irrespective of the family needs of workers. The doctrine of separate spheres and the sexual division of labor it spawned also allowed employers to assume that employees were predominantly people without child-rearing obligations and to establish work rules and procedures that ensured the uninterrupted supply of labor to the firms (penalties for tardiness, procedural rules for obtaining days or portions of days off, etc.). In short, workers' time was controlled by the firms in exchange for access to jobs.

Finally, the transition to industrialization broke the symbiotic relationship between personal well-being and collective well-being. In the agrarian household, producing and rearing children who subsequently became law-abiding, productive members of society generated significant material benefits for parents. Industrialization and the new employment contract encouraged men to look to their jobs for monetary rewards, future security, and increasingly personal fulfillment (Ehrenreich, 1984). Although family life remains the locus of emotional fulfillment and personal identity for many, particularly working-class men, the attractions of family life clearly have waned for others in the late 20th century (Bernard, 1981). Women have been slower to heed the siren call of paid employment, partially because its rewards have been structurally blocked for many of them. But as the labor market becomes more open and less discriminatory, it seems likely that the powerful lures of money, status, and social integration through market work will affect them as well. Although the goals of parenting have changed little throughout the tumultuous economic changes of the past century, some believe that the motivations of parents to fulfill those goals have eroded (Coleman, 1993). Investments in children rather than market skills and experience seem rather foolhardy from a purely economic perspective; indeed, some demographers are seriously asking the question why people in advanced capitalist countries continue to have children at all (Friedman, Hechter, & Kanazawa, 1994).

THE SECOND OR POSTINDUSTRIAL REVOLUTION

Although the preceding analysis tells us much about male workers and employers, it does not reveal much about the changing role of mothers in the family and labor market. After all, if mothers continued to occupy their separate spheres with adequate financial support from men (whether in intact households or not), employers would be free to control workers' time without harming children's care or well-being. But the history of the 20th century has told a different story.

The underlying assumption of the separate spheres family/gender system was that the productivity gains of industrialization would require far fewer adult workers to produce enough food, clothing, and shelter for the entire population. Hindsight shows that those productivity gains were not equally distributed among all households, so that many adult married women worked in the formal or informal labor force throughout the 20th century, particularly immigrants and women of color (Amott & Matthaei, 1991; Kessler-Harris, 1982). Moreover, in the early 20th century, homemakers continued to produce essential goods and services for the household because no market equivalents existed (e.g., sewing, baking, caring for the sick or infirm), although they were not paid for the production of these commodities. By the end of the 20th century, it has become clear that whatever release from provisioning industrialization bestowed on human populations has been transferred more to the elderly population in the form of retirement than to childbearing women. Thus the fundamental premise on which the stability of the breadwinner/housewife system was predicated proved to be false. Women, even mothers with children, were needed in the provisioning work of industrial society, and that provisioning work increasingly took place outside the home.

In fact, much of the heralded economic growth of the late 20th century, particularly in the rapidly expanding service sectors, was due to the movement of ever more productive functions from the home to the marketplace. Not surprisingly, the bulk of the workers hired for this explosive growth in information processing, medical care, and personal services after World War II were women. These were jobs that frequently required high levels of literacy but paid low wages and often had functional equivalents in the domestic labor historically performed by women. One can arguably make the case that many of these functions were performed more efficiently and expertly in the market than at home. The transfer of these functions from home to marketplace could and did benefit many women who lacked male economic support; just as important, it changed the location and temporal fluidity of these tasks. Now these tasks were performed in "industrial time" at workplaces outside the home. Women performing these tasks lost control over the pace and timing of their work and, in particular, lost the ability to interweave these tasks with the care of their own children.

The expansion of the market into previously domestic domains in itself would have created a crisis in child care. However, the growth in women's employment was fueled by other dramatic social changes in marriage and men's economic status as well. The temporal separation of men from family life was paralleled by their decreasing dependency on marriage and children for subsistence. The newly forged emotional basis for marriage proved relatively weak compared to the agrarian interdependency of husband, wife, and children. The increase in divorce, coupled with relatively modest (and often nonexistent) alimony and child support awards for custodial mothers, diminished the logic of relying on male breadwinners for the whole of adult women's lives and fueled women's desires to obtain more education, enter the workforce earlier, and stay longer (Davis, 1989). Moreover, the transition to a postindustrial economy itself weakened the market position of male workers who had expended much time and energy in the early 20th century organizing labor unions to protect wages in occupations that were increasingly disappearing to automation and international competition. Even women in intact marriages stepped up their labor force activity in response to the stagnation or decline in male wages (Treas, 1987). In low-income and inner-city minority communities, the decline in male employment and wages has been so precipitous that marriage itself has suffered, increasing rates of out-of-wedlock childbearing, mother-only households, and subsequent child poverty (Wilson & Neckerman, 1986). Although these trends of increasing divorce, out-of-wedlock births, and stagnant male wages may slow in the future, it is unlikely that mothers' paid labor force participation will ever return to its 19th-century levels.

The Family-Responsive Workplace

Unfortunately, although almost everything else about the organization of households and workplaces has changed since the formulation of the breadwinner/housewife system in the 19th century, the fundamental employment relationship between management and labor has remained male centered and child free. The presumption of free labor sold for a wage to the highest bidder, who then sets hours and working conditions, remains the paradigm for industrial relations in this country. Although governmental regulation of the employment contract has existed for many decades in the form of wage and hour laws, for example, the state has been reluctant to intervene to establish some balance between family and industrial needs despite the proliferation of unsuccessful bills regulating the work-family interface and the increased rhetorical importance of "family values" in political discourse (Burstein, Bricher, & Einwohner, 1995). The Family and Medical Leave Act provides a case in point. Vetoed twice by Republican administrations, it finally was watered down to a 12-week unpaid leave covering establishments with 50 or more employees and signed into law in 1993. By 1996, however, recommendations that the legislation be repealed already were being sent to Congress by industry-weighted groups seeking to eliminate federal "unfunded mandates" to the states (Women's Legal Defense Fund, 1996).

In the absence of state involvement, private employers have been freer to set personnel policies dealing with workers' family obligations in the United States than in any other industrialized nation (Kamerman & Kahn, 1987). However, state sector and private employers also have been subject to mounting pressure from their employees to become more family responsive. Far from acquiescing quietly to the demands of the market, evidence suggests that the growth of women workers and the concomitant growth in men with employed wives have unleashed mounting discontent with the traditional employment contract. Many companies have responded with programs designed to address the family needs of workers for greater schedule flexibility, child care services, and work hours reduction (Friedman, 1990). Indeed, one report indicates that more than two thirds of the Fortune 500 companies have instituted some type of family-responsive program to remain competitive in the skilled labor market (Families and Work Institute, 1991). However, the extent and coverage of these programs remain poorly understood. In an issues paper for the Employee Benefit Research Institute, Nancy Saltford reported that women in professional and managerial positions are much more likely to receive family-friendly benefits such as funded maternity leave, schedule flexibility, and child care assistance than are women in less skilled jobs (cited in Kleiman, 1993). Given the associations between fertility, class, and occupational status, this means that the mothers most in need of family accommodations (e.g., young single mothers with little human capital) are least likely to receive them from their employers.

In general, the economic motivations to institute family-responsive policies remain unclear at best. Although work-family programs have generated enormous interest within professional human resource management and are the subject of numerous publications and books, solid research evidence showing economic benefits to corporations instituting work-family programs has been lacking. Most of the empirical literature on the topic has been based on single case studies of dubious reliability (Raabe, 1990), and some doubt that work-family programs can ever be viewed as economically preferable to the simple exclusion of workers with dependent care responsibilities (Hunt & Hunt, 1982; Kingston, 1990). Even the most optimistic observers of corporate climate admit that very few employers have moved beyond token acknowledgment of the family needs of employees (Galinsky & Stein, 1990; Raabe & Gessner, 1988). Moreover, the policies and practices of small firms, which employ more than one third of the total U.S. labor force, are substantially less generous where known, yet small firms represent the strongest sources of future employment growth (U.S. Bureau of Labor Statistics, 1991).

Given the current economic climate in the United States, workers may face even bigger obstacles to family-responsive policy in the coming years. Although both employers and employees want a "flexible workforce," that term means vastly different things to those two

groups. Pressured by shareholders demanding strong economic performance and international competitors seeking to undermine domestic producers, many companies are downsizing their labor forces,
extracting longer work hours from those that remain, and encouraging
the use of temporary and part-time workers paid lower wages and few,
if any, benefits (Smith, 1993). To employers, this represents a new
flexible workforce. By contrast, employees use the term to indicate
greater willingness to prorate benefits for part-time workers or job-
sharing partners, allow work at home, and encourage creative scheduling such as fewer work days or staggered work hours to accommodate
family schedules. Clearly, the forces of globalization and domestic
economic restructuring are encouraging employers to increase
productivity and exert more control over labor costs, goals that often
are at odds with workers' attempts to increase their family time and
preserve their families' well-being.

The kinds of family-friendly initiatives that come out of this mix of
employer and employee motivations display a schizophrenic quality;
they are designed to help employees cope with their child-rearing or
elder care responsibilities without actually fulfilling those responsibilities themselves. Again from the perspective of employers, the
motivation is to ensure an adequate, trained supply of labor to the
firm. Family-responsive policies that free workers to care for their own
dependents cut into the unfettered supply of labor to the firm and thus
are less likely to be institutionalized in the business community
without considerable external pressure (Glass & Fujimoto, 1995).
Although some classes of workers, particularly those with greater
market power, may get concessions that limit their employers' ability
to schedule work at will, such concessions are unlikely to be extended
to the labor force as a whole. Some examples of the most popular
work-family initiatives succinctly illustrate this point.

"Flextime" has become a commonplace, low-cost policy in the
business community. In two recent corporate surveys, more than two
thirds of the companies surveyed reported the use of flextime
(Families and Work Institute, 1991; Hewitt Associates, 1993). Glass
and Riley (n.d.) show that it was the most common schedule flexibility
policy available to a random sample of childbearing midwestern
employees. However, early evaluation research showed that flextime
was more helpful to workers without families than to parents of minor

children because school and child care schedules tended to be fixed and invariant (Bohen & Viveros-Long, 1981; Christensen & Staines, 1990). More recently, flextime was shown to have no significant effect on the retention of women workers following the birth of children (Glass & Riley, n.d.). Flextime requires that workers continue to work an employer-mandated number of hours and typically requires work throughout the "core" hours of 10 a.m. to 3 p.m. Moreover, most employees must obtain supervisor consent before they change their specific start and end times of work. These restrictions prevent the kind of flexibility parents require to attend school events, consult with teachers or health care workers, and stagger work hours with cooperating spouses to increase parental time with children. The really flexible scheduling options for parents—work at home, compressed workweeks, freedom to schedule particular days or hours at work, freedom to leave work for emergencies, and the like—are far more rare. Work reduction options—job sharing, part-time work with benefits, reduced-hour workweeks, and so on—are even more difficult to find (Hewitt Associates, 1993; Russell, 1988).

The types of child care initiatives that have received considerable attention (and been implemented in some cases) are equally problematic. The lowest cost services for employers to provide are information and referral services and flexible spending accounts for the payment of child care expenses. Information and referral services generally use lists of licensed or registered providers in the local community to assist parents in finding child care. In themselves, these services do nothing to improve the supply, quality, or cost of child care in the community. Just as important, they provide no guarantees to parents that the listed child care providers are trained, have spaces available, or will stay in business. The usual requirement is only that the providers meet variable and often lax state licensing standards. Flexible spending accounts permit employees to use pretax earnings to pay for dependent care, substantially lowering the cost of care for earners in higher earnings brackets. However, federal tax codes already enable most employed parents to avoid the same portion of their child care expenses through the Child and Dependent Care Tax Credit. Moreover, low-income workers who owe no federal income tax obtain no benefit at all from the use of flexible spending accounts because their earnings are effectively not taxed.

Other types of workplace child care assistance are more direct and, hence, less generally available. But even these are imperfect solutions. For example, on-site child care centers have been championed by some as a way in which to keep parents and children together, increase convenience, and decrease absenteeism and turnover. The best on-site centers do just that and frequently more (in the form of subsidies to lower employee costs, sliding fee scales, opportunities for parent involvement, etc.). However, many companies are simply subcontracting employee child care services to for-profit child care chains with little or no direct involvement ("Corporate Centers Important," 1994). When companies do set requirements for centers, they sometimes are designed to accommodate overtime hours, require sick child care, or give preference in admission to children of parents employed full-time or with greater seniority. Again, the motivation is to ensure the supply of labor to the firm by decreasing absenteeism and increasing worker productivity. These are understandable business needs that, unfortunately, conflict with children's needs for parental support and supervision. In the case of preferential admission, parents often are constrained from reducing their work hours or quitting intolerable jobs because their children would lose familiar child care providers in so doing.

Sick child care, whether in the form of home health aides, sitters, or centers, is an egregious redefinition of parental responsibilities; at the very time when children are most in need of the loving care of familiar adults in their home environments, they are asked to tolerate complete strangers in what are perhaps strange or even frightening environments as well. Although care for sick children is supposed to include only "mildly" ill children, the pressure is on parents to redefine their children's illnesses as mild so that they continue to meet their work obligations (Hochschild & Machung, 1989; Nelson, 1990).

Other innovations in child care are similarly problematic; some large corporations are offering emergency nanny care when regular child care arrangements fall apart or overnight child care for parents who must travel as a condition of employment. All are well-meaning attempts to assist employed parents but ignore larger questions about what might be best for children. Placed in proper perspective, all these workplace child care policies might be helpful and appropriate. But given the inability of workers to resist the encroachment of industrial time on family time, these policies may only further cement the control of employers over parents' time and energy.

Patterns and Trends
in Child Care

Given that mothers' employment outside the home is becoming ubiquitous and that fathers are increasingly less (rather than more) available to their children, the use of nonparental child care has been increasing and is likely to continue to increase. This is perhaps the most important consequence of the postindustrial revolution for families. Some parents have found ways in which to minimize the costs associated with nonparental child care; they rely on what might be conceived of as informal child care. This type of child care consists of activities such as sports, lessons, or public arenas for after-school child care (Louv, 1990). Through strategically coordinating shift work (Presser, 1986) to produce "tandem care" (Marshall & Marx, 1991), some parents are able to continue to provide parental child care. However, informal and tandem child care often are not adequate to fulfill all parental child care needs. Hofferth, Brayfield, Deich, and Holcomb (1991) reported that 82% of employed parents of preschool-aged children relied on more than one child care arrangement to fulfill these needs; this suggests that even those parents who use unpaid child care may not be able to do so to the exclusion of paid child care. Accordingly, paid child care has increased rapidly to meet the child care needs of employed parents.

The largest increases in child care for preschool children have been seen in center-based programs (Hofferth et al., 1991). The percentage of preschool children of employed mothers in organized child care facilities increased from 26% in 1988 to 30% in 1996 (Casper, 1996). The use of family day care (a situation in which a few children are cared for in the home of the caretaker) has dropped substantially, from 24% in 1988 to 17% in 1996 (Casper, 1996), whereas the use of paid in-home sitters, nannies, and relative care also has declined. Just as increased female labor force participation drives child care needs, it also diminishes the supply of these traditionally female child care providers. Women who might have provided relative care or been nannies or in-home sitters in a more restricted labor market now face expanded labor market opportunities; the benefits (especially financial) of these new opportunities often outweigh the benefits derived through providing child care. Although approximately a quarter of preschool children of employed parents are cared for by relatives, two out of three of these children are cared for by aging grandparents rather than younger relatives such as aunts or cousins. Finally, paternal child care increased, perhaps in response to the economic recession, in the 2-year period between 1988 and 1991. By 1993, care by fathers had decreased back to its 1988 level. The correlation between care by fathers and economic climate suggests that care by fathers may be driven more by economic factors than by fathers' preferences.

In the following subsections, the child care market is examined. The enormous increase in child care usage over a relatively short period of time has resulted in a lag between the rate of child care use and research on child care. Although recent research has identified some major issues in this area, there still are many gaps in what we currently know about child care. Three major issues are associated with contemporary child care options (Connelly, 1991; Robins, 1991). Culkin, Morris, and Helburn (1991) referred to these issues as the child care "trilemma"—comprised of availability, affordability, and quality. Although these issues appear to be related—parents frequently claim difficulty finding affordable, quality child care—some research has demonstrated that they are empirically uncorrelated (Waite, Leibowitz, & Witsberger, 1991). But the fact that child care cost does not directly affect child care quality does not mean that low-cost quality child care is easy to come by. Indeed, the fact that cost, quality, and supply are uncorrelated may be precisely what makes parents' search for child care so difficult. Unlike other market commodities, parents' willingness to pay more does not ensure greater accessibility or quality in the child care market. In the following subsections, we investigate these issues in more depth. However, a full understanding of the child care trilemma cannot be gained until we understand the role of parental preferences and sources of dissatisfaction with their child care arrangements. Thus, before delving into the issues of availability, cost, and quality, we first examine parental child care preferences.

PARENTS' SATISFACTIONS AND DISCONTENTS

In the 1990 National Child Care Survey, Hofferth et al. (1991) reported that 26% of parents indicated that they would prefer some other type of child care arrangement (or combination of arrangements) than what they currently used. The proportion of parents indicating they would like to change arrangements is consistent with earlier findings that showed almost a quarter of parents would like to change their arrangements (Hofferth & Phillips, 1987). The positive responses to this query seem out of sync with the 96% of parents who indicated they were *very satisfied* or *satisfied* with their child care arrangements. How can it be that parents are both satisfied *and* desirous of different child care arrangements? Hofferth (1992) suggested two explanations. Parents may be satisfied with respect to the available options even though they would prefer other options if given the chance, or their choices may be so constrained due to financial, scheduling, or other factors that they might not be able to use their preferred arrangements and thus profess satisfaction out of guilt. Galinsky (1992) offered evidence for the first of these explanations. She reported that 53% of a representative group of mothers using child care centers in Atlanta, Georgia, said they would have chosen different child care arrangements had they been given more choices. Although the majority of these women expressed satisfaction with their child care arrangements, this satisfaction was situated in a larger sphere of dissatisfaction with the available choices (Galinsky, 1992).

What lies at the heart of the disjuncture between parental preferences and actual child care usage? Hofferth et al. (1991) reported that 60% of parents cited reasons of quality in their preference for alternative modes of child care. The most frequently cited quality concerns fall under the rubric of program-related characteristics (including child/staff ratios, group sizes, and age ranges), provider-related characteristics (warm/loving teaching/parenting style, reliability, training, credentials), and facility-related characteristics (toys, equipment, homelike setting, health/safety issues). Research reveals that quality considerations are salient to parents when they are selecting child care (Galinsky, 1992; Kisker & Maynard, 1991) but that parents are relatively uninformed about what constitutes quality care from a child development expert's perspective (Cost, Quality, and Child Outcomes Study Team, 1995).

The disjuncture between preferences and professed satisfaction with actual arrangements does not prevent us from drawing some tentative conclusions from consistent results. Sonenstein (1991) noted that, judging from use patterns, almost two thirds of all parents prefer parental to nonparental care for their infants of 1 year of age or under. Most of the parents whose behavior did not reflect a preference for parental child care were employed mothers. Yet a Detroit-area representative sample of employed mothers of preschool children showed that 64% of these mothers preferred parental to nonparental care for children under 1 year of age (Mason & Kuhlthau, 1989).

Moreover, there is evidence that parental child care preferences vary with the age of the children. The Detroit study reported a growing proportion of families that preferred nonparental care as children get older (Mason & Kuhlthau, 1989). Other evidence also supports the notion that as children grow older, parents prefer a structured child care atmosphere that emphasizes learning and preparation for school (Hofferth et al., 1991; Kisker, Maynard, Gordon, & Strain, 1989). Given these caveats concerning parental preferences and actual child care arrangements, we now turn to a discussion of the availability and supply of child care.

AVAILABILITY AND SUPPLY

As our dependence on paid child care still is relatively new, institutional arrangements for the market provision of child care may not yet be fully developed. Moreover, the evidence that parents prefer different types of care at different ages suggests that the issue of availability will vary by age (i.e., supply issues may differ across ages of children). Hofferth et al. (1991) dismissed concern over inadequacy in the supply of child care by contending that there was no schism between the demand for child care and the supply of child care. However, their argument did not consider the disjuncture between parental preferences and actual child care options, and their analysis was limited to the child care center arena. Although spaces at child care centers may be increasing with increasing numbers of preschool children, center spaces do not make up the bulk of child care. Other evidence shows that center spaces account for less than one third of preschool children and fewer than one tenth of school-age children (Casper, 1996; Hofferth et al., 1991). Prosser and McGroder (1992) argued that we are not sure what kind of availability problems are associated with noncenter forms of care. Additionally, these authors, as well as others (see Blau, 1991; Brayfield, Deich, & Hofferth, 1993; Cattan, 1991; Marshall & Marx, 1991; Sonenstein, 1991), drew attention to the latent demand for child care emanating from potential labor force entrants who remain out of the labor force due to the lack of affordable child care. Although it is hard to identify the latent demand population, it seems likely that this group is comprised of at least some lower income, often single women whose employment may be contingent on securing child care. In this case, the availability of child care is directly related to its affordability. If affordable child care is not available, then these women cannot work outside of the home.

In general, the availability issue is difficult to divorce from the affordability issue (Connelly, 1991; Kisker & Maynard, 1991). Connelly (1991) stated that problems with obtaining child care many times are more specifically problems obtaining child care at a price families are able or willing to pay. It follows that child care may be in short supply to some groups or in some forms, although in general there appears to be no schism between supply and demand (Kisker & Maynard, 1991). For example, although there appears to be enough slots among various types of child care providers for children who are toilet trained, infant care is in short supply; what does exist is more expensive than care for older preschool children (Sale, 1984). Additionally, after-hours child care is limited in its availability, as is affordable part-time care.

Presser (1992) summarized the state of availability research by saying, "We really do not have an adequate enough understanding of the child care market to say with any confidence . . . whether supply equals demand" (p. 27). In general, much research on supply and demand reflects how this dynamic functions in the formal child care market. But employed parents often use a combination of formal and informal child care to obtain adequate coverage (Hofferth et al., 1991). Relying on data for any one form of child care to ascertain whether or not child care supply is adequate to meet demand involves making spurious connections between a specific type of care and the general demand for child care.

More importantly, evidence of equilibrium in the supply and demand for center care does not indicate that parents are able to obtain the child care of their choice. Although the demand-side economic argument claims that the supply of child care is driven by the preferences of those who demand child care, the research cited previously reveals that this argument is not uncontested.

Parents say that they often have a difficult time locating child care (Galinsky, 1992). Galinsky (1992) reported that parents likened finding out about available sources of care to entering a secret society. She characterized parents as "unsure about where to turn for information and how to judge the information they receive" (pp. 161-162). Hofferth et al. (1991) reported that parents in a national survey relied more often on friends and family rather than resource and referral services to find child care. Sale (1984) also pointed out that informal means of locating care are used more often than are formal means. It is likely that primary reliance on informal networks in child care searches makes locating child care that is in short supply (after hours, infant care, etc.) even more difficult.

Most parents appear to conduct searches before settling on a form of child care (Galinsky, 1992). In the Atlanta study, fully 94% of mothers looked to more than one arrangement before enrolling their children in centers (cited in Galinsky, 1992). In the 1990 National Child Care Survey, Hofferth et al. (1991) showed that in families with employed mothers, the median time between beginning a search for child care and making a commitment to a child care arrangement was 7 weeks. This parental search activity suggests that the discrepancies between what parents want and the type of child care they choose are caused in part by problems with the matching process that links providers to families seeking care. Even if one optimistically assumes that the supply of child care slots is adequate, the evidence cited shows that parents are unable to easily locate providers that meet their needs, whereas providers are inefficient in marketing their services (with suboptimal outcomes on both sides as a result).

CHILD CARE QUALITY

The term "quality care" is given various meanings in child care research. In the 1990 National Child Care Survey, the measure of quality was multifaceted (Hofferth et al., 1991). Some researchers have noted that although child care quality most often is employed to refer to care characteristics that lead to developmental outcomes for children, parents often use a different measuring stick for quality (Kisker & Maynard, 1991). Sonenstein's (1991) study of welfare mothers revealed that parents may be more concerned about location, convenience, and hours than about the developmental outcomes with which child care experts are concerned. Parents' concern about location, convenience, and hours need not be interpreted as a lack of concern for other aspects of child care quality. Parents who work nonstandard shifts, who work overtime, or who live far away from high-quality care often must prioritize their scheduling needs over concern for developmental outcomes even though that may not be their preference. The fact that most parents indicate that quality concerns drive their desire to change child care arrangements suggests that parents are having a difficult time finding quality providers within the location, cost, and hours "window" structured by their jobs.

How parents weigh children's needs (developmental) against their own (convenience) remains a black box in child care research (Kisker & Maynard, 1991). To complicate matters, it is unclear whether parents are aware of the schism between their own needs and their children's needs. Because of their limited understanding of the developmental consequences of child care for their children, parents may cite high satisfaction with their child care arrangements even if they are of poor quality (Cost, Quality, and Child Outcomes Study Team, 1995). Just as important, parents may have adequate knowledge but be unable to monitor the quality and consistency of providers' care. The inherent danger of inadequate consumer knowledge of child care quality is that providers' incentive to provide quality child care may be reduced (Cost, Quality, and Child Outcomes

Study Team, 1995). From a developmental perspective, child care quality is related to staff/child ratios, staff turnover, staff wages, staff education, administrators' prior experience, and specialized training (Cost, Quality, and Child Outcomes Study Team, 1995; Hayes, Palmer, & Zaslow, 1990). Additionally, state licensing standards have been found to have a strong effect on the quality of care; child care centers in states with more stringent licensing standards generally were of higher quality than those in states with more lenient standards (Cost, Quality, and Child Outcomes Study Team, 1995; Kagan, 1991; Phillips, Howes, & Whitebook, 1992).

Because child care has increasingly been viewed as a good forum for school preparation, the primary developmental outcomes of concern are those that indicate a child's preparedness for learning. Data from approximately 100 for-profit and nonprofit centers in Colorado, Connecticut, North Carolina, and California revealed that children in higher quality child care had more developed skills in advanced language and pre-math, better social skills, better relationships with teachers, and more positive views of themselves and their child care situations (Cost, Quality, and Child Outcomes Study Team, 1995). At-risk children proved to especially benefit from high-quality care; higher quality child care was related to better language skills for nonwhite minorities. Additionally, children whose mothers had lower levels of education exhibited stronger relationships between high-quality child care and their positive attitudes about their child care situations and their own competence (Cost, Quality, and Child Outcomes Study Team, 1995). These research findings reveal that, indeed, child care quality is related to increased preparedness for learning.

Although there is a general consensus on what factors are important to children's developmental outcomes, this knowledge has not translated into child care policy. Alarmingly, in the most elaborate and representative child care study to date, the Cost, Quality, and Child Outcomes Study Team (1995) found poor to mediocre quality at most child care centers it studied. Only 14% of centers were rated as developmentally appropriate, whereas fully 74% were rated as mediocre and 12% were rated as poor quality (or developmentally harmful) centers. Fully 49% of all centers had scores of 4 or less—at least one point below the quality designation of *good.*

More specifically, infant and toddler care (in which a majority of children were less than 2½ years old) was found to be of poorer quality than care of older children. Fully 40% of infant and toddler rooms were given poor quality ratings, indicating that the health and welfare of young children were compromised in these settings. The hazards in infant and toddler care were unsanitary conditions that may lead to disease, lack of nurturing care that inhibits emotional development, and the absence of developmentally appropriate toys that serves to inhibit intellectual and social abilities.

Preschool care (in which the majority of children were over 2½ years old but not yet in kindergarten), on the other hand, was of higher quality than the average infant/toddler care. Approximately 25% of these centers met developmentally appropriate standards. However, 10% of these centers still fell below the minimum standard. This means that 1 in 10 preschool children is exposed to care that fails to encourage the social and intellectual skills that are vital to a children's later educational success.

Another quality concern lies in the fact that many children are cared for in more informal, unregulated settings such as family day care, relative care, and babysitters in the home. Although some of this care undoubtedly is of good quality, we know little about informal care because it is mostly hidden and unregulated. Additionally, there is evidence that even in regulated sectors of non-center-based child care, the quality of care may be low. Sale (1984) asserted that the licensing of family day care programs does not ensure high-quality programs. In fact, licensure often indicates only that the family day care meets *minimal* safety and health standards. Compared to child care centers, it is expensive for states to regulate family day care homes. Thus they tend to go unregulated (Sale, 1984). Nelson (1990) reported that most estimates indicate that close to 50% of all family homes remain unregulated even if they might subject themselves to some form of registry. If the quality of care in child care centers that are regulated is relatively poor, then it is likely that care also is relatively poor in these more informal arenas. The lack of standards in day care allows extreme variability. Although some care facilities may be of high quality without the incentive of regulation, others certainly are of dangerously low quality because there is no imposed floor beyond which facilities are prevented from operating.

The provision of child care through the market in the United States differs greatly from the governmental provisions of child care in other Western nations. In contrast to Sweden, where the state takes a more active role in the provision of child care, the United States relies more on the open market in the for-profit and nonprofit sectors. The minimal governmental involvement in the United States might help explain why much of child care in the United States is of low quality.

The growth of the for-profit market in day care centers has quickened, and little regulation accompanies this unfettered free market. The quality distinction between for-profit and nonprofit child care has long been taken for granted (Kagan, 1991). Kagan (1991) explained that "convention holds that nonprofit providers offer superior child care because . . . they are altruistically motivated to serve children rather than make money" (p. 90). However, for-profit providers argue that they would not be able to satisfy customers and stay in business if they did not provide good child care. Most research supports the conventional wisdom, finding that nonprofit centers are almost uniformly higher in quality than for-profit centers (Cost, Quality, and Child Outcomes Study Team, 1995; Kagan, 1991; Phillips et al., 1992). Although the latest evidence from the Cost, Quality, and Child Outcomes Study Team (1995) indicated that there was no overall difference in the quality of services between for-profit and nonprofit sectors, this finding is due to the low quality of the church-affiliated sector of nonprofit child care. Although two sectors of nonprofit care (independent nonprofit and publicly owned nonprofit) were of higher quality than for-profit care (independent for-profit, local chain, and national system), the church-affiliated sector contributed to the appearance that nonprofit and for-profit child care services were of similar quality. Church-affiliated centers had lower staff/child ratios, fewer trained and educated teachers, lower education levels for administrators, lower labor cost, less cost per child per hour, and lower overall quality. Due to the separation of church and state, the church-affiliated sector generally remains outside the arm of governmental regulation; thus no minimum quality level is guaranteed for the children in this sector.

Interestingly, although a two-tiered system of child care quality exists, low-income children are not necessarily disadvantaged in this system. Children from low-income families or families in poverty are more likely to be in nonprofit care (as are those from high-income families), and so they do benefit from the higher quality of this sector (Kagan, 1991). At risk are those children from working-class and middle-class families who are disproportionately located in church-affiliated and for-profit centers.

As noted, the issue of child care quality is difficult to abstract from issues of child care affordability and availability. Connelly (1991) argued that both the availability of child care and the quality of child care are inextricably linked (e.g., waiting lists at some high-quality centers may be long, whereas other child care centers are underused). However, the price parents pay for child care has not been shown to be affected by quality characteristics such as group size, caregiver/child ratios, and the education of the caregiver (Waite et al., 1991).

COST AND AFFORDABILITY

Data from the Survey of Income and Program Participation showed that in 1993, employed parents with preschool-aged children spent an average of $79 per week on child care. This amount represents a $15 increase from the $64 per week families paid on average in 1988 (Casper, 1995). Combining family payments for all children in pre-school, organized day care costs averaged $63.58 and the average family day care cost was $51.52 per week, whereas in-home babysitters were significantly more expensive at an average of $68.31 and care by relatives was less expensive at $42.04 per week (Casper, 1995). The cost of day care tended to decrease with the increasing ages of children (Casper, 1995). Part-time mothers paid more per hour, which suggests that there is some penalty for using fewer hours of care. On average, children of employed mothers spent 37 hours in paid arrangements; for the subgroup of mothers employed full-time, this average was 42 hours; for those mothers working part-time, it was 23 hours.

The cost of child care varies little across income groups. This cost invariance illustrates the plight of low-income families (Marshall & Marx, 1991). Marshall and Marx (1991) summed consistent findings of surveys to show that parents spend on average 9% to 11% of their incomes on child care. This proportion is then taken as a general rule of thumb concerning what parents can afford to pay for child care. However, low-income families pay a larger proportion of their incomes to child care than do higher income families (Marshall & Marx, 1991). Again, the lack of affordable child care contributes to the absence of some women in low-income families from the labor market (Marshall & Marx, 1991).

The economic paradox in child care is that although demand for care has increased, this increase has not been accompanied by much increase in cost. Much evidence shows that families judge child care affordability using the measuring stick of mother's income (Marshall & Marx, 1991). If child care accounts for too great a proportion of this income, then cost-benefit analysis shows that families are better off in the short run if they use maternal child care, which costs the mothers' forgone incomes. This ceiling on child care cost underlies the latent demand phenomenon. Some women forgo paid employment because the cost of child care exceeds what families could reasonably pay to justify their labor force participation. Thus, in general, child care providers are inhibited from increasing their fees. Fee increases *unaccompanied by increased income for women* would result in fewer mothers working and thus less manifest demand for child care.

Various subsidies for child care also serve to keep child care costs low (Culkin et al., 1991). Demand-side governmental subsidies given to child care consumers, as opposed to supply-side subsidies given to child care providers, may serve to cap the amount of money parents are willing to pay for child care. Subsidies and tax credits of any given amount may serve as a disincentive to acquiring higher cost child care in that they cap the amount parents think they can afford to pay for child care. In a study using data collected in the Seattle (Washington) and Denver (Colorado) Income Maintenance Experiments, families in the treatment group were eligible for a tax-based subsidy for use in the child care market, whereas those in the control group did not receive the subsidy treatment. Treatment group families were more likely to use market care than were families in the control group (Robins & Spiegelman, 1978). The Cost, Quality, and Child Outcomes Study Team (1995) concluded that government agencies involved in securing child care for low-income children played a part in keeping the cost (and thus maybe the quality) of child care low by offering insufficient child care payments and reimbursement plans.

Additionally, supply-side subsidies by both private and governmental agencies serve to limit child care costs in both for-profit and nonprofit centers. Perhaps the largest child care subsidies come from child care workers themselves. Their forgone earnings (based on the differences between the wages a staff member could earn in another occupation given relevant demographic and human capital factors and his or her wages as a child care worker) function to keep child care costs low (Cost, Quality, and Child Outcomes Study Team, 1995). Even centers that offer mediocre-quality care receive donations and use forgone earnings of staff members to account for more than one fourth the full cost of child care (Cost, Quality, and Child Outcomes Study Team, 1995).

The lack of a direct relationship between child care quality and child care cost might be related to the ceiling on the price of child care and the existence of subsidies to child care providers. The Cost Quality Survey showed that nonprofit centers were able to offer superior quality care in large part because of the in-kind donations of space, utilities, and materials by the nonprofit institutions with which they were affiliated (Cost, Quality, and Child Outcomes Study Team, 1995). Knowing that their client base was unable to pay more in fees, these centers used interorganizational linkages and even corporate sponsorship to enhance their programs.

Effects of Increased Parental Employment on Families

Thus far, we have focused on changes in the location and amount of parents' productive activities and the responses of employers and child care providers to those changes. In this section, we turn to the responses of parents themselves to their changing work roles and the consequences of these new family arrangements for children. Although it is difficult to disentangle the effects of changing marriage and fertility patterns from transformations in the labor market because they are so intertwined, we focus on the latter. We recognize that children's overall well-being also is affected by family structure, racial and gender inequality, schooling, community resources, and the like, but we argue that specific forms of these social conditions frequently flow from the underlying changes in the relationship between production and reproduction created by industrialization.

One obvious consequence of increased paternal employment is a decrease in time spent in the home. Although the increase in women's labor force participation logically implies decreased time spent in the home by mothers, the decrease in home time has not been limited to mothers; in fact, the decreased time is a result not only of the increased labor force participation of women but also of employers' preferences for longer work hours and premium pay for overtime work (Schor, 1992). Schor (1992), with estimates from the National Income and Product Accounts of the United States, found that the average employed person worked 163 more hours in 1987 than he or she worked in 1963. These average hours were most noticeably increased for women. Women on average worked 1,406 hours in 1963 and 1,711 hours in 1987. The 305-hour increase translates into 7½ weeks of work. Men's hours on average changed from 2,054 to 2,152 for an overall increase of 98 hours or 2½ extra weeks. The increase in work time has not gone unnoticed. Research compiled in 1996 showed that a full 61% of women and 41% of men thought they had less leisure time in 1996 than they had 6 years earlier in 1990 ("Where Does the Time Go?" 1996).

How have families accommodated the increase in work hours? The increase has necessarily translated into less time spent in the home. Schor (1992) found that although men had increased the amount of time they spent on household work by approximately 3 hours per week, that increase did not match the decrease in women's time spent in domestic labor. The result was an overall decrease in time parents spent with children (Nock & Kingston, 1988) and an increase in the time children spent with nonparental caregivers. For latchkey kids, longer family workdays resulted in greater time spent in "self-care."

This decrease in time with children does not fit with formerly predominant cultural notions of what children "need" from their parents (Hochschild & Machung, 1989). However, as Hochschild and Machung (1989) pointed out, our definitions of what children need have changed as women have increasingly entered the labor force. To square children's situations with new work norms, the quality time paradigm of child care has replaced the quantity time paradigm. In their book, *Quality Parenting*, Albert and Popkin (1987) suggested that if parents worked hard, certain encounters with children could transcend the level of ordinary interactions to become "quality" interactions; these quality interactions were then posited to be a fine substitute for quantity of exposure to parents.

Parents' behavior has reflected this quality time logic. An analysis of detailed time diaries from a 1981 national sample of married couples revealed that although employed women with preschool children spent less time with their children overall than did non-employed mothers, the largest proportion of the difference (23%) came from the discrepancy in time spent homemaking. Employed mothers cut down on home-based activities that involved children only peripherally more than they cut down on activities that involved children directly (e.g., play, education, talking). However, employed mothers still spent less time than nonemployed mothers in so-called quality activities with their children, suggesting that employed mothers could not completely compensate for their increasing absence (Nock & Kingston, 1988).

Hewlett (1991) pointed out that although quality time may be attractive in theory, parents may have difficulty putting the concept into practice at the end of a demanding workday. Furthermore, some authors (Hochschild & Machung, 1989; Louv, 1990) have contended that the time crunch problem is much harder to alleviate than "quality-over-quantity" rhetoric suggests. In his journalistic exploration of childhood in America, Louv (1990) found parents rebelling against "time pollution" or

> the feeling that the essence of what makes life worth living, the small moments, the special family getaways, the cookies in the oven, has been taken away. We yearn so deeply for time—not quality time but free time, dream time, time to be with our families. (p. 24)

In other words, there is a growing concern that quality time cannot compensate for the common absence of parents. Hewlett (1991) criticized recent studies of parent-child interactions for ignoring the importance of "just being together" (p. 73), and Hochschild and Machung (1989) critiqued the quality time movement by saying that "our idea of what a *child* needs . . . reflects what *parents* need" (p. 230; emphases in original).

It appears that families are not faring so well under employment situations dominated by industrial time. Parents are aware that they are sacrificing the company of their families for the financial benefits of paid employment. A 1991 Gallup poll showed that one half of employed mothers and two thirds of fathers thought they spent too little time with their children (cited in Hugick & Leanord, 1991). Schor (1996) reported that more and more parents are demonstrating an interest in limiting their work spheres to have more time for family, although the work-and-spend cycle of the American economy often prevents parents from cutting work hours at the expense of income (Schor, 1992). However, there is mounting evidence that most parents would choose not to increase financial remuneration if it meant an increase in work time (Presser, 1989; Schor, 1996).

This time deficit increases problems with the supply of child care, especially in nonstandard or expanded hours of work. Additionally, the longer parents work, the more the cost of child care becomes an issue, as does the quality of care as children spend more and more of their time there. The increasing time deficit only serves to exacerbate the preexisting incompatibility of industrial time with family time. The following evidence about children's well-being shows that families are not faring so well under the mandate of industrial time.

CHILDREN'S WELL-BEING

As the economic rationality behind having children fades, the childbearing decision increasingly has come to be seen as a matter of individual choice and responsibility. This perception of childbearing and child rearing in turn provides a rationale for the relegation of child care to the private arena and away from an awareness of the collective nature of child rearing. This development has produced harsh consequences for children; the effects of this process on children are exacerbated by the increasing demands of industrial time on parents.

In his 1984 presidential address to the Population Association of America, Preston (1984) showed that the status of children has declined in sharp contrast to that of the elderly. These two groups of dependents were compared on such measures as percentage of group in poverty, suicide rate, public expenditure pattern (especially in the areas of education vs. health), and labor force participation. Although more elderly had been in poverty in 1970, that pattern had shifted by 1982. Additionally, although suicide is rare in children, the rate was increasing. Finally, public funds for children have been cut since the late 1970s, with welfare reform promising even larger cuts in the 1990s. Preston gave several demographic factors that can help account for these unsettling developments. Marital instability threatens the interests of children who still are located primarily in the privacy of the home, whereas much responsibility for the elderly has been absorbed by the state. Also, given the swelling of the ranks of the elderly, they comprise a large and powerful demographic group, whereas the dwindling numbers of children are neither able to mobilize on their own behalf nor protected by a strong sense of collective responsibility on the part of adults. These factors conspire to make children a very disadvantaged group of dependents.

More recent evidence shows that children's well-being has not improved since the mid-1980s. In fact, evidence concerning the change in children's well-being from 1985 to 1992 suggests that well-being may be declining further. A national study on the well-being of children reports that the levels of low-birthweight babies increased in the period between 1985 and 1992, although the increase was not large (Blakely & Voss, 1995). Infant mortality rates dropped, as did the child death rates, but these drops were not significant. There was little change in high school dropout rates or in numbers of teens who neither attended school nor worked. In this 7-year period, births to unmarried teens increased in the aggregate, the juvenile violent crime arrest rate increased, and the rate of violent teen deaths increased. In the aggregate, the proportion of children in poverty increased slightly and resulted in a national child poverty rate of 19.2%. Finally, in each of the 50 states, single-parent families increased. Blakely and Voss's work shows that Preston's earlier analysis of the well-being of children continues to be valid.

Hewlett (1991) contended that economically disadvantaged children suffer from a resource deficit, whereas mainstream children are more affected by the time deficit. Although this categorization shows how children are negatively affected by the lack of differing resources, the dichotomization is not altogether accurate. To be sure, economically disadvantaged children are resource poor, but these resources are not limited to the financial sphere. The time deficit is salient for both professionals who work long hours and the under-employed who moonlight to make ends meet. Additionally, those workers who have borne the brunt of downsizing and outsourcing also are engulfed in a time shortage. In this case, time is directed to finding other jobs, often ones that require longer hours at lower pay to support the workers' families. Either way, work consumes time. As work consumes time, parents spend less time with children. The lack of sensitive, responsive, consistent care from overworked parents or substitute providers can lead to decreased cognitive and social skills (Parcel & Menaghan, 1994) and promote attachment insecurity that encourages uncooperative and problematic behavior in children (Belsky, 1990). These developments, in collusion with financial problems generated by stagnant wages, help pave the way for the harsh outcomes for children discussed earlier.

Conclusions

This chapter has traced the encroachment of industrial time on family time, the subsequent imbalance between production and reproduction in mothers' and fathers' lives, and the crisis in child care that the implicit employment contract of the 20th century has produced. We then looked in some detail at the current child care market, emphasizing the trilemma of quality, cost, and availability as well as the problems in each sphere. Finally, we reviewed the available research on the impact of these changes on families' time together and children's well-being. Although larger macroeconomic pressures of advanced capitalism can be blamed for the encroachment of industrial time on family time, the impact of those pressures are felt by individual parents and children, particularly young children not yet in school. The sources of our collective acquiescence to this state of affairs are both political and personal, as are the sources of potential resistance. We close by considering each of these forces in turn.

Politically, the tendency to reduce jobs and increase work hours among those who remain employed has led to insecurity among voters and fears of real economic scarcity. In such a climate, ethnocentrism flourishes, resentment toward state spending on the needs of "others" increases, and the rhetoric of individual self-sufficiency expands. The

United States is particularly vulnerable to these tendencies because of the importance of individualist ideology in the historic formation of the state, strong masculinist politics in the two-party system of governance, and generally weak class formation relative to the class politics of Western Europe. The needs of the caregivers of children, whether mothers, fathers, or child care workers, are not often acknowledged in national politics despite the symbolic importance of references to family values in political discourse (Bonnar, 1991). Those family values frequently are merged with excessive individualism and freedom from government interference to promote an ideology of minimal state support for families rather than state responsibility for the well-being of families.

Despite widespread public sentiment that something is wrong with the state of family life today, political mobilization among parents is rare, and ideological splits between traditionalists (such as the Christian Coalition) and modernists (such as the Children's Defense Fund [Louv, 1990]), prevent the formation of public policies that place children's needs for security and care ahead of the needs of industry for an unfettered supply of labor. Yet parents could be a prominent political force if they spoke in coalition with other organizations with an interest in either labor issues or children's well-being such as labor unions, professional organizations, neighborhood organizations, and churches. Given that many of the issues affecting families actually are work-family issues, the natural places to attempt political reform are in concert with those organizations devoted to the regulation of labor.

In the personal realm, the structure of opportunity in market-based economies tilts clearly toward paid market involvement and away from noneconomic family pursuits. Not just money but also status, interpersonal influence, and respect increasingly flow from market work rather than from family caregiving. Bettering one's own human capital, increasing one's wages, and securing one's stable employment are concerns of both women and men, of both mothers and fathers, across a wide spectrum of class and ethnic differences (see, e.g., Blum & Deussen, 1996). Although altruistic sacrifice to accommodate family caregiving still is abundant and indeed still is expected of mothers, such sacrifices lead to decreased power within marriage (England & Kilbourne, 1990), increased vulnerability in the event of divorce (Arendell, 1986), and immediate earnings penalty in the labor force (Felmlee, 1995). Challenging this state of affairs at the personal level requires great commitment and moral courage. Fortunately, the affective bonds between parents and children are indeed strong enough to generate such commitment, as the increasing numbers of parents who wish to cut back their work hours, lobby for family-responsive employment practices at work, and support family-friendly community groups attest. However, whether public sentiment in favor of the protection and revival of family time has grown strong enough to resist the powerful inertial forces of market capitalism has yet to be determined.

References

Albert, L., & Popkin, M. (1987). *Quality parenting*. New York: Random House.

Amott, T., & Matthaei, J. (1991). *Race, gender, and work: A multicultural economic history of women in the United States*. Boston: South End.

Arendell, T. (1986). *Mothers and divorce*. Berkeley: University of California Press.

Belsky, J. (1990). Parental and nonparental child care and children's socioemotional development: A decade in review. *Journal of Marriage and the Family, 52*, 885-903.

Bernard, J. (1981). The good-provider role: Its rise and fall. *American Psychologist, 36*, 1-12.

Blakely, R. M., & Voss, P. R. (1995). *Indicators of child well-being in the United States, 1985-1992: An analysis of related factors*. Madison: University of Wisconsin–Madison, Applied Population Laboratory.

Blau, D. M. (1991). The quality of child care: An economic perspective. In D. Blau (Ed.), *The economics of child care* (pp. 145-174). New York: Russell Sage.

Blum, L., & Deussen, T. (1996). Negotiating independent motherhood: Working-class African American women talk about marriage and motherhood. *Gender & Society, 10*, 199-211.

Bohen, H. H., & Viveros-Long, A. (1981). *Balancing jobs and family life: Do flexible work schedules help?* Philadelphia: Temple University Press.

Bonnar, D. (1991). The place of caregiving work in industrial societies. In J. Hyde & M. Essex (Eds.), *Parental leave and child care* (pp. 195-205). Philadelphia: Temple University Press.

Brayfield, A., Deich, S. G., & Hofferth, S. L. (1993). *Caring for children in low-income families: A substudy of the National Child Care Survey, 1990*. Washington, DC: Urban Institute Press.

Brenner, J., & Ramas, M. (1984). Rethinking women's oppression. *New Left Review, 144*, 33-71.

Burstein, P., Bricher, M. R., & Einwohner, R. (1995). Policy alternatives and political change: Work, family, and gender on the congressional agenda. *American Sociological Review, 60*, 67-83.

Casper, L. M. (1995). What does it cost to mind our preschoolers? In U.S. Bureau of the Census, *Current Population Reports* (Series P70, No. 52). Washington, DC: Government Printing Office.

Casper, L. M. (1996). Who's minding our preschoolers? In U.S. Bureau of the Census, *Current Population Reports* (Series P70, No. 53). Washington, DC: Government Printing Office.

Cattan, P. (1991, October). Child care problems: An obstacle to work. *Monthly Labor Review*, pp. 3-9.

Christensen, K. E., & Staines, G. L. (1990). Flextime: A viable solution to work/family conflict? *Journal of Family Issues, 11,* 455-476.

Coleman, J. (1993). The rational reconstruction of society. *American Sociological Review, 58,* 1-15.

Connelly, R. (1991). The importance of child care costs to women's decision making. In D. Blau (Ed.), *The economics of child care* (pp. 87-118). New York: Russell Sage.

Corporate centers important to working dads. (1994, August). *Employee Benefit Plan Review,* p. 38.

Cost, Quality, and Child Outcomes Study Team. (1995). *Cost, quality, and child outcomes in child care centers: Public report* (2nd ed.). Denver: University of Colorado at Denver, Economics Department.

Culkin, M., Morris, J. R., & Helburn, S. W. (1991). Quality and the time cost of child care. *Journal of Social Issues, 47,* 71-86.

Davis, K. (1989). Wives and work: A theory of the sex-role revolution and its consequences. In S. Dornbusch & M. Strober (Eds.), *Feminism, children, and the new families* (pp. 67-86). New York: Guilford.

Degler, C. N. (1980). *At odds: Women and the family in America from the Revolution to the present.* New York: Oxford University Press.

Ehrenreich, B. (1984). *The hearts of men: American dreams and the flight from commitment.* Garden City, NY: Anchor Doubleday.

England, P., & Kilbourne, B. (1990). Markets, marriages, and other mates: The problem of power. In R. Friedland & A. Robertson (Eds.), *Beyond the marketplace: Rethinking economy and society* (pp. 163-187). New York: Aldine de Gruyter.

Families and Work Institute. (1991). *Corporate reference guide to work-family programs.* New York: Author.

Felmlee, D. (1995). Causes and consequences of women's employment discontinuity, 1967-73. *Work and Occupations, 22,* 167-187.

Friedman, D. E. (1990). Corporate responses to family needs. *Marriage and Family Review, 15,* 77-98.

Friedman, D., Hechter, M., & Kanazawa, S. (1994). A theory of the value of children. *Demography, 31,* 375-401.

Furstenberg, F. (1988). Good dads, bad dads: Two faces of fatherhood. In A. Cherlin (Ed.), *The changing American family and public policy* (pp. 193-215). Washington, DC: Urban Institute Press.

Galinsky, E. (1992). The impact of child care on parents. In A. Booth (Ed.), *Child care in the 1990s: Trends and consequences* (pp. 159-171). Hillsdale, NJ: Lawrence Erlbaum.

Galinsky, E., & Stein, P. (1990). The impact of human resource policies on employment: Balancing work-family life. *Journal of Family Issues, 11,* 368-383.

Glass, J., & Fujimoto, T. (1995). Employer characteristics and the provision of family responsive policies. *Work and Occupations, 22,* 380-411.

Glass, J., & Riley, L. (n.d.). *"Family friendly" policies and employee retention following childbirth*. Unpublished manuscript, Department of Sociology, University of Iowa.

Hareven, T. K. (1982). *Family time and industrial time: The relationship between the family and work in a New England industrial community*. Cambridge, MA: Cambridge University Press.

Hartmann, H. (1981). The unhappy marriage of Marxism and feminism: Toward a more progressive union. In L. Sargent (Ed.), *Women and revolution* (pp. 1-42). Boston: South End.

Hayes, C. D., Palmer, J. L., & Zaslow, M. J. (1990). *Who cares for America's children?* Washington, DC: National Academy Press.

Hewitt Associates. (1993). *Work and family benefits provided by major U.S. employers in 1993*. Lincolnshire, IL: Author.

Hewlett, S. A. (1991). *When the bough breaks*. New York: Basic Books.

Hochschild, A., with Machung, A. (1989). *The second shift: Working parents and the revolution at home*. New York: Avon Books.

Hofferth, S. L. (1992). The demand for and supply of child care in the 1990s. In A. Booth (Ed.), *Child care in the 1990s: Trends and consequences* (pp. 3-25). Hillsdale, NJ: Lawrence Erlbaum.

Hofferth, S. L., Brayfield, A., Deich, S., & Holcomb, P. (1991). *National Child Care Survey, 1990*. Washington, DC: Urban Institute Press.

Hofferth, S. L., & Phillips, D. (1987). Child care in the United States, 1970 to 1995. *Journal of Marriage and the Family, 49*, 559-571.

Hugick, L., & Leanord, J. (1991, September). Job dissatisfaction grows: "Moonlighting" on the rise. *Gallup Poll Monthly*, pp. 2-15.

Hunnicutt, B. (1988). *Work without end: Abandoning shorter hours for the right to work*. Philadelphia: Temple University Press.

Hunt, J., & Hunt, L. (1982). The dualities of careers and families: New integrations or new polarizations? *Social Problems, 29*, 499-510.

Kagan, S. L. (1991). Examining profit and nonprofit child care: An odyssey of quality and auspices. *Journal of Social Issues, 47*, 87-104.

Kamerman, S. B., & Kahn, A. J. (1987). *The responsive workplace: Employers and the changing labor force*. New York: Columbia University Press.

Kessler-Harris, A. (1982). *Out to work: A history of wage-earning women in the United States*. New York: Oxford University Press.

Kingston, P. (1990). Illusions and ignorance about the family responsive workplace. *Journal of Family Issues, 11*, 438-454.

Kisker, E., & Maynard, R. (1991). Quality, cost, and parental choice of child care. In D. Blau (Ed.), *The economics of child care* (pp. 127-144). New York: Russell Sage.

Kisker, E., Maynard, R., Gordon, A., & Strain, M. (1989). *The child care challenge: What parents need and what is available in three metropolitan areas*. Princeton, NJ: Mathematica Policy Research, Inc.

Kleiman, C. (1993, February 8). Study shows job status skews family benefits. *Chicago Tribune*, sec. 4, p. 3.

Lasch, C. (1977). *Haven in a heartless world: The family besieged*. New York: Basic Books.

Laslett, P. (1983). *Family forms in historic Europe*. New York: Cambridge University Press.

Louv, R. (1990). *Childhood's future*. Boston: Houghton Mifflin.

Marshall, N. L., & Marx, F. (1991). The affordability of child care for the working poor. *Families in Society, 72*, 202-211.

Mason, K. O., & Kuhlthau, K. (1989). Determinants of child care ideals among mothers of preschool-aged children. *Journal of Marriage and the Family, 51,* 593-603.

Nelson, M. (1990). *Negotiated care.* Philadelphia: Temple University Press.

Nock, S. L., & Kingston, P. W. (1988). Time with children: The impact of couples' work-time commitments. *Social Forces, 67,* 59-85.

Parcel, T., & Menaghan, E. (1994). Early parental work, family social capital, and early childhood outcomes. *American Journal of Sociology, 99,* 972-1009.

Phillips, D. A., Howes, C., & Whitebook, M. (1992). The social policy context of child care: Effects on quality. *American Journal of Community Psychology, 20,* 25-51.

Presser, H. (1986). Shift work among American women and child care. *Journal of Marriage and the Family, 48,* 551-563.

Presser, H. (1989). Can we make time for children? The economy, work schedules, and child care. *Demography, 26,* 523-543.

Presser, H. (1992). Child care supply and demand: What do we really know? In A. Booth (Ed.), *Child care in the 1990s: Trends and consequences* (pp. 26-32). Hillsdale, NJ: Lawrence Erlbaum.

Preston, S. (1984). Children and the elderly: Divergent paths for America's dependents. *Demography, 21,* 435-457.

Prosser, W. R., & McGroder, S. M. (1992). The supply of and demand for child care: Measurement and analytic issues. In A. Booth (Ed.), *Child care in the 1990s: Trends and consequences* (pp. 42-55). Hillsdale, NJ: Lawrence Erlbaum.

Raabe, P. (1990). The organizational effects of workplace family policies. *Journal of Family Issues, 11,* 477-491.

Raabe, P., & Gessner, J. C. (1988). Employer family-supportive policies: Diverse variations on the theme. *Family Relations, 37,* 196-202.

Robins, P. K. (1991). Child care policy and research: An economist's perspective. In D. Blau (Ed.), *The economics of child care* (pp. 11-42). New York: Russell Sage.

Robins, P. K., & Spiegelman, R. G. (1978). Substitution among child care modes and the effect of a child care subsidy program. In P. Robins & S. Weiner (Eds.), *Child care and public policy: Studies of the economic issues* (pp. 87-102). Lexington, MA: Lexington Books.

Russell, C. (1988, May). Who gives and who gets. *American Demographics,* pp. 16-18.

Sale, J. S. (1984). Family day care homes. In J. Greeman & R. Fuqua (Eds.), *Making day care better* (pp. 21-43). New York: Teachers College Press.

Schor, J. (1992). *The overworked American.* New York: Basic Books.

Schor, J. (1996, March). *Time, work, and money: Escaping the cycle of work and spend.* Paper presented at the Conference on Our Time Famine, Iowa City, IA.

Smith, V. (1993). Flexibility in work and employment: The impact on women. In S. Bacharach (Ed.), *Research in the sociology of organizations* (pp. 195-217). Greenwich, CT: JAI.

Sonenstein, F. L. (1991). The child care preferences of parents with young children: How little is known. In J. Hyde & M. Essex (Eds.), *Parental leave and child care* (pp. 337-353). Philadelphia: Temple University Press.

Treas, J. (1987). The effect of women's labor force participation on the distribution of income in the United States. *American Review of Sociology, 13,* 259-288.

U.S. Bureau of Labor Statistics. (1991). *Employee benefits in small private establishments, 1990* (Misc. Pub. No. 2388). Washington, DC: Government Printing Office.

Waite, L. J., Leibowitz, A., & Witsberger, C. (1991). What parents pay for: Child care characteristics, quality, and costs. *Journal of Social Issues, 47,* 33-48.

Where does the time go? (1996, February 28). *Iowa City Press Citizen,* p. A3.

Wilson, W. J., & Neckerman, K. (1986). Poverty and family structure: The widening gap between evidence and public policy issues. In S. Danziger & D. Weinberg (Eds.), *Fighting poverty: What works and what doesn't* (pp. 236-259). Cambridge, MA: Harvard University Press.

Women's Legal Defense Fund. (1996). *Memorandum on Family and Medical Leave Act.* Washington, DC: Author.

10

An Agenda for Family Policy
in the United States

GEORGE T. MARTIN, JR.

Because of the vital role it plays in reproduction and socialization, the family historically has been a central focus of social policy. The focus is on the family with dependent children, the social unit that carries the greatest responsibility for societal regeneration. Today, at least in the developed world, it is impossible for the family to be a self-sufficient institution. The well-being of a family is determined by its connections to a highly complex society, especially to its paid labor force.

Because of its unique importance to society and because of its increased dependence on forces outside its control, the family has attracted growing attention from government policy in recent years. Virtually all societies have comprehensive policies that support family functioning. However, there is a wide range among nations in the level and extent of these family policies. National family policies typically have four cornerstones: cash benefits to supplement the incomes of adults who raise children, comprehensive health services for pregnant women and for children, paid work leaves for parents to care for newborns and ill family members, and a child care program. The nations with the most comprehensive and effective policies are the developed welfare states such as Sweden. The United States, the focus of this analysis, is a welfare state laggard and is one of the few developed nations that lacks a family policy.

Because women bear inordinate responsibility for unpaid family labor (i.e., caring work and housework), they are more negatively affected by the lack of a comprehensive family policy than are men. The absence of a family policy further disserves the economically disadvantaged families in society. They cannot afford the services and benefits that a family policy would provide, whereas the economically advantaged can purchase such services and benefits in the marketplace. Ultimately, the lack of a family policy is a liability to the society as a whole to the extent that it increases the social costs of inadequate attention to family needs and of political conflict between the "haves" and the "have-nots."

A family policy is a public policy that addresses the particular needs of the family as well as social interests. What are its general parameters? An agenda for a family policy in the contemporary United States must deal with the twin realities of secular economic decline and conservative political ascendancy. Both realities circumscribe the possibilities of achieving an ambitious and progressive family policy. A family policy agenda will be subjected to the related tests of achievable reform. Are public costs minimized while returns to the public are maximized? Is social need readily and demonstrably amenable to programmatic intervention? Is policy adoptable in the face of conservative or fractured national politics? Does policy benefit the broadest possible constituency? Such an achievable family policy agenda is a more urgent task now than ever before given the significant changes that are taking place in the family.

The Family in Change

There is widespread concern about the condition of the family. Indeed, the structure and purpose of the family are changing, creating new social needs. The crisis of the family actually is a crisis of policy, which lags behind the new needs of families. The process by which some family functions are externalized (removed from the family) plays a central role in the current transition in the family. To the extent that such activities become publicly sponsored, they are both *socialized* and externalized. An example is compulsory free public schooling that externalized and socialized a major part of the family's traditional social activity. The development of the need for extra-familial child care and elder care represents an extension of the same trend.

We are not witnessing the death of the family; rather, we are witnessing its differentiation. The traditional family, in which women marry and have children while being supported by and subordinated to men breadwinners, has been the model for social policy. As a result, throughout history married women and previously married, especially widowed, women have fared better under social policy than have never-married women, including unwed mothers (Abramovitz, 1988). The contemporary transition is from one dominant model of the family to diversity. In addition to the traditional family, there now are large numbers of single-parent families and families in which the wives and mothers also work in the paid labor force.

SOCIETAL CHANGE

Specific societal changes are the driving forces in the current transition in family form and purpose (Martin, 1991). For most of human history, the family fulfilled production tasks. Capitalism, especially capitalist industrialization, and urbanization steadily encroached on this purpose of the family. Products formerly made for use in the family now are produced by corporations for profit. In the not-too-distant past, families produced much of their own food, clothing, and shelter. At home, they churned butter, raised buildings, baked bread, sewed clothing, cultivated gardens, and preserved vegetables for winter. This no longer is the case. Today, even farmers buy their bread.

In losing its production function, the family lost something else. The enormous labor required for production required the services of all the family members; it was an important focus of social life. Children were an economic asset because they could work. Production required cooperation and interaction; it was an activity around which intra- and interfamily communal life was organized. Thus the family lost a basis of its solidarity along with its productive function—the cooperative dependence of its members. Additionally, children have become economic liabilities.

In addition to displacing production from the family, capitalism has accelerated consumption in the family and remolded it into a sanctuary from the travails of modern life. It now is the responsibility of the family to provide the emotional connections that citizens lack in their public lives, in which they experience alienation. Zaretsky (1976) analyzed this development of a personal life apart from society and work as a new basis for the oppression of women. Women are responsible for the maintenance of personal life. They do it in the family as unpaid mothers and wives, they do it outside the family as low-paid secretaries and waitresses, and they do it in the welfare state as underpaid social practitioners—caseworkers, nurses, and teachers (Martin, 1990).

WOMEN'S ENTRY INTO THE PAID LABOR FORCE

Industrial capitalism transformed peasants into proletarians, and women were among the first proletarians. However, because of their caring and domestic responsibilities as well as other reasons, women have lagged behind men in entering the paid labor force. The first group of women to become proletarians were poor and working class, for whom protective policies were created during the Progressive Era of the early 20th century in the United States. Still, only 24% of all women of working age were in the labor force in 1920. As late as 1960, only 38% of women, as compared to 83% of men, were in the paid labor force. The gradual increase of 14 percentage points in women's labor force participation between 1920 and 1960 was largely accounted for by middle-class women with educations, and with few or no small children, entering the workforce (Matras, 1990, pp. 131-133).

Since the 1960s, economic and political changes have led the last group of women—married women whose husbands are present and who have small children—to enter the paid labor force. These changes include the decline in real earnings for U.S. workers, compelling many mothers to work. Between 1980 and 1994, the average real weekly earnings, including overtime, for nonagricultural private-sector employees declined from $275 to $256. Another important change has been the opportunities created through the activities of the feminist movement, which opened many jobs to all categories of women. In 1960, only 19% of married women with children under 6 years of age were in the paid labor force; by 1994, that figure had more than tripled to 62%. This last wave of women to enter the paid labor force is producing an equalization of labor force participation rates for men and women. In 1960, the men's labor force participation rate was 2.2 times that of the women; in 1994, it was only 1.3 times that of the women.[1]

Such a major change as mothers going outside the home to work was bound to have serious ramifications for the family. The impact was heightened by other major social changes that were occurring simultaneously—the transition to a service economy and the post-1960s cultural/sexual liberalization and pluralization. As a result of all these changes, the family has undergone an unprecedented transition, the effects of which policy is only beginning to try to accommodate. One indication of this transition is the changes in time use by women and men. In the United States between 1965 and 1986, average paid labor for women increased by 31%, whereas that for men decreased by 14%; in the same period, women's average unpaid housework (including child care) decreased by 16%, whereas that for men increased by 81%. In 1986 in the United States, the share of all unpaid housework done by women was 64%, down from 79% in 1965. Parallel changes in the same period were noted in comparable nations (United Nations, 1991, p. 102). Although their proportion of domestic labor is slowly trending downward, women still do the bulk of it—even if they have full-time jobs outside the home. This is the contemporary dual burden of paid work outside the home and unpaid work (the "second shift") in the home for working women who also are wives and mothers (Hochschild & Machung, 1989).

Work in the paid labor force has provided new economic resources to many women. For white couples in the United States, the proportion of wives who were 100% dependent on their husbands declined from 84% in 1940 to 31% in 1980 (Sorenson & McLanahan, 1987). With their own economic resources, more women have been free to delay or leave marriages. Work in the paid labor force also has provided more women greater incentive to have few or no children because of the burdens of the second shift. In fact, being a full-time parent is incompatible with many of the most desirable careers in the labor force. In the absence of work not having become substantially more family friendly, many working women choose to deemphasize family. Many others try to have both and struggle with the dual burden; the need for exquisite timing becomes routinized in their lives.

Although the U.S. family has undergone major change in the past quarter century, it also is significant that similar changes have been going on in comparable nations. This fact points to structural changes engendered by transformations in the global capitalist economy as being the underlying cause of the changes in the family. This casts considerable doubt on the argument that family changes are due to the fact that the United States has been experiencing moral decline or decay. It may be the case that changes in the family are more *noticeable*—even alarming—in the United States because the nation lacks a comprehensive family policy that could mitigate some of the most negative effects of the global changes. At the least, the current changes in the family make the absence of a family policy in the United States more conspicuous.

Despite the fact that it lacks a comprehensive package of policies that are addressed to families per se, the United States does have a range of social programs that bear on the family. Even though they cannot fully compensate for the lack of a comprehensive family policy, current programs—in the areas of income security, work, and health— provide some support to families.

Income Security

Because of its reliance on the paid labor market, the family is exposed to the hardships of unemployment, underemployment, and poverty. The effects of economic hardship are not the same for all groups in society; they are modulated in impact and content by social class, gender, race, and age. The people who are most vulnerable to changing economic conditions are those with the more tenuous ties to the paid labor force. Prominent among the most vulnerable are caregivers, caregivers' children, and the aged.

EARNERS AND CARERS

Welfare state income security programs are decidedly oriented to the labor market, not to the family. This is consistent with the focus in social policy on the traditional family with one breadwinner—the father and husband. Social rights accrue primarily to earners, whereas carers are left largely to fend for themselves, perpetuating a gendering of citizenship. Working women are obliged to make a choice because "full access to social rights is ensured only if their caring commitments are organized so that they do not interfere with formal employment" (Leira, 1992, p. 172).

The overarching purpose of income security programs is to prevent poverty—what Shaw (1907/1958) called "the worst of crimes"—and they have been the prime components of social policy since its inception in Elizabethan England in the 16th century (Martin, 1990, p. 43). Compared to similar nations, the United States has a persistently high poverty rate, and children comprise a group that has experienced large increases in poverty. A 1995 comparative study of 18 nations found that poor children in the United States were poorer than those in 15 other nations. The United States ranked below nations such as Italy that are considerably less affluent than the United States (Bradsher, 1995b). In 1975, when the overall poverty rate stood at 12% of the population, it was 17% for children under age 18. In 1993, the poverty rate for all Americans had risen to 15%; for children, the rise was to 23%. In 1993, there were 15.7 million children under age 18 living below the poverty level.

Homelessness represents the lowest depth of poverty in the contemporary United States. Although there are other factors involved in the etiology of homelessness, experts tend to put poverty at the head of the list. Families have become the most rapidly growing segment of the homeless population and in 1992 constituted 34% of all homeless people. The great majority of these homeless families are headed by women who have several children, most of whom are under age 7 (Lee et al., 1992, p. 119).

For the United States to have such a high number and rate of poor children seriously calls into question the effectiveness of its income security programs. These questions relate to the income security programs themselves and to phenomena external to the programs. The most important external phenomenon that is family related is the issue of child support.

CHILD SUPPORT

Divorce has become ubiquitous in the developed world, whereas effective supportive policies for divorced families lag behind. A leading researcher of divorce patterns recently concluded after a comprehensive comparative study that

> we should accept the fact that most developed nations can now be seen as high divorce rate systems, and we should *institutionalize* divorce— accept it as we do other institutions, and build adequate safeguards as well as social understandings and pressures to make it work reasonably well. (Goode, 1993, p. 345; emphasis in original)

The principal reason behind the rise in divorce in the developed world is that the capitalist economy has made individuals relatively independent economically outside family units.

Increased divorce, coupled with remarriages, produces more "blended" families—families in which there are biological children, adoptive children, and stepchildren. The blended family is an example of the kinds of departures from the traditional family model that have become more common in recent decades. In the United States in 1990, one out of four married-couple family households with children had at least one nonbiological child, a fraction that has been gradually rising.

These demographic changes are reflected in the general transition in family composition from one dominant family form to diverse forms. For example, the proportion of children living with their divorced mothers tripled between 1970 and 1993. Many divorced mothers experience considerable economic hardship and uncertainty; downward mobility is a common path for them and their children (Arendell, 1986). In 1995 in the United States, there were 11.5 million custodial parents, of whom 86% were mothers. Lack of financial support from absent parents is a major reason why single-parent families have relatively high poverty rates. In 1991, only 24% of custodial mothers living below the poverty line who sought child support from absent fathers actually received either full or partial payments.

There is some good news despite these discouraging figures; there is a trend toward increased child support compliance. One reason has been a shift in policy focus with the passage of the U.S. Family Support Act (FSA) of 1988, a reform of the Aid to Families with Dependent Children (AFDC) public aid program. To the extent that the FSA has been successful, it has been in improving collection of child support:

> The states have become more aggressively involved in collecting court-ordered child-support payments, taking in a record $6 billion in 1990. New mechanisms include garnishing the wages of parents who owe child support, using the records of the Internal Revenue Service to locate absent parents, and intercepting their tax refunds for past-due child support. All states must now report delinquent parents to credit agencies. (Goode, 1993, p. 172)

Despite the anticipated improvements in child support enforcement, the FSA does nothing with regard to the problem of absent fathers who do not have the means to pay child support. Partly as a result, despite the FSA, the living standards of children continue to decline sharply after their parents divorce (Sullivan, 1995).

There are three major obstacles to securing adequate support payments from absent fathers: courts awarding inadequate sums, a widespread lack of compliance, and the fact that some fraction of all absent fathers are financially unable to support their children. Public attention and the FSA are directed toward the second obstacle— compliance. However, even in the face of the elimination of this obstacle, many single mothers and their children will remain poor because of the other two problems. What may help is a policy shift away from courts and legal contention between mothers and absent fathers to administrative enforcement of child support. Goode (1993, p. 176) sees this shift as a convergence taking place currently in various countries. The administrative approach would involve the following:

1. Public administrative boards would set the amount of child support based on current real costs of child rearing and on relevant data from the involved parties.

2. Support payments would be directly deducted from the absent fathers' incomes.

3. An assured benefit would be paid in the cases in which absent fathers are determined not to have incomes. Absent fathers with low incomes would pay a proportion of their incomes. Any difference between what the absent fathers contribute and the standard set by the administrative board would be made up with an assured benefit.

In a model child support program based on policies such as these, the poverty among eligible children could be reduced considerably (Oellerich & Garfinkel, 1983). Using such an administrative system eliminates parental jockeying over the children and ensures the government's interest that children not be raised in poverty. Despite the high costs entailed by establishing an assured benefit administrative system, much of the cost could be retrieved by the savings from substantial reductions in public aid and from the saved costs of tending to the social problems engendered by poverty (e.g., poor health).

PUBLIC AID

A piece of erroneous conventional wisdom is that welfare creates family dissolution. The fact is that, as noted by Ellwood (1988), "Virtually every careful social science study that has investigated this issue has found that the welfare system has had little effect on the structure of families" (p. 22). Thus welfare cannot be blamed for the rise either in female-headed households or in out-of-wedlock births. The welfare system responds to changes in the family caused by social changes; it does not create changes in the family. It is important, too, to recognize that households headed by women are not poor because of changes in family composition. For example, even though African American poverty is concentrated in female-headed households, in only about 17% of cases did poverty begin with family changes such as divorce or separation (Bane, 1986).

Although the poverty population is mixed in its composition, one large group of poor persons commands the special attention of social policy: female-headed households. In 1993 in the United States, 14% of all families were below the poverty level; however, in families headed by single mothers, the poverty rate was 39%. Research has found several problems for poor women raising children alone— among them, they work for low wages and get less support from absent fathers than do nonpoor women raising children alone (Ellwood, 1984).

The rise in women-headed households has been especially pronounced among African Americans. Largely because of high and rising unemployment rates, the proportion of African American men in stable jobs has been in a long-term decline. Thus the increasing delay of first marriage and the low rate of remarriage among African American women (compared to that among white women), which produced more female-headed households, is directly tied to the high rates of joblessness for African American men (Wilson & Neckerman, 1986). Subsequent research has found an association between the increase in the families headed by women and the declining economic fortunes of young men—not only African American young men but also Hispanic and white ones (Holmes, 1995). Other data support the connection between fatherless families and out-of-work fathers. In 1994 in the United States, in approximately 5,000 neighborhoods where at least 50% of families had no fathers present, fully 52% of men were out of the labor force (Lewin, 1995). Data such as these have been the basis for a growing concern with the "feminization of poverty" (Pearce, 1978).

The growth in female-headed families is not confined to the United States. For example, between 1961 and 1981, the number of one-parent families (about 90% of which are female headed) more than doubled in the United Kingdom (Graham, 1984, pp. 30-31). Thus the "feminization of poverty," although more acute in the United States, is a growing problem in other nations as well. This may be a result of their common failure to equalize women's opportunities in the labor force and to equalize men's responsibilities in the family. The United States ranked last in the 1980s among seven welfare states and socialist nations in social policy measures to deal with female poverty (Goldberg & Kremen, 1987). It is likely that the problem is more acute in the United States because of two factors: its racial divisions and its weak welfare state.

A comparative study of eight welfare states by Kamerman and Kahn (1987) found that the United States stood last in providing income to single-mother families. For nonworking single mothers with two children in Sweden, family income was 94% of the net wage of the average production worker, the highest among the eight nations. Single mothers with two children in the United States had incomes that were only 44% of the net wage of the average production worker. For low-wage, single working mothers with two children, Sweden again was first; such families there had incomes that were 123% of the net wage of its average production worker. In the United States, incomes of similar families were only 69% of the net wage of the average production worker. These rankings correspond to others on the level of support for general welfare state activity; the more developed welfare states do better at providing income security for single mothers.

Thus, compared to policies of other developed nations, U.S. social welfare policy has not responded as well to the rise in female-headed households. Instead of adopting a comprehensive policy to support family integrity in a time of social change, the United States has only tinkered with its limited and piecemeal welfare system. A major example of this is the FSA, which in large measure represents a recurrent historical reaction to welfare—"workfare," or mandatory work for welfare recipients. This reaction became even more extreme with the Republican Congress elected in 1994.

The Personal Responsibility and Work Opportunity Reconciliation Act of 1996 ended the federal guarantee of cash assistance for poor children that was inaugurated with the Social Security Act of 1935. The entitlement program, AFDC, was terminated. States now operate their own welfare programs with block grants from the federal government. The highlights of the 1996 law were the establishment of mandatory work requirements and time limits for recipients.

Workfare also has met with little success in the United States (Morris & Williamson, 1987; Walsh, 1988) or in other nations including Canada (Evans & McIntyre, 1987). For poor mothers of young children to work and to remain responsible parents, they need access to adequate child care and health care. In addition, many need basic work skills training. Ultimately, workfare cannot measurably reduce poverty in the absence of decent-paying jobs. The availability of such jobs is predicated on an effective full-employment policy and an above-poverty minimum wage, among other reforms.

FAMILY-ORIENTED
INCOME SECURITY

The incomes of those raising children can be supported by building a minimum income floor for families. Such a floor could be cobbled together in the United States with an integrated approach to reforms in child support, the minimum wage, child care, health care, and the Earned Income Tax Credit (EITC).

The EITC, which dates back to 1975, provides an annual earnings supplement to parents who maintain a household for a child, provided the parents' income falls below a specified level. If parents do not owe any taxes or owe a tax lower than the EITC, then they receive a payment from the Internal Revenue Service. In 1995, a family with two children qualified for the tax credit if the family earned less than $26,673. The maximum credit was $3,114 in 1995—for a family with two children earning about $9,000. The credit is available only to families with earnings, and it benefits a broader constituency than the chronically poor. A federal commission concluded in 1995 that many middle-class families periodically are eligible when job losses or serious illnesses temporarily reduce their incomes (Bradsher, 1995a). With expansion, the EITC could approximate the family allowances found in other welfare states.

Currently, the EITC functions as an antipoverty program for the working poor. Calculations indicate that 4.5 million poor Americans who work will have their incomes raised above the poverty line under the 1996 benefit schedule (Passell, 1995). The EITC traditionally has appealed to both conservatives (because it rewards work) and liberals (because it helps the poor).

Work

Short of a comprehensive full-employment policy, there are a number of meaningful reforms that could be made to improve the lot of working families in the United States in addition to expanding the EITC. The working poor would be helped substantially by raising the minimum wage. In 1968, the minimum wage of $1.60 represented 54% of the average hourly wage. Then, the United States exceeded the goal in developed nations, that is, that the minimum wage represent 50% of the average industrial wage. However, since then, there has been considerable slippage. The 1994 minimum wage of $4.25 represented only 35% of the average hourly wage. At the desired 50% level, the minimum wage in 1994 would have been $6.07. Changes in the minimum wage adopted in 1996 will raise it to $5.15 on July 1, 1997. However, this still falls short of what is needed to help keep low-wage workers out of poverty. Perhaps the simplest and most effective single thing to do to help poor families would be to fix the minimum wage at 50% of the average hourly wage and build in an automatic cost-of-living adjustment such as presently exists for social security benefits.

Workers who raise families have social needs other than adequate income. Child care at work sites and flexible working hours ("flextime") are the supports that employed parents most desire (Galinsky, 1992). Flextime allows workers to put in their required hours at flexible times and so permits them to arrange their hours for child care. Both child care and flextime provide considerable benefits to employers in the form of reduced employee turnover, improved employee recruitment, higher employee morale, and reductions in employee tardiness and absenteeism. Although there are costs involved for providing child care, the employer costs for implementing flextime are quite low. Yet only a minority of private employers extend these necessary supports to working parents. Research indicates that about one out of five or six unemployed women cannot work because she is unable to make satisfactory child care arrangements (U.S. Commission on Civil Rights, 1984, p. 96).

Kentucky's Family Resource Centers provide an example of the possibilities of using public schools as a base to extend needed child care and social services to families that need them. Kentucky's Education Reform Act of 1990 authorized funding for these centers in all public schools in which at least 20% of the students are eligible for school lunch funding. The Family Resource Centers provide child care (full-time preschool care for 2- to 3-year-olds and after-school care for 4- to 12-year-olds), classes for new and expectant parents, referrals to health and social service agencies, and other services. Preliminary data indicate that children who have participated in the Kentucky program show improvements in classroom performance (Family

Resource Coalition, 1993, p. 48). Although the Family Resource Centers are intended to improve the educations of disadvantaged children, they also demonstrate the possibility of operating various programs in conjunction with public schools, including child care. (Child care was further analyzed in Chapter 9 of this volume.)

PARENTAL LEAVE

In addition to flextime and child care, other steps need to be taken to help families meet their child care needs. One is parental leave. All developed nations except Australia and the United States now provide paid and job-protected maternity leave for working women. The length of leave ranges from 10 to 52 weeks, the rate of pay ranges between 50% and 100% of salary, and in the Nordic nations there has been a transition from maternal to parental leave (United Nations Children's Emergency Fund [UNICEF], 1994). Sweden has had such a social policy, parental benefit insurance, since 1974. It provides for up to 9 months of any combination of maternity and paternity leave at 90% of pay and guarantees jobs on return to work. Additionally, either parent can receive full pay for working 6-hour days until the child is 8 years old. The father also can take 10 days immediately after birth to care for his family, and either parent can take leave to care for an ill child.

The U.S. Family and Medical Leave Act (FMLA) of 1993 allows a worker to take up to 12 weeks of unpaid leave for the birth of a child or an adoption; to care for a child, spouse, or parent with a serious health condition; or for the worker's own health condition that makes it impossible to work. However, the act exempts employers with fewer than 50 workers. Although this legislation falls short of the Swedish plan, it represents a progressive step for U.S. social policy. Unfortunately, the FMLA likely will have an impact on only one group of working families. "We recognize that, in the end, parental leave is only viable for middle- and upper-income, dual-earner parents who can afford the time off and can live on one paycheck" (Prosser & McGroder, 1992, p. 52).

Working parents of modest and poor means need special attention, especially because they are the most likely to become public aid recipients. The help could come in the form of child care and health care services, two major expenses in family budgets. One scheme, "Help for Working Parents" (modeled on successful programs in France), would have federal and state governments provide vouchers to licensed child care centers; care would be provided free for the poorest families, whereas other families would pay on a sliding scale. Additionally, families that lacked health insurance would have it provided through public auspices (Bergmann & Hartmann, 1995). Such a policy would benefit working-class families, many of whom are caught in a dilemma: When both parents work, the family earns too much money to get subsidies that poor parents receive. Providing adequate child care and health care also would have the benefit of enabling many welfare recipients to work.

Health

The family is at the center of a number of health policy concerns in the United States including maternity care, teenage pregnancy, and domestic violence.

MATERNAL, INFANT, AND CHILD HEALTH

Health care is a vital area of family functioning, in large part because families are the nexus of pregnancy, childbirth, and infant and child development—all of which present unique challenges to health. The health challenges are twofold—to the mother and to the child. In both areas, the United States lags behind comparable nations, sometimes considerably behind. Because of the lack of national health care insurance in the United States, many families are exposed to health risks for financial reasons. Although adopting a national health care plan would be of great assistance to many families, especially poor ones, there is much to be done short of that goal.

With regard to maternal health, in 1993 the United States ranked 18th (tied with two other nations) among world nations in (lowest) maternal mortality (United Nations Development Programme, 1996, p. 188). In a comprehensive comparative study based on a number of measures, the United States stood 18th among 118 nations in overall maternal health in 1995 (Hilts, 1995). The relatively low U.S. position was due largely to its high rate of teenage pregnancy and its low rate of contraceptive use.

In 1995, the United States stood 17th among nations in (lowest) infant mortality; there were 7.9 deaths of children under 1 year of age per 1,000 live births. The U.S. ranked just behind Italy and just ahead of Cuba; Japan was first with an infant mortality rate of only 4.3 per 1,000 live births. A comparison between the United States and France illustrates the "family health care gap" in the United States. In 1994, 96% of children in France were born to mothers who received early prenatal care, compared to 76% of children in the United States. Partly as a result of this difference, the U.S. rate of premature births was 2.6 times the French rate and its infant mortality rate was 23% higher than that for France (James, 1995). France achieves more in infant health despite the fact that the United States spends considerably more on health care in general. Thus the United States has the wherewithal; what is lacking is effective delivery of family health care. Too many expectant mothers do not receive adequate prenatal care, too many infants do not receive adequate neonatal care, and too many children do not receive recommended inoculations, adequate nutrition, and other health care.

There are a few targeted programs that address maternal, infant, and child health in the United States. The Special Supplemental Food Program for Women, Infants, and Children (WIC) has an empirically established record of effectiveness in reducing infant deaths, low birthweight, prematurity, and childhood illnesses (Zuckerman & Brazelton, 1994). Moreover, the program is cost-effective. The U.S. Government Accounting Office is reported to have estimated that for every WIC prenatal dollar spent, $3.50 is saved in future health care costs (Center, 1995). Unfortunately, because it is inadequately funded, only one half of eligible families receive assistance from WIC. Since 1991, the U.S. Department of Health and Human Services has targeted infant mortality with special funds. Family resource programs have operated in 22 cities, providing prenatal and well-baby care, family planning, parenting classes, medical referrals, and help with substance abuse. The services are delivered by vans to neighborhoods. In Oakland, California, the Healthy Start program, for example, has helped to reduce infant mortality by 41% in three districts (Herscher, 1995).

TEENAGE PREGNANCY

There is considerable health risk associated with teen parenting ("children who have children"); it is magnified if the teen mother is unwed. These risks include lower exposure to prenatal care, higher incidences of low birthweight, maternal and infant mortality, and higher exposure to poverty. Children raised in poverty are more likely to suffer from malnutrition, anemia, lead poisoning, and congenital infections and suffer more serious consequences from these problems compared to children raised outside of poverty (Sidel, 1990, pp. 139-140; Zuckerman & Brazelton, 1994, p. 74).

The rise of out-of-wedlock teenage births became a public issue in the United States in the 1980s. The birthrate per 1,000 unmarried women rose from 22 in 1960 to 34 in 1986, an increase of more than 50%. For unmarried women ages 15 to 19, the increase was even more dramatic, rising from 15 to 33 per 1,000 unmarried women, more than a 100% increase. There is indication that this trend is reversing. The National Center for Health Statistics reported that the birthrate among 15- to 17-year-olds fell by 2% in 1992 and by another 2% in 1993 after a 25% rise from 1986 to 1991 (Vobejda, 1994). However, even if the U.S. teenage pregnancy rate (including out-of-wedlock pregnancies) were to stop rising, it would remain the highest among welfare states. The United States leads welfare states in pregnancies, births, and abortions for unmarried women ages 15 to 19. The successes of other welfare states in this area are credited to their sex education programs in schools, to the relatively easy availability of contraception in government health clinics, and to the assurance of confidentiality to teens seeking help (Sidel, 1990, pp. 142-144). Comparative research indicates that the incidence of teenage pregnancy is lower in those nations where contraception, sex education (in and out of schools), and abortion are widely available (Jones et al., 1986, 1989).

The most effective and efficient vehicle for reducing teen pregnancy is sex education in the public schools (Gilchrist & Schinke, 1983) and elsewhere. Officials attributed the 1992 decline in teen birthrates in the United States to better contraceptive use among teenagers and to a leveling off of teenage sexual activity (Vobejda, 1994). Although the overwhelming majority of Americans favor sex education in public schools, only four states require it in all schools. An additional problem is that sex education often is not contraception education and is, therefore, not effective as a way in which to prevent pregnancy. Abstinence is the only message commonly given, and it is not convincing to many teenagers. Government leadership for a thorough and honest sex education policy is needed. As Edelman (1987) noted, the teen parenthood problem and its costs

> are not the inevitable outcomes of increased adolescent sexual activity, but of our inability as a society to deal in a preventive way with the implications of that increase: to provide early comprehensive sex and family-life education in our homes, schools, and other institutions and to give sexually active teens access to family-planning services and counseling. (p. 53)

New evidence indicates that teenage pregnancy also is, to some extent, a product of sexual abuse (Steinhauer, 1995). Research conducted by the Alan Guttmacher Institute during 1989-1991 found that at least one half of the children born to teenage girls were fathered by adults. Such data have implications for social policy to deal with teenage pregnancy. For example, in addition to increased sex education and family planning services, it may be advisable to increase the prosecution of state age-of-consent laws. In most cases, these laws prohibit anyone age 18 or older from having sexual relations with anyone under age 16. However, presently the laws rarely are applied.

VIOLENCE

Violence is a major problem in the lives of U.S. families. In 1992, there were nearly 1 million substantiated dispositions of maltreatment of children by their adult caretakers. Of these dispositions, 48% involved neglect, 22% involved physical abuse, 13% involved sexual abuse, and 5% involved emotional abuse. Child maltreatment is a serious matter; child abuse and neglect is the leading cause of trauma death for children age 4 or under, ranking ahead of death from motor vehicle accidents, fires, or other traumas (Action Alliance for Children, 1995, p. 4).

Domestic violence is subject to underreporting and other distortions that make it notoriously difficult to measure, even in nations such as the United States where national statistical accounting generally is quite advanced. Comparative data are even more difficult to acquire and assess. The World Health Organization (WHO) made the first major step in the development of a reliable indicator of child maltreatment (UNICEF, 1994, p. 42). For 1985-1990, the United States ranked 2nd worst among 23 developed nations on the WHO comparative measure; only the former Czechoslovakia was worse.

Spousal abuse also is a problem for U.S. families, and it is primarily abuse of wives by their husbands. About one third of all female homicide victims are killed by their husbands or boyfriends. Elder abuse—the abuse of live-in elderly relatives—has been the newest addition to the abysmal domestic violence problem in the United States.

Domestic violence and violence against women are problems that have been brought to public attention with the help of feminists and their organizations. Recognition has, in turn, led to increased programs directed to preventing and treating the problems. The most recent step in this process was the inclusion in the 1994 U.S. crime legislation of the Violence Against Women Act. This act makes domestic violence crimes federal offenses and provides funding for public education and treatment programs for offenders, among other measures. Federalization puts domestic violence on the national agenda and commits new resources to dealing with it.

School-based programs to prevent sexual abuse of children have developed in the United States in recent years. The first national study to assess their effectiveness found that they do help children in encounters with potential child molesters but that many programs are inadequate (Goleman, 1993). The most effective programs were long term—given every few years to the same children—and involved parents. One promising initiative in the provision of support services for families to prevent abuse and neglect is the Family Preservation and Support Services Program, enacted as part of the Omnibus Budget Reconciliation Act of 1993. Money is provided for new services that will address the current imbalance in federal programs that entitle states to open-ended funding for out-of-home care but very limited funding for home and community-based prevention.

The family preservation movement in child welfare developed out of the idea that, in the absence of serious contraindications, children are better off in their original homes than elsewhere, including foster placement. Combined with the principle of the least-restrictive alternative, family preservation results in the following hierarchy of alternatives: home of origin, adoption, foster care by a relative, long-term foster care by a stranger, and, finally, institutionalization. Studies of family preservation approaches, including the Homebuilders program and the family systems model, have indicated high levels of success maintaining intact families while they are receiving social services (Schuerman, Rzepnicki, & Littell, 1994). However, it always is a delicate balancing act to develop policy that both protects children from harm and protects families from dismemberment.

Frontiers

Looking into the near future, it is apparent that new issues are looming for consideration in a comprehensive family policy. As if the family has not experienced enough social change in recent decades, more is in store in the future, including the impacts of technological advances.

TECHNOLOGY

Technology is quickly and radically altering the social landscape with regard to procreation. The first "test tube baby" conceived through in vitro fertilization (IVF) was born in England in 1978. The first surrogate birth, in which an embryo was transferred to a woman with no genetic connection to it, happened in 1986, and in 1992 a postmenopausal South African grandmother gave birth to her own granddaughter, having served as the surrogate for the daughter's embryo. In 1994, nearly 9,000 children conceived in laboratories were born in the United States.

New reproductive technologies (NRTs) carry potential challenges to the nature of the family as well as to the parameters of family policy by altering the nature of parenthood and by introducing new actors such as surrogates. "People are creating new relations that separate genetic, gestational and social parentage" (Russell, 1994, p. 287). The surrogate (gestational) mother creates a new form of blood kinship, a relationship that can exist only through technology. "By this is . . .

breached the important symbolic conjunction of conjugal and procreative activity, and the equally important opposition between acts
undertaken for 'love' and those undertaken for money" (Franklin,
1993, p. 545).

NRTs are biomedical interventions in the natural process of birthing and include amniocentesis, donor insemination, embryo freezing
and transfer, IVF, and other technologies. The NRTs are largely being
developed privately and for profit. They serve as yet another example
of the encroachments of commodity capitalism on the functioning of
the family. One criticism made of Marx's pessimistic prognosis for
capitalism is that he failed to anticipate its immense adaptive potential,
highlighted by its penetration of every nook and cranny of human
existence in the pursuit of profit. By itself, technology is neutral in its
social implications. However, when it enters the marketplace, it has
significant social implications. "Thus, the new developments in
reproductive relations are neither inherently liberating nor automatically dehumanizing. It is the context of commodification of childbirth
that must be analyzed to chart the way forward" (Russell, 1994,
p. 312). Although NRTs carry promise for extending procreative
choices (e.g., they have made it possible for gay and lesbian couples
to have their biological offspring), they also carry potential danger,
especially for women.

NRTs have further widened the gap in modern society between the
biological act of reproduction and the social activity of parenting.
Donor insemination is a good example of the disjuncture between the
biological and social aspects of modern family life. In the United States
in 1994, there were more than 400 sperm banks as well as 11,000
physicians and 125 fertility clinics involved in donor insemination.
Donor anonymity has been the standard practice, but it is being widely
questioned today (Orenstein, 1995). The Sperm Bank of California,
opened in Oakland in 1982 as an outgrowth of a feminist health clinic,
pioneered the new policy direction: identity release. Almost four fifths
of the bank's clients request "yes donors" that allow donor-insemi-
nated children, when they become 18 years old, to find out the identity
of their donors. (Sweden made donor identification mandatory in
1989.) Existing law that denies paternal rights to donors in many
jurisdictions prevents potential court actions (Bartholet, 1993, pp.
222-223).

NRTs have exploded onto the scene at a time of increasing conservative hegemony in social policy. This accents the normal gap between technological innovation and sociocultural lag. This growing gap is a source of contradiction in societies. "Certainly it is striking to contrast the flourishing of NRTs, whilst infant mortality rates amongst inner-city blacks in the USA remain shockingly high" (McNeil, 1993, p. 503). Such contradictions reflect the growing polarization in U.S. society, in which the "haves" maximize their access to more benefits and services, whereas the "have-nots" experience worsening conditions. Conservative social policy only deepens this polarization because in its reliance on market solutions, it reinforces the already commanding position of the haves in society. Additionally, market-based policy extends the process of commodification into unprecedented areas—with unknown risks.

Such policy as has been developed with regard to NRTs has focused on quality control and has avoided the conundrum of issues that it raises for family life. Only a very few nations have addressed even the quality control issue in social policy. The Human Fertilisation and Embryology Act in the United Kingdom is one example. However, even the naming of the act conflates the natural with the technological. After all, fertilization is a natural act, whereas embryology is a branch of science. This misnaming "replicates the source of many of the confusions encountered by legislators attempting to formulate regulatory guidelines in unfamiliar territory" (Franklin, 1993, p. 556). A more accurate name for the act could have been the Human Embryo Research and Infertility Services Regulation Act. The muddled nature of the policy efforts to deal with the NRTs is reflected in their politics as well. For example, both the National Organization for Women and the New York State Catholic Conference, usually in opposing camps with regard to reproductive issues, endorsed the banning of payment for surrogacy adopted by New York in 1992.

In 1995, the U.S. Food and Drug Administration proposed federal regulations for sperm and ova banks that set guidelines on testing for HIV, syphilis, and hepatitis as well as on donor screening, retrieval, processing, labeling, storage, and distribution of reproductive tissue (Dieges, 1995). This kind of regulation will address the quality control issues that are currently paramount in dealing with the NRTs. However, around the corner looms the more contentious and muddled arena of social, political, and moral questions posed by NRTs.

The current haphazard and problematic development of NRTs raises into high relief other policies that pertain to parenting, especially adoption. Adoption is a nontechnological and traditional activity that furthers the interests of society in two important ways: It provides children who need parents with parents who want children. One experienced student of the subject, who has a biological child and an adopted child and who was not successful in conceiving an IVF child, argues that society is rushing too fast to embrace the NRTs while it continues to present impediments to adoption:

> We drive people away from adoption by surrounding it with burdensome regulations, by artificially limiting the number of children available out of all those desperately in need of homes, and by characterizing it as a grossly inferior form of parenting. We lure people into infertility treatment by encouraging them to believe that their efforts to pursue the dream of childbirth will be worth it, and by glorifying procreation. We subsidize procreation by using our health insurance, free medical care, and tax systems to reimburse the costs of childbirth as well as the costs of most infertility treatment. At the same time we make those who choose adoption pay every step of the way to parenthood. (Bartholet, 1993, pp. 213-214)

Thus, at the same time that society needs to regulate the NRTs, it may need to deregulate adoption to make it easier. However, deregulation is difficult in an environment in which there are divergent interests involved among birth parents, adoptive parents, and state agencies. That is why two efforts to streamline adoption—the 1993 Hague Convention at the international level and the Uniform Adoption Act (UAA) in the United States—may not pass muster in the United States. The UAA proposes the following: Set an 8-day period after childbirth for the consenting birth mother to revoke the adoption, allow open adoptions, and permit screened independent bodies to directly place adoptions. The Child Welfare League, other groups, and adoption agencies oppose the 8-day period as unfair to the birth mother and oppose independent placement as reducing quality control of adoptions (Giang, 1992). Until these issues are resolved, stalemate will be the result in this important area of needed reform.

PARENTING

Biological reproduction through new technologies and the focus on custody in divorce proceedings have contributed to an increasing gap between the biological and social dimensions of being a parent. Leach (1994) defined this gap in the following way:

> We know much more about the reproductive biology and genetics of parenthood than we know about the social, emotional and psychological impacts of parenting, and we devote far greater research resources to producing physically healthy babies than to rearing emotionally stable children. Indeed, while family planning, artificial baby foods and a host of childcare aids have dramatically reduced the burdens of traditional mothering roles, those roles themselves have been invalidated and have not been replaced with a workable restructuring of gender roles and relationships. What is needed now is something that cannot be produced by further scientific advance or a new technical fix: a reappraisal of the importance of parenting and fresh approaches to the continuing care and education of children in, and for, changing societies. (pp. xiv-xv)

The growing interest in the subject of parenting skills is slowly being reflected in policy. For example, the U.S. Violent Crime and Law Enforcement Act of 1994 provides funds for services to children and their families. One of the prevention programs included is the Family and Community Endeavor Schools Grant Program, which will fund community-based organizations for nutrition, mentoring, family counseling, and parenting programs at schools—all for at-risk children.

Family Support Programs of Richmond, Virginia, is an example of the kinds of local private efforts that are under way to provide parenting education (Vogel, 1992). It is an outgrowth of the Richmond Child Guidance Clinic and is supported by the United Way, corporate contracts, grants, and some modest fees. It provides parent education workshops, parent support groups, and a 24-hour hotline for parents and child care providers, among other services. The services provide for extensive evening hours as well as work-site and community-site programming to increase accessibility.

There are two dangers associated with the upsurge in interest in parenting programs. Unless consciously guided to do otherwise, the tendency is for such programs to reinforce the traditional perception that the responsibility—sole or major—for child rearing lies with mothers. Substantial effort is needed to ensure that both fathers and mothers are involved in such programs. A second danger presented by the current programs is that they single out one group of mothers (perhaps single, young, and poor) for special attention—and blame. The result may be that parenting programs become as stigmatized as welfare is. This produces two negatives: Other parents (married, middle class) may avoid the programs and the programs may deflect needed attention away from other, more basic and material problems of single, young, and poor mothers such as their poverty:

> A lack of parenting skills is associated implicitly with women who do not constitute a "nuclear married family." There is ample evidence to show that one of the major pressures on lone mothers, as on teenage mothers, comes from poverty. Nor is there any reason to believe that "the poor," like "the young" or "the single," should possess fewer skills of parenting than the rich, the older or the married. (Edwards, 1995, p. 256)

For these reasons, care must be given to the specification of what exactly is included in the realm of parenting skills—that it is empirically based and sensitive to the cultural differences that exist between social classes and ethnic and racial groups. Whatever the substantive content of parenting programs and whatever social class or ethnic group is served, all need to deliberately strive to include fathers, including fathers who are estranged from their families.

FATHERING

In the contemporary discussion of female-headed families, poverty, and welfare, the subject of fatherhood is virtually absent (at least beyond child support maintenance issues). In large part, this is because many fathers also are absent from their families; in the United States in 1994, 27% of children under age 18 were in families in which the fathers were absent. Even when fathers are present, despite the effects of feminism and the fact that more mothers are working in the paid labor force, women still carry a highly disproportionate burden of child care (and housework), even when the women's incomes are higher than the men's (Sidel, 1990, pp. 202-203).

However, there is good reason for a renewed emphasis on fathering. Until about 20 years ago, mothers almost always were awarded custody of children in divorce cases. Since then, however, many states have legalized joint custody. Although mothers still are overwhelmingly the custodial parents, in 1990 in the United States 16% of divorces involving children resulted in joint custody and 9% resulted in paternal custody (Hoffman, 1995). These legal advances come at a time when evidence is accumulating that there is a connection between the nature of a father's relationship to his children and the likelihood that he will maintain support. Fathers with joint custody are more likely to keep up support payments than are fathers without custody.

Local programs that support fathering may serve as examples for state and national policy innovation. For example, many public school districts in Minnesota offer a variety of programs to encourage responsible fatherhood including a Father's Resource Center that provides parenting classes, anger workshops, and legal clinics dealing with custody and support matters, among other services (Lewin, 1995). Education for fathering is not something that should wait until fatherhood comes along. Conceptions and behaviors about fathering are shaped from the earliest experiences of children. Education for fathering (and parenting) is best begun in elementary schools:

> We could begin with parenting and child-care courses in middle school. Both boys and girls need to learn how to care effectively for children and that child care is mother's and father's responsibility. Boys especially need to learn that caring for a baby does not undermine masculinity. (Berry, 1993, p. 219)

CARING FOR PARENTS

In addition to their responsibilities for the maintenance of personal life in the family, women face an increasing burden of elder care. The population of aged parents in the United States, especially those who need care, is increasing, and only about 5% of them are in nursing homes at any given time (McLeod, 1995). According to a 1989 study by the Older Women's League, women spend an average of 17 years of their lives caring for children and 18 years aiding aged parents. Full-time women workers are four times as likely as full-time working men to be primary caregivers to the elderly. A national study in the United States in the 1980s revealed that 72% of all carers for the elderly were women and that adult daughters comprised the largest single group of carers (29%). Many of these caregivers do not receive formal support:

> The fact is that many caregivers never access formal support systems at all. Others are confused by the sheer multiplicity of agencies, charging policies, and eligibility criteria and by the lack of service coordination. Still other caregivers delay their use of services until the situation has deteriorated to the point where agency staff have little choice but to encourage placement in long-term care. (Gottlieb & Gignac, 1994, p. 228)

That this heavier workload of caring is stressful for women has been documented. A 1992 study of 33 firms in Portland, Oregon, found that women with responsibilities for both children and elderly (or disabled) adults experienced more stress and were absent more often than employees with little or no such care tasks (Brody, 1992).

There are incremental policy changes that could help parents who care for their parents. Social security could be reformed to meet their special needs. Schorr (1986, p. 69) proposed the following reforms of social security that would help women: (a) upgrading benefits for the "old old," usually defined as people age 85 or older, perhaps by revising the benefits to increase with age rather than decrease as they currently do; (b) liberalizing maximum benefits for families; and (c) restoring a general minimum benefit. These reforms would be especially helpful for those families who care for their elderly members, a growing segment of all families.

Conclusion

The increased stresses from without experienced by the family have been discussed and analyzed. On top of those, there are increasing internal stresses within the family. These stresses can result from the generic conflicts that spring from the structure of the family. Families are intergenerational structures, and generations often have opposing interests. Thus parent-child conflicts are inherent in the family. Some of them, most notably parental child abuse, call for mediation by society and the application of government authority against parents in the interests of the child. Additionally, there are inherent structural conflicts between parents, of which custody and support issues emanating from divorce are only the most prominent examples. The point of looking at the endogenous sources of stress for the family is that they, like the exogenous sources of stress, have been increasing over recent decades. In fact, qualitatively new sources of internal stress have been created by social and technological changes such as the conflicts that exist between grandparents and their in-laws over visitation rights with grandchildren.

For several decades now, there has been much lip service paid to the need to strengthen the family in the United States. Even the 1994 Republican "Contract With America"—a generally conservative anti-government tract—included a Family Reinforcement Act that would promote child support enforcement, tax incentives for adoption, and an elderly dependent care tax credit. Despite the rhetoric, however, there has been a dearth of action with regard to developing a systematic family policy. Part of the problem has been disagreement about what constitutes a family and what is desirable policy to promote the family. This disagreement has become highly politicized. In the polarized public discourse that results, there is little room for discussion of the pragmatic things that could be done to support family functioning.

The loudest voices in the public discourse are those who represent, on the one hand, feminist groups (the liberal camp) that lobby for full equality for women, especially within the paid labor force, and, on the other, antifeminist groups (the conservative camp) that lobby for what they refer to as "family values"—a set of positions that argue for the restoration of the traditional patriarchal family. Each side often operates politically as vetoes on the other's legislative moves, resulting in a general stalemate. Much of the polarization results from a decades-long focus on a single issue that is very divisive—abortion. Indeed, the two sides are best recognized publicly for their self-chosen appellations: The liberals are pro-choice and the conservatives are pro-life.

Thus, today, the constituency with the greatest organic interest in family policies, women, is divided. This stands in contrast to the

1910s-1920s, when maternalist family policies (e.g., mothers' pensions, child and female labor laws) and egalitarian policies (the franchise for women) were championed by virtually all politically active women. The contemporary women's movement is dominated by an interest in gender-neutral equality programs. As a result, contemporary Second Wave feminism has not been an effective voice for children and families. "Feminist scholars have studied the social organization of mothering in theory but not the actual experiences of child raising, and the movement as a whole has not significantly influenced child welfare debates or policies" (Gordon, 1992a, p. 269). As Skocpol (1992) noted, "Contemporary feminists may also be able to learn lessons from the maternalists of old who, in their self-conceptions and public rhetoric, stressed solidarity between privileged and less privileged women, and honor for values of caring and nurturance" (p. 538). Women who are homemakers or for whom being homemakers is a central identity in their lives are not addressed by a feminist rhetoric that either ignores or trivializes homemaking.

First Wave feminism articulated a vision of the modern woman as living in a world of special difference (e.g., pregnancy), whereas Second Wave feminism represents the view of woman as living in a world of equality (e.g., equal pay for equal work). First Wave feminism was rooted in the Progressive movement that emanated from settlement house leaders such as Jane Addams and other reformers, for whom women and children deserved special attention and care; it included organizations such as the National Congress of Mothers. At that time, honoring motherhood and other special attributes of women "could symbolically and relatively unproblematically connect many elite, professional, middle class, and poor American women" (Skocpol, 1992, p. 538). Second Wave feminism has focused on work because work represents the desires of its principal social base—the generation of women who were behind the social change of the 1960s and forward—referred to as women's entry into the paid labor force. It includes organizations such as the National Organization for Women. These women, as a whole, do not place a high priority on their reproductive ("special") lives except for the right to abortion, which guarantees them the possibility of delaying or opting out of reproduction.

The focus of contemporary feminism on paid work and on reproductive freedom has left the field of speaking for mothers, especially the large number of mothers who have not entered the paid labor force, to cultivation by the right. As Gordon (1992b) noted,

> The feminist reproductive rights movement faces the task of finding a program that equally defends women's individual rights to freedom, including sexual freedom, *and* the dignity of women's need and capacity for nurturance and being nurtured, with or without biological motherhood. (p. 153)

Although a majority of married mothers now are in the paid labor force, there are sizable minorities who are not—about one quarter of married mothers with children ages 6 to 17 and about two fifths of married mothers with children under age 6.

What is needed to overcome the right's co-optation of motherhood under the "family values" slogan (which in reality attacks the gains in women's work and reproductive rights made by Second Wave feminists) is for the left to find ways in which to address the concerns of all mothers. Feminism can profit from finding an appropriate voice and program for "valuing family." The FMLA may represent a frontier in melding the issues of Second Wave feminism and motherhood, according to Vogel (1993). It addresses the special concern of birth and mothering without treating pregnancy as a disability; pregnancy leave thus becomes parenting leave. The FMLA conceives of the worker as both an individual and a family member, and leave is provided on a gender-neutral basis that allows room for recognizing the special needs of new mothers.

However, the FMLA provides only for those mothers (and others) who work. What is needed is a family policy focus that also addresses the needs of mothers who do not work. The WIC program, which essentially represents a maternalist approach, addresses the needs of mothers who do not work but does so only for poor mothers who qualify for the program. There are various ways in which the WIC program could be universalized. One possibility would be to expand on what Marmor (1983) has suggested—a universal health insurance program for children, called "Kidcare," which would include coverage for preventive programs such as prenatal care and child care. Such a

Children's Health Security program could meet the needs of many constituencies, including married working mothers of modest to middle-class means and unmarried mothers who need health care and child care for their children to contemplate working. The costs of such a program could be minimized by using the public schools and by charging an affordable sliding-scale fee for enrollment. Short of adopting such a universal program, targeted efforts can be mounted to address specific needs. The success of Oakland's Healthy Start program in reducing infant mortality is an example. Such a program may survive the current retrenchment in social policy because it is limited in scope, is cost-effective, and builds on the political support enjoyed by the HeadStart program.

In conclusion, we live at a time when families with dependent children in the United States face increasing economic pressures and other stresses, many of them caused by social changes out of the control of individual families. Although many of these families receive some help from private and public sources, much more is needed in the form of policy that addresses their needs. At a time of growing government decentralization and downsizing, it is even more critical that the needs for government intervention and support be rank ordered. Thus far, despite the political rhetoric that is aimed at family functioning, it remains a relatively low priority for policy attention. This is a regrettable fact, one that potentially carries with it quite perilous outcomes for all of society.

A comprehensive family policy is required to meet both the new changes and the recurrent problems that contemporary families face. This family policy must take into consideration mothers, fathers, children, and the family as well as work needs of mothers and fathers. Such a policy could stand as a true testament to this society's devotion to valuing its families.

Note

1. Unless otherwise noted, statistical data come from U.S. Department of Commerce (1995).

References

Abramovitz, M. (1988). *Regulating the lives of women: Social welfare policy from colonial times to the present.* Boston: South End.

Action Alliance for Children. (1995, July/August). A nation's shame: Fatal child abuse and neglect in the U.S. *Children's Advocate,* p. 4.

Arendell, T. (1986). *Mothers and divorce: Legal, economic, and social dilemmas.* Berkeley: University of California Press.

Bane, M. J. (1986). Household composition and poverty. In S. Danziger & D. Weinberg (Eds.), *Fighting poverty: What works and what doesn't* (pp. 209-231). Cambridge, MA: Harvard University Press.

Bartholet, E. (1993). *Family bonds: Adoption and the politics of parenting.* Boston: Houghton Mifflin.

Bergmann, B. R., & Hartmann, H. I. (1995, May 1). A program to help working parents. *The Nation,* pp. 592-595.

Berry, M. F. (1993). *The politics of parenthood: Child care, women's rights, and the myth of the good mother.* New York: Penguin Books.

Bradsher, K. (1995a, June 7). Earned Income Tax Credit, under siege by G.O.P., gets a defender. *New York Times,* pp. A16, A22.

Bradsher, K. (1995b, August 14). Poor children in U.S. are among worst off in study of 18 industrialized countries. *New York Times,* pp. A7, A9.

Brody, J. E. (1992, December 9). For mothers who also work, rewards may outweigh stress. *New York Times,* pp. B8, C16.

Center, J. (1995, June 6). Why punish poor children? *San Francisco Chronicle,* p. A19.

Dieges, J. (1995, May/June). Sperm and ova banks come into the regulatory fold. *Children's Advocate,* pp. 4-5.

Edelman, M. W. (1987). *Families in peril: An agenda for social change.* Cambridge, MA: Harvard University Press.

Edwards, J. (1995). "Parenting skills": Views of community health and social service providers about the needs of their "clients." *Journal of Social Policy, 24,* 237-259.

Ellwood, D. T. (1984). The hope for self-support. In M. Carballo & M. Bane (Eds.), *The state and the poor in the 1980s* (pp. 19-49). Boston: Auburn House.

Ellwood, D. T. (1988). *Poor support: Poverty in the American family.* New York: Basic Books.

Evans, P. M., & McIntyre, E. L. (1987). Welfare, work incentives, and the single mother: An interprovincial comparison. In J. Ismael (Ed.), *The Canadian welfare state: Evolution and transition* (pp. 101-125). Edmonton: University of Alberta Press.

Family Resource Coalition. (1993). Kentucky looks at the first year of its statewide program and charts a course for the future. *Report, 12,* 47-48). (Family Resource Coalition, Chicago)

Franklin, S. (1993). Postmodern procreation: Representing reproductive practice. *Society as Culture, 3,* 522-561.

Galinsky, E. (1992). Work and family: 1992. *Report, 11*(2), 2-3. (Family Resource Coalition, Chicago)

Giang, K. M. (1992, May/June). The tale of two adoption laws. *Children's Advocate,* pp. 4-5, 10.

Gilchrist, L. D., & Schinke, S. P. (1983). Teenage pregnancy and public policy. *Social Service Review, 57,* 307-322.

Goldberg, G. S., & Kremen, E. (1987). The feminization of poverty: Only in America? *Social Policy, 17,* 3-14.

Goleman, D. (1993, October 6). Abuse-prevention efforts aid children. *New York Times,* pp. B9, C13.

Goode, W. J. (1993). *World changes in divorce patterns.* New Haven, CT: Yale University Press.

Gordon, L. (1992a). Family violence, feminism, and social control. In B. Thorne & M. Yalom (Eds.), *Rethinking the family: Some feminist questions* (rev. ed., pp. 262-286). Boston: Northeastern University Press.

Gordon, L. (1992b). Why nineteenth century feminists did not support "birth control" and twentieth-century feminists do: Feminism, reproduction, and the family. In B. Thorne & M. Yalom (Eds.), *Rethinking the family: Some feminist questions* (rev. ed., pp. 140-154). Boston: Northeastern University Press.

Gottlieb, B. H., & Gignac, M. A. M. (1994). Family support and care of the elderly: Program and policy challenges. In S. Kagan & B. Weissbourd (Eds.), *Putting families first: America's family support movement and the challenge of change* (pp. 216-242). San Francisco: Jossey-Bass.

Graham, H. (1984). *Women, health and the family.* Brighton, IL: Wheatsheaf Books.

Herscher, E. (1995, August 4). Infant death rate drops in Oakland. *San Francisco Chronicle,* p. A21.

Hilts, P. J. (1995, July 26). Maternal health ranking puts U.S. in 18th place. *New York Times,* pp. B10, C8.

Hochschild, A., with Machung, A. (1989). *The second shift: Working parents and the revolution at home.* New York: Viking.

Hoffman, J. (1995, April 26). Divorced fathers make gains in battles to increase rights. *New York Times,* p. A1.

Holmes, S. A. (1995, April 25). Low-wage fathers and the welfare debate. *New York Times,* pp. A7, A12.

James, B. (1995, January 12). U.S.-French prenatal care study. *International Herald Tribune,* p. 7.

Jones, E. F., Forrest, J. D., Goldman, N., Henshaw, S., Lincoln, R., Rosoff, J. I., Westoff, C. F., & Wolf, D. (1986). *Teenage pregnancy in industrialized countries.* New Haven, CT: Yale University Press.

Jones, E. F., Forrest, J. D., Goldman, N., Henshaw, S., Lincoln, R., Rosoff, J. I., Westoff, C. F., & Wolf, D. (1989). *Pregnancy, contraception, and family planning services in industrialized countries.* New Haven, CT: Yale University Press.

Kamerman, S. B., & Kahn, A. J. (1987). Universalism and income testing in family policy: New perspectives on an old debate. *Social Work, 32,* 277-280.

Leach, P. (1994). *Children first.* New York: Vintage Books.

Lee, M. A., Haught, K., Redlener, I., Fant, A., Fox, E., & Somers, S. A. (1992). Health care for children in homeless families. In P. Brickner, L. Scharer, B. Conanan, M. Savarese, & B. Scanlan (Eds.), *Under the safety net: The health and social welfare of the homeless in the United States* (pp. 119-138). New York: Norton.

Leira, A. (1992). *Welfare states and working mothers: The Scandinavian experience.* Cambridge, UK: Cambridge University Press.

Lewin, T. (1995, June 18). Creating fathers out of men with children. *New York Times,* p. A1.

Marmor, T. R. (1983). Rethinking national health insurance. In T. Marmor (Ed.), *Political analysis and American medical care: Essays* (pp. 187-206). Cambridge, UK: Cambridge University Press.

Martin, G. T., Jr. (1990). *Social policy in the welfare state.* Englewood Cliffs, NJ: Prentice Hall.

Martin, G. T., Jr. (1991). Family, gender, and social policy. In L. Kramer (Ed.), *The sociology of gender* (pp. 323-345). New York: St. Martin's.

Matras, J. (1990). *Dependency, obligations, and entitlements.* Englewood Cliffs, NJ: Prentice Hall.

McLeod, B. W. (1995, August 21). Elder care, prime social issue of the 21st century. *San Francisco Examiner,* p. A13.

McNeil, M. (1993). New reproductive technologies: Dreams and broken promises. *Science as Culture, 3,* 483-506.

Morris, M., & Williamson, J. B. (1987). Workfare: The poverty/dependence trade-off. *Social Policy, 18,* 13-16, 49-50.

Oellerich, D. T., & Garfinkel, I. (1983). Distributional impacts of existing and alternative child support systems. *Policy Studies Journal, 12,* 119-130.

Orenstein, P. (1995, June 18). Looking for a donor to call dad. *New York Times Magazine,* pp. 28-35, 42, 50, 58.

Passell, P. (1995, July 13). Economic scene: Semi conductor semi-success. *New York Times,* pp. C2, D2.

Pearce, D. (1978). The feminization of poverty: Women, work and welfare. *Urban and Social Change Review, 11,* 28-36.

Prosser, W. R., & McGroder, S. M. (1992). The supply of and demand for child care: Measurement and analytic issues. In A. Booth (Ed.), *Child care in the 1990s: Trends and consequences* (pp. 42-55). Hillsdale, NJ: Lawrence Erlbaum.

Russell, K. (1994). A value-theoretic approach to childbirth and reproductive engineering. *Science and Society, 58,* 287-314.

Schorr, A. L. (1986). *Common decency: Domestic policies after Reagan.* New Haven, CT: Yale University Press.

Schuerman, J. R., Rzepnicki, T. L., & Littell, J. H. (1994). *Putting families first: An experiment in family preservation.* New York: Aldine de Gruyter.

Shaw, B. (1958). *Major Barbara.* New York: Longman. (Originally published 1907)

Sidel, R. (1990). *On her own: Growing up in the shadow of the American Dream.* New York: Penguin Books.

Skocpol, T. (1992). *Protecting soldiers and mothers: The political origins of social policy in the United States.* Cambridge, MA: Harvard University Press.

Sorenson, A., & McLanahan, S. (1987). Married women's economic dependency, 1940-1980. *American Journal of Sociology, 93,* 659-687.

Steinhauer, J. (1995, August 2). Study cites adult males for most teenage births. *New York Times,* p. A14.

Sullivan, J. F. (1995, July 26). A second look at child-support laws, as New Jersey adheres to old standards. *New York Times,* pp. A11, B5.

United Nations. (1991). *The world's women: Trends and statistics 1970-1990.* New York: Author.

United Nation's Children's Emergency Fund. (1994). *The progress of nations: The nations of the world ranked according to their achievements in child health, nutrition, education, family planning, and progress for women.* New York: United Nations.

United Nations Development Programme. (1996). *Human development report 1996.* New York: Oxford University Press.

U.S. Commission on Civil Rights. (1984). Equal opportunity and the need for child care. In R. Genovese (Ed.), *Cities and change: Social needs and public policies* (pp. 92-105). New York: Praeger.

U.S. Department of Commerce. (1995). *Statistical abstract of the United States.* Washington, DC: Bureau of the Census.

Vobejda, B. (1994, October 26). Birthrate among teenage girls declines slightly. *Washington Post,* p. A3.

Vogel, C. (1992). Program providers' roundtable on work and family issues. *Report, 11*(2), 12-15. (Family Resource Coalition, Chicago)

Vogel, L. (1993). *Mothers on the job: Maternity policy in the U.S. workplace.* New Brunswick, NJ: Rutgers University Press.

Walsh, J. (1988, September 14-20). It's the rage on Capitol Hill, but does workfare work? *In These Times,* p. 2.

Wilson, W. J., & Neckerman, K. M. (1986). Poverty and family structure: The widening gap between evidence and public policy issues. In S. Danziger & D. Weinberg (Eds.), *Fighting poverty: What works and what doesn't* (pp. 232-259). Cambridge, MA: Harvard University Press.

Zaretsky, E. (1976). *Capitalism, the family and personal life.* New York: Harper & Row.

Zuckerman, B., & Brazelton, T. B. (1994). Strategies for a family-supportive child health care system. In S. Kagan & B. Weissbourd (Eds.), *Putting families first: America's family support movement and the challenge of change* (pp. 73-92). San Francisco: Jossey-Bass.

Name Index

Abelda, R., 16, 17, 18
Abramovitz, M., 9, 101, 102, 291
Acock, A. C., 20
Adams, J., 24, 96
Adams, M., 219-249
Ahrons, C. R., 160, 167, 168, 180, 182, 183, 184, 185
Alanen, L., 247, 248
Albert, A. A., 242
Albert, L., 278-279
Albiston, C. R., 160
Allegro, T., 245
Allen, K. A., 201
Allen, K. R., 13, 22, 175, 196-219
Allen, W., 80
Allison, P., 170
Alvarez, F. B., 20
Alwain, D. F., 24
Amaro, H., 203
Amato, P. R., 28, 157, 159, 174-175, 176, 178, 179, 186
Ambert, A. M., 8-9, 22, 167, 179, 184
Amott, T., 254, 258
Anderson, E. R., 178, 181, 182
Andrzejewski, J., 206
Aquilino, W. S., 186
Aravosis, J., 18
Arditti, J., 155, 169, 170
Arendell, T., 1-34, 95, 100, 105, 106, 154-188, 284, 296
Aries, P., 48, 49, 50, 51

Asamen, J. K., 9, 10
Astone, N. M., 86-87
Atwood, J. D., 3, 4
Axtell, J., 50

Babcock, B. A., 100
Baber, K. M., 13, 201
Backett, K., 20
Badinter, E., 48
Bales, R. F., 223
Bandura, A., 228
Bane, M. J., 69, 71, 154, 298
Bardwell, J. R., 242
Barnett, R. C., 95, 96, 98, 101
Barringer, F., 146
Bartholet, E., 310, 312
Bartko, W. T., 241, 246
Bartlett, K. T., 105
Basow, S. A., 24
Bates, J. E., 28
Baumrind, D., 6, 25, 26, 176
Baydar, N., 174, 187
Becker, M., 105
Beer, W. R., 181, 183
Behlmer, G. K., 49
Belkin, L., 144
Bell, A. P., 211
Bellah, R., 11
Bellissimo, A., 176
Belous, R. S., 69

Belsky, J., 5, 24, 25, 282
Bem, S. L., 221, 229-230, 231, 235, 240, 242, 244, 246
Bengtson, V. L., 199
Benjamin, M., 167
Benkov, L., 196, 212, 213
Bentancout, H., 6
Berger, B., 11
Berger, P., 11
Bergmann, B. R., 97, 110, 111, 145, 304
Berkner, L. K., 47
Bernard, J., 254, 256, 257
Bernstein, A. C., 180
Berry, G. L., 9, 10
Berry, M. F., 315
Bianchi, S. M., 161, 185
Bigler, R. S., 231
Blair, S. L., 19, 95
Blakely, R. M., 281
Blakeslee, S., 160
Blankenhorn, D., 92, 102, 104, 155
Blau, D. M., 269
Blau, F. D., 97
Bleier, R., 221
Bloch, R. H., 53
Block, J., 159, 175, 178
Block, J. H., 159, 175, 178
Blum, L., 283
Blumstein, P., 197
Bohannon, P., 160
Bohen, H. H., 263
Bolduc, D., 237, 238
Bolgar, R., 175, 176, 187
Bond, J. T., 20
Bonnar, D., 283
Booher Feagin, C., 14
Booth, A., 155, 178, 179, 186, 200
Booth, C. C., 23, 158-159
Bould, S., 12
Boulding, E., 234
Bowlby, J., 7
Boxer, A., 203
Bozett, F. W., 201, 211
Bradbard, M. R., 237
Bradsher, K., 295, 301
Brayfield, A., 265, 267-271
Brazelton, T. B., 305, 306
Brenner, J., 254, 255, 256
Bretherton, I., 7
Bricher, M. R., 260

Brillon, L., 14, 15, 27, 28, 29, 31, 32, 33
Bronfenbrenner, U., 27
Brooks, J. B., 1, 24, 25
Brooks-Gunn, J., 17, 181, 182, 185, 187
Broverman, D. M., 244
Broverman, I., 244
Brown, L. S., 198-199, 214
Bruner, J. S., 226, 235, 236
Bumpass, L. L., 71, 73, 74, 75, 83, 146, 147, 157
Burgoyne, J., 179
Buriel, R., 33
Burke, P., 203
Burstein, P., 260
Burton, L. M., 80
Butler, J. P., 221

Cahill, S. E., 21, 221, 229, 232, 233-234, 235, 236, 237, 243
Caldera, Y. M., 244
Cancian, F. M., 134
Carlson, L., 27
Carson, D. K., 33
Casper, L. M., 265, 269, 275
Casper, V., 208
Castellino, D. R., 17, 18, 28
Cattan, P., 269
Chafetz, J. S., 246
Chambers, D., 170
Chan, S., 33
Chang, B.-H., 6
Chao, R. K., 26, 32, 33
Chase-Lansdale, P. L., 159, 174, 175, 178, 179, 187
Chatters, L., 15, 29, 30
Chauncey, G., Jr., 202
Cheal, D., 11, 12
Cherlin, A., 23, 71, 75, 80, 83, 85, 87, 97, 106, 157, 158, 159, 163, 164, 168, 170, 176, 178, 180-181, 182, 183, 184, 185, 186, 187
Cherry, L., 239
Chodorow, N., 21, 226, 227-228, 244, 245, 246
Christensen, K. E., 263
Clark, D., 179
Clarkson, F. E., 244
Clingempeel, W. G., 181, 182
Cochran, S. W., 242

Cohen, K. M., 209
Coiro, M. J., 18, 25
Coleman, J., 257
Coleman, M., 179
Collins, P. H., 3, 30, 94, 199
Collins, R., 84, 222
Coltrane, S., 84, 95, 219-249
Condry, J., 10
Connell, R. W., 138, 245, 246
Connelly, R., 266, 269, 275
Cook, J. A., 201
Cook, K. V., 237
Coontz, S., 111, 112
Copelon, R., 100
Corsaro, W. A., 223
Cossette, L., 237, 238
Cott, N. F., 55
Cowan, C., 20, 22, 23, 24, 158
Cowan, G., 238
Cowan, P., 20, 22, 23, 24, 158
Cox, M. S., 20, 24, 160, 164, 174
Cox, R., 160, 164, 174
Cranston, M., 48
Crawley, B., 30
Crnic, K. A., 23, 158-159
Crockenberg, S., 5
Crosbie-Burnett, M., 212
Crouter, A. C., 27, 241, 246
Cunningham, A., 197
Curran, D. J., 177
Curtin, R. B., 159
Czapanskiy, K., 106

Dahlstrom, E., 11
Dail, P. W., 33
Danziger, S., 86
Darling-Fisher, C. S., 19
Davis, K., 256, 259
Deal, J., 181, 182
Deaux, K., 239
DeFrain, J., 25
Degler, C. N., 47, 53, 54, 254
Deich, S. G., 265, 267, 268, 269, 270, 271
DeMaris, A., 163, 166
D'Emilio, J., 203, 204, 207
Demo, D. H., 8, 20, 198, 200, 210, 211, 214
Demos, J., 7, 47, 49
Denzin, N. K., 247
Depner, C. E., 160, 167, 169

Deschamps, D., 84, 85
Deussen, T., 283
DeVault, M. L., 112
Devore, W., 33
Dickerson, B. J., 17
Dickie, J. R., 20, 25
Dieges, J., 311
DiLapi, E. M., 202
Dill, B. T., 94
Dinnerstein, D., 227, 244
DiPietro, J. A., 241
Dizard, J., 11
Dodge, K. A., 28
Donnelly, D., 167
Dornbusch, S. M., 26
Dorr, A., 10
Downey, D. B., 176
Duberman, M. B., 202
Duncan, G. D., 162
Dunn, J., 155, 179

Eastman, G., 1, 5, 24
Eccles, J. S., 246
Edelman, M. W., 307
Edwards, J., 314
Eggebeen, D., 8
Ehrenreich, B., 257
Einwohner, R., 260
Elder, G. H., Jr., 199
Ellwood, D. T., 298, 299
Ellwood, M. S., 176
Elmen, J. D., 26, 176
Emery, R. E., 159, 167, 171, 176, 178
England, P., 100, 283
Engstler, A., 8
Epstein, C. F., 221
Epstein, S., 7, 21
Erikson, E. H., 225
Eskridge, W. N., Jr., 207, 209
Estes, S., 254-284
Etaugh, C., 221, 237, 246
Etzioni, A., 92
Evans, P. M., 300

Faderman, L., 203
Fagot, B. I., 232, 238, 239, 240, 241, 244
Falk, P. J., 205, 211

Fant, A., 18, 295
Farley, R., 80
Fay, R. E., 210
Feagin, J. R., 14
Felmlee, D., 284
Fenstermaker, S., 243
Ferber, M. A., 97
Ferree, M. M., 21, 93
Ferron, J., 28
Ficher, I., 211, 213
Fine, M. A., 177, 186
Fineman, M. A., 93, 104, 105, 107, 108,
    111, 112
Finkelhor, D., 167
Finlay, B., 18, 20
Fish, L. S., 161
Fish, M. C., 201
Fishel, A. H., 167
Fivush, R., 231, 232
Flaherty, D. H., 48
Flaks, D. K., 211, 213
Flax, J., 11
Fleming, S., 49
Fliegelman, J., 53
Folbre, N., 16, 17, 18
Fonow, M. M., 201
Fox, E., 18, 295
Fraleigh, M. J., 26
Frank, S., 7, 45-63
Frank, S. M., 57, 58, 59, 60
Frankel, D. M., 143
Franklin, S., 310, 311
Fraser, N., 9, 112, 114
Freedman, A., 100
Freedman, E. B., 203, 204
Freud, S., 224, 226
Frey, R. G., 173
Friedman, D. E., 20, 258, 261
Fu, V. R., 32
Fuchs, V. R., 145
Fujimoto, T., 262
Furstenberg, F. F., Jr., 80, 97, 106, 128,
    157, 158, 163, 164, 168, 170, 175,
    176, 178, 180-181, 183, 184, 185,
    186, 187, 256
Furukawa, S., 13, 158

Gadlin, H., 11
Gagnon, J. H., 210
Galinsky, E., 20, 261, 267, 268,
    270

Gallo, F., 69
Gamble, W. C., 24
Ganong, L. H., 179
Garasky, S., 175
Garcia Coll, C. T., 14, 15, 27, 28, 29, 31,
    32, 33
Garfinkel, I., 100, 107, 162, 298
Garrett, P., 28
Gebhard, P. H., 210
Gergen, K. J., 3
Gergen, M. M., 3
Gerson, K., 95, 119-150
Gessner, J. C., 261
Giang, K. M., 312
Gibbs, J. T., 30
Gignac, M. A. M., 316
Gilchrist, L. D., 306
Gjerde, P. F., 159, 175, 178
Glass, J., 254-284
Glazer, N., 102
Glenn, E. N., 93
Glenn, N. D., 69
Glenn, S. A., 60
Glick, P. C., 77, 157
Goetting, A., 19, 24
Goffman, E., 219, 221
Goldberg, G. S., 299
Goldberg, W., 26
Goldfield, E. C., 226
Goldscheider, F. K., 70
Goleman, D., 308
Goode, W. J., 296, 297
Goodman, M., 49
Goodman, N., 229, 232
Goodman, P., 210
Goodnow, J. J., 241
Gordon, A., 268
Gordon, L., 9, 101, 102, 112, 114, 318,
    319
Gordon, M., 8
Gottlieb, B. H., 316
Gottman, J. M., 157
Gottman, J. S., 201
Graham, H., 299
Graves, S. B., 10
Greely, S., 33
Greenberger, E., 26
Greif, G. L., 163, 166, 169
Gresham, J. H., 101
Greven, P. J., 47
Griswold, R. L., 62
Groeneveld, L. P., 74

Gross, P., 182
Grossbart, S., 27
Grossberg, M., 56
Gubrium, J., 4
Gutman, H. G., 61

Haas, B., 27, 28
Hagan, M. S., 174, 181, 182
Hale-Benson, J. E., 30, 242
Halttunen, K., 58
Hamburg, D., 19
Hamill, S., 26
Hamner, T. J., 24, 28
Hannan, M. T., 74
Hardesty, C., 245
Hare, J., 200
Hareven, T. K., 7, 47, 58, 60, 254, 255
Harold, R. D., 246
Harrison, A., 33
Harry, J., 211
Hartmann, H. L., 102, 110-111, 138, 256,
    304
Hartsock, N. C. M., 246
Harwood, R. L., 31
Hashima, P. Y., 28
Haught, K., 18, 295
Hayes, C. D., 272
Haynes, J., 178
Hechter, M., 258
Helburn, S. W., 266, 276
Helmbrecht, L., 212
Henderson, K. V., 20, 24
Hendrick, H., 9
Herdt, G., 197, 203
Herek, G. M., 203
Hernandez, D. J., 68, 71, 74, 76, 77, 82,
    83
Herrell, R. K., 203, 209
Herrerías, C., 169
Herscher, E., 305
Herz, D. E., 95
Hess, B. B., 21
Hetherington, E. M., 26, 155, 156, 159,
    160, 164, 174, 175, 176-177, 178,
    179, 181, 182, 187
Hewitt, N. A., 200
Hewlett, S. A., 281
Hilts, P. J., 305
Hochschild, A., 19, 21, 23, 94, 95, 96, 97,
    112, 113, 119, 264, 278, 279, 293
Hoffer, P. C., 49

Hofferth, S. L., 265, 267, 268, 269, 270,
    271
Hoff-Ginsberg, E., 17, 28
Hoffman, C. D., 238
Hoffman, J., 315
Hoffman, L. W., 96
Hoffman, S. D., 162
Hogan, D. P., 70, 71, 74, 87
Holcomb, P., 265, 267, 268, 269, 270, 271
Holden, K., 162
Hollier, A., 181, 182
Holmes, W. M., 155, 157, 160, 162
Holstein, J., 4
Horowitz, J. A., 1, 22, 26
Hort, B., 240
Howes, C., 272, 274
Hughes, C. B., 1, 22
Hugick, L., 280
Hull, N. E. H., 49
Hunnicutt, B., 257
Hunt, J., 261
Hunt, L., 261
Huston, A. C., 239, 241, 244

Inkeles, A., 223
Irving, H. H., 167

Ja, D. Y., 6, 32
Jacklin, C. N., 241, 245
Jacob, H., 74
Jacobs, J. A., 145
Jacobs, J. E., 246
Jacobson, L., 242
James, B., 305
Jargowsky, P. A., 69
Jeffrey, K., 58
Jencks, C., 147
Joe, J. R., 33
Johnson, M., 95
Johnson, M. M., 227
Johnson, M. P., 19
Johnston, J. R., 178
Joseph, G., 211, 213

Kaestle, C. F., 50, 51
Kagan, S. L., 272, 274, 275
Kahn, A. J., 260, 299-300
Kain, E. L., 28, 69, 74
Kamerman, S. B., 260, 299-300

Kanazawa, S., 258
Karraker, K. H., 236, 238, 239
Kaufman, M., 246
Kay, H. H., 74
Keith, B., 157, 159, 174-175, 176, 178,
    186
Kellan, S., 161, 162
Kelley, M. L., 30, 32, 33
Kenote, T., 33
Kerber, L. K., 53
Kessler, S. J., 230, 243
Kessler-Harris, A., 254, 258
Kett, J. F., 55, 60
Khader, A. B., 48
Kiernan, K. E., 178
Kilborn, P. T., 145
Kilbourne, B. S., 100, 283
Kimmel, D. C., 203
Kimmel, M. S., 245, 246
Kingston, P. W., 261, 278, 279
Kinsey, A. C., 210
Kisker, E., 268, 269, 271
Kitson, G. C., 155, 157, 160, 162, 163
Kittay, E. F., 102, 110, 112, 113
Klassen, A. D., 210
Kleiman, C., 261
Kline, M., 178
Koepke, L., 200
Kohlberg, L., 225, 226, 229
Kohn, M. L., 27
Kolchin, P., 61
Kosters, M. H., 143
Krause, H. D., 172
Kremen, E., 299
Krogh, M., 86-87
Kroll, J., 50
Kuhlthau, K., 268
Kuhn, A. L., 54
Kunkel, D., 10
Kurdek, L. A., 177, 186, 187-188
Kurz, D., 92-114, 162, 165, 179

Laird, J., 197, 199, 206, 211-212, 214
Lamb, M. E., 24
Lancel, S., 48
LaRossa, M. M., 22, 172, 200
LaRossa, R., 22, 172, 200
Lasch, C., 254
Laslett, P., 46, 254
Lather, P., 200, 201
Leanord, J., 280

Lederman, H. P., 26
Lee, M. A., 18, 295
Leibowitz, A., 266, 275
Leinbach, M. D., 238, 239, 240, 244
Leira, A., 295
LeMasters, E., E., 25
Lerner, R. M., 17, 18, 28
Lester, G. H., 162, 164
LeVine, R. A., 5, 7
Levitan, S. A., 69
Levy, E. F., 214
Levy, G. D., 231, 232
Lewin, E., 202
Lewin, T., 299, 315
Lewis, E., 15, 29, 30
Lewis, J., 53
Lewis, J. M., 20, 24
Lewis, M., 239
Liben, L. S., 231
Lin, C. Y. C., 32
Lin, S.-L., 157
Lindner, M., 181, 182
Lisansky, J., 6
Liss, M. B., 221, 237, 246
Littell, J. H., 309
Lobar, S. L., 33
London, H., 33
Loomis, L. S., 178
Lorber, J., 221, 244
Lorde, A., 199
Losh-Hesselbart, S., 228
Louv, R., 265, 279
Luker, K., 147
Luria, Z., 236
Luscher, K., 8
Luster, T., 27, 28
Luxton, M., 102
Lystra, K., 54
Lytton, H., 241, 244

Maccoby, E. E., 26, 105, 155, 159, 160,
    161, 162, 163-164, 165, 166, 167,
    168, 169, 172, 221, 222, 223, 226,
    228, 229, 241, 245
Machung, A., 19, 21, 23, 94, 95, 96, 97,
    119, 264, 278, 279, 293
Madsen, R., 11
Mahoney, M. R., 179
Malcuit, G., 237, 238
Malveaux, J., 101
Marcus, E., 207

Marin, G., 6
Marmor, T. R., 319
Marshall, N. L., 265, 269, 275-276
Marsiglio, W., 170, 182, 183, 184
Martin, A., 212
Martin, C. E., 210
Martin, C. L., 226, 231
Martin, E. P., 80
Martin, G. T., Jr., 9, 17, 34, 289-320
Martin, J. M., 80
Martin, T. C., 73, 74, 75, 157
Martinez, E. A., 31
Marx, F., 265, 269, 275-276
Masnick, G., 71
Mason, K. O., 268
Masterpasqua, F., 211, 213
Matras, J., 292
Matthaei, J., 254, 258
May, D., 50
May, L., 159, 173
Maynard, R., 268, 269, 271
McAdoo, H. P., 15, 30
McBride, B. A., 20
McCall, L., 57
McDannell, C., 57
McFarlane, A. H., 176
McGroder, S. M., 269, 303
McHale, S. M., 27, 241, 246
McIntyre, E. L., 300
McKenna, W., 230, 243
McKinney, M. H., 17, 18, 28
McLanahan, S. S., 24, 96, 155, 159, 293
McLeod, B. W., 315
McLoyd, V. C., 28
McNeil, M., 311
Mead, G. H., 226, 244
Melton, G. B., 203
Menaghan, E., 282
Mencher, J., 202
Merton, R. K., 242
Messner, M. A., 245, 246
Meyer, E. T., 14, 15, 27, 28, 29, 31, 32, 33
Miller, D., 33
Mills, C. W., 2
Mills, D. M., 181
Mills, G., 20
Mirowsky, J., 96
Mishel, L., 143
Mitchell, J., 225, 227
Mitchell-Kernan, C., 87

Mnookin, R. H., 26, 105, 155, 159, 160, 161, 162, 163-164, 165, 166, 167, 168, 169, 172
Modell, J., 47, 49
Moore, K. A., 18, 25
Moorman, J. E., 74, 75
Moran, G. F., 49, 50, 51, 60
Moran, P. B., 200
Morgan, C. S., 245
Morgan, D. H., 9, 11, 12
Morgan, E. S., 47, 49, 51
Morgan, L., 163
Morgan, S. P., 170
Morris, J. T., 237
Morris, M., 300
Morrison, D. R., 159, 178
Mounts, N. S., 26, 176
Murray, C., 102

Nasar, S., 145
Neckerman, K., 75, 86-87, 259
Nelson, K., 231
Nelson, M., 264, 273
New, R. S., 161
Newman, K. S., 16
Ng'Andu, N., 28
Nock, S. L., 278, 279
Norman, G. R., 176
Norton, A. J., 74, 75
Norton, E. H., 100
Norton, M. B., 48, 49, 53

O'Boyle, C., 239
O'Brien, M., 244
Oellerich, D. T., 298
Ogbu, J. U., 5, 27, 28
Okin Moller, S., 21
Olson, M., 178
O'Neil, R., 26
Oppenheim, D., 24
Orenstein, P., 310
Osmond, M. W., 11, 198
Owen, M. T., 20, 24

Padavic, I., 102
Palermo, G. B., 10
Palmer, J. L., 272
Papernow, P. L., 181, 182, 185, 187

Parcel, T., 282
Paris, J., 175, 176, 187
Parke, R., 245
Parsons, T., 11, 46, 223
Passell, P., 301
Patterson, C. J., 84, 197, 201, 211
Patterson, G. R., 25
Payne, C. K., 26
Pearce, D., 101, 299
Perdue, B. J., 1, 22
Perry-Jenkins, M., 241
Peters, M. F., 199
Peterson, G. W., 222, 223, 228
Pettit, G. S., 28
Phillips, D. A., 267, 272, 274
Phillips, R., 143
Phillips, S. J., 33
Piaget, J., 225, 226
Pies, C., 206, 212
Pine, C., 33
Pine, M., 33
Pleck, E. H., 58
Pleck, J. H., 19, 95, 161
Polatnik, M., 138
Pollock, L., 48
Pomerleau, A., 237, 238
Pomeroy, W. B., 210
Popenoe, D., 12, 69, 70, 74, 83, 92, 103,
    112, 155
Popkin, M., 278-279
Porter, J. R., 242
Powell, B., 176
Power, M. B., 229
Power, T. G., 30
Presser, H. B., 8, 16, 23, 265, 269, 280
Preston, S., 280
Prosser, W. R., 269, 303

Raabe, P., 261
Rabin, B. E., 10
Radin, N., 245
Rafkin, L., 197
Ramas, M., 254, 255, 256
Raphael, J., 108
Rapp, R., 11
Rashid, H., 30
Redlener, I., 18, 295
Reskin, B. F., 102, 138
Rheingold, H. L., 237
Rhoades, K., 27, 28
Riessman, C. K., 20, 155

Riley, L., 262, 263
Risman, B. J., 163, 245
Ritter, P. L., 26
Rivers, C., 95, 96, 98, 101
Roberts, D. F., 26
Roberts, P. G., 100, 103, 107
Robins, E., 24
Robins, P. K., 178, 266, 276
Robinson, C. C., 237
Rohrbaugh, J. B., 202, 208, 212
Roland, A., 31
Rollins, B. C., 222, 223, 228
Romney, D. M., 241, 244
Rosenkrantz, P. S., 244
Rosenthal, R., 242
Ross, C. E., 96
Ross, M. N., 143
Ross, S., 100
Rossi, A. S., 75, 83, 221
Rotella, E., 94, 99
Rubenstein, W. B., 198, 204, 205, 206, 207
Rubin, J. Z., 236
Rubin, L., 16
Ruiz, J., 3, 4
Russell, C., 263
Russell, K., 309, 310
Ryan, M. P., 54
Rzepnicki, T. L., 309

Sahler, O. J., 158
Sale, J. S., 269, 273
Saltford, N., 261
Saluter, A. F., 94
Sandefur, G., 155
Sanderson, J., 172
Sandquist, K., 104
Saum, L. O., 49
Savin-Williams, R. C., 209
Scanzoni, J., 167
Schinke, S. P., 306
Schor, J. B., 23, 144, 280
Schorr, A. L., 316
Schuerman, J. R., 309
Schultz, J. A., 50
Schultz, S., 208
Schutze, Y., 9
Schwandt, T., 3
Schwartz, L. L., 13
Schwartz, P., 83, 84, 197
Scoon-Rogers, L., 162, 164
Scott, J., 24

Seligmann, J., 85
Sellers, C., 55
Seltzer, J. A., 97, 161, 162, 168, 170, 171,
  185
Setiadi, B., 6
Shahar, S., 50
Shakin, D., 238
Shakin, M., 238
Shaw, D. S., 159, 178
Shon, S. P., 6, 32
Shorter, E., 48, 51
Sidel, R., 16, 17, 18, 27, 93, 100, 103,
  306, 314
Signorella, M. L., 231
Silverstein, L. B., 104, 108
Singer, B., 84, 85
Sklar, K. K., 54
Skocpol, T., 318
Skolnick, A., 11
Skolnick, J., 11
Slater, P. G., 50
Slater, S., 202
Slim, H., 48
Small, S. A., 1, 5, 24
Smith, D. E., 102, 199
Smith, D. S., 52, 55
Smith, E. W., 18, 25
Smith, V., 262
Smock, P. J., 162
Snipp, M., 6, 33
Somers, S. A., 18, 295
Sonenstein, F. L., 268, 269, 271
Soren, D., 48
Sorenson, A., 293
Spalter-Roth, R. M., 110-111
Spanier, G., 182-183
Speier, M., 248
Spiegelman, R. G., 276
Stacey, J., 4, 20, 69, 206, 213,
  214
Stack, C., 83, 105
Staines, G. L., 263
Stanley-Hagan, M., 178
Stannard, D. E., 50
Staples, R., 27, 29
Starnes, C. E., 20
Steif, T., 18, 25
Stein, P., 261
Steinberg, L., 26, 176
Steinhauer, J., 307
Stern, M., 236, 238, 239
Sternglanz, S. H., 238

Stevenson, B., 60
Stolberg, A. L., 176
Stone, L., 47, 48, 49, 51, 52
Strain, M., 268
Strikwerda, R., 159, 173
Sugarman, S., 74
Sullivan, J. F., 297
Sunley, R., 54
Sussman, G. D., 48, 51
Sweet, J. A., 71, 73, 74, 75, 83
Sweig-Frank, H., 175, 176, 187
Swidler, A., 11, 137

Tardiff, T., 17, 28
Taub, N., 100
Taylor, R., 68-88
Taylor, R. L., 14, 15, 29, 30
Teachman, J., 162
Teitler, J. O., 175, 176, 178,
  184
Terry, P. A., 17, 18, 28
Testa, M., 86-87
Therborn, G., 9
Thoits, P., 96
Thompson, K., 206
Thompson, L., 20, 93, 246
Thomson, E., 159
Thorne, B., 11, 21, 93, 156, 198, 234,
  242, 247, 248
Thornton, A., 75
Tiedje, L. B., 19
Tipton, S., 11
Trattner, W. I., 49
Treas, J., 259
Triandis, H. C., 6
Tronto, J., 173
Trumbach, R., 47, 52
Tschann, J. M., 178
Tseng, H.-M., 32, 33
Tucker, M., 15, 29, 30, 87
Tuer, M. D., 159, 178
Tuma, N. B., 74
Turner, C. F., 210
Turner, J., 49
Turner, P. H., 24, 28

Uchitelle, L., 143, 145
Uhlenberg, P., 8
Ullian, D., 246
Ulrich, L. T., 53

Van Cleave, N. J., 161
Vega, W. A., 6, 30, 31, 32
Vicinus, M., 202
Victor, S. B., 201
Villarruel, F. A., 17, 18, 28
Vinovskis, M. A., 7, 45-63
Viveros-Long, A., 263
Vobejda, B., 18, 306
Voeller, B., 210
Vogel, L., 313, 319
Vogel, S. R., 244
Volling, B. L., 24
Voss, P. R., 281
Vygotsky, L. S., 226, 235, 236

Waite, L. J., 70, 266, 275
Walker, A. J., 20, 93, 246
Walker, S., 242
Wall, H. M., 49
Wallerstein, J., 160
Wallisch, L., 160, 167, 168, 180, 182, 183,
    184, 185
Walsh, J., 300
Webster-Stratton, C., 25
Weinberg, D., 86
Weinberg, M. S., 211
Weiss, R., 21
Weitzman, L. J., 99, 100, 165
Wenk, D., 245
Wentworth, W. M., 242
West, C., 21, 220, 230, 243
Weston, K., 85, 197, 211, 213
White, L. K., 183, 186, 187, 200
White, M., 7

Whitebook, M., 272, 274
Wickens, E., 208
Wilkerson, M. B., 101
Williams, E., 245
Williams, W., 100
Williamson, J. B., 300
Willis, W., 30
Wilson, W. J., 15, 16, 75, 80, 87,
    259
Wimbush, D. D., 30
Winter, J. A., 226
Wirth, L., 46
Wishy, B., 49, 53
Witsberger, C., 266, 275
Wolfe, A., 11
Wood, J. T., 241, 244
Wootton, B. H., 95
Wyche, K. F., 95

Yellowbird, M., 6, 33

Zaretsky, E., 7, 11, 292
Zaslow, M. J., 272
Zelizer, V. A., 7, 8
Zicklin, G., 204, 205, 207, 208,
    209-210
Zigler, E., 15, 25
Zill, N., 18, 25
Zimmerman, D. H., 21, 220, 230, 243
Zinn, M. B., 3, 14, 15, 16, 21, 94
Zuckerman, B., 305, 306
Zuckerman, M., 49
Zuniga, M. E., 30

Subject Index

Abortion:
  availability of, 306
  legalization of, 71
Abortion rights, 318
Acculturation, 14
Achievement:
  child care effects on, 272
  parenting style and, 26, 177
  poverty and, 18
Adolescence/adolescents:
  lesbian and gay male, 209
  19th century concepts, 60
  postdivorce adjustment, 175-176
  pregnancy and, 82, 155, 306-307
  stepfamily adjustment, 187
Adopted children, 77-78
  lesbian and gay parents, 207-208, 209,
    211
  social policy and, 312
Adult children:
  Asian American families, 32
  caring for parents, 7, 315-316
  returning home, 12
Advertising, influence of, 10
Affection, provision of, 69
Affective value, 8
African American(s):
  unemployment, 17, 299
  urban areas and, 29, 61
African American families:
  blended, 77
  divorce and, 87, 157

extended, 29, 79, 80
gender socialization and, 241
19th century, 60-61
nonparental adult male influence, 83
nuclear, 77
parenting practices, 29-33
poverty in, 17, 29, 86
racial socialization, 29-30
in urban areas, 29, 61
African American men:
  pool of eligible, 75, 87
  single fathers, 147
  unemployment and, 299
African American women:
  divorced, 73
  head of family, 61-62, 63, 81, 86-87,
    103, 299
  marriage and, 299
  never married, 63, 71
  remarriage and, 75, 299
Age:
  postdivorce adjustment, 175-176
  stepfamily adjustment, 184-185,
    187
Aggression, television's effects on, 10
Aging parents, care for, 7, 315-316
Agrarian household, 255-256, 257
AIDS, 206-207, 212
Aid to Families with Dependent Children
    (AFDC), 17, 18, 109, 114, 297, 300
Alimony, 99-100
Appearance, gender and, 220

Artificial insemination:
    lesbian mothers using, 85, 211, 212
    reproductive technologies and, 309-310
Asian and Pacific Islander families:
    extended, 80
    nuclear, 77
    parenting styles, 31-32
    single parent, 81
Asian immigrants, 13
Aunts:
    African American families, 30
    living with, 78, 79
Authoritarian parenting, 25-26, 177, 182
Authoritative parenting, 26-27, 176-178
Authority, 6
    noncustodial parent, 171
    patriarchal, 9, 21, 32, 53, 106
    stepparent, 181, 185
Autonomous behavior, boys learning,
    245-246
Autonomous males, 122, 125-126, 140
Autonomy of children, 6

Behavior:
    disparity between values and, 135-136
    gendered, 220, 221, 231-232
    postdivorce, 175-176
Behaviorist theories, gender identity and,
    228
Belongingness, racial and ethnic identity
    and, 15
Bicultural children,1 4
Biculturalism, in lesbian and gay families,
    198-199
Biological imperative, 11
Birth rates, 12
    child labor and, 255
    19th century, 55
    teenagers, 306
    unmarried women, 82
Blended families, 77-78, 158, 212, 296
Boys:
    gender identity and, 238-239, 241,
        244-246
    gender stereotype transmission, 244-246
    stepfamily adjustment, 187

Capitalism, 291-292
Caregiving behavior, gender stereotypes
    about, 21

Child abandonment, historical context of,
    48-49
Child abuse, 49, 307
Child and Dependent Care Tax Credit, 263
Child care:
    availability and supply of, 96, 268-271
    child outcomes and, 272, 280-282
    cost and affordability, 266, 275-277
    deductible, 111
    employer assistance, 261, 263-265, 302
    employment and, 254-284, 302-303
    extended families and, 266
    fathers providing, 266
    government role in, 110
    informal, 265, 266, 270, 273
    male commitment to, 63
    overseeing, 7, 23
    para-parenting and, 83-84
    patterns and trends in, 265-277
    poverty and, 96, 109, 274-275
    professionals and, 8, 96, 98, 109, 264,
        265-277
    quality of, 266, 268, 271-275, 277
    satisfactions and discontents with,
        267-268
    social policies, 102, 283
    tandem, 265
Child-centered parents, 49, 54, 173
Child characteristics, parenting competency
    and, 24-25
Child custody, 163-168
    joint, 105-106, 160-161, 166-168, 315
    lesbian and gay parents, 87, 204, 205
    19th century, 56
Child development, 1
    child care and, 271, 272
    gender identity and, 219-249
    interaction style and, 25
    lesbian and gay families, 197
    professionals and, 8
    socioeconomic status and, 28
Child labor, 255-256
Child outcomes:
    child care and, 272, 280-282
    divorce and, 155, 159-160, 174-179,
        281
    gender socialization and, 242-244
    lesbian and gay parenting, 196-197, 205
    parent's employment and, 280-282
    remarriage and, 186-188
Child poverty:
    increase in, 17-19, 281

single mothers and, 69, 86, 93, 99-101,
    155, 162, 298-299
  See also Poverty
Child rearing, 69
  burdens of, 95-99
  costs of, 23
  gender differences, 19-22
  gender identity development and,
    219-249
  labor intensive, 94
Children:
  attitudes about, 69
  emotional value, 8
  gender identity, 21-22, 219-249
  health of, 304-305
  latchkey, 92, 278
  rights of, 9, 51-52
  suicide by, 281
Child support payments, 17, 99-100,
    107-108, 120, 161-163, 296-298
Christian fatherhood, 56-57
Cognitive development, gender identity
    and, 225-226, 228-232
Cohabitation, 71, 75, 146, 158
Collectivist orientation, 6
  agrarian household and, 257
  Asian Americans, 32
  Hispanics, 31
  Native Americans, 33
  19th century, 60
Colonial America, parenting in, 46-52
Communication:
  gender identity and, 230, 232-234
  joint custody and, 167
  nonresidential fathers, 171
Companionship, provision of, 69
Conflict, 5
  immigrant families, 14
  joint custody and, 106, 167
  marital, 97, 159, 175, 178-179
  noncustodial fathers, 173
  postdivorce, 173, 177, 178-179
  remarriage and, 181
  visitation, 172
Conformity:
  Asian Americans, 33
  socioeconomic status and, 28
Consumer-oriented society, 6
Contemporary society, parenting in, 5-14
Contraceptive availability, 71, 306
Contradictions, 5
  postmodern perspective, 201, 202

Control over children, 6
  noncustodial parent, 171
  single parents', 159
Coparenting, 95-96, 103-109, 166-168,
    173
Cousins, living with, 79
Cultural differences:
  immigrants, 14
  kinship obligations, 6
  parenting practices, 29-33
Cultural ideologies, primary, 11-12
Cultural images, of stepfamilies, 182
Cultural values, 6
Culture, 4
  gay, 197, 203
  gender scripts and, 231
  masculine, 130, 132-137
Custodial fathers, 163-164, 166,
    315
Custodial mothers, 163-165
Custody, 163-168
  See Child custody

Day care:
  need for subsidized, 110
  overseeing, 7
  See also Child care
Deadbeat dads, 119-120
Death:
  child abuse and, 307
  infant, 281, 305
  of spouse, life after, 81, 179
  spouse abuse and, 308
Defense of Marriage Act, 206
Demographic factors, 63, 69
  children's well-being and, 281
Demographic patterns:
  custodial mothers versus fathers,
    164
  divorce, 157-159
  family composition and, 296
  remarriage, 157-159
Dependency:
  agrarian household, 259
  derivative, 112-113
  inevitable, 112
  prolonged period of, 6
  socialization and, 222
  welfare and, 114
Discipline, 9
  African American families, 30

Asian Americans, 32
Colonial America, 49
gender and, 241
Hispanics, 31
Native Americans, 33
socioeconomic status and, 28
Discrimination, 15
African Americans and, 61
immigrants, 14
same-sex marriages and, 205-206
Disengaged parenting style, 177
Divorce, 154-179
adjustment to, 159-160
African American families, 87
after remarriage, 157, 158, 182
autonomous males and, 125
child outcomes in, 155, 159-160,
174-179, 281
demographic patterns, 157-159
economic consequences of, 99-100
economic support after, 161-163
father participation after, 97, 105-106,
127-129
increase in, 63, 68, 70, 72-74, 94, 146,
147, 157
involved fathers and, 127-129
living arrangements after, 160-161
living with grandparents after, 80
maternal custody in, 21
multiple, 188
postindustrial economy, 259
poverty and, 94
rising rates of, 12
second marriages and, 157, 158
single-parent families and, 81
social policies and, 103
standard of living and, 100
stereotypes, 99
Domestic feminism, 55
Domestic violence, 103, 106, 107, 307-308
Dual earner families:
standard of living, 16
work schedules, 63

Earned income credit, 111, 301
Economic change, 19th century, 55
Economic consequences, of divorce, 99-100
Economic factors:
divorce, 74
extended families and, 78
remarriage, 75, 163, 186

visitation, 169
Economic growth, 143
Economic pressure, 63
Economic reforms, 110
Economic stratification, 15-19
Economy, structural changes in,
142-143
Education:
African American families, 30
Asian Americans, 32
historical practices, 51
19th century, 55, 59-60
overseeing, 7
prolonged period of, 6
sex, 306-307
television's effects on, 10
Education level:
age at marriage and, 71
custodial mothers versus fathers, 164
father's role and, 122
poverty and, 18
women's, 145, 164
Egalitarian relationships, 28, 197
Elder care, 7, 315-316
Employment:
child care and, 254-284
child care assistance and, 261, 263-265,
302
children's well-being and, 280-282
effects of increased, 277-282
family policy, 301-304
future prospects, 6, 16, 23
historical perspective, 255-260
nature of, 15-16
parental competence and, 25
shared parenting and, 167
Environment, interaction with, 225, 229
Escape fantasy, 136
Ethnicity, 14-15
familism and, 6
parenting practices and, 29-33
Extended families:
African Americans, 29
Asian American, 32
child care and, 266
Colonial America, 46-47
Hispanic, 30
immigrants, 14
lesbian and gay, 213
living with, 78-80
Native American, 33
stepfamily as, 179-188

Familism, 6, 12, 31
Family:
    definitions of, 12-13, 68-88
    functions of, 7, 69
    problems facing, 92-114
    routines of, 69
    size of, 12, 55, 69
    traditional, 63, 68, 69, 102-103, 247
Family allowances, 111
Family and Medical Leave Act of 1993,
    102, 260, 303
Family leave, 105, 110
Family policy:
    agenda for, 289-316
    aging parents and, 315-316
    child support and, 296-298
    health and, 304-309
    income security and, 294-301
    parenting, 313-315
    reproductive technology and, 309-312
Family preservation policy, 308-309
Family Preservation and Support Services
    Program, Omnibus Budget
    Reconciliation Act of 1993, 308
Family rituals and traditions, 178
Family Support Act of 1988, 107, 297, 300
Family systems paradigm, 156
Family values, 92, 101, 317, 319
Father(s):
    autonomous orientation, 122, 125-126
    child care by, 63, 266
    custodial, 163-164, 166, 315
    disengaged from child rearing and care, 8
    gay, 84-85, 87, 196-214
    gender stereotype transmission, 244-246
    innovative, 173
    involved, 122, 126-129, 131-132,
        139-140, 141
    joint custody satisfaction, 167-168
    masculine culture and, 132-137
    noncustodial, 170-174
    nurturing, 120, 122, 126-129,
        131-132, 139-140
    time spent with children of divorce, 97
    traditionalization, 172-173
    See also Single fathers
Father-child attachment, 24, 147
Fatherhood:
    serial, 186
    social construction of, 119-150
Father's role, 7, 8, 19-20
    changes in, 119-150

Colonial America, 51
    coparenting and, 95-96, 103-109
    family policy and, 314-315
    future of, 148-150
    Hispanics, 31
    industrialization and, 256
    mother's remarriage and, 186
    19th century, 56-59
    noncustodial fathers, 170-174
    postindustrial economy, 259
    slave families, 61, 62
    social change and, 120, 123-129
    stepfathers, 183-184
    traditional, 102, 120, 122, 123,
        124-125, 129-130, 137-138, 247
Female(s). See Women
Feminine socialization, 220-221, 224, 232,
    244-245
Feminist groups, family policy and, 317,
    318-319
Feminist movement, 63, 224, 293
Feminist perspective:
    gender socialization, 246-248
    lesbian and gay families, 198-199
    on mother's role, 92-114
Feminization of poverty, 17, 101, 299
Fertility rates, 12
First Wave feminism, 318
Flexible workforce, 261-262
Flextime, 105, 262-263, 302
Food stamps, 17-18
Freedom, ideal of, 11
Freudian theory, gender and, 224-225
Friends:
    influence on family, 47-48
    para-parenting by, 83
    stepparents as, 183

Gay civil rights, 203, 205, 207, 209
Gay culture, 197, 203
Gay men, partnership rights, 206-208
Gay parenting, 13, 84-85, 87, 196-214
    child outcomes, 196-197, 205
    gender stratification, 22
    historical perspective, 202-210
    innovation and, 214
    prevalence and diversity of, 210-214
    theoretical perspectives, 198-202
Gender:
    intergenerational transmission of
        stereotypes about, 244-246

parenting satisfaction and, 24
power and, 21, 93, 137-139
sex versus, 220-221
socialization, 219-249
socially constructed, 219-220
transition to parenthood and, 23
Gender differences, socially constructed,
    134-135
Gender division of labor, 95-97, 122,
    137-138, 161, 168, 184, 241
Gender gap, in income, 143, 144-145
Gender identity, 21-22
    children in lesbian and gay families, 197
    socialization of, 219-249
Gender-neutral child rearing, 224
Gender roles:
    ideologies about, 102
    learning, 130
    lesbian and gay families, 197
    socialization, 219-249
    stepparents, 184
    television's effects on attitudes about, 10
    traditional, 93
Gender schema, 229-231, 246
Gender scripts, 231-232, 246
Gender stratification, 17, 19-22
Girls:
    gender identity and, 238-239, 241,
        244-246
    gender stereotype transmission, 244-246
    stepfamily adjustment, 187
Government:
    care work and, 110-113
    child care subsidies, 276-277, 302-303
    welfare reform, 18
Government intervention:
    child care, 272, 274
    growth of, 9
    lesbian and gay parents and, 204-206
Grandparents, 12
    African American families, 30
    child care by, 266
    child rearing by, 13
    living with, 78
    living with parent in home of, 79
Great-grandparents, 12

Health, family policy and, 304-309
Health care, need for, 101, 111, 304,
    319-320
Heterosexism, 199

Hispanic families:
    blended, 77
    extended, 79, 80
    nonparental adult male influence, 83
    nuclear, 77
    parenting styles, 30-31
    single parent, 81
Hispanic women:
    divorced, 73
    never married, 71
Historical context of parenting, 45-63
Historical perspective:
    employment and child care, 255-260
    lesbian and gay parenting in, 202-210
Homelessness, 18, 295
Hostility, of noncustodial fathers, 173
Household work:
    gender division of, 19, 95-97, 122,
        137, 161, 184, 241
    shared, 104

Identity development, 7
    gender, 219-249
Illness, poverty and, 18
Immigrants, 13, 256
    kinship obligations, 6
    19th century, 60
Immigration Reform and Control Act of
    1986, 13
Impression management, gender, 221
Income, 15-19
    child care and, 274-277
    decline in real, 16, 292, 302
    divorce and, 74
    gender gap in, 143, 144-145
    joint custody and, 167
    male workers, 142-143, 162
    postdivorce, 162
    redistributing, 112
    single fathers, 162
    working women and, 99, 110-111,
        144-145
Income guarantees, 111
Income security, family policy and, 294-301
Independence:
    of children, 6
    male, 132, 135
    women's economic, 144-146
Independent thought, socioeconomic status
    and, 28
Individualist orientation, 6, 11-12

Industrialization, 46, 58, 63, 256-258
Infant(s):
    child care for, 268, 273
    gender development, 238-240
    health of, 304-305
    mortality rates, 281, 305, 311
Infanticide, 48, 49
Infant schools, 50
Initiative, socioeconomic status and,
    28
In-laws, living with, 78, 79
Innovation:
    fathers and, 173
    lesbian and gay families and, 199, 214
Interaction:
    gendered socialization through,
        222-223, 225, 229, 232-234
    parent-child relationships formed
        through, 3
    style of, 25
Interactionist synthesis of gender
    socialization, 234-237
Interactionist theories of gender, 232-237
Interpersonal skills, 222
    African American families, 30
    television's effects on, 10
In vitro fertilization, 309
Involved fathers, 173
    See Nurturing fathers

Joint custody, 105-106, 160-161, 166-168,
    315

Labor, gender division of, 95-97, 122,
    137-138, 161, 168, 184, 241
Language skills:
    child care effects on, 272
    socioeconomic status and, 28
Latinos, 13
    See also Hispanic families
    child poverty, 17
    unemployment, 17
Learning:
    environment for boys versus girls, 245
    gender identity, 228
    parenting behaviors, 3
Legal issues, lesbian and gay parents and,
    204-206
Leisure time, 23, 166
Lesbian(s):

couple satisfaction, 200
partnership rights, 206-208
Lesbian families, 84-85, 87, 196-214
    child outcomes, 196-197, 205
    gender stratification, 22
    historical perspective, 202-210
    innovation and, 214
    prevalence and diversity of, 210-214
    theoretical perspectives, 198-202
Life course perspective, on lesbian and gay
    families, 199-200
Life satisfaction, 24, 98
Living alone, 146
Living arrangements:
    postdivorce, 160-161
    shifts in, 69-70, 76-85
Longevity, 12
Low-income families, 18
    child care and, 274-276, 303-304
    See also Poverty

Male(s), see Men
Male commitment:
    avoidance of, 132-133, 140
    emerging patterns of, 121-123
    social factors, 130-150
Male dominance:
    erosion of, 137-141
    norms of, 103
Male rebels, 119-120
Male violence, 93, 106, 107, 108, 246
Manufacturing jobs, 143
Marginality, lesbian and gay families and,
    199
Marital property, 100
Marital separation, single-parent families
    and, 81
Marriage:
    agrarian interdependency and, 259
    alternatives to, 146
    attitudes about, 69
    changes in, 69, 70-72
    conflict in, 97, 159, 175, 178-179
    equality in, 104, 138, 140, 145
    parental competence and, 25
    postponing, 70-71, 293
    same-sex, 205-206, 207
    separation of parenthood and, 147
    social policies, 112
    women's disenchantment with, 20
    women's employment and, 21

Masculine culture, 130, 132-137
Masculine personality, 131, 227-228
Masculine socialization, 220-221, 224,
    232, 244-245
Masculinity, Victorian concepts of, 57
Mate selection, parental power over, 52
Maternal custody, 161
Maternity leave, 261, 303
Meanings, 4
Men:
    age at first marriage, 70-71
    autonomous, 122, 125-126, 140
    childhood experiences of, 130-131
    difficulties in relationships with
        women, 125
    economic entitlement and, 142-144
    household work and, 95-97, 122,
        137-138, 161
    indifferent, 141
    living alone, 146
    nonparental adult, influence of, 82-83
    postdivorce income, 162
    postindustrial economy, 259
    psychological diversity among, 130-132
    remarriage and, 74, 157
    stereotypical, 227
    unemployed, 299
    violent, 93, 106, 107, 108, 246
    work hours, 278
Middle class:
    child care and, 275
    gap between working class and, 16
    government subsidies for, 111
    involved fathers, 126
    male identity, 57
    Victorian era, 62
Middle-class bias, in research, 27
Minimum wage, 302
Minorities, single mother poverty and, 101
Mobility, downward, 15, 100
Moral nature of children, 55
Mother(s):
    custodial, 163-165
    failure to support, 95-103
    gender stereotype transmission, 244-246
    gender stratification, 19-22
    health of, 304-305
    joint custody satisfaction, 167-168
    lesbian, 84-85, 87, 196-214
    parenting burdens, 22, 95-99
    See also Single mothers; Working
        mothers

Mother-child attachment, 24
Mother's role, 7, 8, 19-22
    Colonial America, 51, 52-53
    feminist perspective, 92-114
    industrialization and, 256
    19th century, 54-56
    postindustrial revolution, 258-260
    slave families, 61
    stepmothers, 184
    traditional, 102-103

Native American families, parenting styles
    of, 33
Neighbors, influence of, 47-48
Networks, parental competence and, 25
New reproductive technologies, 309-312
Normative creativity, lesbian and gay
    families and, 199
Nuclear family, 11
    decline in numbers of, 68, 76-77
    defined, 12-13
    elements of, 69
    history of, 46-48
Nurturance:
    Asian Americans, 32
    Native Americans, 33
    19th century, 53
Nurturing behavior:
    gender stereotypes, 21
    girls learning, 245-246
    learning, 3, 245-246
Nurturing fathers, 120, 122, 126-129,
    131-132, 139-140, 173
Nutrition, poverty and, 18

Obedience, 19th century views on, 54
Obligation, ideal of, 11
Occupational segregation, 17, 19
Oral tradition, African American families,
    30
Ova banks, 311

Parallel parenting, 168
Para-parenting, 83-84
Parent(s):
    caring for aging, 7, 315-316
    expectations of, 4
    noncustodial, 168-174
    See also Father(s); Mother(s)

Parent education programs, 25, 313-314
Parental characteristics, parenting styles
    and, 24-27
Parental determinism, 11
Parental leave, 261, 303-304
Parental satisfaction, 24
Parent-child relationships
    formed through social interaction , 3
Parenthood:
    separation of marriage and, 147
    transitions to, 22-23
Parenting:
    activities of, 3-4, 6
    co-, 95-96, 103-109, 166-168, 173
    in contemporary society, 5-14
    cultural variations, 29-33
    defining, 1, 158
    double standard about, 164
    emerging form of, 8
    family changes, 6-10
    family policies, 313-315
    historical overview, 45-63
    individuals' definitions, 4-5
    19th-century America, 52-62
    noncustodial parents, 168-174
    nuptial behavior and, 70-75
    parallel, 168
    patterns, 68-88
    personal costs and rewards, 22-24
    postdivorce, 159-160
    professionals and, 8-9
    situated in place and time, 4
    social constructionist approach to, 1-34
    trends, 68-88
Parenting styles:
    authoritarian, 25-26, 172,
        176-178
    authoritative, 26-27, 176-178
    parental characteristics and, 24-27
    permissive, 26, 177
    postdivorce adjustment and, 176-178
    socioeconomic status and, 27-29
    stepparents, 181-182
Partnership rights, for lesbians and gay
    men, 206-208
Part-time working women, 97, 99, 102,
    110, 111, 144, 165
Paternity establishment, 107-108
Paternity leave, 104-105, 110, 303
Patriarchal authority, 9, 21, 32, 53, 106
Peer groups, 6
Permissive parents, 26, 177

Personal Responsibility and Work
    Opportunity Reconciliation Act of
    1996, 18, 300
Personality characteristics, 222
Physical punishment:
    Colonial America, 49
    gender and, 241
Play, gender-typical, 241
Poor, working, 18
Postindustrial revolution, 258-260
Postmodern perspective, on lesbian and gay
    families, 200-201
Poverty, 17-19
    child care and, 96, 109, 274-275
    divorce and, 94
    effects on parenting, 27-28
    feminization of, 17, 101, 299
    income security programs and, 295
    minorities and, 15, 29
    para-parenting and, 83-84
    racialization of, 17, 101, 299
    remarriage and, 75
    single mothers and, 69, 86, 93, 99-101,
        155, 162, 298-299
Power:
    gender and, 21, 93, 137-139
    heterosexist society and, 199
    of noncustodial fathers, 172
Prejudice, 15
Preschool care, 269, 273. See also Child
    care
Procreation technology, 309-312
Professionals, child care provision by, 8-9,
    96, 98, 109, 264, 265-277
Psychoanalytic theories of gender:
    contemporary, 226-228
    Freudian, 224-225
Psychological well-being:
    children's postdivorce, 174-179
    parental functioning and, 24
    postdivorce income and, 162
    stepfamilies and, 186-188
Public assistance:
    declining value of, 17-18
    See also Welfare; Aid to Families With
        Dependent Children

Race, 12, 14-15
    economic stratification and, 16, 99
    parenting practices, 29-33
    poverty and, 17, 99, 101, 299

Racial ethnic variations, 12
Racialization of poverty, 17, 101, 299
Racial socialization, African American
    families, 29-30
Racism, 15, 114
Reciprocity, historical tradition of, 7
Reflexive insight, 201
Relationship satisfaction:
    lesbian and gay families and, 200
Religion, 9
    African American families, 30
    Hispanics, 30
Religious influences, 9
Remarriage, 12, 154-158, 179-188, 296
    African American women and, 75, 299
    child outcomes, 186-188
    custodial mothers versus fathers, 164
    demographic patterns, 157-159
    divorce after, 157, 158, 182
    economic factors, 163, 186
    increase in, 74-75
    involved fathers and, 127-129
Reproductive technologies, 309-312
Research:
    gender socialization, 237-242
    middle-class bias, 27
Romantic movement, 53

Scaffolding, 226, 236
Schema, gender, 229-231, 246
School. See Achievement; Education
Scripts, gender, 231-232, 246
Second shift, 19, 94, 95-99, 293,
    294
Second Wave feminism, 318
Segregation:
    African Americans and, 61
    occupational, 17, 19
Self-esteem, racial and ethnic identity and,
    15, 30
Self-fulfilling prophecy, gender identity
    and, 242-243
Self-fulfillment, 12
Self-regulation, gender identification and,
    233-234, 235
Separate spheres doctrine, 11
Serial fatherhood, 186
Service sector
    expansion of, 15-16, 143, 258-259
Sex, gender versus, 220-221
Sex education, 306-307

Sex role. See Gender roles
Sexual orientation, of children in lesbian
    and gay families, 197
Sexual revolution, 71
Sick child care, 264
Single fathers, 86, 127
    African American, 147
    cohabitating, 158
    income, 162
    increase in, 81
    nonparental adult female influences, 83
    postdivorce, 163-164, 166
    white, 147
Single mothers, 12, 13, 80
    African American, 61-62, 86-87, 103,
        299
    cohabitating, 158
    divorced, 21, 163-165
    increase in, 63, 68, 70, 94
    living with extended family, 79
    never married, 63, 68, 71-72, 82, 94,
        154, 155
    nonparental adult male influence, 83
    para-parenting and, 84
    parenting styles, 176-177
    percent of, 147
    postdivorce, 163-165
    poverty and, 17, 69, 86, 93, 99-101,
        155, 162, 298-299
    remarriage and, 75
    socioeconomic status, 82
    stigmatization of, 103
Single parents, 13
    challenges for, 163-168
    control demands, 159
    increase in number of, 70, 281
    living with grandparents, 80
    never married, 82
    para-parenting and, 83-84
    shared parenting, 105
Slavery, 60-61
Social changes, 7-8, 11-12, 23
    father's role and, 120, 123-129
    masculine beliefs and ideals and,
        135
    parental expectations and, 4
    procreation technology and, 309-312
    working women and, 292-294
Social competence, parenting style and,
    177
Social constructionist approach to
    parenting, 1-34

Social construction of fatherhood,
   119-150
Social construction of gender, 134-135,
   219-220, 243-244
Social construction of reality, lesbian and
   gay families and, 199, 200
Social context of transition to parenthood,
   23
Social cues, gender identity and, 240
Social development, 7, 10
Social factors, men's commitments and,
   130-150
Social institutions, relationships between
   family and, 11
Social interaction. *See* Interaction
Socialization:
   of children in lesbian and gay families,
      197
   extended households, 80
   gender, 21-22, 219-249
   interaction and, 222-223, 225, 229,
      232-234
   men's fathering attachments, 130-131
   racial, 29-30
Social learning theory, gender and, 228
Social lives, of single mothers, 165
Social location of families, 15
Social norms, gender identity and, 232-233
Social policies, 101-103
   care work and, 94, 110-113
   child care, 254, 260-265, 283
   employment, 301-304
   father participation, 104-105
   income security, 294-301
   joint custody, 105-106
   marriage, 112
   parenting and, 313-315
Social skills, child care effects on, 272, 273
Social status, 5
   heterosexist society and, 199
Social supports, 94
   government role, 110-113
   parental competence and, 25
Social values, 222
Social welfare state, 9
Sociodemographic changes, 69
Socioeconomic factors, in remarriage, 75
Socioeconomic status:
   parenting styles and, 27-29
   single mothers, 82
Socioeconomic stratification, 15-19
Sodomy laws, 204

Special Supplemental Food Program for
   Women, Infants, and Children,
   305, 319
Sperm banks, 310-312
Standard of living, 16
   divorce and, 100
   remarriage and, 186
States, block grants to, 18
Stepfamilies, 12, 13, 296
   dissolution of, 157, 158, 182
   formation of, 154-158, 179-188
   gay male, 212
Stepparenting, 77, 179-188
   quasi-, 158
Stonewall generation, 203
Strain:
   on mothers, 24
   postdivorce, 164
Stratification, systems of, 14-22
Stress:
   caring for parents and, 316
   domestic life and, 102
   economic, 15
   income and, 28
   mother's role and, 96-97
Suicide, child, 281
Supportive detachment, 8

Technological changes, 23
Technology, procreation, 309-312
Television:
   authoritative parenting and, 26
   influence of, 9-10
Tensions, 5
   immigrant families, 14
   postmodern perspective, 201
   remarriage and, 181
Time deficit, 23, 165, 279-280
Time spent with children, 8
   custodial mothers versus fathers, 164
   employment and, 278-280, 281-282
   noncustodial parents, 168-174
   working mothers, 69, 278-280
Toddlers:
   child care for, 269, 273
   gender development, 239-240
Toys, gender-stereotyped, 239, 240-241
Traditionalization, men and, 172

Uncles, living with, 78, 79

Underemployment, minorities and, 15
Unemployment:
    divorce and, 74
    increasing, 17
    minorities and, 15, 61, 299
    social class and, 16
Unemployment insurance, 110-111
Urban areas:
    blacks in, 29, 61
    lesbians and gay men in, 203
Urbanization, 46, 63

Values:
    cultural, 6
    cultural tradition of masculinity and,
        133
    disparity between behavior and,
        135-136
    gender scripts and, 231
    immigrants, 14
Victorian era, 54-57, 62
Violence:
    against gay people, 209
    family policy and, 307-309
    male, 93, 106, 107, 108, 246, 307-308
    postseparation, 179
Visitation, 168-174
    lesbian and gay parents and, 205

Welfare, 96
    dependency and, 114
    family policy and, 298-300
    health care benefits, 111, 304, 319
    inadequacy of, 100, 102, 109
    income security and, 295
    paternity determination and, 108
Welfare reform, 18, 100-101, 109, 281,
    300
Western culture, transformation of, 11-12
White families:
    blended, 77
    divorce and, 157
    extended, 79, 80
    gender socialization and, 241
    nonparental adult male influence, 83
    nuclear, 77
    poverty, 86
    single parent, 81
White single fathers, 147
White women:

divorced, 73
never married, 71
Women:
    age at first marriage, 70-71
    caring for aging parents, 7, 315-316
    divorced, 72-74
    educational level, 145
    living alone, 146
    moral worth, 53
    never married, 71-72
    postdivorce income, 162
    remarriage and, 74-75, 157
    stereotypical, 227
    violence against, 93, 106, 107, 108,
        246, 307-308
    work hours, 278
Work. See Employment
Workfare, 300
Work hours, 256-257, 261, 278
Working class:
    child care and, 275, 303-304
    father's role and, 122, 126
    gap between middle class and, 16
    involved fathers, 126
    job uncertainties, 16
    19th century, 60
Working mothers, 8, 19
    benefits to men of, 139-140
    burdens of, 95-99
    child care and, 254, 258-284, 302-303
    feminists and, 318-319
    income of, 99, 110-111, 144-145
    involved fathers and, 126, 127
    male commitment to child care and, 63
    19th century, 60
    part-time work, 97, 99, 102, 110, 111,
        144, 165
    postdivorce, 164
    postindustrial revolution,
        258-260
    promotions for, 97
    roadblocks, 124
    satisfaction of, 98
    shared parenting and, 104
    stereotypes of, 93
    time spent with children, 69, 278-280
    work hours, 278
Working poor, 18
Working women:
    age at marriage, 71
    committed employment,
        144-146

marital dynamics and, 21
social change and, 292-294
standard of living and, 16
Workplace:
equity in, 144
family-responsive, 60-265

nature of, 15-16
Work schedule, 63, 105, 261, 262-263,
271, 302

Zone of proximal development, 226, 236

About the Editor

Terry Arendell, Ph.D., is Associate Professor and Chair of the Department of Sociology at Colby College. Her interests include interpretive sociology, family, gender, feminist theory, and qualitative research methods. She is the author of *Fathers and Divorce* (Sage Publications) and *Mothers and Divorce: Legal, Economic, and Social Dilemmas,* and has published in various scholarly journals, including *Symbolic Interactionism, Gender & Society,* and *Signs.*

About the Contributors

Michele Adams is a doctoral candidate in the Department of Sociology at the University of California, Riverside. Her current research projects include an analysis of cohabitation as an alternative family form, the relationship of the media to gender socialization, and the study of violence prevention and intervention at the family level.

Katherine R. Allen, Ph.D., is Professor of Family Studies in the Department of Family and Child Development at Virginia Polytechnic Institute and State University, Blacksburg. She is a faculty affiliate in the Center for Gerontology and a core teaching faculty member in the Women's Studies Program. She is active in the National Council on Family Relations. She currently serves as Deputy Editor of *Journal of Marriage and the Family* and is a member of the editorial boards of *Family Relations* and *Journal of Social and Personal Relationships*. She is the author of more than 40 articles and books on the topics of family diversity, feminist pedagogy, and qualitative research methods.

Scott Coltrane, Ph.D., is Associate Professor of Sociology at the University of California, Riverside. His research on families and gender has been published in various scholarly journals, including the *American Journal of Sociology, Social Problems, Sociological Perspectives, Journal of Marriage and the Family, Journal of Family Issues, Gender & Society,* and *Sex Roles.* He is coauthor, with Randall Collins, of *Sociology of Marriage and the Family* (1995) and author of *Gender and Families* (Pine Forge Press) and *Family Man: Fatherhood,*

Housework, and Gender Equity (1996). His research focuses on the social construction of gender in family contexts, with special emphasis on issues of inequality and possibilities for social change.

Sarah Beth Estes is a doctoral candidate in sociology at the University of Iowa. Her recent research investigates mothers' post-partum job changes, focusing on the potential trade-offs between financial compensation and family responsive working conditions. She is also interested in the allocation of adults' time between paid work and domestic labor, and the legitimacy processes involved in the pursuit of social change by collective actors.

Stephen M. Frank recently received his Ph.D. in American history at the University of Michigan and is seeking academic employment. His book on fatherhood in the nineteenth-century American North is forthcoming from Johns Hopkins University Press. His work has previously appeared in the *Journal of Social History*.

Kathleen Gerson, Ph.D., is Professor of Sociology at New York University, where she teaches courses on gender, work, family, and social change. She is the author of several books, including *No Man's Land: Men's Changing Commitments to Family and Work* (1993) and *Hard Choices: How Women Decide About Work, Career, and Motherhood* (1985), as well as numerous articles on gender, work, and family change. She is now at work on a study of how children growing up in diverse types of families have responded to the gender revolution at home and at the workplace.

Jennifer Glass, Ph.D., is Associate Professor of Sociology at the University of Iowa. Her research interests include work and family issues, gender stratification, organizations, and mental health. She is currently researching the effects of employer family responsiveness on mothers' job moves. Another project focuses on the effects of different types of child care (especially father care) on mother's child care satisfaction, job satisfaction, and mental health.

Demie Kurz, Ph.D., is Co-Director of Women's Studies at the University of Pennsylvania and has an appointment in the Sociology Department. She has written extensively on issues of gender and the family. She is the author of the recent book *For Richer, For Poorer: Mothers Confront Divorce* (1995), which analyzes the social and economic impact of divorce on a diverse group of divorced mothers. She has also written on issues of violence against women in the United

States, including social science debates over how to define and measure domestic violence.

George T. Martin, Jr., Ph.D., is Professor of Sociology at Montclair State University. His most recent publications are "In the Shadow of My Old Kentucky Home," in *This Fine Place So Far From Home* (1995), edited by C. L. B. Dews and C. L. Law, and *The Ecology of the Automobile* (1993). He has published widely in scholarly journals and anthologies.

Ronald L. Taylor, Ph.D., is Director of the Institute for African American Studies and Professor of Sociology at the University of Connecticut. He is the editor and/or author of five books, including *The Black Male in America* (with Doris Wilkinson), *Minority Families in the United States* (1994), and *Black Youth in the United States* (1995), and more than 30 journal articles and book chapters on a range of topics involving African Americans. He is currently editor of the journal *Race & Society* and is a member of the editorial boards of *Journal of Research on Adolescents* and *Journal of African-American Male Studies*. He serves as referee and consultant to a number of foundations and government agencies.

Maris A. Vinovskis, Ph.D., is Professor of History in the Department of History and a research scientist at the Institute for Social Research at the University of Michigan. He has written various articles and books on the history of the American family. His latest book is *Education, Society, and Economic Opportunity: A Historical Perspective on Persistent Issues* (1995).